CONTACT AND CONFLICT

CONTACT AND CONFLICT

INDIAN-EUROPEAN RELATIONS IN BRITISH COLUMBIA, 1774–1890

Robin Fisher

UNIVERSITY OF BRITISH COLUMBIA PRESS

VANCOUVER

CONTACT AND CONFLICT

INDIAN-EUROPEAN RELATIONS IN BRITISH COLUMBIA, 1774-1890

©The University of British Columbia 1977
Reprinted 1978
All rights reserved

Canadian Cataloguing in Publication Data

Fisher, Robin, 1946-
Contact and conflict

Includes bibliography and index.

ISBN 0-7748-0108-5

1. Indians of North America—British
Columbia—History. 2. Acculturation.
I. Title.
E78.B9F58   971.1′004′97   C77-002016-X

International Standard Book Number 0-7748-0108-5

Printed in Canada

This book has been published with the help of a gift to scholarly publishing made in honour of Dr. Harold S. Foley for his distinguished services to the University of British Columbia, and grants from:

The Humanities Research Council of Canada, using funds provided by the Canada Council

Simon Fraser University

The Leon and Thea Koerner Foundation

The Hamber Foundation

To my mother and father,
and the memory of Wilson Duff

Contents

Photographic Credits

Plate 13 is from the Public Archives of Canada (PA 44328). Plates 1, 3, 9, and 21 appear courtesy of the British Columbia Provincial Museum, Victoria. Plates 2, 4, 5, 6, 7, 8, 10, 11, 12, 14, 15, 16, 17, 18, 19, 20, 22, 23, 24, are from the collection of the British Columbia Provincial Archives.

Cover photograph is from *Northwest Coast Indian Artifacts from the H. R. MacMillan Collections*, The University of British Columbia.

ILLUSTRATIONS

Abbreviations

BCHQ	*British Columbia Historical Quarterly*
CC	British Columbia, Colonial Correspondence (Inward Correspondence to the Colonial Government), MS, Provincial Archives of British Columbia
CO.42	Great Britian, Colonial Office. Original Correspondence, Canada, 1874, microfilm, Public Archives of Canada
CO.60	Great Britain, Colonial Office. Original Correspondence, British Columbia, 1858–1871, microfilm, University of British Columbia Library
CO.305	Great Britain, Colonial Office. Original Correspondence, Vancouver Island, 1846–1867, microfilm, University of British Columbia Library
HBCA	Hudson's Bay Company, Archives, microfilm, Public Archives of Canada
PABC	Provincial Archives of British Columbia
PAC	Public Archives of Canada
RG10	Canada, Department of Indian Affairs, Black Series, Western Canada, Record Group 10, MS, Public Archives of Canada
TS	Typescript
UBCL	University of British Columbia Library
WDP	William Duncan Papers, microfilm, University of British Columbia Library

Preface

The history of the fur trade in North America has been shown as a retreat in the face of settlement.[1]

In Canada the relationship between the native Indians and the immigrant Europeans has not, until recently, been a major concern of historians. In contrast to other former British settlement colonies in Australasia or Africa, the aboriginal people have been seen as a peripheral rather than a central concern in the study of Canada's past; or, as some have put it, the Indian provides a "background" for Canadian history.[2] Some of the major themes of Canadian historical writing have perpetuated a limited view of the indigenous Canadian.

The staple-Laurentian thesis, the most creative idea to emerge out of the study of Canadian history, holds that Canada's development can be explained in terms of the production of certain staples for export to metropolitan markets. Both Harold Innis and Donald Creighton make the point that the culture of the hunting Indians was essential to the fur trade, and Creighton adds that, while the fur trade preserved the Indians from extinction, settlement drove them towards degradation.[3] It was in the writings of these two authors that I found the germ of the idea that I have developed in this book. Yet both these historians deal with the Indians only as they respond to the European economic system, accommodating to European demands rather than acting in terms of the priorities of their own culture. A further effect of staple theory history has been that the Indians drop from view with the decline of the fur trade. Having ceased to be an important factor in the European economy, the Indians are given little attention during the disruptive settlement period.

Attempts to apply Frederick Jackson Turner's frontier thesis to Canada have also done little to elucidate the role of the Indians. The frontier thesis is confidently ethnocentric because it is predicated on the notion of the "existence of an area of free land"; land which, of course, really belonged to the

[1]Harold H. Innis, *The Fur Trade in Canada*: *An Introduction to Canadian Economic History* (Toronto: University of Toronto Press, 1956), p. 386.

[2]Diamond Jenness, *The Indian Background of Canadian History*, Canada, Department of Mines and Resources Bulletin no. 86 (Ottawa: J. O. Patenaude, 1937); George F. G. Stanley, "The Indian Background of Canadian History," Canadian Historical Association, *Papers* (1952): 14–21.

[3]Innis, *The Fur Trade*, p. 389; Donald Creighton, *The Empire of the St. Lawrence* (Toronto: Macmillan, 1970), pp. 16, 200–201.

Indians. Turner himself simply dismissed the Indians as "a consolidating agent," a common danger demanding united action on the part of the settlers.[4] In his view the Indians were merely an impediment to the drive westwards. Work on comparing frontier experiences has tended to produce a smug self-satisfaction with the Canadian example, as if a comparative lack of interracial violence were sufficient evidence of a superior Indian policy.[5]

The writing of Canadian history has been whiggish to the extent that it deals with the successful. The overriding concern has been with central politics, and, as non-participants in the development from colony to nation, the Indians have been neglected. Bernard De Voto's comment that American history "has been written as if history were a function solely of white culture — in spite of the fact that till well into the nineteenth century the Indians were one of the principal determinants of historical events,"[6] is equally applicable to Canadian.

In the historical writing of British Columbia the situation is little different. Even though the Indians formed the majority of the population of British Columbia until the 1880's, they receive little attention in the general histories of the province. Some more detailed studies have failed to achieve very high standards of historical accuracy. Works like Forrest E. LaViolette's *The Struggle For Survival* and the sections that deal with British Columbia in E. Palmer Patterson's *The Canadian Indian: A History Since 1500* are based on superficial research and consequently contain numerous errors of fact and interpretation.[7] More promising is the recent publication of works dealing with particular aspects of the history of Indian-European relations.[8] But British Columbia historians have, by default, left the study of the Indians' role in the province's history largely to the anthropologists, and Wilson Duff's *The*

---

[4]Frederick Jackson Turner, *The Frontier in American History* (New York: Holt, Rinehart and Winston, 1962), pp. 1, 15; see also Wilbur R. Jacobs, *Dispossessing the American Indian: Indians and Whites on the Colonial Frontier* (New York: Scribner's, 1972), p. 149.

[5]See, for example, George F. G. Stanley, "Western Canada and the Frontier Thesis," Canadian Historical Association, *Report* (1940): 111; Paul F. Sharp, "Three Frontiers: Some Comparative Studies of Canadian, American, and Australian Settlement," *Pacific Historical Review* 24 (1955): 373.

[6]Bernard De Voto, "Introduction," in Joseph Kinsey Howard, *Strange Empire* (Toronto: Swan, 1965), pp. 15–16.

[7]Forrest E. LaViolette, *The Struggle For Survival: Indian Cultures and the Protestant Ethic in British Columbia* (Toronto: University of Toronto Press, 1961); E. Palmer Patterson, *The Canadian Indian: A History Since 1500* (Don Mills, Ont.: Collier-Macmillan Canada, 1972).

[8]Robert E. Cail, *Land, Man, and the Law: The Disposal of Crown Lands in British Columbia, 1871–1913* (Vancouver: University of British Columbia Press, 1974); and Jean Usher, *William Duncan of Metlakatla: A Victorian Missionary in British Columbia*, National Museum of Man Publications in History, no. 5 (Ottawa: National Museums of Canada, 1974).

Indian History of British Columbia,[9] more than ten years after its publication, is still the best general work in the field. In 1958 the authors of a study of the contemporary social adjustment of the Indians of British Columbia were "impressed by the lack of historical writings dealing with the social history of White and Indian relations in British Columbia."[10] Today the remark has almost as much validity as it did then.

One of my purposes is to establish the role of the Indians in the history of British Columbia, but this volume is not an Indian history.[11] It is a history of the contact of two cultures, of Indian-European relations. Though some historians have tried to put the Indian at "the centre of his own history," they have generally proceeded to write descriptions of Indian and European relations.[12] Since the historian relies largely on written, and therefore European, sources, which inevitably impose limits on his appreciation of the Indian side of the story, it is perhaps more valid to deal with Indian-European relations rather than with so-called Indian history. These sources obviously contain distortions resulting from ignorance and prejudice, but they still reveal much about what the Indians were doing and, sometimes, about what they were thinking.[13]

The Indians' response to the intrusion of European culture is an important part of the history of British Columbia, and much can be gleaned from the usual historical sources about the behaviour of the Indians in contact with the white man. Moreover, the imbalance that would be created by relying solely on records written by Europeans can be partially corrected by utilizing the work of anthropologists. Anthropological literature provides the historian

[9]Wilson Duff, *The Indian History of British Columbia: Vol. 1. The Impact of the White Man*, Anthropology in British Columbia Memoir no. 5 (Victoria: Provincial Museum, 1964).

[10]H. B. Hawthorne, C. S. Belshaw, and S. M. Jamieson, *The Indians of British Columbia: A Study of Contemporary Social Adjustment* (Toronto: University of Toronto Press, 1958), p. 48.

[11]Nor does this book attempt to describe in any systematic way the traditional cultures of the Indians of British Columbia. Those wanting to investigate these cultures should begin with bibliographical guides such as Wilson Duff and Michael Kew, "A Select Bibliography of Anthropology of British Columbia," *BC Studies* 19 (1973): 73–121; or George Peter Murdock, *Ethnographic Bibliography of North America* (New Haven: Human Relations Area Files, 1960).

[12]Patterson, *The Canadian Indian*, pp. 28, 37, 38, and passim.

[13]T. O. Ranger has pointed out that the problems of dealing with the history of one group on the basis of the writings of another are by no means confined to the study of indigenous people responding to the impact of European culture. Scholars who have reconstructed the role of "inarticulate peasant movements" in Europe have necessarily had to rely on sources from outside such movements (Ranger, *Revolt in Southern Rhodesia 1896–1897: A Study of African Resistance* [Evanston: Northwestern University Press, 1967], p. x).

with descriptions of Indian cultures as well as insights into the Indians' response to the impact of Europeans.

There are, nevertheless, implicit tendencies towards ethnocentrism in a study of this kind. In a sense to write about the British Columbia Indian is unhistorical, for the political entity certainly had no meaning to the Indians for most of the period under discussion. There are also dangers in making generalizations about the Indians of British Columbia as if they were culturally similar. There were many subtle and not so subtle variations in the Indian cultures of the area, as well as a fundamental division between the coastal and interior tribes.

This volume does not describe every aspect of Indian-European relations in the years covered but attempts to draw out the essence of that relationship. It does not, like a Franz Boas ethnography, attempt to include all the information collected; rather, like all history, this work is by necessity selective. For the period of the maritime fur trade the sources are scattered and fragmentary anyway. Most of the information comes from voyagers' journals, and there are years in which several accounts are written followed by periods in which there is no information at all. This results in the kind of history that may not be congenial to those accustomed to the comparative certainties of political history. The greater amount of space devoted to the settlement period is also a reflection of the sources.

Variations in culture and contact experience notwithstanding, the Indians of the area that became British Columbia did have something in common during the period 1774 to 1890; and that was the European. Throughout this period most of the Indians were in contact with, and had to adjust to, the representatives and products of an alien culture. Naturally neither culture was monolithic, and therefore neither was uniform in its response to the other. Geography introduced another variable. The degree of contact and the pace of change were not the same among all the Indian groups at a given time. Nevertheless, at least one generalization can be made about the history of Indian-European contact in British Columbia; there was a fundamental change in the nature of Indian and European relations with the passing of the fur trade and the establishment of settlement, and this volume examines the differing nature of race relations on the fur-trading and settlement frontiers.

In British Columbia there was a sharply definable shift from fur trade to settlement. Although there were transitional phases either side of that date, in 1858 the fur trade essentially came to an end and the settlement frontier was born. Based on this premise, my contention is that the fur trade brought only minimal cultural change to the Indians and that it was change that they could control and adapt to. Settlement, on the other hand, was disruptive because it introduced major cultural change so rapidly that the Indians began to lose control of their situation. During the fur-trading period Indians and Europeans shared a mutually beneficial economic system. Because the fur traders were involved in an enterprise that required the co-operation of the Indians, they did not try to alter their social system radically, to undermine their beliefs, or to destroy their means of livelihood. Indeed, fur traders, at least to some extent, had to accommodate to Indian ways. With settlement, however, new groups of Europeans arrived who were in no way dependent on the Indians and who therefore not only had no desire to accommodate to Indian demands, but also no compunction about disrupting their traditional way of life.

The settlement frontier has been defined broadly to include other groups besides farming settlers. Gold miners, settlers, missionaries, and government officials, in different ways, all required the Indians to make major cultural changes, and the whites now had the power to force change. During the fur-trading period there was the kind of reciprocity between the two races that is implied by the word "relationship," but with settlement the word "impact" more appropriately describes the effect of one culture on the other.

The transition from fur trade to settlement and the change in the nature of the interaction between the two races were accompanied by a modification of the attitudes that the Europeans held towards the Indians. Because attitudes are powerful determinants of actions, chapter four examines the changing image of the Indian through the period. The maritime fur traders had only limited contact with the coast Indians, and so their opportunities to understand the cultures were limited. The land-based fur traders lived more closely with the Indians, and their letters and journals record much information that is relatively unencumbered with misconceptions and prejudice. Settlers, by contrast, had no need to comprehend the Indian way of life, and their image tended to be founded on preconceptions rather than frontier experience. This chapter will attempt to probe beyond the realm of official despatches[14] and uncover the attitudes of a larger number of the participants. Although the student still has to rely on the surviving records left by the literate and articulate, chapter four draws more on travellers' accounts and the writings of residents than on official papers.

By 1890 the developments that had commenced with the advent of settlement were complete. As the Europeans consolidated their hold on the country, the traditional Indian cultures were disrupted and the Indians' current needs were often neglected. Governmental action constituted an attack on Indian cultures and reflected the fact that the Indians had become largely irrelevant to the development of the province by white settlers.

---

[14]Philip Curtin has prefaced his study with a similar remark (see Curtin, *The Image of Africa: British Ideas and Action, 1780–1850* [Madison: University of Wisconsin Press, 1964], p. vii).

I would like to thank many people who helped to make this book possible. My indebtedness to my teachers in New Zealand, who first showed me the way, is too great to be repaid. I particularly appreciate the assistance of Anne Yandle and the staff of Special Collections, University of British Columbia Library, who have been consistently helpful over a number of years. Frances Gundry and Kent Haworth at the Provincial Archives of British Columbia always answered my questions helpfully and guided me through the eccentricities of the collection. My research was also facilitated by the cooperation of the Public Archives of Canada; the Department of Indian Affairs and Northern Development; the Glenbow Historical Library and Archives, Calgary; the Alexander Turnbull Library, Wellington; the Mitchell Library, Sydney; and the Church Missionary Society Archives, London. I wish to thank the governor and committee of the Hudson's Bay Company for their permission to use and publish from the company archives.

I acknowledge the work of Nancy, Elsie, Dru, and Carole of the office of the Dean of Arts, Simon Fraser University, who typed the final manuscript so rapidly.

Finally, and most importantly, I owe deep gratitude to Coralie, for all she did to make this work possible, and to my doctoral supervisors, Margaret A. Ormsby and Wilson Duff who, in different ways, rendered invaluable assistance. While all these people contributed to whatever merit this book may have, the errors are mine.

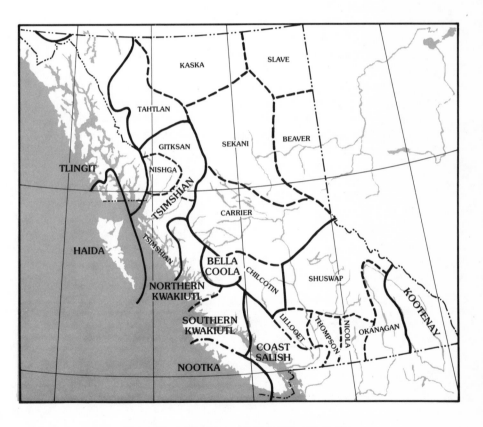

Major Ethnic Divisions of British Columbia Indians

1

The Maritime Fur Trade

... we found to our cost, that these people, ... possessed all the cunning
necessary to the gains of mercantile life.[1] —JOHN MEARES, 1790

Historians have usually characterized the maritime fur trade on the northwest coast as a trade in which gullible Indians were exploited by avaricious and unprincipled European traders. Stanley Ryerson has asserted that the maritime fur trade "depended on ruthless exploitation of Indian labour... backed whenever necessary by force or open threats of force."[2] Others, with less obvious ideological commitments, have made similar comments. H.H. Bancroft wrote of Captain James Cook buying furs from the "guileless savage,"[3] while F.W. Howay, the most meticulous student of the trade, described it as a predatory affair, "merely a looting of the coast."[4] Like much historical writing on Indian-European relations, these conclusions pass judgments on European behaviour and fail to analyse Indian responses. In fact, the Indians of the northwest coast exercised a great deal of control over the trading relationship and, as a consequence, remained in control of their culture during this early contact period.

The first recorded encounter with the Indians of what was to become British Columbia was in July 1774 when the Spanish navigator Juan Pérez met a group of Haida off the northwest point of Langara Island. The record of this initial contact is to be found in the diaries of two Franciscan friars, Juan Crespi and Thomás de la Peña, who were aboard the *Santiago*. According to these reports the first responses of the Indians to the presence of Europeans were tentative, curious, and peaceful.

A group of Haida came out to the *Santiago* in their canoes. They could not be convinced to come aboard, but they did paddle around the vessel throwing feathers on the water. The act was a sign that they came in peace, and al-

[1]John Meares, *Voyages Made in the Years 1788 and 1789, from China to the North West Coast of America* ... (London: Logographic Press, 1790), pp. 141–42.
[2]Stanley B. Ryerson, *The Founding of Canada: Beginnings to 1815* (Toronto: Progress Books, 1960), p. 262.
[3]Hubert Howe Bancroft, *History of British Columbia* (San Francisco: History Company, 1890), p. 4.
[4]F. W. Howay, "An Outline Sketch of the Maritime Fur Trade," Canadian Historical Association, *Report* (1932): 14.

though the Spaniards could not know its significance, Crespi concluded that these Indians were a "peaceful and very docile people." The Indians' desire to trade soon became greater than their fear of the strangers, and when other canoes paddled out to the vessel, the exchange of goods began. The sailors offered clothes, beads, and knives, and in return the Haida traded some sea otter furs along with a variety of handmade articles. Carved plates and spoons, mats, and hats were all obtained, but the diarists were most impressed with what appear to have been chilcat blankets and with the ornately carved wooden boxes that were offered to them.[5] The *Santiago* spent two days in the area and then moved on without any of its crew having made a landfall. The expedition met in a similar way with the Indians of the west coast of Vancouver Island, but again no one set foot on land.

This first fleeting contact between the two cultures was not renewed for four years,[6] and a decade was to pass before the first fur-trading expedition came to the coast. In 1778 the brilliant, meticulous James Cook, leading his third expedition to the Pacific, spent nearly a month refitting at Nootka Sound. While he was there, his crews obtained a number of sea otter skins from the Indians, and the story has often been retold of how these pelts fetched fabulous prices in China. However, rumours of the profits to be made by selling sea otter furs in China were not confirmed until the publication of the official account of Cook's third voyage in 1784 and Captain James King's revelation that some of the best skins had sold for $120.[7] In the following year the first fur-trading vessel, appropriately named *Sea Otter*, arrived at Nootka under James Hanna.

In the next few years, as explorers began to probe the sounds and circle the islands, the continental foreshore was opened to the maritime fur trade. For the first three seasons all the trading vessels were British, but in 1778 the first American ships arrived on the coast. In 1792 the trade began to burgeon. That season there were twenty-one vessels engaged in the trade, nearly double the number of the previous year, and more than half of them were British. But in

[5]The sources for the previous two paragraphs are Juan Crespi and Thomas de la Peña, Diaries, 20 and 21 July 1774, in Geo. Butler Griffin, ed., *Documents from the Sutro Collection*, Publications of the Historical Society of Southern California (Los Angeles: Franklin Printing Co., 1891), 2: part 1, pp. 121–23, 187–94; Juan Pérez, Diary, 20 and 21 July and 8 August 1774, in Margaret Olive Johnson, "Spanish Exploration of the Pacific Coast by Juan Pérez in 1774" (Master of Letters thesis, University of California, Berkeley, 1911), pp. 58–64, 87.

[6]In 1775 Juan Francisco de la Bodega y Quadra passed up the coast in the schooner *Sonora*. Although he discovered and named Bucareli Bay on the west coast of Prince of Wales Island, he did not make a landfall between latitudes 49° and 54° 40' N.

[7]James Cook and James King, *A Voyage to the Pacific Ocean . . . in His Majesty's Ships the "Resolution" and the "Discovery." In the Years, 1776, 1777, 1778, 1779, and 1780* (London: G. Nicol and T. Cadell, 1784), 3: 437.

the next year the American outnumbered the British, and this trend continued until by 1801 the trade was dominated by American vessels, most of them out of Boston. The peak years of the maritime fur trade were from 1792 to about 1812. By 1825 the Hudson's Bay Company was becoming active on the northwest coast, and the maritime fur trade had virtually ceased to exist as a separate entity.

During the very early years of the trade pelts were relatively easily acquired, and some European traders made considerable profits. On 2 July 1787 Captain George Dixon was tacking into a bay that was later to become famous as Cloak Bay when some Haida approached in their canoes. The Haida could not, at first, be tempted to trade; "their attention seemed entirely taken up with viewing the vessel, which they apparently did with marks of wonder and surprise."[8] Only after the Indians had satisfied their curiosity about the vessel could they be induced to trade. Later in the day Dixon ran his snow, the *Queen Charlotte*, further up the bay and a scene is described "which absolutely beggars all description." The crew was "so overjoyed, that we could scarcely believe the evidence of our senses," because the Indians were falling over each other to trade their cloaks and furs: "they fairly quarrelled with each other about which should sell his cloak first; and some actually threw their furs on board if nobody was at hand to receive them." In half an hour Dixon obtained 300 furs. A month later, when he left the islands that he had named the Queen Charlottes, his vessel had 1,821 furs in its hold.[9] In 1789, two years after Dixon's visit, the crew of the American ship *Columbia* emulated his example. John Kendrick, the master of the *Columbia*, made one of the best deals ever when in a few minutes he traded 200 pelts at the rate of one chisel each at the Indian village of Kiusta on the northern end of Graham Island.[10] In the first years of the trade these furs, so cheaply purchased, brought high prices in China. It was claimed that the 560 sea otter pelts that Hanna collected on his first trip realized $20,600,[11] and that the Dixon and Portlock expedition sold 2,552 furs for $54,875.[12] Prices such as these moved Dixon's associate,

---

[8]George Dixon, *A Voyage Round the World; but more Particularly to the North-West Coast of America: Performed in 1785, 1786, 1787 and 1788, in the "King George" and "Queen Charlotte,"* ... (London: G. Goulding, 1789), pp. 199–200. Although Dixon's name appears on the title page of this work, it was actually written by William Beresford who was supercargo on the *Queen Charlotte*.

[9]Ibid., pp. 201, 228.

[10]"Robert Haswell's Log of the First Voyage of the *Columbia*" [June 1789], in Frederic W. Howay, ed., *Voyages of the "Columbia" to the Northwest Coast 1787–1790 and 1790–1793* (Boston: Massachusetts Historical Society, 1941), p. 96.

[11]Dixon, *A Voyage*, pp. 315–16. The author notes elsewhere that the currency used in most of these transactions in China was Spanish dollars, p. 312.

[12]George Dixon, "Remarks on the Voyages of John Meares, Esq. in a Letter to the Gentleman," in F. W. Howay, ed., *The Dixon-Meares Controversy* ... (Toronto: Ryerson [1929]), p. 30.

Nathaniel Portlock, to remark that his branch of commerce was perhaps "the most profitable and lucrative employ that the enterprising merchant can possibly engage in."[13]

Yet even in these early years the Indians were not passive objects of exploitation. Rather they vigorously asserted their demands. Northwest coast Indians were, for example, never very interested in baubles and beads as trade items. Cook noted in his journal that European beads could not supplant the Nootkans' own ornaments.[14] So the old stereotype of the avaricious trader stealing Indian furs for a few trinkets never applied to the maritime fur trade.

Furthermore, the comparatively easy trading and high profits of the first frantic years were not to continue. As vessels visited the coast with increased frequency, the trade settled into a more consistent pattern, and it was one over which the Indians exercised a great deal of control. It was, after all, Indian demands that had to be satisfied before sea otter pelts exchanged hands.

For one thing, the Indians rapidly lost their curiosity about the Europeans and their vessels. A ship under full sail was an impressive sight, but to the trading Indians it became commonplace. In contrast to the curiosity with which the *Queen Charlotte* was received in 1787, the Indians of Cloak Bay wandered all over Jacinto Caamaño's ship *Aranzazú* in 1792 "without showing wonder at anything, nor was there any object of which they did not appear to know the use."[15] As in most contact situations, the initial phase, when the white men were inexplicable and were perhaps even regarded as supernatural beings, soon passed. It quickly became apparent to the Indians that their visitors were quite human, and though some of their behaviour might be curious, many of their demands and desires were familiar.

As the Indians grew accustomed to the presence of the Europeans, they also became shrewder in trading with them. Even after his brief encounter with a group of Haida in 1774, Pérez declared that the Indians were expert and skillful traders.[16] The members of Cook's expedition reached similar conclusions. As one of them put it, "they are very keen traders getting as much as they could for everything they had; always asking for more give them what you

[13]Nathaniel Portlock, *A Voyage Round the World; but more Particularly to the North-West Coast of America: Performed in 1785, 1786, 1787 and 1788 . . .* (London: J. Stockdale, 1789), p. 382.

[14]James Cook, Journal, 30 March and 26 April 1778, in J. C. Beaglehole, ed., *The Journals of Captain James Cook on his Voyages of Discovery: The Voyage of the "Resolution" and "Discovery," 1776–1780* (Cambridge: Hakluyt Society, 1967), part 1, pp. 297, 302, 314; see also Crespi, *Diary*, 21 July 1774, Griffin, 2: part 1, p. 192.

[15]Jacinto Caamaño, Journal, 19 July 1792, "The Journal of Jacinto Caamaño," *"British Columbia Historical Quarterly* 2 (1938): 215 (hereafter cited as *BCHQ*). Cook made similar remarks about the Nootka Indians as early as 1778 (see Cook, *Journal,* 12 April 1778, Beaglehole, part 1, p. 301).

[16]Pérez, "Diary," 20 July 1774, Johnson, p. 59.

would." The consequence of their astuteness was that the Indians of Nootka "got a greater middly and variety of things" from *Resolution* and *Discovery* than any other people that the vessels had visited.[17] When John Meares left on a trading expedition to the coast in 1787, he was warned that "it appears that the natives are such intelligent traders, that should you be in the least degree lavish, or inattentive in forming bargains, they will so enhance the value of their furs, as not only to exhaust your present stock, but also to injure, if not to ruin, any future adventure."[18]

The Indian demand for metals, particularly iron, was recognized by most early traders. Cook's ships left Nootka with hardly any brass left on board, and his crews had also traded a considerable amount of iron.[19] Like the explorers, the early fur traders found that the coast Indians were most partial to iron. Members of the Spanish expedition led by Pérez had noted that the Indians particularly wanted large pieces with a cutting edge, and Dixon's staple medium of exchange was "toes," or iron chisels.[20] Early in 1789 the crew of the *Columbia*, trading in the Straits of Juan De Fuca, were mortified to see seventy prime pelts escape them "for want of Chizels to purchase them."[21]

Another indication of Indian control of the maritime fur trade was the rapid increase in the price of furs in the early 1790's. In those years traders who hoped to follow the example of those who were first in the field and purchase large numbers of furs cheaply were often disappointed. John Boit returned to the coast in 1795 and found that the price of pelts at Dadens on Langara Island had increased 100 per cent since 1792 when he had been there on the *Columbia*.[22] Archibald Menzies observed a similar rate of increase in Johnstone Strait when he returned there with Vancouver in 1792,[23] while another member of Vancouver's expedition claimed that prices generally had quadrupled since the earliest voyages.[24] At Nootka, where Meares had

[17]Beaglehole, *Journals*, part 1, p. 302n.2; and Cook, *Journal*, 18 April 1778, Beaglehole, part 1, pp. 302–3.

[18]The Merchant Proprietors to John Meares, 24 December 1787, Meares, *Voyages*, appendix no. 1, unpaginated.

[19]Cook, *Journal*, 18 April and 29 March 1778, Beaglehole, part 1, pp. 302, 296.

[20]Peña, *Diary*, 21 July 1774, Griffin, 2, part 1, p. 123; Dixon, *A Voyage*, pp. 200–201.

[21]"Haswell's Log of the First Voyage," 19 April 1789, Howay, "*Columbia*," p. 81.

[22]John Boit, Journal, 9 June 1795, "Journal of a Voyage Round the Globe, 1795 and 1796 [in the *Union*]," University of British Columbia Library (hereafter cited as UBCL).

[23]George Vancouver, *A Voyage of Discovery to the North Pacific Ocean, and Round the World; . . . Performed in the Years 1790, 1791, 1792, 1793, 1794 and 1795 in the "Discovery" Sloop of War and Armed Tender "Chatham," . . .* (London: G. G. and J. Robinson, 1798), 1: 348.

[24]Edmund S. Meany, ed., *A New Vancouver Journal of the Discovery of Puget Sound by a Member of the "Chatham's" Crew* (Seattle: University of Washington Press, 1915), p. 40.

traded ten skins for one piece of copper in 1786, the asking rate six years later was one pelt for one piece of copper.[25] Price increases such as these led the Spaniard Alejandro Malaspina to conclude that the great profits of Cook's and Portlock's voyages were no longer attainable.[26] There were, of course, other factors that affected prices, including the growing scarcity of furs. However, the depletion of the sea otter was not as significant in the early 1790's as it was to be after the turn of the century. The Indians had learned to demand higher prices while furs were still relatively plentiful.

Not only did the Indians quickly learn to demand a greater quantity of goods for their furs, but they also became very discriminating about the nature of the goods they acquired. It is a commonly held view that the Indian taste in trade goods was "strangely whimsical and constantly variable." By citing examples from widely differing points in time and place it is possible to create the impression that Indian demands were merely fickle[27] and to obscure those patterns that their requests conformed to. Initially the Indians wanted articles that had meaning and use within pre-contact society. They already possessed both iron and copper at the time of contact, but not in plentiful supply. For this reason iron and other metals were highly valued and in great demand in the early years of the trade. The iron chisels brought by the traders were sufficiently similar to indigenous tools to be readily understood, hence the heavy initial demand for them. As the market became saturated with these items, their value dropped, other needs began to operate, and new demands were made. The trade meant that the furs were not used for clothing as much as they had been prior to the arrival of the Europeans. The need for an alternative arose, and the Indians turned their attention to trading cloth, clothing, and blankets. The demand for blankets particularly remained fairly constant, and they became a staple in the trade. As a garment they served an important function for the Indians. But the blanket was also an article that could be easily counted and compared. It was, therefore, a useful medium of exchange both in the fur trade and for Indian potlatches. During the later years of the

---

[25]Cecil Jane, trans., *A Spanish Voyage to Vancouver and the North-West Coast of America being the Narrative of the Voyage Made in the Year 1792 by the Schooners "Sutil" and "Mexicana" to Explore the Strait of Fuca* (London: Argonaut Press, 1930), p. 90; see also Vancouver, *A Voyage*, 1: 349.

[26]Alessandro Malaspina, "Politico-Scientific Voyages Around the World . . . from 1789–1794," UBCL, 2: 244.

[27]F. W. Howay, "The Voyage of the *Hope*: 1790–1792," *Washington Historical Quarterly* 11 (1920): 28; Howay, "The Maritime Fur Trade," p. 8; Paul Chrisler Phillips, *The Fur Trade* (Norman: University of Oklahoma Press, 1961), 2: 54; Hubert Howe Bancroft, *History of the Northwest Coast* (San Francisco: A. L. Bancroft and Co., 1884), 1: 370–71.

trade the Indians acquired some more exotic tastes. A liking for rum, smoking tobacco, and molasses gradually developed, and muskets also became an important trade item.[28]

Naturally, there were exceptions to this pattern, since the Indian market was as much subject to fads as any other. Yet most of these were also related to Indian usages. The popularity of the iron collars forged aboard the brigantine *Hope* has been seen as the height of Haida faddishness, but this demand was consistent with the Haida taste in personal ornamentation. Copper bracelets, for example, were frequently worn, and Joseph Ingraham made his collars from the pattern of one he had seen a Haida woman wearing.[29] The same point can be made about the ermine skins that William Sturgis sold with considerable profit at Kaigani.[30] Ermine pelts were an important wealth item among the coast Indians. But demand for these kinds of articles was temporary, and the market quickly became glutted.

There were other factors that created the impression that the Indians would take a great variety of goods. At times they would receive as presents items, such as beads and trinkets, that they would not accept in trade.[31] Often when Indians accepted these baubles they were as an additional gift to facilitate trade and not as a part of the actual trading transaction. These presents added to the diversity of goods that changed hands but not to the number of articles that would buy furs.

Trading Indians paid great attention to the quality of the goods that they acquired, and trade articles were examined closely and carefully before bargains were struck.[32] Iron that contained flaws or was too brittle was of little value to the Indians because they worked it while it was cold. Indians showed great "judgement and sagacity" when selecting firearms; woollen goods of insufficient quality were turned down, and porcelain imitations of

[28]This kind of pattern has been delineated for other areas of the Pacific (see Dorothy Shineberg, *They Came for Sandalwood: A Study of the Sandalwood Trade in the South-West Pacific* [Melbourne: Melbourne University Press, 1967], pp. 145, 150).

[29]Howay, "Voyage of the *Hope*," p. 10; Joseph Ingraham, Journal, 12 July 1791, in Mark D. Kaplanoff, ed., *Joseph Ingraham's Journal of the Brigantine "Hope" on a Voyage to the Northwest Coast of North America 1790–1792* (Barre, Mass.: Imprint Society, 1971), p. 105.

[30]F. W. Howay, ed., "William Sturgis: The Northwest Fur Trade," *BCHQ* 8 (1944): 22.

[31]Vancouver, *A Voyage*, 1: 349.

[32]C. P. Claret Fleurieu, *A Voyage Round the World, Performed during the Years 1790, 1791, and 1792, by Etienne Marchand . . .* (London: T. N. Longman and O. Rees, 1801), 1: 449.

dentalia shells were treated with contempt.[33] Usually the Indians knew what they wanted when they were trading, and they were determined to get it. Nor were Indian traders easily diverted from their purpose. One captain hoped that a few hours of conviviality in the house of a chief would bring him more furs, "but, no sooner was traffic mentioned, than from being the engaging master of the house, he became a Jew chapman and dealer."[34] There are numerous comments in the journals of trading expeditions to the northwest coast about the enterprise of Indian traders whose trading acumen meant that many captains "had the sorrow to see valuable furs escape us, the acquisition of which was the principal object of the expedition, for want of suitable objects to exchange."[35]

As vessels came in search of furs with increasing frequency, the Indians became very tough-minded manipulators of competition. They forced prices upwards, particularly at places often visited by traders. As a consequence, in the early years furs were found to cost more at Nootka than at other places.[36] Later, harbours such as Newitty, Massett, and Kaigani became centres of trade and of high prices. At Kaigani John D'Wolf found in 1805 that the Indians were "so extravagant in their demands. . .that it was quite impossible to trade."[37] When more than one vessel was at anchor, the Indians would move from one to another comparing prices and bargaining to force them upward; and, as one trader observed, it was easy to increase one's price but always impossible to reduce it.[38] The American Richard Cleveland, while on the northern coast in 1799, was told by another captain that he could expect ten other vessels from Boston to be trading in the area that year. He was, therefore, anxious to dispose of his "articles of traffic" before competition reduced their value, because, he said,

[33]Meares, *Voyages*, p. 368; James Burney, Journal, 24 April 1778, "Journal of the Proceedings of His Majesty's Sloop *Discovery*—Chas. Clerke, Commander, 1776–1779," Provincial Archives of British Columbia (hereafter cited as PABC); John D'Wolf, *Voyage to the North Pacific and a Journey through Siberia more than Half a Century Ago* (Cambridge: Welch, Bigelow, and Company, 1861), p. 19; M. Camille de Roquefeuil, *A Voyage Round the World, between the Years 1816–1819* (London: Sir R. Phillips and Co., 1823), p. 87; G. H. Von Langsdorff, *Voyages and Travels in Various Parts of the World, during the Years 1803, 1804, 1805, 1806 and 1807* (Carlisle: George Philips, 1817), p. 413.
[34]Fleurieu, *A Voyage*, 1: 422.
[35]Roquefeuil, *A Voyage*, p. 92.
[36]"John Hoskins' Memorandum on the Trade at Nootka Sound" [August 1792], Howay, *"Columbia,"* p. 486; Peter Puget, Log, 27 April 1793, "Log of the Proceedings of His Majesty's Armed Tender *Chatham* . . . Commencing 12 Day of January 1793," UBCL, p. 40.
[37]D'Wolf, *Voyage*, pp. 17, 18.
[38]Samuel Dorr to Ebenezer Dorr, 16 August 1801, Ebenezer Dorr, Dorr Marine Collection, 1795–1820, PABC.

the Indians are sufficiently cunning to derive all possible advantage from competition, and will go from one vessel to another, and back again, with assertions of offers made to them, which have no foundation in truth, and showing themselves to be as well versed in the tricks of the trade as the greatest adepts.[39]

Even the captains of solitary vessels who felt that Indian prices were exorbitant were informed that other traders would soon follow who would be willing to pay what was asked.[40] Such exploitation of competition by the trading Indians was one of the reasons why, far from making huge profits, many fur-trading voyages were ruinous to their promoters.[41] As the Indians raised their prices, captains were apt to overestimate the value of their cargo and, therefore, their margin of profit.

Indian traders were not above adding a few tricks to the trade. When Cook was at Nootka, he found that the Indians were not quite as "guileless" as Bancroft believed. The explorer discovered that the Indians were deceiving his men by selling containers of oil that were partly filled with water. In fact, "once or twice they had the address to impose upon us whole bladders of water wi[t]hout a drop of Oil in them."[42] Another captain found a Nootkan trying to pass off a land otter pelt as a sea otter in the dusk of evening.[43] Meares went as far as to claim that in their commercial transactions the Indians would play a thousand tricks. He was probably exaggerating when he added that Europeans were "more or less, the dupes of their cunning,"[44] but it is undeniable that Indians behaved with confidence when they were trading.

The Indians were able to assert their demands with such vigour that European captains had to modify their trading methods to accommodate them. In the early years of trade Dixon had largely coasted along the shoreline and relied on the Indians to paddle out to him to trade. He was convinced "that this plan was attended with better and speedier success than our laying at anchor could possibly be."[45] Only four years later, in 1791, Ingraham collected 1,400 sea otter skins off the Queen Charlotte Islands, and he attributed his success to the opposite tactic of remaining at one village until no further

[39]Richard J. Cleveland, *Voyages and Commercial Enterprises of the Sons of New England* (New York: Leavitt and Allan, 1865), p. 94.

[40]"Haswell's Log of the Second Voyage of the *Columbia*," 25 April 1792, Howay, "*Columbia*," p. 323.

[41]Howay, ed., "William Sturgis," p. 20.

[42]Cook, *Journal*, 18 April 1778, Beaglehole, part 1, p. 302; cf. Bancroft, *History of British Columbia*, p. 4.

[43]Roquefeuil, *A Voyage*, p. 97.

[44]Meares, *Voyages*, p. 148.

[45]Dixon, *A Voyage*, p. 204.

furs could be secured. The Indians preferred this approach to paddling out four or five miles to a moving vessel.[46] The tendency was for captains to have to spend more and more time in one place instead of moving about. It also became apparent that one season was insufficient time to gather a profitable cargo. Crews began to winter on the coast and, by 1806-08, to trade all year round.[47] At first most trading was conducted over the side of vessels with the Indians remaining in their canoes, but increasingly they had to be allowed to come on deck to display their wares.

Changes such as these occurred because the Indians preferred to trade at their leisure. They had plenty of time at their disposal and liked to use it to bargain over prices. Though captains were invariably in a hurry to fill their holds, Indian concepts of time operated increasingly. Many "would wait alongside several hours—nay all day—to obtain their price."[48] D'Wolf complained that the Kaigani Indians would lie about the deck for days on end endeavouring to extort unreasonable prices for their furs, while affecting the utmost indifference as to whether they sold them or not.[49]

Other Indian usages had to be observed by captains hoping to acquire furs. The journals show that a considerable amount of Indian ceremonial accompanied trading. One observer noted that it was a constant custom to begin and terminate commercial transactions with strangers with singing.[50] Although traders often found such ceremonies irritating and time-consuming, they had to be patiently accepted before the exchange of goods began. However fixed European notions of the nature of trade might be, traders also had to accede to the custom of gift exchange with Indian leaders. This ritual was observed in spite of the feeling on the part of some captains that furs exchanged as presents were sure to prove the dearest.[51]

European traders were also adapting to the patterns of northwest coast Indian society by conducting most of their trading with Indian leaders rather than with the general population. Some of the trading was done with individual families, but the people did not possess such an abundance of furs as their leaders. Those chiefs who had the good fortune to be in the right place at the right time were able to dominate the trade. So great was the power and influence of some of these leaders that European traders found it in their interests to cultivate their friendship even though they had to be treated with much of

---

[46]Ingraham, *Journal*, 2 September 1791, Kaplanoff, p. 146.
[47]Howay, "The Maritime Fur Trade," p. 10.
[48]Ingraham, *Journal*, 2 September 1791, Kaplanoff, p. 147.
[49]D'Wolf, *Voyage*, p. 18.
[50]Fleurieu, *A Voyage*, 1: 283.
[51]Meares, *Voyages*, p. 120; Ingraham, *Journal*, 5 and 11 August 1791, Kaplanoff, pp. 126, 130; "John Hoskins' Narrative of the Second Voyage of the *Columbia*," January 1792, Howay, "*Columbia*," p. 265.

the deference that they expected from their own people. Richard Cleveland was one trader who generally could not abide the presence of Indians on the deck of his ship. When he was at Kaigani, however, the Indian leader named Kow had to be indulged with hospitality on board. "It would," said Cleveland, "have been folly to have prevented him."[52] Indian leaders who were unwittingly insulted had to be mollified, while supposed insults from Indians were often tolerated in the hope of driving a bargain.[53]

European traders were further subject to Indian trading patterns to the extent that those Indians who sold them furs were often middlemen who had' their own markup. The first Europeans to arrive on the coast noticed how Indian traders made efforts to prevent other Indians from trading with them. While he was at Nootka, Cook, who by 1778 was an experienced observer of the behaviour of indigenous peoples, noted that the Indians whom he first encountered attempted to monopolize the trade with the *Resolution* and the *Discovery*. Whenever strangers were allowed to trade with the ships, the transactions were managed by the people of Yuquot and in such a way as to increase their own prices while lowering the value of the English commodities. On other occasions the local Indians used force to prevent outsiders from trading with the ships.[54] It was evident that these explorers had not arrived in a commercial desert and that definite trading patterns already existed. Much is often made by European historians of the trading abilities of the Yankee captains out of Boston, but it is less frequently remembered that the Indians also had a long tradition of trading among themselves.

Many, perhaps most, of the furs that changed hands during the period of the maritime fur trade were not captured by the Indians who traded them. When captains were exhorted, as they often were, to wait a day or two so that Indian traders could gather more furs, it did not mean that those Indians intended to hunt for them. Indian leaders on the outer coast collected furs from those who lived deeper inland either as plunder or by trade. Some chiefs quite frankly told white traders that if they would wait they would go and fight for furs which they would then bring to sell.[55] No doubt this method of gathering pelts was not uncommon. It was well known that Maquinna con-

---

[52]Richard Cleveland, Log, 27 June 1799, Log Kept by Capt. Richard Cleveland, 10 January 1799 to 4 May 1804, UBCL.

[53]Cleveland, Log, 17 June 1799; Meares, *Voyages*, p. 128; D'Wolf, *Voyage*, p. 18; and "Hoskins' Narrative," July 1791, Howay, "*Columbia*," p. 198.

[54]Cook, *Journal*, 1 and 18 April 1778, Beaglehole, part 1, pp. 299, 302. See also Charles Clerke, *Journal* [April 1778], Beaglehole, part 2, p. 1326. Cook did not anchor at Yuquot (called Friendly Cove by Europeans) but at Ship Cove (now called Resolution Cove) on the southwest tip of Bligh Island. But it seems likely that the people who had a summer village at Yuquot were the ones controlling the trade with the expedition.

[55]Ingraham, *Journal*, 2 August 1791, Kaplanoff, p. 121.

trolled a trading network with the Indians who lived near the mouth of the Nimpkish River on the east coast of Vancouver Island. When European explorers established the insularity of Vancouver Island, they also found that the Indians who had villages along Johnstone and Queen Charlotte Straits were quite familiar with their merchandise. These Indians, in contrast to the Coast Salish to the south, had passed through the stage of high demand for iron and were also much sharper traders.[56] Maquinna nevertheless made considerable profit in his trade with these people.[57] Wickaninish, the chief at Clayoquot Sound, exercised a similar control over the trade of that area.[58] The Haida likewise traded with mainland groups. By 1799 it was considered that not half of the furs traded at the Queen Charlottes were collected there.[59] Indians on the outer coast exchanged European goods with inland Indians at 200 and 300 per cent profit margins,[60] and in this way furs were collected at the central locations of the trade with European vessels. Thus, one seaman observed, "we see the untutored Indian influenced by true Mercantile principles."[61]

The Indians of the northwest coast, rather than feeling exploited by the European traders, usually became annoyed when opportunities to trade escaped them. If Europeans rejected offers to trade, particularly when furs were offered by the Indians in the form of reciprocal presents, the refusal could be, and sometimes was, taken as an insult.[62] Indian groups also became dissatisfied when the maritime fur trade passed them by. Sea otters were rare at Nootka Sound by the turn of the century, and vessels were neglecting the area in favour of visiting the more lucrative inner harbours.

It has been argued that because trading captains seldom expected to return to a specific locality, they were frequently able to defraud Indian traders and regularly took violent action against them.[63] In fact, there was more continu-

[56]Vancouver, *A Voyage*, 1: 331–32, 346, 349; Jane, *A Spanish Voyage*, pp. 74–75; Archibald Menzies, Journal, 20 July 1792, in C. F. Newcombe, ed., *Menzies' Journal of Vancouver's Voyage, April to October 1792*, Archives of British Columbia Memoir no. 5 (Victoria: W. H. Cullin, 1923), p. 88.

[57]"Hoskins' Narrative," January 1792, Howay, "*Columbia*," p. 265.

[58]Meares, *Voyages*, p. 142; Bernard Magee, Log, 31 May 1793, "Log of the *Jefferson*," UBCL.

[59]*Eliza*, Journal, 5 May 1799, "Journal of the *Eliza*, February-May 1799," UBCL, p. 45. Although this manuscript includes a title page attributing the authorship of the journal to Sturgis, it is clear from the text that he was not the author.

[60]Ibid., 4 March 1799, p. 13.

[61]Puget, "Log of the *Chatham*," p. 52.

[62]Ibid., 27 July 1793, p. 71; Edward Belcher, *Narrative of a Voyage Round the World Performed in Her Majesty's Ship "Sulpher," during the Years 1836–1842 . . .* (London: H. Colburn, 1843), 2: 111.

[63]See Howay, "The Maritime Fur Trade," p. 9; and Criston I. Archer, "The Transient Presence: A Re-Appraisal of Spanish Attitudes toward the Northwest Coast in the Eighteenth Century," *BC Studies* 18 (1973): 29.

ity in the trade than might be expected. There are records of some 330 fur-trading vessels coming to the northwest coast during the forty years between 1785 and 1825. Of this total 40 per cent spent more than one season trading on the coast, and about 23 per cent made three or more visits.[64] Not only did many vessels and captains return to the coast more than once, but also a large percentage of the trade was done with a few Indian leaders at a limited number of entrepôts. So a European trader who made more than one voyage was very likely to return to the same place to trade, particularly if relations with the Indians had been amicable during the first visit. The possibility of a return trip militated against the indiscriminate use of fraud and violence.

During this early contact period there was a certain amount of interracial violence, but its extent should not be exaggerated. Such were the demands made by the Indians on European traders that it was considered that "a man ought to be endowed with an uncommon share of patience to trade with any of these people."[65] Of course, many trading captains lacked their fair share of patience, and caught in the squeeze between increasing costs on the northwest coast and declining prices in China, they were apt to become annoyed with Indians who made what they considered to be unreasonable demands. When coasting became unfruitful and vessels had to stay longer in one place, the extended contact added to the possibility of friction. Given these circumstances, what is surprising is not that there were some outbreaks of violence, but that they were not more frequent.

It is clear that the hostility of the Indians has been overemphasized in European records. Captains often came to the coast expecting the Indians to be warlike and therefore perceived hostility where it did not exist. This possibility was exemplified while Cook was at Nootka. The Indians whom he had been dealing with suddenly armed themselves and became aggressive. Cook first thought that the actions were directed against his men, but then he realized that they were aimed at another group of Indians who were attempting to trade with his ships. Other captains, lacking Cook's experience, were not so discerning. In fact, one of his own crew was still suspicious that there

---

[64]The figures are based on Howay's own compilations of the visits of trading vessels to the northwest coast (see "A List of Trading Vessels in the Maritime Fur Trade, 1785–1794," *Transactions of the Royal Society of Canada*, 3d ser., 24, section 2 [1930]: 111–34; "A List of Trading Vessels in the Maritime Fur Trade, 1795–1804," ibid., 25, section 2 [1931]: 117–49; "A List of Vessels in the Maritime Fur Trade, 1805–1814," ibid., 26, section 2 [1932]: 43–86; "A List of Trading Vessels in the Maritime Fur Trade, 1815–1819," ibid., 27, section 2 [1933]: 119–47; "A List of Trading Vessels in the Maritime Fur Trade, 1820–1825," ibid., 28, section 2 [1934]: 11–49). The percentages of vessels making more than one visit are probably a little conservative since the records for some of the single season voyages are of dubious authenticity. For the same reason the total figure is only approximate.

[65]Ingraham, *Journal*, 12 August 1791, Kaplanoff, p. 132.

was a strategy between the two parties of Indians to catch the visitors off their guard and attack them with a combined force.[66] A member of Cook's expedition recorded an account of the Nootka welcoming ceremonies but added that, although intended as a sign of friendship, these ceremonies could as easily be taken as an indication of enmity.[67] In a situation where neither race was familiar with the behaviour patterns of the other, the possibility of misunderstanding leading to violence was as great as the degree of mutual suspicion.

Seeing the situation in racial terms, Europeans tended to assume that all Indians were equally hostile and that all hostility was directed towards them. That these "savage" Indians were "only waiting an opportunity for to Massacre the whole of us in cold blood" was a common enough belief among fur traders.[68] Because the Indians were often warlike towards each other, it was assumed by some Europeans that their "intentions towards us white people, are at all times bad, no doubt."[69]

Occasionally the anticipation of violence brought its expected result. When trading over the stern of his ship, Richard Cleveland was in the habit of mounting two four pound cannon and a pair of blunderbusses, all loaded, on the tafferel.[70] This practice was hardly conducive to relaxed relations. Some captains on occasion took Indian hostages, either to prevent expected attacks or to force reluctant traders. Indians in canoes were sometimes fired upon, and the shelling of Indian villages by angry traders was not unknown. Indian stealing could result in violence. Because the traders operated largely outside Indian social sanctions, European property was not regarded in the same way as the property of other Indians. The traders were aliens and seemed extremely wealthy to the Indians, and their goods were looked upon as fair game. Yet Indians stole lightheartedly and laughed when they were detected, "as if they considered it as a piece of Dexterity and did them credit ra[ther] than any dishonour."[71] European captains saw the matter differently. They treated theft seriously, and the punishment that they meted out was sometimes savage. Naturally the Indians did not remain passive in the face of such treatment; they reacted in kind.

Indian retaliation for outrages committed against them has been seen as the major reason for their attacks on fur traders and their vessels.[72] One of the

[66]Cook, *Journal*, 4 April 1778, David Samwell, *Journal*, 4 April 1778, Beaglehole, part 1, p. 299, part 2, p. 1093.

[67]King, *Journal* [April 1778], Beaglehole, part 2, p. 1406–7.

[68]"John Boit's Log of the Second Voyage of the *Columbia*," 18 June 1792, Howay, "*Columbia*," p. 388.

[69]"Remarks on the Voyage of the *Eliza*, 1789–1799," UBCL, p. 56.

[70]Cleveland, *Voyages*, p. 91.

[71]Samwell, *Journal*, 25 April 1778, Beaglehole, part 2, p. 1100.

[72]Howay, "The Maritime Fur Trade," p. 9; and "*Columbia*," p. xxvii.

best documented of these cases was Koyah's attack on the brigantine *Lady Washington* in June 1791. Koyah was the leading figure at the Haida village on Anthony Island. The early contacts with his people had been peaceful enough.[73] For example, Robert Haswell on the *Columbia* noted that the Indians "pillaged any little triffling thing they could find a good opportunity to take unobserved," but he added that "as we took no rash meens with them it never interrrupted our trade."[74] Other traders were much less tolerant. When pilfering occurred on John Kendrick's *Lady Washington*, he reacted by capturing Koyah and mistreating him in a way that was shattering to the Indian leader's prestige. Kendrick apparently flogged Koyah, painted his face, cut off his hair, and took a large number of pelts from him. John Hoskins arrived after the event on the *Columbia*'s second voyage and was told that "Coyah was now no longer a Chief but an 'Ahliko' or one of the lower class; they now have no head Chief, but many inferior Chiefs."[75] When Kendrick returned to the village on the *Lady Washington* in 1791, almost certainly in revenge for the treatment he had received, Koyah attacked the vessel. Although the Haida gained the initial advantage, the result was a considerable loss of Indian life and further loss of face by Koyah.[76] In an effort to re-establish his lost prestige, Koyah led attacks on other vessels.

Yet, even if the Indians had taken revenge for all insults against them, it would be fallacious to reverse the proposition and say that all attacks were motivated by revenge.[77] The "revenge only" explanation is an obvious corollary of the view that the Indians were exploited by the maritime fur traders and overlooks other possibilities. According to this view the Indian only reacts in response to European action, he does not take the initiative. Rather than having reasons of his own for attacking whites, he must wait for the European to insult him. This explanation is as naive as the notion that Indians attacked ships simply because of their natural treachery and ferocity. The simple misconstruing of European behaviour could have been the reason for some Indian attacks. The violation of Indian social customs, either wittingly or unwittingly, would also be likely to produce conflict. When the *Columbia* was in Clayoquot Sound in 1792, Hoskins tried repeatedly to visit a group of

---

[73]Dixon, *A Voyage*, p. 215.

[74]"Haswell's Log of the First Voyage," 11 June 1789, Howay, "*Columbia*," p. 98.

[75]"Hoskins' Narrative," July 1791, Howay, "*Columbia*," p. 200. To have had his hair cut off would have been particularly degrading for a northwest coast Indian since short hair signified a slave.

[76]The various accounts of this incident have been gathered together in F. W. Howay, "The Ballad of the Bold Northwestman: An Incident in the Life of Captain John Kendrick," *Washington Historical Quarterly* 20 (1929): 114–23.

[77]This point has been made in the context of the South Pacific by Shineberg, *They Came for Sandalwood*, p. 199.

mourning Indian women in spite of Wickaninish's warnings not to. The captain of the ship, Robert Gray, a few days earlier had declined an invitation to a potlatch which "by no means pleased" his hosts.[78] This kind of disregard for Indian protocol was likely to produce hostility. Through ignorance of Indian social usages, white traders probably offended Indian sensibilities on many occasions.

There were many possible motives behind Indian attacks on vessels, most of them more complex than revenge or innate treachery. There was a delicate balance of gains and losses to be weighed up by Indian leaders who contemplated an attack. The immediate advantage of gaining wealth by plunder had to be assessed against the long term disadvantage of losing trade. One of the most famous and successful Indian assaults was that led by Maquinna on the American ship *Boston* in 1803. Many motives seemed to have operated. Grievances had accumulated against the whites over twenty-five years of contact.[79] There was also dissatisfaction among the Nootka because the fur trade was passing them by. Four days before the attack on the *Boston*, there had been an angry exchange between the Captain, John Salter, and Maquinna over a musket which had been presented to the chief but which he claimed was defective. So the Indians attacked the *Boston* and killed her crew, with the exception of John Jewitt and John Thompson who were taken as captives. Maquinna was astute enough to realize the possible consequences of the destruction of the *Boston*.[80] Actions such as this tended to deter other traders, and two summers were to pass before another vessel came to Nootka Sound.

The balance of actual power on the coast was quite fine. European captains relied on the assumed superiority of their firearms over Indian weapons. They thought that the "terror" which these arms inspired constituted their strength and security "against the multitude."[81] This assumption is also implicitly accepted by historians who argue that fur traders imposed their will on the Indians. In fact, the smoothbore musket, the weapon that Europeans relied on, was notoriously unreliable and inaccurate. It was liable to misfire, particularly under damp conditions; it emitted a cloud of smoke that obscured vision; and it took a long time to reload. Where accuracy and rapid fire were required, the Indian bow was probably superior. In close fighting the seamen had, in effect, one shot. The coast Indians probably used hand weapons more than the bow, and by the time the struggle became hand to hand, they were

---

[78]"Hoskins' Narrative," January and February 1792, Howay, "*Columbia*," pp. 265, 269.

[79]John Jewitt, Journal, 6 November 1803, *A Journal Kept at Nootka Sound...* (Boston: J. Jewitt, 1807), p. 13.

[80]Jewitt, *Journal*, 19 and 26 March 1803, pp. 3, 5.

[81]Fleurieu, *A Voyage*, 1: 421.

better armed and more experienced. For similar reasons the Indians did not necessarily become more efficient fighters and hunters by the acquisition of firearms. Initially muskets probably made little difference to indigenous people who already possessed projectile weapons. When hostilities developed, the Indians had the additional advantages of numbers and knowledge of the territory. In their attacks on trading vessels the northwest coast Indians employed some of the strategies that they had used in pre-contact times. Tactics designed to catch the foe off his guard and mount a surprise attack were viewed as treachery by Europeans, but to the Indians they were a means of ensuring success with a minimum loss of life. Such tactics were used by Koyah in his attack on the *Lady Washington* and, more successfully, by the Nootka when they overwhelmed the *Boston* in 1803 and the *Tonquin* in 1811.[82] Europeans did have the power to destroy Indian villages at long range with cannonfire, but the destruction of property was not new to the Indians, since it was a part of their own warfare. Villages were totally destroyed by Indian raiding parties, not at such a range, but equally effectively. These tactics may well have held less terror for the Indians than Europeans thought. When the Indians, for their part, mounted a determined and concerted attack on a vessel, they stood a good chance of success. What is surprising, therefore, is not that a few vessels were captured but that there were not more attacks.[83]

Because the Indians had considerable control over both the trade and the power relationship between themselves and the Europeans, they experienced little cultural disruption during the period of the maritime fur trade. There were changes in Indian cultures, just as there had been before the arrival of the European. The fur trade did not introduce change into a static society, although it probably did quicken the pace of change. But, as far as it is possible to determine, the developments took already existing directions rather than new ones.

The nature of the evidence makes it difficult to be precise about the type or degree of change that the Indians were experiencing. Traders who recorded

[82]In this case the word "Nootka" is used in its broadest sense, as the attack on the *Tonquin* probably occurred in Clayoquot Sound. The attack left no survivors, and there are, therefore, no eyewitness accounts. The most reliable account is in W. Kaye Lamb, ed., *Journal of a Voyage to the Northwest Coast of North America during the Years 1811, 1812, 1813 and 1814, by Gabriel Franchère* (Toronto: Champlain Society, 1969), pp. 124–27.

[83]Howay lists only fifteen incidents that could possibly be described as attacks on vessels, and at least five of these are highly doubtful cases (see Howay, "Indian Attacks upon Maritime Fur Traders of the North-West Coast, 1785–1805," *Canadian Historical Review* 6 [1925]: 287–309). I have developed the argument outlined in this paragraph in greater detail in "Arms and Men on the Northwest Coast, 1774–1825," *BC Studies* 29 (1976): 3–18.

their observations of the Indians paid particular attention to those aspects of the culture that were relevant to their own purpose. As has been shown, they left information on the nature of Indian trading patterns and the kinds of goods that they demanded. They also left records on such subjects as the nature of leadership in Indian society and the availability of Indian women. Changes that the Indians were experiencing, though less prominent in the journals, can be deduced by a careful reading of, and between, the lines.

Because European traders preferred to deal with Indian leaders, it is possible that their role has been exaggerated in the journals. Yet it is also clear that the role of certain individuals within Indian society was being enhanced as a result of the fur trade. Chiefs who were dominant in the trade greatly increased their wealth and, in a culture where the two were closely related, their prestige. Because of their position, some chiefs were able to gather more sea otter pelts; therefore, they traded more European goods and so were able to acquire even greater numbers of furs. The trade placed the rich in a position to add to their wealth increasingly.

A number of such individuals emerge in the journals of traders, but the most famous was Maquinna, who has received particular attention because of the centrality of Nootka Sound in the early history of the northwest coast. Probably newly succeeded to chieftainship when the fur trade began,[84] Maquinna was able to tap the wealth of his own people and of neighbouring groups. During the Nootka Sound controversy, he was fêted by both the Spanish and the English, and he was recognized as the leading trading chief in the area. By Indian standards Maquinna became exceptionally wealthy. In 1803, for example, it is reported that he gave a potlatch at which he dispensed two hundred muskets, two hundred yards of cloth, one hundred chemises, one hundred looking glasses, and seven barrels of gunpowder.[85]

There were other Indian leaders whose power was comparable to that of Maquinna. It is possible that Wickaninish, the leader at Clayoquot Sound, was even more powerful. On the northern Queen Charlottes, Cunneah, who resided at Kiusta, was the first mentioned and best known chief. Also very

---

[84]The Spaniard, Moziño, who wrote what might be considered the first ethnography of the Nootka Sound Indians, claimed that Maquinna's father died in 1778 (José Mariño Moziño, *Noticias de Nutka: An Account of Nootka Sound in 1792* [Toronto and Montreal: McClelland and Stewart, 1970], p. 31). There is some evidence that this Maquinna died in 1795, in which case his name and position were taken over by another individual (see Charles Bishop, Journal, 5 October 1795, in Michael Roe, ed., *The Journal and Letters of Captain Charles Bishop on the North-West Coast of America, in the Pacific and in New South Wales 1794-1799* [Cambridge: Hakluyt Society, 1967], pp. 107–8). It is therefore untrue to say that it was the same Maquinna who met Cook and Vancouver and captured the *Boston*; probably they were three different men; cf. Howay, "Indian Attacks," p. 304.

[85]Jewitt, *Journal*, 24 November 1803, p. 12.

important was Kow, who initially lived at Dadens but during the 1790's moved across Dixon Entrance and established himself permanently at his summer village at Kaigani.[86] Like Maquinna, these leaders acquired great wealth. In 1799, when the author of the *Eliza* journal visited the house of Kow, the chief proudly displayed his wealth. The house was lined with boxes of goods acquired in the trade, but Kow drew particular attention to his hoard of ermine skins which were valued as gold or silver. By virtue of his collection of 120 of these pelts, Kow claimed that, next to Cunneah, he was the wealthiest chief in the area.[87]

Their wealth enabled these chiefs to acquire the labour force to do the work of preparing pelts for market. Considerable time and effort went into drying and stretching a sea otter pelt, and the trade probably placed a premium on the labour of slaves. Preparing pelts was often women's work, so the trade may also have provided an impetus for increased polygamy in the houses of chiefs. Certainly, those leaders who became more wealthy because of the fur trade could afford more wives.

In time women also acquired new economic value as prostitutes on trading vessels. Prostitution for economic gain was something that the Indians learned from the European. The early voyagers who came via the Pacific found the northwest coast inhospitable, and one of the reasons for this feeling was the modesty of Indian women compared to the amorous Polynesians.[88] During the early contact period the women of Nootka Sound, for example, were said to be unable to bear even "the most trifling attacks of gallantry."[89] But the attitudes of Indian women were soon to change. In 1792 Peter Puget, who was with Vancouver, was astonished that the women of Nootka had so completely changed their ideas about chastity.[90] The Haida were also jealous of their women at first, but in time "Ladies of Easy access" became common.[91] The pattern was not consistent for all the coast. The Vancouver expedition was probably the first to enter Smith Inlet, and there the women immediately solicited the company of members of the crew.[92] It is possible that in this case,

[86]Cf. Ingraham, *Journal*, 10 July 1791, Kaplanoff, p. 102; and *Eliza*, "Journal," 27 March 1799, p. 13.

[87]*Eliza*, "Journal," 27 March 1799, p. 28. Kow owned these ermine skins before Sturgis glutted the Kaigani market with them in 1804 (see Howay, "William Sturgis," p. 22).

[88]Samwell, *Journal*, 6 April 1778, Beaglehole, part 2, p. 1095; [John Nicol], *The Life and Adventures of John Nicol Mariner* (Edinburgh and London: W. Blackwood, 1822), p. 89. Nicol was a member of the crew of Portlock's *King George* on the coast in 1786 and 1787. See also Puget, "Log of the *Chatham*," p. 134.

[89]Meany, *A New Vancouver Journal*, p. 36.

[90]Puget, "Log of the *Chatham*," 16 April 1793, p. 40.

[91]Dixon, *A Voyage*, p. 225; Bishop, *Journal*, 30 July 1795, Roe, p. 83.

[92]Vancouver, *A Voyage*, 1: 377.

as in others, one should make a distinction between hospitality and prostitution. It seems that usually the wives of chiefs could not be tempted, and it is likely that prostitution was largely confined to "the inferior class."[93] If this observation was accurate, then this European vice brought little demoralization to Indian society. Slave girls, and among some groups unmarried women generally, did not break Indian social sanctions by going aboard ships.

The new wealth brought by the fur trade was not evenly spread among Indian groups. Disparities in wealth, and therefore in power, undoubtedly increased. Differences developed in the economic activities of Indian groups, since some specialized in trading and others in trapping. Trading Indians were freed by the trade goods that they acquired from some of the activities that had hitherto consumed much of their time, and they were now able to spend more time bargaining with Europeans. Those groups that concentrated on hunting devoted more of their time to that task. Capturing a sea otter was time-consuming, particularly as the animals became scarcer, so many Indians probably spent most of their time hunting for pelts.[94] The growth of disparities in wealth between Indian groups may have increased excuses for warfare, although, at the same time, the fact that warfare tended to disrupt trade may have militated against intertribal conflict. While rivalry between Indian groups hoping to profit from the trade may have added to the incidence of hostility, economic motives had also been powerful in indigenous warfare. The fur trade did not bring new reasons for attacks.

When attempting to assess in a more general way the impact of the maritime fur trade on Indian society, historians and anthropologists have tended towards opposite interpretations. Historians have adhered to a guilt-induced mythology and argued that the effect on the Indians was disastrous. Howay set the pattern when he claimed that the trade "seriously dislocated the finely balanced economic and social fabric of the Indians."[95] Anthropologists, on the other hand, have inclined towards the view that the trade stimulated Indian culture. Some anthropologists have pointed to the new prosperity

[93]Puget, "Log of the *Chatham*," p. 49. European captains sometimes thought that they were being offered the daughter of a chief. Caamaño once thought that he was being accorded the privilege, but as the Haida girl wore no labret, it is unlikely that she was of high rank (Caamano, "Journal," July 1792, p. 216).
[94]Puget, "Log of the *Chatham*," p. 50.
[95]F. W. Howay, W. N. Sage, and H. F. Angus, *British Columbia and the United States: The North Pacific Slope from Fur Trade to Aviation* (Toronto: Ryerson, 1942), p. 13. In support of his contention Howay cites *The Indians of Canada*, but on the page referred to Jenness is discussing the impact of settlement. Howay's is a typical backwards extrapolation which sees the impact of settlement on the Indian population beginning with the fur trade (see Diamond Jenness, *The Indians of Canada*, National Museum of Canada Bulletin 65 [Ottawa: Queen's Printer, 1960] p. 261). The pagination of this edition is the same as the 1934 edition which Howay probably read.

brought to the Indians, which facilitated increased artistic and ceremonial life and led to a golden age of northwest coast Indian development.[96] It has even been argued by Marius Barbeau that such a major Indian art form as the totem pole actually originated from the stimulation provided by the fur trade.[97] However, the arguments to the contrary are convincing, and Barbeau's view can no longer be accepted.[98] But there is little doubt that the trade did facilitate an increase in Indian wood carving, particularly among the Haida. This development of Indian art is evidence that for the initial contact period the anthropological interpretation is closer to the truth. The flourishing of northwest coast carving illustrates that the maritime fur trade largely produced an elaboration of existing culture patterns rather than radical social change.

Naturally, the enrichment thesis cannot be advanced without reservations. All that it claims is that the fur trade was more beneficial than detrimental to the Indians, even though they did pay a price other than furs for their new wealth. A major part of that price was disease, which was certainly one aspect of the situation that the Indians had little control over. The absence of accurate figures makes it impossible to determine exactly what happened to the Indian population during this period, but it is possible that estimates of the impact of disease have been exaggerated. It is evident that many crews were infected with venereal disease when they came to the coast, particularly when they had called at Hawaii on the way.[99] But we do not know whether they brought mostly mild or severe forms of the disease, how many fatalities were caused by it among the Indians, or, for that matter, whether the Indians had venereal disease prior to European contact. There is, however, one certainty about venereal disease, and that is that exposure to it does not, of necessity, lead to infection. The means of transmitting venereal disease is very specific, and it can only be passed on to one person at a time, so its impact was probably more limited than smallpox, an epidemic disease transferred by a com-

---

[96]Duff, *The Indian History of B.C.*, pp. 57–58; J. A. Wike, "The Effect of the Maritime Fur Trade on Northwest Coast Indian Society" (Ph.D. dissertation, Columbia University [1951]), p. 92.

[97]See, for example, Marius Barbeau, "Totem Poles: A By Product of the Fur Trade," *Scientific Monthly*, December 1942, pp. 507–14.

[98]Wilson Duff, "Contributions of Marius Barbeau to West Coast Ethnography, "*Anthropologica* 6 (1964): 63–96; and Phillip Drucker, "The Antiquity of the Northwest Coast Totem Pole," *Journal of the Washington Academy of Sciences* 38 (1948): 389–97.

[99]See, for example, William Robert Broughton, *A Voyage of Discovery to the North Pacific Ocean: . . . Performed in His Majesty's Sloop "Providence," and her Tender, in the Years 1795, 1796, 1797, and 1798* (London: T. Cadell and W. Davis, 1804), p. 48.

mon medium. Smallpox probably was introduced by Europeans,[100] although again it is not known how virulent the forms were. The journals do not contain numerous accounts of wholesale depopulation resulting from smallpox. Reports tend to be of isolated cases and often of Indians with pock-marked faces who were apparently survivors of the disease.[101] Frequently the contemporary comments about population decline were based on the observation of deserted villages. Voyagers would attribute the supposed depopulation to disease, whereas villages were clearly abandoned for a variety of reasons. Seasonal migrations, the exhaustion of resource areas, and moves to be closer to the centres of the fur trade were all reasons for an Indian band to relocate its village. Furthermore, most voyagers came to the coast in the summer months when the Indians were more mobile, and there was a greater number of "deserted" villages.

It is, of course, as impressionistic to argue that the impact of disease in this period has been exaggerated as it was for voyagers to assert that there was considerable depopulation. It is interesting to note, however, that where statistical studies of the impact of European-introduced diseases on the indigenous people of the Pacific have been made, it has been found that the population decline was often less than had been assumed. The demographer Norma McArthur has questioned the assumption that European diseases caused wholesale depopulation. She has argued that for an epidemic to initiate substantial decline in a previously stable population, age-selective mortality is a pre-requisite. Contemporary accounts emphasize deaths when disasters strike, but the effect of an epidemic on the birth rate is far more significant. Unless the childbearing sector of the population in particular is struck by the disease, within a few years birth and death rates return to their normal levels. Therefore, if the population was increasing before the epidemic, in the absence of further outbreaks it will soon increase again.[102]

Many conclusions about the nature of culture change among the coast Indians during the fur-trading period are based on the assumption that there was major population decline as a result of the introduction of diseases and

---

[100]Less equivocal statements have been made on this point but not, unfortunately, supported by any evidence (see Robert E. McKechnie, *Strong Medicine: History of Healing on the Northwest Coast* [Vancouver: J. J. Douglas, 1972], p. 75).

[101]See, for example, Peter Puget, "A Log of the Proceedings of His Majesty's Ship *Discovery* . . . from the 4th Day of January 1791, to the 14th Day of January 1793," UBCL, p. 134; and Fleurieu, *Voyage*, 1: 438. An exception to the generalization is Bishop's claim that two-thirds of the Kaigani people had died of smallpox, although he also notes that they were still numerous at the time of his visit (Bishop, *Journal*, 30 July 1795, Roe, p. 83).

[102]Norma McArthur, *Island Populations of the Pacific* (Canberra: Australian National University Press, 1967), p. 347 and passim.

new weapons. It has been held, for instance, that one consequence of devastating disease was that individuals were probably elevated to social positions that they would not normally have attained. According to this argument, epidemics left vacancies in the higher social ranks that had to be filled by people from the lower classes.[103] If, however, the impact of disease was much less than has been assumed, such deductions about the nature of social change become less tenable. But whatever its effect, disease was the only importation that the Indians had to accept.

Otherwise, the Indians were selective in their attitude to those aspects of European culture that confronted them. They were not in contact with the whole scope of western culture and met only a very select number of its representatives, mostly young men who came with very limited intentions and demands. These demands could be handled by existing Indian social patterns and offered little threat to Indian leadership. Once satisfied with furs, the traders left the coast. There was no reason for the Indians to believe that such a small number of transitory visitors would seriously dislocate their culture. Even the more permanent Spanish establishment at Nootka had only a very limited impact on the Indians. The erratic Spanish commander Estéban Martinez thought that the building base would give them dominion over the coast Indians from Nootka to Monterey.[104] But whatever Europeans thought about the ease with which "savages" could be subjugated, the Indians proved to be resilient. In January 1795, when the Spanish abandoned Nootka, the Indians tore down the buildings, rebuilt their own summer houses, and Friendly Cove became Yuquot again.

During the maritime fur trading period the Indians of the northwest coast were not, like some pre-Marxist proletariat, the passive objects of exploitation. Rather they were part of a mutually beneficial trading relationship. The overwhelming impression that emerges from the journals is that the Indians were intelligent and energetic traders, quite capable of driving a hard bargain. The confidence that the Indians showed in their trading with the Europeans was indicative of the power relationship between the two races. By making a concerted effort the Indians could have destroyed any of the vessels that came to their villages. Far from being the victims of "an unequal trade with a primitive people,"[105] the Indians met the maritime fur trade and moulded it to serve their own ends.

---

[103]See for example Wayne Suttles, "Post-Contact Culture Change Among the Lummi Indians," *BCHQ* 18 (1954): 45.

[104]Warren L. Cook, *Flood Tide of Empire: Spain and the Pacific Northwest, 1543–1819* (New Haven and London: Yale University Press, 1973), p. 129.

[105]Howay, Sage, and Angus, *British Columbia*, p. 12.

2

The Land-Based Fur Trade

We are traders, and apart from more exalted motives, all traders are desirous of gain. Is it not self evident we will manage our business with more economy by being on good terms with the Indians than if at variance.[1] —JOHN MCLOUGHLIN, 1843

With the decline of the maritime fur trade and the establishment of land-based operations, trading methods changed, but the essential nature of the contact between the two races remained the same. The fur trade continued to be a reciprocal relationship between Indian and European. The Indians still to a large extent controlled both the trade and their culture, and European traders did not attempt any major interference with their way of life. The mutually beneficial nature of the land-based fur trade was indicated by the continued absence of major interracial conflict. Even those critics of the Hudson's Bay Company who have supposed, on dubious authority, that the Indians in its territories were usually entirely dependent on the company have had to admit that the area west of the Rockies was an exception.[2]

During the period of the maritime fur trade some trading captains and their backers had toyed with the idea of establishing shore factories in order to tap the source of furs more efficiently. Apart from the short-lived Spanish establishment at Nootka and the even more temporary shore posts built by Meares, Kendrick, and Gray, these plans came to nothing. The trade remained maritime and therefore, to a degree, transitory until the 1820's. It was not until after the advent of the Hudson's Bay Company west of the Rockies that the first trading fort was built on the coast of what was to become British Columbia. Inland, however, forts were built from the first decade of the nineteenth century.

The first approach from the east was in 1793. In July Alexander Mac-

[1] John McLoughlin to the governor, deputy governor and committee, 15 November 1843, in E. E. Rich, ed., *The Letters of John McLoughlin from Fort Vancouver to the Governor and Committee, Second Series, 1839–1844* (London: Hudson's Bay Record Society, 1943), p. 118.

[2] James Edward Fitzgerald, *An Examination of the Charter and Proceedings of the Hudson's Bay Company, with Reference to the Grant of Vancouver's Island* (London: T. Saunders, 1849), pp. 152–53.

kenzie, having completed the first overland crossing of North America, came down the Bella Coola River and reached tidewater on Bentinck Arm. He just missed meeting the members of the Vancouver expedition who had been in the area in the armed tender *Chatham* a few weeks earlier. The first thrust had been made, but little was done with Mackenzie's discoveries for more than a decade. Not until the North West Company sent another of its servants, Simon Fraser, over the mountains was the first permanent fur-trading post established in 1805 at McLeod Lake. In the following year Fraser established what was later named Fort St. James at the south end of Stuart Lake and also a post on Fraser Lake. In 1807 Fort George was built at the confluence of the Fraser and Nechako rivers. These forts were to be the major centres of the fur trade in the area named New Caledonia, which was vaguely defined but can be roughly detailed as including the area from 51° to about 57°. The key to unlocking this rich fur region was access to the sea, but geography imposed restrictions. In 1808 Fraser made his famous journey down the wild and treacherous river that bears his name, but it proved to be neither the Columbia, as he had expected, nor a satisfactory route to the sea, as he had hoped. The Columbia River was still the most feasible route to the Pacific, and the North West Company had sent David Thompson to explore its possibilities. Moving with less determination than Fraser, Thompson did not reach the mouth of the Columbia until July 1811. On his arrival he found the men of John Jacob Astor's Pacific Fur Company already constructing Fort Astoria. Two years later, during the War of 1812, the North West Company acquired this fort, and it was renamed Fort George. The Nor'westers now possessed a viable outlet from New Caledonia to the sea. The route was via the upper Fraser Valley, Fort Kamloops (established in 1812), the Okanagan Valley, and the Columbia. The North West Company had control of the Pacific slope, but it was not until after its amalgamation with the Hudson's Bay Company in 1821 that the fur resources of the region were exploited systematically.

In 1824 the Hudson's Bay Company efficiency expert, Governor George Simpson, came to look over the Columbia enterprise. Travelling at a frantic pace, he made the journey from York Factory in record time, and he arrived at Fort George with "oeconomy" on his mind. Besides tightening up the slack that the servants had allowed to develop in the running of individual posts, Simpson's attention was concentrated on two areas where the company faced major opposition. In the Snake country and on the northwest coast Simpson was to institute methods of dealing with opponents that he had forged in the fire of the Athapaska campaign against the North West Company. Peter Skene Ogden, the feisty ex-Nor'wester, was directed to lead a series of expeditions into the Snake country through the 1820's with the object of completely exhausting the fur reserves of this frontier area and thereby excluding rival trappers. Eliminating competition on the coast was not so easy. Compared to the relatively unsophisticated Indians of the Snake country, those of the northwest coast had had forty years' experience of trading with Europeans. They knew, and could benefit from, the advantages of rivalry between fur traders.

The company's coastal push was planned by Simpson in the winter of 1825 –26 at Fort George, expounded by him before the London committee in 1826, and begun in 1827 by the establishment of Fort Langley on the Fraser about thirty miles from its mouth. Simpson came back to the coast in 1828 and made further plans with Chief Factor John McLoughlin, who was now in charge of the area west of the Rockies. Two more coastal forts were founded in the early 1830's. In 1831 Fort Simpson was built at the mouth of the Nass River, but this position soon proved unsatisfactory and the fort was moved to a site on the Tsimshian Peninsula. The area around the mouth of the Nass was the "grand mart" for both land and sea furs,[3] so Fort Simpson was the company's most important coastal station. In 1833 Fort McLoughlin was founded on Milbanke Sound, completing a chain of forts up the coast as far north as latitude 54° 40′, the boundary between British and Russian America. These forts were to be supplied and supplemented by the vessels that the company operated. The schooner *Cadboro* was acquired in 1827 and used in the establishment of Forts Langley and Simpson. The party that built Fort McLoughlin was transported in the brig *Lama*, which had been purchased in 1831. In 1835 the legendary steamship *Beaver* was acquired by the company. These forts and vessels were to be the means by which the Hudson's Bay Company hoped to break the hold of American and Russian traders on the coast. But it was to be no simple task. Naturally, their European opponents were not anxious to give up a lucrative commerce, and much has been written of the strategies and policies by which the company tried to eliminate these rivals. Less attention has been given to the reactions of the trading Indians to these developments.[4]

The Hudson's Bay Company inaugurated its coastal enterprise among Indians who had lost none of their trading acumen. They were still discriminating about types and quality of goods and could still drive a hard bargain. In spite of all their trading experience, the company men found the Indians of the northwest coast to be "tiresome in their bargaining."[5] Sometimes their demands were so exorbitant that the company's traders found it impossible to

[3]George Simpson to William Smith, 17 November 1828, in Frederick Merk, ed., *Fur Trade and Empire: George Simpson's Journal, . . . 1824–1825; . . .* (Cambridge, Mass.: Harvard University Press, 1931), p. 300.

[4]An exception is E. E. Rich, "Trade Habits and Economic Motivations among the Indians of North America," *Canadian Journal of Economics and Political Science* 26 (1960): 35–53.

[5]Sir George Simpson, *Narrative of a Journey Around the World during the Years 1841 and 1842* (London: H. Colburn, 1847), 2: 192.

deal with them. The Indians were still not above using a certain amount of artifice when trading. According to Simpson, a favourite trick was to doctor a land otter pelt and pass it off as a sea otter. Furthermore, said Simpson, "when a skin is rejected as being deficient in size, or defective in quality, it is immediately, according to circumstances, enlarged, or coloured, or pressed to order, and then is submitted, as a virgin article, to the buyer's criticism by a different customer."[6] In short, these Indians were still "sagacious enough to pursue their own interest without persevering industry,"[7] and, most of all, they were still masters of the art of manipulating competing traders.

During the 1820's and 1830's there was still competition on the coast, and it enabled the Indians to continue to assert their demands with confidence. When the company moved into the coastal trade, its officers thought that a couple of years would be sufficient to eliminate any opposition.[8] By increasing the price of furs beyond their opponents' ability to pay, they hoped that they would soon have a monopoly of the trade with the coast Indians. But the company had reckoned without the fact that the Indians were already exacting high prices. Higher prices caused large losses,[9] and even then it was to be more than ten years before anything like a monopoly situation was achieved. All three coastal forts were affected by the activities of American trading vessels during the 1830's, and tariffs had to be adjusted accordingly. Even Fort Langley, somewhat removed from the outer coast, was not immune. From the beginning it was found that the Indians visiting the fort had great difficulty in bartering at company prices after American traders had visited them and supplied them with goods much more cheaply.[10] In the north the Russian traders provided the Indians with a second alternative market, and competition was even more intense at Fort Simpson. The Fort Simpson journals for the 1830's are replete with references to Indians holding out for higher prices in the expectation that American vessels would soon be in the area or because they knew they could do better at the Russian forts. Just a few miles across Dixon Entrance, Kaigani Harbour was still a great centre of trading with the Ameri-

---

[6]Ibid., p. 188.

[7]Duncan Finlayson to James Hargrave, 10 March 1832, in G. P. de T. Glazebrook, ed., *The Hargrave Correspondence 1821–1843* (Toronto: Champlain Society, 1938), p. 88.

[8]E. E. Rich, ed., *Part of a Despatch from George Simpson Esqr. Governor of Ruperts Land to the Governor & Committee of the Hudson's Bay Company London March 1, 1829. Continued and Completed March 24 and June 5, 1829* (London: Hudson's Bay Record Society, 1947), p. 85.

[9]E. E. Rich, *The History of the Hudson's Bay Company 1670–1870* (London: Hudson's Bay Record Society, 1959), 2: 639.

[10]Fort Langley, Journal, 21 September 1827, Hudson's Bay Company Archives (hereafter cited as HBCA), B-113/a, Public Archives of Canada (hereafter cited as PAC).

cans. The Kaigani Indians were "reckoned to be the most difficult Indians on the coast to deal with,"[11] and their proximity to Fort Simpson forced up the tariff. The Fort Simpson Indians themselves were described as being "in their glory" when competition was in the area and "chuckling at their high prices."[12]

Company vessels operating up and down the coast encountered a similar situation. When opposing vessels were working the same area, the Indians took every advantage of the situation, just as they had done when all the trade was maritime. John Work, having been relieved from the struggle against the opposition in the Snake country, spent some time in 1835 cruising the coast in the *Lama* in search of furs. The obstinacy of the Indian traders provoked the normally stoic Work into fulminations against them. An American captain named Allen was the most frequently mentioned opponent, and in April 1835 both his brig, *Europa*, and the *Lama* were at Newitty at the same time. Nothing made the Indians happier than such a situation, but Work was distinctly displeased. "It is annoying in the extreme," he wrote in his journal, "to see the advantage which the black vagabonds endeavour to make of this circumstance."[13] As they were accustomed, the Indians were moving from one vessel to the other trying to raise the price. The technique, perfected during the maritime fur trade, was applied to both the forts and the vessels that the company operated on the coast.

Because of the opposition, the Indians demanded prices that were said to be "most extravagant."[14] In spite of the company's strong desire to lower the tariff, it was "deemed not prudent to do so"[15] as long as competition persisted. John McLoughlin found it necessary to maintain three price levels in his territory. One pertained in the interior, a second on the coast, and a third at coastal forts when competitors were in the area. The third was exorbitant by the standard of the other two.[16] But even this degree of orderliness was difficult to maintain. Increases in price anywhere on the coast tended to have repercussions throughout the entire system. One of the senior traders at Fort Simpson, Dr. John Kennedy, spent a whole day in May 1837 bargaining with some Tsimshian for sea otter pelts. At the end of the day he had achieved nothing. The difficulty was that Kennedy did not want to give more than eight blankets per pelt at the fort, although he had recently given the Kaigani Haida

---

[11]John Work, Journal, 23 February 1835, Journals, 1823–1851, PABC.

[12]Fort Simpson, Journal, 5 August 1839, HBCA, B-201/a.

[13]Work, Journal, 23 April 1835.

[14]Finlayson to Hargrave, 19 March 1832, Glazebrook, p. 88.

[15]Work, Journal, 18 February 1835.

[16]J. S. Galbraith, *The Hudson's Bay Company as an Imperial Factor 1821–1869* (Berkeley and Los Angeles: University of California Press, 1957), pp. 138–39. See also Charles Wilkes, *Narrative of the United States Exploring Expedition, during the Years 1838, 1839, 1840, 1841, 1842* (London: Whittaker, 1845), 4: 299.

ten blankets per pelt to prevent some sea otter from falling into the hands of the Russians. The Haida had acquainted the Tsimshian with the price that they had received and thus caused Kennedy "a good deal of trouble." The following day the Tsimshian were still holding out for a higher price.[17] Fort Langley was similarly affected. The Kwakiutl were in frequent contact with American traders, and because of the high prices they were offered, the Indians were able to divert trade that would normally have gone to Fort Langley.[18] Even prices at Fort Simpson—hundreds of miles away, but the storm centre of competition—had an impact on returns at Fort Langley. The Kwakiutl were again responsible. They redirected furs from the Musqueam, a Salish group living at the mouth of the Fraser River, to Fort Simpson. "This evil" arose from the fact that the difference between the tariffs at Fort Langley and Fort Simpson generally exceeded 100 per cent.[19]

As was the case during the maritime fur trade, competition influenced not just the flat rate of exchange but also the quality of the articles obtained by the Indians. Blankets were the trading staple, but at times even the famous Hudson's Bay blanket proved unacceptable. When their blankets were inferior to those of the Americans or Russians, company traders had to build up the price with other goods.

Dealing in a competitive market was not new to the northwest coast Indians, but the advent of the land-based fur trade did result in some innovations in their trading techniques. One of the most obvious was the way in which local Indians would congregate around a newly established fort and attempt to control its trade. "Home guards" were a feature of the first three coastal forts,[20] and after Fort Victoria was built in 1843, the Songhees moved from Cadboro Bay and "considered themselves specifically attached to the Establishment."[21] Fort Simpson was typical of the pattern. After the fort was

---

[17]Fort Simpson, Journal, 20 and 21 May 1837, HBCA, B-201/a. This evidence convincingly contradicts H. G. Barnett's claim that at Fort Simpson "values were arbitrarily assessed by the white traders and the Indian took what he could get" ("Applied Anthropology in 1860," *Applied Anthropology* 1 [1942]: 20).

[18]Work, Journal, 25 September 1835.

[19]That is, the former paid 5s. for a large beaver, while the latter paid upwards of 10s. (James Douglas to Simpson, 18 March 1838, in E. E. Rich, ed., *The Letters of John McLoughlin from Fort Vancouver to the Governor and Committee, First Series, 1825–1838* [London: Hudson's Bay Record Society, 1941], p. 281).

[20]Simpson to governor and committee, 25 November 1841, HBCA, D-4/59; A. C. Anderson, Diary, January 1834, in James Robert Anderson, "Notes and Comments on Early Days and Events in British Columbia, Washington and Oregon . . . ," PABC, p. 16; James MacMillan, Journal, 13 June and 31 July 1829, James MacMillan and Archibald McDonald, "Fort Langley Journal, 27 June 1827–30 July 1830," PABC.

[21]Douglas and Work to governor, deputy governor and committee, 6 November 1847, HBCA, A-11/72.

removed to its second location, a large population of Tsimshian gathered around its walls. The site had previously been a temporary camping place for the various Tsimshian tribes on their way north to the Nass River for the spring eulachon fishing, but now it became a large winter village. The Tsimshian who established themselves at Fort Simpson, like the home guards at the other coastal forts, made every effort to control the trade of the fort. These Indians were agents and dealers more than hunters and trappers. They set themselves up as middlemen between other Indians and the company traders. Because traders tended to assess Indian industriousness in terms of their zeal for hunting furs, fort Indians were often accused of laziness. James Douglas once complained that the Fort Langley Indians had to be "literally dunned into something like exertion."[22] But these Indians were keenly aware of the benefits of controlling a fort. They were often pleased when they learned that a fort was to be built in their midst and became angry and hostile when they heard that a fort was to be relocated or abandoned. The Nishga Indians of the Nass River were extremely annoyed when they discovered that Fort Simpson was to be moved to the territory of the coast Tsimshian, and their threatening attitude resulted in a rather undignified retreat by the company traders.[23] The final departure from Fort McLoughlin when it was abandoned in 1844 was only carried off gracefully by planning the move for a time when the local Indians were away fishing.[24]

Indians as well as whites coveted the monopoly situation, and home guards, anxious to keep the trade entirely in their hands, were jealous of the visits of other Indians to their fort.[25] These Indian traders were able to influence the trade even though their interests ran counter to those of the company. The 1834 season was a poor one at Fort Simpson partly because the Tsimshian considered the price offered by the company too low and they were determined to withhold their furs.[26] They also made every effort to persuade all visiting Indians to do the same. These Indian brokers could not always maintain a total dominance. The Fort Langley Indians could not regulate

[22]Douglas to governor, deputy governor and committee, 14 October 1839, Rich, *McLoughlin's Letters, Second Series*, p. 216.

[23]William Fraser Tolmie, Journal, 21 June 1834, *The Journals of William Fraser Tolmie: Physician and Fur Trader* (Vancouver: Mitchell Press, 1963), p. 290.

[24]Charles Ross to Simpson, 10 January 1844, HBCA, D-5/10; Charles Ross to Donald Ross, 10 January 1844, in W. Kaye Lamb, ed., "Five Letters of Charles Ross, 1842–1844," *BCHQ* 7 (1943): 110. Fort Taku was abandoned in the same year, and there the Indians were "extremely incensed by the desertion of their establishment" (Douglas to Donald Ross, 12 March 1844, Donald Ross Papers, PABC).

[25]Simpson to governor and committee, 25 November 1841, HBCA, D-4/59.

[26]Fort Simpson, Journal, 20 November 1834, HBCA, B-201/a.

the actions of the feared southern Kwakiutl, and the Tsimshian were seldom able to dictate to the obstreperous Haida. But these coastal Indians did maintain highly profitable monopolies over the Indians of the interior.

The first white men to cross the continental divide found evidence that the interior Indians had trading links with those of the coast. Mackenzie discovered that bands even as far east as the Sekani of the Finlay and Parsnip rivers possessed iron that had come from the coast, and Simon Fraser found similar evidence. The travels of Samuel Black in the northern interior, in particular, had awakened the company to the nature of intertribal trading patterns in the area.[27] Company strategists were aware that most of the furs traded at the coast actually came from the interior, and the coastal operation was developed to tap that trade. The fort on the Nass River, for instance, was established primarily to intercept furs coming out from the interior. The Indians, however, were not eager to relinquish these old trading connections and the profits that they brought. At first the Nishga were apprehensive about their trade monopoly and therefore were unco-operative.[28] It became evident, particularly after the fort was relocated, that Indian trade patterns were to be continued and even strengthened. One tribe of the Fort Simpson Tsimshian under a series of leaders named Legaic maintained a tightly controlled monopoly over the Gitksan of the upper Skeena River. Tsimshian parties went up the river to trade at the villages around the junction of the Skeena and Bulkley rivers and then returned to the fort to realize a handsome profit.[29] The Gitksan were prevented from coming down to the fort and sharing directly in the high coastal prices. Because Legaic's relationship with the fort gave him access to new sources of wealth and power, he was strong enough to enforce this monopoly strictly, and those Indians who tried to break it were severely punished.

To the north and south of Fort Simpson other Indian groups reaped the benefits of similar trading patterns. The Indians of Milbanke Sound acted as dealers between the Indians of the interior and Fort McLoughlin.[30] To the

[27]Alexander Mackenzie, Journal, 9 July 1783, in W. Kaye Lamb, ed., *The Journals and Letters of Sir Alexander Mackenzie* (Cambridge: Hakluyt Society, 1970), p. 287; Fraser to gentlemen proprietors of the North West Company [August 1806], in W. Kaye Lamb, ed., *The Letters and Journals of Simon Fraser, 1806–1808* (Toronto: Macmillan of Canada, 1960), p. 232; Samuel Black, Journal, 15 and 16 July and 13 August 1824, in E. E. Rich, ed., *Journal of a Voyage from Rocky Mountain Portage in Peace River to the Sources of Finlay's Branch and North West Ward in Summer 1824 [by Samuel Black]* (London: Hudson's Bay Record Society, 1955), pp. 112, 116, 161–62.
[28]Aemilius Simpson to McLoughlin, 23 September 1830, Rich, *McLoughlin's Letters, First Series*, p. 311.
[29]Fort Simpson, Journal, 25 August 1839, HBCA, B-201/a.
[30]A. C. Anderson to Simpson, 5 March 1845, HBCA, D-5/13.

north the Tlingit were famous as middlemen, and it was apparent to the company that they were draining off a large quantity of furs from the interior of northern New Caledonia to sell to the Russians.[31] The Stikine leader named Shakes had a monopoly on the Stikine similar to that of Legaic on the Skeena. He travelled up the Stikine River annually to trade and jealously guarded the privilege. Trading with the interior Indians was a traditional aspect of the Tlingit way of life, and so they had a highly developed sense of jurisdiction over trading trails and the right to trade with certain groups.[32] The "grand mart" of the Stikine Indians was a village 150 miles in from the sea and 60 miles from Dease Lake.[33] The company, desiring to intercept this kind of trade, planned to establish a fort on the Stikine River in 1834. Ogden was delegated to carry out the plan, and he was, not unexpectedly, opposed by the Russians. This opposition prompted another round of diplomacy. But the Russians were not the only opponents of the scheme. For all that they tried to conceal it, the company officers also faced strong opposition from the leaders of the Stikine Indians, who were concerned about their monopoly with the up-river Indians. These Indians "assumed a tone" that even a troubleshooter like Ogden "was not in the habit of hearing." The Indians were worried that the company's men might proceed up the river and injure their trade, and they appeared to be determined to prevent it. To deprive them of their trade, said the Indians, would reduce them to the state of slaves.[34] The mood of the Tlingit was one of the reasons why Ogden decided in 1834 against establishing in the area. After the 1839 agreement by which the Russian American Company leased the mainland coastal strip to the Hudson's Bay Company for ten years, the company did take possession of Fort Stikine and built another fort near the mouth of the Taku River, but it still had to contend with Tlingit middlemen. During the expedition to establish these forts, Douglas went so far as to suggest that relying on Indian enterprise to bring furs to the coast, "may prove in the end the safest and the least expensive way of improving the important territory in question."[35]

The Oblate missionary Father A.G. Morice claimed that the Hudson's Bay

[31]Rich, *Part of A Despatch*, p. 12.

[32]Aurel Krause, *The Tlingit Indians: Results of a Trip to the Northwest Coast of America and Bering Straits*, trans., Erna Gunther (Seattle and London: University of Washington Press, 1970), pp. 115, 126ff; Kalervo Oberg, "The Social Economy of the Tlingit Indians" (Ph.D. dissertation, University of Chicago, 1937), pp. 104–5.

[33]Simpson, *Narrative*, 1: 210.

[34]Rich, *History of the H.B.C.*, 2: 637; Ogden, "Report of transactions at Stikine," Rich, *McLoughlin's Letters, First Series*, pp. 319–21; see also Tolmie, *Journal*, 21 June 1834, p. 285.

[35]Douglas to McLoughlin, 10 October 1840, Fort Vancouver, Correspondence Inward, 1840, signed by James Douglas, PABC.

Company enjoyed the strictest monopoly in the interior of New Caledonia.[36] In fact, the Indian trade with the coast precluded any absolute monopoly. As long as trade routes remained open and a competitive market on the coast stimulated prices, the Indians of the interior could maintain a degree of independence from the forts in their territory. Both conditions pertained at least until 1840.

The company traders knew that to secure the trade in the interior competition on the coast had to be destroyed and that the failure to do so left the interior Indians with the possibility of acquiring higher prices from the coastal Indians. The trade between the coastal Tsimshian and the Gitksan has already been mentioned. These upper Skeena people in turn traded with the Carrier, who had trading contacts with the Sekani. The Indian traders who formed the links in these chains knew all about price differentials and realized that this trade could afford "a very handsome profit to the native speculator."[37]

The North West Company had introduced the debtor system among the Indians of the interior, and the Hudson's Bay Company continued it after it took over the area. Under this system the Indians were sold goods and equipment in the fall and were expected to pay for them in furs the following spring. One of the reasons for retaining the debtor system was the supposition that it made the Indians less susceptible to the higher prices paid by the coast traders, but after seven years in charge of the New Caledonia district, Ogden doubted that the system was having the desired effect. The interior Indians were still "clandestinely" selling their furs to coastal Indians. Accounts of the trade by other traders in the interior provide evidence to support Ogden's claim, and there is no doubt that the coastal trade had an adverse effect on the takings at inland posts.[38]

By the early 1840's the company had considerably reduced, although not entirely eliminated, competition on the coast. The 1839 agreement with the Russians removed almost completely that source of opposition. By contracting under the same agreement to provide the Russian posts with supplies, the Hudson's Bay Company took an important source of revenue out of the hands of American captains, and there was some reduction in the number of American vessels from about 1840. But American traders did not completely

[36]A. G. Morice, *The History of the Northern Interior of British Columbia Formerly New Caledonia [1660–1880]* (Toronto: William Briggs, 1904), p. 149.

[37]John McLean, *Notes of a Twenty-Five Years' Service in the Hudson's Bay Territory* (London: R. Bentley, 1849), 1: 303.

[38]Peter Skene Ogden, "Notes on Western Caledonia [1844]," Ross Papers; Fort Babine, Journal, 19 June 1825, HBCA, B-11/a; A. C. Anderson to Simpson, 5 March 1845, HBCA, D-5/13.

disappear. They continued to be something of a nuisance to the company on the coast, and the effects of their activities were still felt in the interior.[39]

Although the company was moving closer towards the establishment of a trading monopoly, the Indians still formed the second half of a mutually beneficial economic partnership. Contemporary critics of the company often assumed that it had an absolute control over the Indians. Frequently, however, these assertions were based on politics rather than facts and revealed the prejudice of the critic not the realities of the frontier. As a monopoly, the company offended current economic dogma in England, and since monopolies in general were pernicious, critics reasoned, this particular monopoly must have been bad for the Indians. In the United States the company was vilified by those who saw it as a hindrance to settlement. Missionaries and humanitarians also tended to denigrate the influence of the company on the Indians, claiming, for example, that the company held the Indians in slavery.[40] But these views were based, at best, on superficial knowledge of the fur trade west of the Rockies and, at worst, on total ignorance.

Certainly the Indians involved in the trade became dependent on the company for European goods, but no more than the company was dependent on the Indians for furs. Some forts even had to rely on the Indians for their very sustenance, and were therefore doubly dependent. Indians who were relied on for provisions took every advantage of their position, just as they did in other aspects of the trade.[41] Some company traders appreciated the restrictions that their dependence placed upon them in their dealings with the Indians. Soon after the establishment of Fort Langley, the company traders, irritated by Indian stealing, wanted to demonstrate their "disapprobation of so knavish a behaviour." They refused to allow any Indian to land near the fort, yet at the same time they realized that the "want of fresh Provisions will soon compel us to concede a little in regard to this restriction." Naturally, the journals are not littered with such comments, for the admission of dependence was not in accord with the white sense of superiority. But Fort McLoughlin was similarly dependent, and Duncan Finlayson pointed out in a letter to his superiors

[39]W. H. McNeill to H.B.C. Board of Management, 26 August 1852, Fort Simpson, Correspondence Outward, 20 November 1851–2 November 1855, PABC; Ogden, "Notes on Western Caledonia," Ross Papers.

[40]See *The Hudson's Bay Question* [*from the "Colonial Intelligencer"*] (London: W. Tweedie, 1857), p. 24; Frank E. Ross, "The Retreat of the Hudson's Bay Company in the Pacific North-West," *Canadian Historical Review* 18 (1937): 263; and [Herbert Beaver], "The Natives of the North West Coast of America," *Extracts from the Papers and Proceedings of the Aborigines Protection Society* 2 (1841): 140.

[41]William Bean to John Tod, 20 June 1840, HBCA, B-37/a.

that their living would be precarious as long as the Indians had to be relied on for food.[42]

Like Europeans, Indians became fur traders because they perceived that there were benefits to be gained, and during the fur trade the Indians still had other options. Some preferred not to be involved in the trade and found it possible to exercise that choice. In 1829 a fort was established within the territory of the Chilcotin Indians in spite of some grave reservations about the prospects of the area.[43] These fears were quickly realized. The post was abandoned the year after its foundation but apparently subsequently reoccupied. Relations between the Chilcotin and the traders were always uneasy, and the Indians were evidently not at all interested in hunting for furs to trade at the fort. There was constant bickering about prices, and the men in the fort were frequently afraid of an attack. An Indian spokesman said that the company traders were always short of trade goods, maintained a high tariff, and rejected poor quality furs. The Indians, according to their representative, could see no advantage in the presence of the whites and expected them to leave the fort so that they would have an opportunity to burn it down. In reply the head trader had to concede that the Indians were at liberty to act as they pleased, to hunt or not to hunt, because there was no compulsion in the trade.[44] Essentially the Chilcotin had opted out of the fur trade, and there was little that the company could do but recognize the fact by abandoning the post in 1844.

When the trading partnership was established, however, the Indian and the fur trader shared certain interests, and the best evidence that both recognized them is the relative lack of hostility between the two groups. Individual traders, driven to exasperation by unco-operative Indians, would sometimes rail against them. Ogden once remarked that he would be willing to spend a year or two exterminating all the adult males of the Snake country. In 1835 Work found the daring of the Haida to be insufferable and thought that the traders' own safety would eventually compel them "to come to extremities with these people, and let them feel our force by destroying a number of them."[45] But such verbal tirades and threats seldom became more than that.

[42]MacMillan and McDonald, "Fort Langley Journal," 1 and 2 September 1827; Duncan Finlayson to McLoughlin, 29 September 1836, Rich, *McLoughlin's Letters, First Series*, p. 324.

[43]William Connolly to George McDougall, 28 January 1830, HBCA, B-188/b/7; Report of William Connolly to governor and council of the Northern Department, 4 March 1830, HBCA, D-4/123; see also Tod to Edward Ermatinger, 18 February 1830, Ermatinger Papers, UBCL.

[44]See, for example, Fort Chilcotin, Journal, 23 December and 2 January 1839, HBCA, B-37/a.

[45]Ogden, Journal, 22 January 1828, in Glyndwr Williams, ed., *Peter Skene Ogden's Snake Country Journals 1827–28 and 1828–29* (London: Hudson's Bay Record Society, 1971), p. 52; Work, Journal, 1 June 1835.

The nature of the fur traders' relationship with the Indians restrained any desire for wholesale extermination. Unlike other frontier situations, the fur trade placed no premium on dead Indians. When Captain T. Spaulding of the American vessel *Lausanne* made the ridiculous claim that the company was actually murdering hundreds of Indians every year,[46] McLoughlin countered by pointing out that as fur traders they were unlikely to benefit from the destruction of their source of supply and that it was therefore in their interest to maintain friendly relations with the Indians.[47]

Normally the officers of the company were circumspect about the punishment that they gave to Indians responsible for outrages against traders. They certainly believed in the necessity of retaliation when white men were injured or killed. McLoughlin's view in such cases was "that the honour of the whites was at a stake" and that to leave offences unpunished "would lower us in the opinion of the Indians."[48] Fur traders demanded revenge and often in the heat of the moment demanded it in violent terms, but there were definite limits within which they could act. Even Simpson's "rod of iron" approach had to be modified to suit different circumstances. In those parts of the Hudson's Bay Company's territories where the Indians were dependent, they were to be kept in a "proper state of subordination," but in areas like the Pacific Northwest where the Indians retained a large degree of independence "mild and cautious measures" would have to be used.[49] Punishment, when administered, should be specific and effective. Rather than the indiscriminate killing of a number of Indians, the guilty parties should be discovered and an example made of them. These were the views of many of the company's officers,[50] and James Douglas was a particularly strong exponent of such methods. He advocated moderate punishment and the taking of "due allowance for the ignorance of the Party with whom I was dealing."[51] This was advice from a mature trader, who had learned from long, and sometimes bitter, experience.

[46]Ross, "Retreat of the H.B.C.," p. 263.

[47]McLoughlin to governor, deputy governor and committee, 15 November 1843, Rich, *McLoughlin's Letters, Second Series,* p. 118.

[48]McLoughlin to governor, deputy governor and committee, 10 July and 7 August 1828, Rich, *McLoughlin's Letters, First Series,* pp. 57, 63–65; Frank Ermatinger, Journal, 13 July 1828, "Earliest Expedition Against Puget Sound Indians," *Washington Historical Quarterly* 1 (1907): 17.

[49]Simpson to A. Colvile, 20 May 1822, Merk, p. 179.

[50]Governor and committee to McLoughlin, 28 October 1829, Merk, p. 318; Eden Colvile to Sir J. H. Pelly, 15 October 1849, in E. E. Rich, ed., *London Correspondence Inward from Eden Colvile, 1849–1852* (London: Hudson's Bay Record Society, 1956), p. 2.

[51]Douglas to A. C. Anderson, 20 April 1841, Douglas to Angus McDonald, 25 January 1842, and Ogden and Douglas to Tolmie, 18 April 1848, Fort Vancouver, Correspondence Outward, PABC.

In his youth Douglas had been much rasher. In 1828, while stationed at Fort St. James, he had learned that an Indian accused of murdering a trader was hiding in a nearby Indian village. Rushing precipitately into the village, Douglas was responsible for the Indian being beaten to death. The Carrier Indians were aroused by the action, not so much by the killing itself, but by the fact that the victim was a guest in their village. The Indians felt that they deserved recompense from Douglas, and his life was subsequently endangered on more than one occasion.[52]

The Fort St. James affair involved only an individual Indian, at least initially, and that was the way that the company liked to keep such disputes. This approach is clearly illustrated in the Fort McLeod journal for 1823. A group of Indians was induced to discuss the question of responsibility for some murders at Fort George. The Chief Trader, George McDougall, discounted any thought of indiscriminate killing of those Indians who came to negotiate, partly because they were the best beaver hunters and also men of influence, "who if once destroyed would leave only the most worthless probably to trouble us again." The company men were also fairly certain that the murders had been the work of individuals and not of a large group. Following the Fort George murders, the Carrier Indians warned the traders that, should any wholesale killing of Indians occur, they would retaliate and would not leave a white man alive in western Caledonia.[53] Clearly it was not in the interests of the company to become embroiled in the kind of large scale interracial conflict that would threaten if they were injudicious in their dealings with the Indians.

The monotonous and uncouth life led by many traders undoubtedly had a brutalizing effect on them, and there were incidents of individual cruelty towards Indians. On a couple of occasions Indians who made off with traders' women had their ears cut off, and once, on a similar pretext, an Indian was castrated at Fort Vancouver.[54] In considering such behaviour it ought to be remembered that the company's punishment of its own servants who were found guilty of misdemeanours was often just as brutal, a fact which may

---

[52]See Margaret Ormsby, "Sir James Douglas," *Dictionary of Canadian Biography* (Toronto: University of Toronto Press, 1972), 10: 239. The major accounts of this affair are listed in W. N. Sage, *Sir James Douglas and British Columbia* (Toronto: University of Toronto Press, 1930), p. 48n.1., although one account not mentioned is provided by John Tod, "History of New Caledonia and the Northwest Coast," PABC.

[53]George McDougall to John Stuart, 29 December 1823, HBCA, B-119/a; Fort McLeod, Journal, 3 November 1823 and 1 January 1824, ibid.

[54]McLoughlin to Simpson, 16 March 1831 and McLoughlin to governor, deputy governor and committee, 17 January 1837, Rich, *McLoughlin's Letters, First Series*, pp. 227, 185–86; Tod to Edward Ermatinger, 10 April 1831, Ermatinger Papers.

explain the undercurrent of cruelty in the trader's life, even though it does not excuse mistreatment of Indians. There were isolated cases of rather indiscriminate punishment being meted out to groups of Indians. Following the murder of a trader named Alexander McKenzie and four other men by the Indians of the Port Townsend area in 1828, an expedition was mounted to take revenge. The party destroyed a good deal of Indian property, and the hotheads of the group were disappointed that they were not allowed to do more "to the rascals themselves."[55] These examples are, however, exceptions to the company's general rule of limiting the use of violence against Indians. From violence, as Ogden succinctly put it, "we have nothing to gain; on the contrary, everything to lose."[56]

The Indians, for their part, also curbed much of the violence that friction with the traders could well have produced. The history of the land-based fur trade west of the Rockies is remarkable for the virtual absence of mass attacks on forts. The assertion that forts were in a constant state of siege and that "hostility and avoidance marked the interrelations between whites and Indians" is not substantiated by the evidence.[57] There were murders of individual traders, but concerted assaults on posts were rare and hostility was not the norm. The killing of individual traders was sometimes the result of personal disagreements, as was the case with the Fort George murders. On other occasions company men were unknowingly the victims of Indians' notions of revenge, which apparently was the motive for the murder of Samuel Black at Fort Kamloops in 1841. This killing was clearly perpetrated by an individual and was said to be regretted as much by the rest of the Indians as it was by the traders.[58] When an Indian was killed while in the employ of the company, the traders could expect trouble from other Indians who would regard them as accessories after the fact.

Company men also sometimes found their posts the location of conflict between rival groups of Indian traders. Such dissension was a frequent occurrence at posts like Fort Simpson where a number of Indian groups often traded. What was essentially a fight between Indians could be taken by the inexperienced trader as an attempt to overrun the fort. Traders sometimes exacerbated intertribal differences. An attempt to please one group of Indians could cause offence to another. When John Tod allowed a band of Indians to

[55]McLoughlin to governor, deputy governor and committee, 10 July 1828 and [7 August 1828], Rich, *McLoughlin's Letters, First Series*, pp. 57, 63–65; Ermatinger, "Journal," 3 July 1828, p. 28.

[56]Ogden to Tod and D. Manson, 22 October 1845, quoted in Morice, *History of the Northern Interior*, p. 176.

[57]H. G. Barnett, "Social Forces, Personal Conflicts and Cultural Change," *Social Forces* 20 (1941): 163–64.

[58]Tod, "History," pp. 25, 12ff.

settle near Fort Kamloops in 1846, an attack on the fort was only narrowly averted, for they turned out to be the enemies of the Nicola Indians.[59] Efforts to break through Indian trading monopolies were naturally resented, and a fort established on Dease Lake was attacked in the winter of 1838–39, probably by coastal Indians who feared the loss of their trade.[60] The contact between races provided numerous possibilities for misunderstanding, and so incidents like these are not surprising.

Isolated in their little outposts, fur traders were highly vulnerable. The Indians probably had the power to destroy them, and yet they refrained, not because they feared the white traders but because they valued their presence. This attitude is in marked contrast to the Indian behaviour towards white trappers who, unlike the traders, operated in direct competition with the Indian. An American, Joseph Meek, was for eleven years a fur trapper in the Rocky Mountains, and he later admitted that where the influence of the company was great "their men could go where we dare not go unless we had force."[61] Nevertheless, the company traders were a tiny minority among a large population of Indians, and only slightly less vulnerable in their forts than a trapping party moving about in the Indians' territory. Company men set great store on the strength of their forts to protect them from any Indian attacks, but the numerous occasions on which forts were totally destroyed by fire indicate how easily the Indians could have removed them. When the Carrier warned that they might eliminate all traders from New Caledonia in 1824, they probably could have made good their threat, and some traders were well aware of just how fragile their situation could become.[62]

A measure of the traders' weakness was their frequent bravado about their strength. Isolated among an alien population, they assumed that the only way to control the Indians was to overawe them. Traders attempted to impress the Indians with ostentatious displays of power, which often took the form of a demonstration of the destructive capabilities of muskets or cannon. Such displays were possibly more for the benefit of the whites than the Indians. They were reassuring, particularly if the Indians appeared to be suitably impressed. One such incident occurred soon after Fort Victoria was founded in 1843. The Songhees threatened to attack the company establishment with assistance from some neighbouring tribes. The Chief Trader, Roderick

[59]Ibid., pp. 88ff.

[60]Simpson, *Narrative*, 1: 211.

[61]*British and American Joint Commission for the Settlement of the Claims of the Hudson's Bay and Puget's Sound Agricultural Companies* (Montreal: J. Lovell; Washington: Government Printer, 1865–1869), 8: 64.

[62]Fort McLeod, Journal, 1 January 1824, HBCA, B-119/a; Morice, *History of the Northern Interior*, p. 200.

Finlayson, fired a cannon load of grapeshot into an empty Indian house, completely destroying it. The action produced the desired effect. Apparently the Songhees and their allies were impressed, and the quarrel was settled by negotiation.[63]

Yet Indians were not always overawed by the ways in which whites tried to express their power. In 1846 the frigate H.M.S. *Constance* anchored at Esquimalt, and Finlayson asked Captain Courtenay to drill some of his men in the use of their arms in order to impress the Indians. The Songhees this time were unmoved. When a chief was asked what he thought of the exercise, he pointed out the stupidity of fighting in the open compared to the Indian method of fighting from behind cover. "The Captain was not at all pleased at the savage's reply," Finlayson observed. At Fort McLeod, John Tod once had it explained to him by the Indians why the bow and arrow was more effective than the musket.[64] Fur traders who thought such displays ensured their security had not necessarily accurately assessed the Indian view of the situation. They could not conceive that the Indians might have found the continued presence of the company to their benefit.

It was argued, in the context of litigation on the land question in the twentieth century, that the establishment of forts by the Hudson's Bay Company constituted a conquest of the area that became British Columbia.[65] In reality, the Indians accepted the existence of trading posts out of self-interest rather than fear, and therefore they can hardly be described as a conquered people during the fur-trading period.

Another measure of the reciprocity of the traders' dealings with the Indians was the nature of their relationship with their Indian wives. The temporary liaisons that were typical of the maritime fur trade continued, but in addition there were more permanent relationships. There was evidently some concern that Indian women and their children were being deserted by traders, for the Council of the Northern Department passed an order in 1824 requiring all officers and servants to make adequate provision for their Indian women, not only while they were resident in the country but also after their departure.[66]

[63]Roderick Finlayson, *History of Vancouver Island and the Northwest Coast*, Saint Louis University Studies, Series B (Saint Louis: Saint Louis University Press, 1945), 1: 79–80.

[64][Roderick Finlayson], *Biography of Roderick Finlayson* [Victoria, 1913], p. 17; Tod, "History," p. 34.

[65]Canada, Parliament, Senate, *Journals*, 16th Parl., 1st sess., 1926–27, Appendix to the Journals of the Senate. . . . Special Joint Committee of the Senate and House of Commons Appointed to Inquire into the Claims of the Allied Indian Tribes of British Columbia . . . , *Report and Evidence* (Ottawa: F. A. Acland, King's Printer, 1927), p. vii.

[66]Minutes of the Council of the Northern Department, 10 July 1824, in R. Harvey Fleming, ed., *Minutes of the Council of the Northern Department of Rupert Land, 1821–1831* (London: Hudson's Bay Record Society, 1940), pp. 94–95.

Probably there were discrepancies between the ideal of the order and the reality of its execution, but some traders did build lasting relationships based on mutual respect with their Indian wives. The pull of the metropolitan society was still strong, and traders were aware that their frontier marriages might be frowned upon in the "civilized" world. Charles Ross, in a letter to his sister, felt it necessary to deny that he was ashamed of his Indian wife. While she was not exactly fitted to grace a nobleman's table, he said, she suited the sphere in which she had to move.[67] John Work described his wife as "an affectionate partner" who took "good care of my children and myself"; but in his opinion it was out of the question for an Indian wife to join "civilized society."[68] Work's views notwithstanding, some traders did take their Indian wives with them when they left the fur trade.[69] The tedium of much of their existence prompted traders, even those who were initially determined not to do so, to seek the companionship of Indian women. Apart from the personal advantages, such unions were often also good business. Although wives involved the company in additional expenses, even the economy-minded Simpson saw that they were "a useful link between the traders and the savages." In fact, during the Athapaska campaign he had positively urged traders "to form connections" with the daughters of Indian leaders because "connubial alliances are the best security we can have of the goodwill of the Natives."[70]

John Kennedy's marriage to a daughter of Legaic is a good example of an alliance that helped to facilitate trade. From Legaic's point of view the marriage was part of a pattern whereby he married his daughters to the leaders of Indian groups with whom he traded. It was only logical to establish a similar alliance by marriage with this new, and particularly wealthy, tribe that had arrived in the area. The marriage was part of the reason for moving Fort Simpson into Tsimshian territory and for Legaic's pre-eminence after 1834. For their part, the company traders had the benefit of a leader "of weight and standing among the Natives,"[71] who could attract furs in their direction.

---

[67]Ross to Mrs. Joseph MacDonald, 24 April 1843, Lamb, "Five Letters of Charles Ross," p. 107.

[68]Work to Edward Ermatinger, 15 February 1841 and 1 January 1836, "Letters of Edward Ermatinger from John Work, William Tod, Jane Klyne McDonald, and Archibald McDonald, 2 January 1828–14 November 1856," UBCL.

[69]Ibid.; Daniel Williams Harmon, Journal, 8 May 1819, in W. Kaye Lamb, ed., *Sixteen Years in Indian Country: The Journal of Daniel Williams Harmon, 1800–1816* (Toronto: Macmillan, 1957), pp. 194–95; Ross Cox, *Adventures on the Columbia River . . .* (New York: J. & J. Harper, 1932), p. 311.

[70]Simpson, *Narrative*, 1: 231; Simpson to governor, deputy governor and committee, 18 May 1821, in E. E. Rich, ed., *Journal of Occurrences in the Athapaska Department by George Simpson, 1820, and 1821, and Report* (London: Hudson's Bay Record Society, 1938), p. 392.

[71]Work, Journal, 25 August 1835.

William McNeill, who served the company as commander of the *Lama* and then of the *Beaver*, apparently married a Kaigani woman, thus establishing a similar alliance with that group.[72] Marriages such as these had little impact on the social organization of groups like the Tsimshian who had matrilineal exogamous clans since the children would take the inheritance of the mother.[73] These marriages served the company's end much more adequately than having servants disappear over the fort wall to spend the night with Indian women. Still, it is true that relations of any kind could bring trouble for the traders. The Fort George murders in 1823 were apparently motivated by jealousy over an Indian woman.[74] But, more importantly, a marriage union could greatly enhance the economic union between trader and Indian.

The company's drive for profit even affected the most personal aspects of the lives of its servants and officers, but for the Indians this same singlemindedness defined the limits of the traders' impact on their culture. Like those who had come by sea, the land-based fur traders made limited demands on the Indians and did not attempt to initiate major cultural change. On the contrary, the company had a considerable investment and interest in keeping much of the Indian way of life intact. Obviously it did not want to see the kind of radical change that would prevent the Indians from being efficient fur hunters. For this reason there was little intrusion on Indian land during the fur-trading period. The Indians retained their village sites, and their hunting and fishing grounds were unmolested. The company was often chided by humanitarians for its lack of philanthropic concern for the Indians and for doing little to "raise their level of civilization." Although it had moments when it tried to deny these charges, the company really had little interest in making major "improvements" to the Indian way of life. "Philanthropy," wrote Simpson in a pointed understatement, "is not the exclusive object of our visits to these Northern Regions, but to it are coupled interested motives." In short, he concluded, "Beaver is the grand bone of contention."[75]

Their efforts to acquire furs from the Indians did sometimes lead traders to attempt to modify Indian behaviour. They preferred, for instance, to see the Indians gathering furs rather than engaging in internecine warfare. When "War, and not Skins" seemed to occupy the Indians' attention, traders became concerned about returns. The obvious response was to try to settle disruptive

---

[72]Dorothy Blakey Smith, ed., *The Reminiscences of Doctor John Sebastian Helmcken* (Vancouver: University of British Columbia Press, 1975), p. 108.

[73]See Leonard Broom et al., "Acculturation: An Exploratory Formulation . . . ," *American Anthropologist* 56 (1954): 980; and Viola E. Garfield, *Tsimshian Clan and Society* (Seattle: University of Washington Press, 1939), p. 231.

[74]Fort McLeod, Journal, 6 February 1824, HBCA, B-119/a.

[75]Simpson to governor, deputy governor and committee, 18 May 1821, Rich, *Journal of Occurrences*, p. 356.

intertribal conflicts by negotiation. Although Simpson denied it before the 1857 committee on the Hudson's Bay Company,[76] traders did sometimes try to act as mediators between warring parties of Indians. They wanted the Indians to recognize that the forts were neutral ground where all were free to trade; the Indians were told that their disputes should be settled elsewhere.[77] Traders also tried to act as peacemakers in intertribal conflicts that had no connection with the fur trade. In 1835 John Work was concerned about the effects of continued hostility between the Fort Simpson Tsimshian and the Kaigani Haida. He saw that peaceful relations between the two groups would enable the Haida to come to the fort more frequently, so he took Legaic's son to deliver a message from his father to the Kaigani in the hope that it would facilitate a settlement.[78] In all efforts of this kind, however, the company men could use only moral suasion. They were in no position, and had no desire, to use force. Consequently their peacemaking attempts often met with failure. Sometimes traders were simply told to mind their own business,[79] while on other occasions would-be mediators had to desist because their efforts only excited the Indians' derision.[80]

"Conjuring" (the word that Work used to describe Kwakiutl winter cere-monial) was another activity that the traders thought diverted the Indians' attention from hunting. The existence of slavery in Indian society also dis-turbed some company men. But these were integral parts of the Indian way of life and could not easily be eliminated, or even modified, particularly as the traders had to move with extreme care in their occasional efforts to bring ‹ about change. The need for great caution was explained by Douglas in a letter to the governor and committee of the company. He wrote that "undesirable" practices could be discouraged

> by the exertion of moral influence alone, carefully avoiding direct colli-sion either with their selfish feelings or inveterate prejudices, as I don't feel justified in exposing our interests to the shock of excitement and desperate animosity which more active measures, on our part, might provoke.[81]

[76]Great Britain, Parliament, House of Commons, *Report from the Select Com-mittee on the Hudson's Bay Company; together with the Proceedings of the Com-mittee, Minutes of Evidence, Appendix and Evidence* [London: 1857], p. 92.

[77]Fort Simpson, Journal, 25 April 1839, HBCA, B-201/a; Roderick Finlayson to McLoughlin, 11 January 1845, HBCA, B-226/b.

[78]Work, Journal, 20 February 1835.

[79]Duncan Cameron to Donald Mason, 11 November 1844, quoted in Morice, *History of the Northern Interior*, pp. 216–17.

[80]Letter of John McLeod [1823], "Journals and Correspondence of John McLeod . . . 1812–1844," PABC.

[81]Douglas to governor, deputy governor and committee, 18 October 1838, Rich, *McLoughlin's Letters, First Series*, p. 238.

As long as the traders had to be so circumspect about interfering with Indian social customs and the Indians were still in a position to reject these efforts, control of their society remained in Indian hands.

There were some changes in Indian culture that were brought about inadvertently by the land-based fur traders. The shift from trading with vessels to trading at forts reduced the wealth of those Indian groups living on the outer fringes of the coast. As the traders moved inland, the groups who had reaped the benefits of the maritime fur trade experienced a declining standard of living. It appears that the Nootka could make no effective response to this experience, and they lapsed into obscurity as far as European traders were concerned.[82] The Queen Charlotte Haida, on the other hand, made definite efforts to accommodate themselves to the changed situation. In 1825 the botanist Dr. John Scouler was on the coast, and later he recorded some perceptive observations of the Indian inhabitants. He noted that when the sea otter had abounded around the Queen Charlottes, the Haida were among the most wealthy Indians on the coast, but that with the depletion of the fur-bearing animals they became poorer. To offset this decline in wealth, the Haida looked for other sources of income. They began to cultivate potatoes and sell them in large quantities both to the mainland Indians and, after it was established, at Fort Simpson. The potato became their staple trading article, but Scouler also reported that the Haida "fabricate most of the curiosities found on the coast," and these too were traded. The Haida were turning the superb artistry of their wood carving to profit. Not only were "curiosities" carved in wood, and later in argillite, produced for export, but also their fine cedar canoes were manufactured for sale.[83] In these ways the Haida supplemented their trade in potatoes and regained some of the wealth they lost by the passing of the fur trade from their shores.

Disease was still a factor which the Indians could not control, and for the historian the difficulties of accurately assessing its impact still remain. Permanent contact with Europeans undoubtedly did little to reduce the incidence of venereal disease among the Indians. Mercury treatment was a frequent necessity at the forts, and there are references to cases of both gonorrhoea and syphillis,[84] both of which were passed on to the Indians.

---

[82]John Scouler, Journal, 31 July and 3 August 1825, "Dr. John Scouler's Journal of a Voyage to N.W. America," *Quarterly of the Oregon Historical Society* 6 (1905): 193–94.

[83]John Scouler, "Observations of the Indigenous Tribes of N.W. Coast of America," *Journal of the Royal Geographical Society of London* 11 (1841): 219; John Dunn, *History of the Oregon Territory and British North American Fur Trade* . . . (London: Edwards and Hughes, 1844), pp. 293–94.

[84]Simpson, Journal, Merk, p. 99; Simpson *Narrative*, 1: 207; Joseph McGillivray, "Report of Fort Alexandria," 1827, HBCA, B-5/e; MacMillan and McDonald, "Fort Langley Journal," 7 September 1827.

Smallpox was also taking Indian lives. Reports of outbreaks became more frequent in the 1830's, and there are comments about the "dreadful ravages" of smallpox taking "great numbers" of Indians. But the evidence is seldom more specific. Douglas wrote in 1838 that reports indicated that smallpox had killed one-third of the Indian population on the northern coast, but the Reverend Herbert Beaver, writing the following day, claimed that the disease had only taken one in three of those attacked.[85] All such estimates have to be treated with caution, particularly when they were based on Indian reports. Dr. William Fraser Tolmie, who by profession took a great interest in the incidence of disease, claimed that experience had taught him to place little faith in Indian accounts of the severity of outbreaks because of their tendency to exaggerate misfortune.[86] By 1838 deaths from smallpox should have been decreasing as a result of a fairly extensive programme of vaccination of Indians by company traders.[87] Besides venereal disease and smallpox, measles and respiratory diseases were also prevalent among the Indians. The combined effect of all these complaints was undoubtedly a quickening of the death rate, but the exact degree of mortality cannot be ascertained.

With the possible exception of loss of trade, and the definite exception of disease, the social change stimulated by the fur trade could be controlled by the Indians. During the period of the land-based fur trade the developments in Indian culture were of two kinds. There were changes that involved the quantitative development of traditional aspects of Indian society, and, secondly, there were qualitative innovations introduced into the culture. There were changes in degree, and there were changes in kind.

Those developments that were an elaboration of existing features of Indian culture after the 1820's were largely a continuation of change begun by the maritime fur trade. Intertribal acculturation was stimulated as more frequent trading contacts between Indian groups provided opportunities for cultural borrowing. Indian art forms continued to flourish, particularly among the tribes of the northern coast, not just because metal tools made wood carving easier but also because new wealth allowed more of the ceremonial that accompanied the erection of a totem pole. There is little doubt that the fur trade produced an increase in the number and size of potlatches among the coastal

---

[85]Douglas to Simpson, 18 March 1838, Rich, *McLoughlin's Letters, First Series*, p. 271; Beaver to Benjamin Harrison, 19 March 1838, in Thomas Jessett, ed., *Reports and Letters of Herbert Beaver 1836–1838* ... (Portland, Ore.: Champeog Press, 1959), p. 88.

[86]Tolmie, *Journal*, 18 August 1833, p. 227. On the tendency of the Indians to generally exaggerate misfortune see Lewis O. Saum, *The Fur Trader and the Indian* (Seattle and London: University of Washington Press, 1963), p. 159.

[87]McLoughlin to governor, deputy governor and committee, 1 August 1838, Rich, *McLoughlin's Letters, First Series*, p. 217; Tod, "History," p. 86.

Indians. It has been suggested that an absence of references to the potlatch in the fur trade literature demands a re-evaluation of its development.[88] In fact, there are numerous contemporary accounts of the ritual to support the equally numerous scholars who contend that the potlatch flourished during the fur trade.[89] The florescence of art and ceremonial that occurred on the northwest coast was perhaps exceptional among North American Indian reactions to European contact, but there is strong evidence that such a response did occur.[90]

The qualitative changes in Indian society included the rise of new leaders who specialized in dealing with European traders. Leaders like Legaic at Fort Simpson and Kwah among the Carrier assumed this role. It was company policy to deal with these leaders and to enhance their authority by bestowing honours upon them. Because of the special treatment they received from the company traders, these leaders were subject to the jealousies of other Indians,[91] but their enormous wealth helped them to withstand challenges to their leadership. In Indian society an individual's position was related to the amount of goods that passed through his hands, so trading chiefs were well placed to maintain and increase their prestige. Legaic's trade monopoly with the upper Skeena Indians "was a very rich privilege," and the traditions record at least one occasion on which he was able to defeat a threat to his life and position posed by the other Tsimshian tribes simply because his wealth was so much greater than theirs. Legaic's rivals were humiliated when confronted by his great wealth.[92] While increased wealth consolidated the power

[88]Saum, The Fur Trader, p. 11.

[89]For an early and very detailed account of a potlatch see Magee, "Log," 9 July 1794. For other references see Moziño, Noticias, p. 33; "Hoskins' Narrative," January 1792, Howay, "Columbia," p. 265; Jewitt, Journal, 12 November 1803, p. 12; Dunn, History, p. 282; [Peter Skene Ogden?], Traits of American-Indian Life and Character, by a Fur Trader (London: Smith, Elder, 1853), pp. 65–67. This last should have been noticed by Saum as the work is frequently cited by him in other contexts. For more recent accounts of the potlatch see Helen Codere, Fighting with Property: A Study of Kwakiutl Potlatching and Warfare 1792–1930, Monographs of the American Ethnological Society, no. 18 (Seattle and London: University of Washington Press, 1966), pp. 89–97; June McCormick Collins, "Growth of Class Distinctions and Political Authority among the Skagit Indians during the Contact Period," American Anthropologist 52 (1950): 336; Phillip Drucker, "Rank, Wealth and Kinship in Northwest Coast Society," American Anthropologist, n.s. 41 (1939): 63; Homer G. Barnett, The Coast Salish of British Columbia (Eugene: University of Oregon Press, 1955), p. 256.

[90]Cf. Robert F. Murphy and Julian H. Steward, "Tappers and Trappers: Parallel Process in Acculturation," Economic Development and Cultural Change 4 (1956): 353; Innis, The Fur Trade, p. 18.

[91]Fort McLeod, Journal, 7 January 1823, HBCA, B-11/a.

[92]Marius Barbeau and William Beynon, unpublished field notes (selections from the "Tsimshian File"), nos. 67 and 89a, in the possession of the Department of Anthropology, University of British Columbia.

of certain leaders, it also increased the possibilities for social mobility in some groups.[93] The establishment of forts often required other social adjustments on the part of the Indians. When the nine Tsimshian tribes moved to Fort Simpson, they all lived at the same place for the first time, and an acceptable order of rank, both for phratries and for individuals, had to be established. Legaic certainly had initial advantages, but his pre-eminence was the result of a continuing process of social reordering.

As well as affecting the social hierarchy within Indian groups, the fur trade produced shifts in the intertribal balance of power. The expansion of the Kwakiutl as far south as Cape Mudge was a post-contact phenomenon,[94] and their new power was partly based on wealth acquired by manipulating the fur trade. Increased concentration on hunting fur-bearing animals brought changes in concepts of land ownership among some groups. The fur trade induced Indians to return to the same trapping territory year after year, and among the Sekani the result was the development of family hunting territories.[95] Simpson may have been describing an intermediate stage in the same development when he noted that around Fort St. James beaver hunting grounds belonged to particular families, while the rights to smaller furs were held in common.[96]

Clearly the fur trade brought change to Indian society, and yet it was change that the Indians directed and therefore their culture remained intact. New wealth was injected into Indian culture but not in a way that was socially disruptive, so the cultures were altered but not destroyed. Fur traders occasionally contemplated modifications of Indian customs, but they lacked the power and, ultimately, the will to effect such changes. The nature of their relationship with the Indians precluded such interference. During the fur-trading period Europeans and Indians were part of a mutually beneficial economic symbiosis, in which neither gained from the hostility of the other. To use a category of acculturation established by Ralph Linton and borrowed by other students of the subject,[97] the Indians were experiencing a period of non-directed cultural change. The situation was sufficiently permissive for the

[93]Collins, "Growth of Class Distinctions," p. 331.

[94]Herbert C. Taylor, Jr. and Wilson Duff, "A Post Contact Southward Movement of the Kwakiutl," *Research Studies of the State College of Washington* 24 (1956): passim.

[95]Diamond Jenness, *The Sekani Indians of British Columbia*, Canada, Department of Mines and Resources Bulletin no. 84 (Ottawa: J. O. Patenaude, 1937): 44.

[96]Rich, *Part of a Despatch*, p. 19.

[97]Ralph Linton, ed., *Acculturation in Seven American Indian Tribes* (Gloucester, Mass.: Peter Smith, 1963), pp. 501ff; Edward H. Spicer, ed., *Perpectives in American Indian Culture Change* (Chicago and London: University of Chicago Press, 1961), pp. 518–20.

Indians to exercise a large degree of choice about those aspects of European culture that they incorporated into their own. It has been pointed out that acculturation, particularly when it is not forced, can be a creative process.[98] The Indians of the northwest coast and New Caledonia provide a case in point. The impact of the fur-trading frontier on their culture was creative rather than destructive. On the other hand, it could well be that the co-operative relationship between the races during the fur-trading period was poor preparation for the Indians when they had to cope with the new and disruptive elements that came with the settlement frontier. Being used to fur traders who were prepared to accommodate themselves to Indian demands to a considerable extent, the Indians were probably ill-equipped to deal with settlers who were not so accommodating.

[98]Broom et al., "Acculturation," p. 985.

3

The Transitional Years, 1849–1858

> The interests of the Colony, and Fur Trade will never harmonize, the former can flourish, only, through the protection of equal laws, the influence of free trade, the accession of respectable inhabitants; in short by establishing a new order of things, while the fur Trade must suffer by each innovation.[1] —JAMES DOUGLAS, 1838

The establishment of the colony of Vancouver Island in 1849 involved a debate between the proponents of the fur trade and of settlement. Was responsibility for the development of the colony to be given to the old fur-trading company or to some new company founded specifically to foster settlement? The most plausible alternative to the responsibility being given to the Hudson's Bay Company was a scheme proposed to the Colonial Office by a clerk in the British Museum named James. E. Fitzgerald. He advocated the founding of a joint stock company to develop Vancouver Island as a settlement colony along Wakefieldian lines.[2] Some officials at the Colonial Office were, quite rightly, dubious about the efficacy of Edward Gibbon Wakefield's principles of systematic colonization, and in the end they opted for the security and the proven financial capacity of the Hudson's Bay Company. The colony of Vancouver Island was granted to the company by a Royal Charter on 13 January 1849.

In many ways the debate that had occurred in Britain prior to the founding of the colony was transferred to Vancouver Island after 1849. Fitzgerald had argued that, because its interests ran counter to those of settlement, the company would not be a vigorous promoter of colonization. Perhaps he was right, although in the end it did not matter much, for Vancouver Island held little attraction for settlers before 1858. Although the grant of the island had gone to the fur-trading company, the Colonial Office appointed Richard Blanshard, a lawyer who had no connection with the company, as the first governor. Blanshard's position was anomalous from the start. He was supposed to represent interests other than the fur trade in a colony where the fur trade was

---

[1]Douglas to governor, deputy governor and committee, 18 October 1838, Rich, *McLoughlin's Letters, First Series*, p. 242.

[2]Fitzgerald to B. Hawes, 9 June 1847, Great Britain, Colonial Office, Original Correspondence, Vancouver Island, 1846–1867, CO.305/1, UBCL (hereafter cited as CO.305).

virtually the only interest. He correctly observed that the colony was really "nothing more than a fur trading post,"[3] and he soon realized that he was a governor with no one to govern. After eighteen months of fussing and frustration Blanshard left Vancouver Island, having expended his energy, money, and health in a post for which he was not suited. With Blanshard's departure the governorship passed to where the real power in the colony lay. On 16 May 1851 James Douglas, chief factor at Fort Victoria and member of the company's three-man board of management for the area west of the Rockies, reluctantly became the governor of Vancouver Island. The fur trade had temporarily reasserted its dominance. Blanshard's period of office was an interlude that, with the exception of one incident, probably went unnoticed by the Indians.

The exception was Blanshard's punishment of the Newitty, a Kwakiutl group living at the northern end of Vancouver Island, who were held responsible for the murder of three British sailors late in the summer of 1850. The company seamen had deserted in Victoria and escaped on the *Norman Morison*, probably heading for a more lucrative career in the gold mines of California. The *Norman Morison* went instead to Fort Rupert; there the men left the ship and later were reported dead, presumably killed by Indians.

It is quite possible that the Indians believed that they had been offered a reward for the capture of the deserters dead or alive. One of the servants at Fort Rupert claimed that the trader in charge, George Blenkinsop, had offered the Indians ten blankets for each of the deserter's heads. The story was in wide circulation at the time, although the company officers denied it. But Blenkinsop definitely did offer the Indians a reward for information on the whereabouts of the three men.[4] In 1850 Blenkinsop was a young man, inexperienced in leadership, and in Douglas's opinion it was an injustice to him to have to take over the responsibility for such a difficult post as Fort Rupert while William McNeill was on furlough.[5] Perhaps as a result of Blenkinsop's inexperience, the Indians gained a mistaken impression of what was being asked of them in return for the reward. It was company practice to offer the Indians

[3]Rich, *History of the H.B.C.*, 2: 761.

[4]Andrew Muir, Diary, 16 and 27 June 1850, "Private Diary, Commencing 9 November 1848 to 5 August 1850," PABC. Muir is possibly an unreliable witness as he was currently waging a bitter feud with the company over working conditions in the Fort Rupert coal mines and would not be likely to miss an opportunity to slander his employer. Blanshard to John Sebastian Helmcken, 6 August 1850, Vancouver Island, Governor (Blanshard), Correspondence Outward, 1849–1851, PABC; Helmcken to Douglas, 28 March 1851, HBCA, A-11/73.

[5]Douglas to Simpson, 24 February 1851, HBCA, D-5/30. A correspondent of Helmcken's concluded on the basis of the doctor's letters that Fort Rupert was "the Lunatic Asylum of the Coast" (D. D. Wishart to Helmcken, 17 August 1850, Helmcken Papers, PABC).

rewards for bringing in deserting servants. Furthermore, from the time of first contact the Indians had assumed that ordinary seamen and, later, company labourers were slaves. Undoubtedly the Indians felt that their view was confirmed by the company's offers of rewards for deserting servants and by the punishment they received on recapture. The Indians certainly claimed that they regarded the three deserting sailors as slaves on the run.[6] In Indian society slaves had few human rights and runaway slaves had none; therefore, in their terms, killing the men was not only permissible but probably desirable. That the three men were killed by Indians was pretty well proven, but exactly which group of Indians was responsible was much less certain.

In Governor Blanshard's mind there was no doubt about where the responsibility lay. The Newitty Indians were guilty of the murders and if necessary would be held responsible as a group. In contrast to the fur traders, Blanshard lacked the ability, and probably the inclination, to delve into the subtleties of Indian motivation. He regarded the Indians as essentially irrational and could see only the need to erect safeguards against any "sudden outburst of fury to which all savages are liable."[7] Blanshard was ill-at-ease in the uncouth frontier environment of Vancouver Island, and his sense of insecurity demanded that strong measures be taken against threatening Indians. "The Queen's name is a tower of strength," he wrote, but only, "when backed by the Queen's bayonets."[8] The governor requested John Sebastian Helmcken, who had arrived earlier in 1850 as a company doctor, to investigate the murders. Helmcken conducted a careful, on-the-spot examination of the evidence and had to confess that he could hardly believe that the Newitty were responsible. He pointed out that the Newitty had given no previous offence to the whites and, moreover, that it was in their interest to maintain friendly relations with the traders. If Newitty killed the sailors, why, he asked, did they not murder other Europeans who were almost as vulnerable? Then there was the further possibility that the Fort Rupert Kwakiutl had implicated the Newitty in the murders out of intertribal jealousy.[9] Apparently Helmcken's reservations and unanswered questions received little attention from Blanshard.

[6]Beardmore's statement regarding the Fort Rupert murders [1850], HBCA, A-11/73; J. H. Pelly to Earl Grey, 14 January 1852, HBCA, A-8/6.

[7]Blanshard to Fairfax Moresby, 27 June 1851, Vancouver Island, Governor, Correspondence Outward.

[8]Blanshard to Helmcken, 6 August 1850, Vancouver Island, Governor, Correspondence Outward.

[9]Helmcken to Blanshard, 17 July 1850, Vancouver Island, Courts, Magistrate's Court, Fort Rupert, Reports to Governor Blanshard, 2 and 17 July 1850, Helmcken Papers.

Aided and abetted by Rear-Admiral Fairfax Moresby,[10] the governor went up the coast on H.M.S. *Daedalus* seeking retribution. He had already asked Helmcken to tell the Indians that the "white man's blood never dries";[11] and when the Newitty proved unwilling, or perhaps unable,[12] to surrender the murderers, their village was destroyed. The following year Blanshard went north again, this time on H.M.S. *Daphne*, and another Newitty village was stormed and destroyed. Later a group of Newitty came alongside the company's brigantine *Mary Dare* with two bodies said, although never proven, to be two of the murderers.[13]

This brutal action came near the end of Blanshard's term of office, and soon Douglas took over. The punishment of the Newitty had been one of Blanshard's few flurries of activity, and in many ways it was misguided. The killing of the three sailors did not even remotely constitute an Indian menace of "serious proportions," nor was the Newitty tribe particularly warlike.[14] Blanshard's reaction to the murders was exactly the one that as a fur trader Douglas had disapproved of, and under his governance fur-trading methods of dealing with the Indians were reinstituted. Still, for the Indians the destruction of the Newitty villages was a foretaste of things to come. Part of the reason for Blanshard's action was that he and Moresby considered the fur traders' methods of protecting themselves from Indian attacks inadequate.[15] The two men were representative of a new set of attitudes that were to impinge on the Indians with the advent of settlement. Methods of dealing with the Indians that the fur traders found quite satisfactory were to be inappropriate as far as settlers were concerned. In the meantime, however, the fur traders remained in control, and they had been very uneasy about Blanshard's handling of the Newitty.[16]

The appointment of Douglas as governor of Vancouver Island was largely the consequence of a recognition by the Colonial Office of the value of his long

---

[10]For Moresby's views on the question of punishment see Barry M. Gough, *The Royal Navy on the Northwest Coast of America, 1810–1914: A Study of British Maritime Ascendancy* (Vancouver: University of British Columbia Press, 1971), p. 92. Because of his specific concerns the author emphasizes the policy of the naval commander, but, as governor, Blanshard must bear all responsibility.

[11]Blanshard to Helmcken, 6 August 1850, Vancouver Island, Governor, Correspondence Outward.

[12]Certainly Douglas was of the opinion that the Newitty "*could* not surrender the criminals" (Douglas to Archibald Barclay, 16 April 1851, HBCA, A-11/73).

[13]Douglas to Barclay, 3 September 1851, ibid.

[14]Cf. Gough, *Royal Navy*, p. 90; and "The Power to Compel: White-Indian Conflict in British Columbia during the Colonial Period, 1849–1871" (Paper given at the Canadian Historical Association Annual Meeting, June 1972), p. 10.

[15]Blanshard to Moresby, 27 June 1851, Vancouver Island, Governor, Correspondence Outward; Gough, *Royal Navy*, p. 92.

[16]Work to Donald Ross, 27 November 1850, Ross Papers.

experience in dealing with the Indians. Douglas accordingly proceeded to apply many of the lessons learned as a fur trader to his new responsibilities. In fact, many critics of his administration would have argued that, because he remained a chief factor in the company until 1858, he was still more of a fur trader than a colonial governor. Douglas's dual role symbolized the transitional phase from fur trade to settlement.

Like other fur traders, Douglas was not at all happy about Blanshard's treatment of the Newitty, and as governor he considered it downright dangerous. He described the action "as unpolitick as unjust"; poorly conceived as well as badly executed. "In all our intercourse with the natives," wrote Douglas summarizing the fur traders' view, "we have invariably acted on the principle that it is inexpedient and unjust to hold *tribes* responsible for the acts of *individuals*." In any terms the punishment meted out to the Newitty was out of all proportion to the crime, but worse still in Douglas's mind were the possible consequences of the operation. Had the Indians made any real attempt to defend themselves, the attackers would have suffered a considerable loss of life.[17] Escalating the violence to such a level might involve the infant colony in a war with the Indians that could only be disastrous. The whites had neither the numbers nor the power to withstand any concerted assault. The fur traders recalled that the war with the Cayuse had stretched the resources of the Oregon Territory to the limit a few years earlier.[18]

Douglas's opinion that Blanshard's action had been mistaken was supported by the Colonial Office. Earl Grey, the secretary of state for the colonies, wrote to Blanshard to inform him that his superiors were by no means satisfied about the prudence of the steps that he had taken.[19] The governor was even ignominiously asked to stand the expenses of his excursion in the *Daedalus* out of his own pocket. Douglas's disagreement with Blanshard's handling of this particular affair was part of a more general difference of opinion about the need for a military presence in the colony. Blanshard believed hostile tribes should be "speedily coerced" and thought that the colony should have a military force for the purpose. Douglas, who strongly advocated modest measures, considered troops an evil to be avoided.[20]

[17]Douglas to Blenkinsop, 27 October and 13 November 1850, HBCA, B-226/b; Douglas to Barclay, 16 April 1851, HBCA, A-11/73.

[18]Work to Donald Ross, 27 November 1830, Ross Papers.

[19]Grey to Blanshard, 20 March 1851, Great Britain, Colonial Office, Despatches to Vancouver Island, 1849–1867, PABC. In 1853 the Royal Navy established new policy guidelines for the use of force against Indians by ships' commanders (see Gough, *Royal Navy*, p. 92).

[20]Blanshard to Moresby, 28 June 1851, Vancouver Island, Governor, Correspondence Outward; Douglas to Barclay, 1 September 1850 and 21 March 1851, HBCA, A-11/72; Douglas to Simpson, 21 May 1851, HBCA, D-5/30.

Douglas was convinced that in the circumstances of the colony expediency required that the old methods of disciplining the Indians be continued, and he was confident of his own ability to administer them. If not exactly a martinet, the new governor certainly believed that stern discipline should be meted out to malcontents, whether Indian or white. In March 1849 he had occasion to deal with some company sailors who had mutinied while their vessel was at Fort Langley. The unruly employees had holed up in the forecastle, and because of the "timidity" of the other officers Douglas had to go and root them out himself. He noted in a letter to Simpson that he thought "a little severity would have a good effect in checking their turbulence."[21] Douglas had the reputation for being a great hand at a flogging,[22] and he was probably originally employed by the company to act as what might euphemistically be termed a policeman. Certainly Douglas was a big, powerful man, quite able to acquit himself well in any activity demanding physical strength. Indians, no less than Europeans, admired physical prowess, and this was undoubtedly an important reason for Douglas's much reported influence over them.[23] In contrast to Blanshard, Douglas was well equipped to cope with the rough and tumble of the frontier. Confident and experienced, he saw little need to administer large doses of indiscriminate force to Indians who committed depredations against Europeans. Capture the individuals responsible and let them be dealt with as British law directs and the justice of the case requires[24]—this was Douglas's recommendation in the particular case of the Fort Rupert murders and the general course that he was to follow himself.

By treating violence as a consequence of the aberrations of individuals, Douglas tacitly denied that it had sociological causes. Those fur traders who were accustomed to co-operating with the Indians did not make the easy assumption of the settler that all Indians were hostile to all Europeans. During the fur trade violence had been on an individual and not a racial level, and Douglas presumed that this state of affairs would continue.

In 1852 there was another incident that, except for the governor's reaction, was similar to the murders near Fort Rupert. A company employee, this time a shepherd named Peter Brown, was killed by Indians in the Cowichan

[21]Douglas to Simpson, 12 March 1849, HBCA, D-5/24.

[22]Pelly to Grey, 14 January 1852, HBCA, A-8/6.

[23]See, for example, Admiral John Moresby, *Two Admirals: Sir Fairfax Moresby John Moresby a Record of a Hundred Years* (London: Methuen, 1913), p. 103; R. C. Mayne, *Four Years in British Columbia and Vancouver Island ...* (London: J. Murray, 1862), p. 54; Edward Cridge, "Characteristics of James Douglas Written for H. H. Bancroft in 1878," PABC; Charles Frederick Morison, "Reminiscences of the Early Days in British Columbia 1862–1876 by a Pioneer of the North West Coast," PABC, p. 15a; Victoria *Evening Express*, 10 March 1864.

[24]Douglas to Blenkinsop, 27 October 1850, HBCA, B-226/b.

Valley. Apparently two Indians were involved; one was a Cowichan and the other was a member of the Nanaimo tribe. When he learned of the murder, Douglas was determined to capture the two individuals, but he was equally determined not to implicate their tribes. For reasons of "public justice and policy" he did not want to involve all the members of the tribes in the "guilt" of two, nor did he want to provide the closely related Cowichan and Nanaimo with a reason to form an alliance against the whites. Douglas sent messages to the tribal leaders demanding the surrender of the murderers, but when these requests produced only evasive replies, he decided that "more active measures" were required. So in January 1853 he assembled a force made up of 130 marines from the frigate *Thetis* and a small group of militiamen who called themselves the Victoria Voltigeurs. Accompanied by this force Douglas went first to the Cowichan Valley and then to Nanaimo and was able to capture the two Indians without loss of life. But the arrests were not a simple matter. When the Cowichan charged his force as a ceremonial test of its courage, Douglas had great difficulty in restraining his men from firing a volley. The Cowichan murderer was finally surrendered by his people, but the Nanaimo Indian was a man of some prestige in his tribe and was more difficult to secure. In the end Douglas had to take him by force of arms. Once captured, the two Indians were tried and hanged before the Nanaimo people. Douglas was highly satisfied with the operation. He considered, in the case of the Cowichan, that the surrender of the killer without bloodshed "by the most numerous and warlike of the Native Tribes in Vancouver's Island" was "an epoch, in the history of our Indian relations."[25]

Douglas had successfully employed the fur-trading principle of selective, rather than indiscriminate, punishment. In fact, he was of the opinion that the success of the venture owed as much to the influence of the Hudson's Bay Company as it had to the use of intimidation. In contrast to its reprimand to Blanshard, the Colonial Office considered Douglas's actions to be "highly creditable."[26]

Three years later, in 1856, a settler named Thomas Williams was shot and wounded by another Cowichan Indian, and Douglas treated this offence in a similar manner. With a naval force and eighteen Voltigeurs Douglas again went to the Cowichan Valley, and the attacker was captured, tried, and exe-

[25]Douglas to John Pakington, 21 January 1853, CO.305/4. For other accounts of the operation see Douglas to Barclay, 20 January 1853, Douglas to Tod, 7 January 1853, HBCA, A-11/74; Douglas, Diary, 3 and 7 January 1853, James Douglas, Private Papers, 1835–1877, PABC; Douglas to Augustus Kuper, 8 November 1852, Vancouver Island, Governor, Correspondence Outward, 1850–1859, PABC.

[26]Douglas to Pakington, 21 January 1853, CO.305/4; Newcastle to Douglas, 12 April 1853, Great Britain, Colonial Office, Despatches to Vancouver Island.

cuted on the spot.[27] Again the Colonial Office had no hesitation in approving the proceedings, although Douglas was reminded that armed force should only be used against the Indians with great caution.[28] In response, Douglas pointed out that force had been a last resort and reiterated that, as in the earlier expedition against the Cowichan, he had operated on the principle that only the guilty were culpable. He assured the Colonial Office that the recent interracial conflict in the Oregon Territory along with Blanshard's "fruitless expedition" against the Newitty were quite sufficient to evince the dangers and difficulties of such operations.[29] The tone of his reply indicated that Douglas had been ruffled by what he thought was a reprimand, but Herman Merivale, the permanent undersecretary at the Colonial Office, wrote to the Hudson's Bay Company explaining that no disapproval had been intended.[30]

Douglas always resented any implication that his handling of the Indians was at all ill-considered. He regarded such imputations as a slight on his years of experience as a fur trader and often cited that experience in defence of his actions. In 1859 Rear-Admiral Robert Baynes wrote to Douglas in the context of the dispute with the United States over the San Juan Islands, and among other things he expressed the belief that, in the event of conflict between the whites, the Indians would take advantage of the situation and prey on all indiscriminately. In a starchily worded reply marked "confidential" Douglas wondered if the admiral was "perhaps not aware of the intense hatred that exists between the Indians and the American." He told Baynes that the Americans did not understand the Indian character, whereas his personal acquaintance with them was of many years' standing.[31]

His early years had taught Douglas the need for limiting punishment of Indians who attacked Europeans. His realization that it was inadvisable to interfere in conflicts between Indians also grew out of his familiarity with them. While he was determined to convince the Indians that the white settlements were "sacred ground," he did not consider it prudent to interfere with the Indians' "domestic broils." Douglas had already told the Colonial Office that he thought it unwise to involve the government in disputes "of which we could learn neither the merits nor the true bearings, and which probably were in accordance with the laws of natural justice." He expounded the principle when unrest developed among the Indians of northern Vancouver Island

[27]Douglas to Henry Labouchere, 6 September 1856, CO.305/7; Douglas to William Smith, 6 September 1856, HBCA, A-11/76.

[28]Labouchere to Douglas, 13 November 1856, Great Britain, Colonial Office, Despatches to Vancouver Island.

[29]Douglas to Labouchere, 24 February 1857, CO.305/8; Douglas to Smith, 18 February 1857, HBCA, A-11/76.

[30]Merivale to John Shepherd, 19 November 1856, HBCA, A-8/8.

[31]Douglas to Baynes, 17 August 1859, CO.305/11.

following an "atrocious massacre" of the Koskimo by Newitty Indians. In fact, he even went so far as to suggest that quarrels between Indians were of some benefit to the colony, since they provided an outlet for violence that might otherwise be directed against the settlers. The minutes on Douglas's letter to the Colonial Office on this subject, along with the Duke of Newcastle's reply, show that his superiors agreed with his "discrete view" of non-interference in purely Indian matters.[32]

Policy makers at 14 Downing Street were confident enough about Douglas's knowledge of the Indians to leave much of the detail of Indian policy in the colony to his discretion. This confidence was well placed. Douglas undoubtedly did know more about the Indian way of life than any other governor of Vancouver Island or of British Columbia during the colonial period. He thought that the Indians were "in many respects a highly interesting people" and worthy of attention.[33] In contrast to the abusive epithets that settlers often used to describe Indians, Douglas characterized the Vancouver Island Indian population as "hospitable, and exceedingly punctilious in their mutual intercourse,—grateful for acts of kindness, and never fail to revenge an injury. Though generally dishonest, they are seldom known to violate a trust."[34] Naturally he sometimes used harsher adjectives, but they were always tempered with a degree of sympathy. As governor, Douglas felt that one of the advantages of attempting to understand the Indians was that knowledge of their attitudes and intentions might forestall serious conflict with the settlers. Douglas said that he was prepared to make every allowance for the "ignorance and impulsive natures" of the Indians,[35] and he was capable of settling disputes according to Indian customs. For instance, when a Stikine Indian was accidentally wounded by a sailor at Victoria, Douglas arranged for the payment of compensation to the relatives.[36] Of course, by using an Indian method to settle the dispute Douglas also revealed that the two races did not stand equal before the law. As the Cowichan discovered, when an Indian wounded a European the statute book declared it to be an offence punishable by death. Nevertheless, Douglas did try to understand Indian society, and he had some sympathy for the predicament of the Indians faced with the encroachment of a foreign civilization.

Although Douglas's fur-trading experience influenced his Indian policy,

---

[32]Douglas to Newcastle, 28 July 1853, CO.305/4; Douglas to Barclay, 2 November 1853, HBCA, A-11/74; Newcastle to Douglas, 15 October 1853, Great Britain, Colonial Office, Despatches to Vancouver Island.

[33]Douglas to Grey, 31 October 1851, CO.305/3.

[34]Douglas to Labouchere, 20 October 1856, CO.305/7.

[35]Douglas to Labouchere, 13 June 1857, CO.305/8.

[36]Douglas to Captain James Prevost, 19 October 1857, Vancouver Island, Governor, Correspondence Outward.

the exigencies of the settlement frontier gradually began to press in on him. The fur traders understood that with the coming of the settlers their days would be numbered. At the time of the establishment of the colony of Vancouver Island, Ogden had assumed in a letter that Simpson would be "fully aware that the Fur trade and Civilization can never blend together and ... the former invariably gives way to the latter." Douglas had also realized for a long time that settlement would bring "a new order of things."[37]

Unlike other colonies, Vancouver Island had not been founded for the purpose of relieving overcrowded conditions in Britain, and settlers arrived only slowly. By 1852 as few as 435 emigrants had been sent to the colony, only 11 had purchased land, and another 19 had applied for land.[38] It has often been assumed that the fur company must have been a bad colonizer because it wanted to retain Vancouver Island as a purely fur-trading preserve.[39] It is true that clearing land for agriculture does little to maintain the habitat of fur-bearing animals, but Vancouver Island was not very important as a source of furs by the 1850's. The company wanted to control the island to ensure the protection of the much more important region of New Caledonia.[40] Nor was the company's decision to charge £1 per acre for land designed to restrain settlement, as Canadian historians have tended to suppose. Archibald Barclay's letter to Douglas outlining the principles of colonization that the company intended to follow is pure Wakefield. The company secretary wrote of the desirability of transferring a cross section of British society to the colony, of disposing of land in a way that would ensure "a just proportion of labour and capital," and of preventing the admission of paupers, squatters, and land speculators.[41] The echoes from *A Letter from Sydney* are unmistakable. The Hudson's Bay Company was thus following what many in Britain, including the Colonial Secretary, Earl Grey, thought was the last word in the theory of colonization. The experience of other colonies was to show that the theory, so promising on paper, was unworkable on the ground. The basic reason for the slow development of colonization on Vancouver Island was not the policy of the company but the few attractions for agricultural settlers. Other colonies seemed to hold greater promise for the potential emigrant, and for those who came as far as the west coast of North America after 1849, California was a much more likely prospect.

---

[37]Ogden to Simpson, 10 March 1849, HBCA, D-5/24; Douglas to governor, deputy governor and committee, 18 October 1838, Rich, *McLoughlin's Letters, First Series*, p. 242.

[38]Andrew Colvile to Pakington, 24 November 1852, HBCA, A-8/7.

[39]Bancroft, *History of B.C.*, pp. 206, 211; Martin Robin, *The Rush for Spoils: The Company Province 1871–1933* (Toronto: McClelland and Stewart, 1972), p. 14.

[40]Galbraith, *H.B.C. as an Imperial Factor*, p. 285.

[41]Barclay to Douglas, December 1849, Fort Victoria, Correspondence Inward, 1849–1859, from the Hudson's Bay Company, London to James Douglas, PABC.

It soon became evident that those colonists who did come to the island were men whose outlook on many matters differed from that of the fur traders. There was a growing group of settlers in opposition to company rule led by the Reverend Robert Staines, and these "free settlers" expected to have "a sore Battle to fight against the Companys."[42] The conflicts that developed between Douglas and men like Staines may have been "Lilliputian,"[43] but they do reflect many of the attitudes of the settlers towards the fur traders. The time had come, the colonists thought, to sever the ties with Vancouver Island's fur-trading past. The British member of Parliament Charles Fitzwilliam considered that Douglas was incompetent for the post of governor because his dealings had been with Indians and not with white men.[44] This attitude was also prevalent in the colony. One of the more supercilious of the settlers wrote to her family that Douglas "has spent all his life among the North American Indians and has got one of them for a wife so can it be expected that he can know anything at all about Governing one of England's last Colonies in North America."[45]

Annie Deans was not the only newcomer who believed that, while Douglas could handle Indians, he "does not seem up to governing a white population at all."[46] For many of the settlers the very quality that had recommended Douglas to the Colonial Office disqualified him as governor. One of the jokes going round the colony was that the letters H.B.C. actually stood for "Here before Christ," and it was indicative of the settler opinion that the fur traders were crude and unrefined. The company men were said to be only one degree removed from the Indians. They had white skins but had been raised and educated up to Indian standards, and only with the arrival of settlers was a degree of civilization introduced to the country.[47] Some fur traders would have agreed with the description: John Tod once remarked that he saw him-

[42]Annie Deans to her cousins, 13 August 1856, Annie Deans, Correspondence Outward, 1853–1868, PABC.

[43]Victoria *Evening Express*, 10 March 1864. For details of the conflict between Staines and Douglas see Hollis G. Slater, "Rev. Robert John Staines, Priest, Pedagogue, and Political Agitator," *BCHQ* 14 (1950): 187–240.

[44]Great Britain, Parliament, *Hansard's Parliamentary Debates*, 3d ser., 151 (1858): 1121.

[45]Annie Deans to her brother and sister, 29 February 1854, Deans, Correspondence Outward.

[46]Charles Wilson, Diary, 8 August 1858, in George F. G. Stanley, ed., *Mapping the Frontier: Charles Wilson's Diary of the Survey of the 49th Parallel, 1858–1862* ... (Toronto: Macmillan, 1970), pp. 29–30; see also George Duncan Forbes MacDonald, *British Columbia and Vancouver's Island* ... (London: Longman, Green, Longman, Roberts and Green, 1862), p. 271; and George Hills (bishop of Columbia), Diary, 26 December 1861, Archives of the Vancouver School of Theology.

[47]Charles Alfred Bayley, "Early Life on Vancouver Island," PABC, p. 2.

self as "half a savage."[48] The settler was never faced with any such confusion of identity: he never got close enough to the Indian for that. While the nature of his occupation demanded that the fur trader should, to some extent, accommodate himself to Indians, settlers had no need and, therefore, no desire to be accommodating and tolerant. The settler came to re-create an alien civilization on the frontier, while the fur trader had to operate largely within the context of the indigenous culture. Although settlers arrived only in small numbers in the early 1850's, they were increasingly to influence colonial affairs in general and Indian policy in particular.

At the time that the colony of Vancouver Island was granted to the company, Douglas was asked by the management for his ideas on how colonization might best be effected. He replied that he had never given the matter a moment's thought and that any attempt to discuss the subject would only reveal his own ignorance. The future governor did, however, offer some thoughts on the difficulties that colonists would face. Among them was the petty theft that the Indians would be tempted into by the careless habits of the settlers.[49] The effect of settlement on relations with the Indians was to give Douglas cause for a great deal of reflection in the next few years.

Douglas was keenly conscious of the deterioration of race relations following the advent of settlement south of the border. In 1846 the old fur-trading preserve had been divided in half by what Douglas regarded as a "monstrous treaty."[50] Following the Oregon Treaty the area north of the forty-ninth parallel continued to be dominated by the fur trade, while to the south settlement prevailed. Almost immediately there was racial conflict in the south. Only a year after the Americans took over, the murders at the Whitman mission and the hostilities that followed set the pattern for the next decade. As far as the fur traders were concerned there was no doubt, after the killings by the Cayuse at Waiilatpu, "that the Americans will, in the end, glut their revenge upon the wretched Indian, although from their want of discipline and means, it will require a length of time to effect the work of destruction."[51] The prophecy turned out to be very accurate. There was warfare with the Indians of Washington again in 1855–56, and it was accompanied by the indiscriminate slaughter of Indians by groups of volunteers. Even Phillip Sheridan, who later showed his lack of sympathy for the native American with the comment about "the only good Indian," criticized the killing of innocent Indians in

---

[48]Tod to Edward Ermatinger, 29 June 1836, Ermatinger Papers.
[49]Douglas to Pelly, 5 December 1848, HBCA, A-11/72.
[50]Douglas and Work to governor and committee, 7 December 1846, ibid.
[51]Despatch from Simpson to Hudson's Bay Company, 24 June 1848, CO.305/1.

Washington for no other reason than to gratify an "inordinate hatred" of them.[52]

Douglas usually could not emphathize with the Americans at all; and he had once declared himself to be more "suspicious of their designs, than of the wild natives of the forest."[53] But he regarded the conflict of 1855–56 as a war of races, of civilization against barbarism,[54] and he acknowledged a moral obligation which bound Christian and civilized nations together "in checking the inroads of the merciless savages."[55] He therefore thought it incumbent on the colony to render some assistance to the Washington authorities, while at the same time he wanted to maintain a façade of neutrality to avoid being identified with the Americans in the mind of the Indians. So he provided the Americans with arms, ammunition, and the use of the *Beaver*, but not with any more active support.

Douglas was most anxious that violence with the Indians in the United States should not spill over the border and threaten the colony. He assumed that there must have been "some great mismanagement" on the part of the American authorities. Nothing else made credible the antagonism of the American Indians, who had been "softened and improved" by fifty years of commercial dealings with the Hudson's Bay Company.[56] His own Indian policies were largely designed to avoid similar mismanagement and the consequent horrors of Indian warfare. The governor also wanted to ensure that the unfamiliarity of the settlers with the Indians did not lead to major conflict on Vancouver Island. For the people in the colony to be reduced in the estimation of the Indians to the level of the Americans would, in Douglas's opinion, invite disaster.[57]

Douglas's prognostication that the carelessness of the settlers would invite depredations by the Indians was borne out from the beginning of colonization. Vancouver Island's first independent settler was Captain Walter Colquhoun Grant, who came to the colony to survey land for the company and to establish a farm. He proved to be incompetent in the first occupation and too irresponsible for the second. When he left the colony, Douglas's parting comment was that the "unfortunate man has been an absolute plague

[52][P. H. Sheridan], *Personal Memoirs of P. H. Sheridan, General United States Army* (New York: C. L. Webster and Company, 1858), 1:88.

[53]Douglas to Simpson, 4 April 1845, HBCA, D-5/13.

[54]Douglas to Smith, 6 November 1855, HBCA, A-11/75.

[55]Douglas to James Tilton, 6 November 1855, Vancouver Island, Governor, Correspondence Outward.

[56]Douglas to William Molesworth, 8 November 1855, CO.305/6.

[57]Douglas to Baynes, 17 August 1859, CO.305/11.

to me ever since he came to the Island."[58] Grant and the settlers he brought with him under his agreement with the company were apprehensive about the Indians, but Douglas was convinced that, instead of thirsting for their blood, the Indians were well disposed and willing to assist them in their labours. He impressed on the inexperienced new arrivals that it was in their own, and in the colony's, interest to cultivate the friendship of these "children of the forest."[59] When Grant, contrary to Douglas's advice, left his property at Sooke unattended, some articles were stolen by unknown parties, presumed to be Indians. The imprudence of the settler had elicited the expected response. Douglas knew that Grant's anxiety about Indian behaviour would become general and that the settlers would clamour for protection until a military force was sent out, a conclusion he wanted to avoid.[60]

In June 1854 a man named Thomas Greenham came rushing into Victoria from the company's Cadboro Bay farm with a wild report that the place had been attacked and overrun by hundreds of Indians. Douglas armed some men and hastened to the spot only to find no sign of Indians and all the residents safe, except for one man who had a cut on the head. Apparently some of the labourers had fled at the sight of the Indians and completely exaggerated the seriousness of the threat. The incident set the whole settlement aflame. The Indian tribes assembled at Victoria and, from mistrust and alarm, took up arms against each other. A relatively minor event had quickly developed into an extremely critical situation. After the excitement had died down, Douglas observed that "a labourer taken from the plough is not to be trusted in circumstances of danger, without some previous training" and that such examples of timidity destroyed the influence of the whites.[61]

During the early years of the colony there were large numbers of free-roaming cattle that were a potential source of interracial conflict. Douglas was aware that the Indians regarded cattle in much the same way as they did wild animals, recognizing none as exclusive property, and he knew that an Indian returning unsuccessful from the hunt would find the settlers' cattle irresistible.[62] To avoid offering such provocation to the Indians, Douglas wanted settlement on Vancouver Island to be confined to a specific area where settlers could protect each other. The company's practice had been to main-

[58]Douglas to Simpson, 24 February 1851, HBCA, D-5/30. Grant did return to the colony for a few months in 1853. For an account of his career see Willard E. Ireland, "Captain Walter Colquhoun Grant: Vancouver Island's First Independent Settler," *BCHQ* 17 (1953): 87–121.

[59]Douglas to Barclay, 3 September 1849, HBCA, A-11/72.

[60]Douglas to Barclay, 1 September 1850 and 21 May 1851, HBCA, A-11/72 and 73.

[61]Douglas to Barclay, 15 June 1854, HBCA, A-11/75.

[62]Douglas to Grey, 15 April 1852, CO.305/3.

tain sufficient men in one place to give some security, but, like settlers everywhere, those on Vancouver Island began to spread out in search of good land.

Isolated and outnumbered, the settlers felt insecure and frequently feared attacks. Douglas often received requests for protection against imagined Indian invasions. He discounted such "idle terrors" and was more concerned that settlers' fears might encourage the Indians to aggression. The colonists were advised to conceal their apprehensions and on all occasions to assume a "bold countenance" with the Indians.[63] Settlers were particularly uneasy about the large numbers of northern Indians, mostly Haida and Tsimshian, who visited Victoria annually from 1854. The Haida particularly had a formidable reputation, and many unfounded rumours were spread about Indian plans to destroy the settlement. But Douglas recognized that the northern Indians had come to benefit from the existence of Victoria and not to end it.[64] The settlement attracted these Indians because it provided a marketplace; they came to trade and to find employment as labourers. It was settler hysteria rather than Indian hostility that produced the demands for protection, and the Indians were probably fortunate that Douglas stood between them and the settlers. In the United States public opinion had a freer rein. At Port Townsend a meeting of citizens resolved to shoot without question all northern Indians found in United States waters.[65] Settler influence was not so strong on Vancouver Island, and Douglas would never have tolerated such extremities.

By the mid-1850's, however, he had become much more conscious of the need for protecting the colony. The migrations from the north were greatly increasing the Indian population around Victoria at a time when events in the United States were raising the spectre of racial warfare. Douglas felt the Vancouver Island Indians had become "restive and insolent" as a consequence of Indian military successes to the south.[66] Then came the news of the Cowichan attack on Thomas Williams, and Douglas began to realize that it required more coercive power to maintain a settlement frontier than the fur traders had needed. He recognized that factionalism among the Indians probably precluded any preconceived or combined attack on the settlements, but he could not discount the possibility that individual disputes could lead to a

[63]Douglas to Tod, 7 January 1853, HBCA, A-11/74; Douglas to Labouchere, 5 May 1857, CO.305/8.

[64]Douglas to Barclay, 13 July 1854, HBCA, A-11/75; Douglas to Newcastle, 8 August 1860, CO.305/14.

[65]C. H. Mason to Douglas, 26 August 1857, CO.305/8. Apparently the Washington government also made it a capital offence for northern Indians to land on American territory (Douglas to McNeill, 21 September 1857, Fort Victoria, Correspondence Outward, 21 December 1856–25 January 1858, Letters Signed by James Douglas [Country Letterbook], PABC).

[66]Douglas to Smith, 18 February 1857, HBCA, A-11/76.

general affray. So he recommended measures to protect the colony, even if only to allay the fears of the colonists.[67] His requests for assistance from the Royal Navy and his advocacy of an armed force became more frequent.

Because of their potential power, Douglas realized that the hostility of the Indians was the worst calamity that the infant colony could face. Hence he felt it necessary to foster their good will; a duty that, according to Douglas, was often rendered difficult by the "recklessness and imprudence" of the colonists.[68] He also recognized the potential value of the Indians as allies. In the event of conflict with the Americans over the San Juan Islands, Douglas thought he could rely on the Indians for assistance, and when the possibility of war between Britain and Russia arose, he suggested that an armed force including both Indians and whites should be raised to defend the colony. The colonists, not unexpectedly, were uneasy about the notion of arming the Indians.[69]

It has been shown that when Douglas perceived a real threat to the security of the colony he acted forcefully and decisively. Yet some settlers remained unconvinced that they were sufficiently protected from the Indians under the Hudson's Bay Company. Aware of their vulnerability, they wanted to use large doses of force to convince the Indians that they were invulnerable. There were continued requests and petitions from colonists for more defensive measures, and some who viewed their position as precarious argued that an abler man than Douglas was required as governor.[70] Many were unimpressed when he used the Indian method of paying damages to settle disputes; they thought that the Indians should be made to "smell powder and ball, instead of perpetuating the old system of doling out blankets to them."[71] Others dismissed such "bribery" as perhaps appropriate to the fur trade but not to a settlement of British subjects. James Cooper, a non-company settler from 1851 to 1857, in testimony before the Select Committee on the Hudson's Bay Company, described this method of dealing with the Indians as probably humane but not judicious. However, when the patently obvious difference between race relations on the British and American sides of the border was

[67]Douglas to Admiral W. H. Bruce, 7 March 1856, Vancouver Island, Governor, Correspondence Outward.
[68]Douglas to Newcastle, 28 July 1853, CO.305/4.
[69]Douglas to Baynes, 17 December 1859, CO.305/11; Douglas to Newcastle, 16 May 1854, Vancouver Island, Governor, Despatches to Her Majesty's Principal Secretary of State for the Colonies, 1851–1859, PABC. In instances where despatches are missing from the CO.305 records this source, which is Douglas's letterbook copies of his despatches, has been used. Margaret A. Ormsby, *British Columbia: a History* (Toronto: Macmillan, 1971), p. 129.
[70]Minutes of the Council of Vancouver Island, 21 June 1855, CO.305/6; Douglas to Sir George Grey, 7 March 1856, CO.305/7; Robert Swanton to Thomas Bannister, 4 January 1856, Great Britain, Colonial Office, Despatches to Vancouver Island.
[71]MacDonald, *British Columbia*, p. 80.

pointed out in implied defence of the company's administration of the colony, Cooper could make no effective rejoinder.[72] Douglas often made the same point in his letters to London. He was undoubtedly aware that the contrast between the "tragic events" taking place in the United States and his reports that on Vancouver Island the Indians continued with their "usual quiet and friendly demeanor" reflected well on his administration.[73]

Nonetheless, the methods of dealing with the Indians that Douglas had learned as a fur trader and applied so successfully in the early years of the colony were used less and less in the later 1850's. In 1855, when the northern Indians returned to Victoria, Douglas assembled the leaders and "spoke to them seriously" about their relations with the whites. There were no major disputes, and in cases of minor infractions of British law the Indians submitted to the decisions of magistrates. Douglas established a four-man police force to deal with the situation created by the continued presence of the northern Indians but noted that what was really required was a force of twenty to thirty men. Both Douglas and the Indians realized that a new relationship was being established between them. Douglas thought that the Indians were beginning to have a clearer idea of the nature and utility of British law, the object of which was to protect life and property. This awareness, wrote Douglas, "may be considered as the first step in the progress of civilization."[74] The Indians themselves were feeling for the first time the full impact of an alien legal system. Even internal disputes were becoming subject to European scrutiny and jurisdiction as long as the Indians remained near the settlements. Whereas earlier Douglas had been prepared to allow the "laws of natural justice" to operate among them, gradually British notions of social control were being applied to the Indians of Vancouver Island.

Settlement impinged on Douglas's relations with the Indians in many areas besides law and order. The availability of armed force and the willingness to use it were not, in themselves, particularly significant in maintaining peaceful relations with the Indians. It has been argued that the Royal Navy provided the "power to compel" on the northwest coast and that its presence in large part accounts for the relatively pacific nature of Indian-white relations.[75] But, as Douglas appreciated, the American example showed that the use of force could not make up for deficiencies in Indian policy.[76] Nor was the governor powerless without the navy's support. The fur traders had maintained a relatively harmonious relationship with the Indians before the navy was very

[72]Great Britain, Parliament, House of Commons, *Report of the Select Committee on the Hudson's Bay Company*, pp. 194–95.
[73]Douglas to Smith, 11 December 1855, HBCA, A-11/75.
[74]Douglas to Lord John Russell, 21 August 1855, CO.305/6.
[75]Gough, "The Power to Compel," passim.
[76]Douglas to Barclay, 22 December 1850, CO.305/3.

active on the coast, and after 1858 Douglas was able to restrain violence between the races on the Fraser and Cariboo gold fields; areas not accessible to naval vessels. Other "tools of statecraft" were required besides the Royal Navy,[77] for peace was not maintained by power alone.

With settlement, Europeans and Indians came into competition for the use of the land. Agricultural settlement was destructive to the Indians' methods of food gathering. In the Fort Victoria area, for example, Indian camas grounds were broken up by the plough.[78] It was true that the Indians no longer relied solely on the old methods of food gathering and that many had become accustomed to cultivating crops both for their own consumption and for sale at the forts. These groups were to come even more directly into competition with the Europeans for the best arable land. If the experience of other colonies meant anything, competition between races for land was likely to produce conflict.

In 1849 Douglas wrote to the Hudson's Bay Company drawing attention to the need for some arrangement to be made for the purchase of Indian land. In reply the company cited the report of a committee of the House of Commons set up to examine the claims of the New Zealand Company. This report argued that aborigines had only "qualified Dominion" over their country, consisting of a right of occupancy but not title to the land. Until the "uncivilised inhabitants" of any country established among themselves "a settled form of government and subjugate the ground to their own uses by the cultivation of it," they could not be said to have individual property in the land. Consequently, while much was left to Douglas's discretion and knowledge of the local situation, the company authorized him to confirm the Indians in the possession of only those lands that they had cultivated or built houses on by 1846 when they came under the sovereignty of Great Britain. All other land was to be regarded as waste and therefore available for colonization.[79] In pursuance of his instructions, Douglas had eleven treaties made with the Indians of the Fort Victoria area and later two at Fort Rupert and one at Nanaimo. Because these treaties were largely based on current British opinion about the nature of aboriginal land tenure, they took little account of Indian realities. In spite of Douglas's familiarity with the Indians the treaties contained a num-

---

[77]Barry M. Gough, " 'Turbulent Frontiers' and British Expansion: Governor James Douglas, the Royal Navy, and the British Columbia Gold Rushes," *Pacific Historical Review* 41 (1972): 18. On the single occasion that navy men went up to the gold fields because of conflict between miners and Indians, the dispute was settled before they arrived (ibid., pp. 23–24).

[78]Gilbert Malcolm Sproat, *Scenes and Studies of Savage Life* (London: Smith, Elder, 1868), p. 55.

[79]Douglas to Barclay, 3 September 1849, HBCA, A-11/72; and Barclay to Douglas, December 1849, Fort Victoria, Correspondence Inward.

ber of "ethnographic absurdities,"[80] including the fact that only "village sites and enclosed fields" were to be reserved: that is, areas of land of which Indian possession could be recognized in European terms. In the Saanich area Douglas found it quite impossible to sort out the real owners from the numerous claimants to the land, so an area of fifty square miles was purchased.[81]

By these treaties the Indians surrendered their lands in return for a few blankets, the reservation of a little land for their use, and the freedom to hunt on unoccupied land and to fish as before. The compensation that the Indians received for these concessions was minimal. Douglas favoured payment by annuity so that the Indians would derive a continuing benefit,[82] but apparently the Indian leaders preferred a lump sum. They were paid in goods, mostly blankets, from the Fort Victoria stores, and the value to the Indians included a markup of approximately 300 per cent over the "department" or wholesale price. The Songhees, for instance, received goods with a retail price of £309.10.0, but the cost to the company had actually been £103.14.0.[83] With the "small exceptions" of village sites and enclosed fields, the land had become "the entire property of the white people for ever."[84]

Douglas did not find these treaties easy to negotiate. He discovered that any discussion of the question of Indian rights invariably produced "troublesome excitements."[85] It is unlikely that the Indians comprehended the full import of the phrase "entirely and forever." In the pre-settlement period the Indians had no way of learning about European concepts of land ownership, and the signatories of the treaties probably thought that they were surrendering the rights to the use of the land rather than title to it. But in spite of the many inadequacies, implicit in these treaties was the notion that the aboriginal race exercised some kind of ownership over the land that ought to be extinguished by the colonizing power.

Because Douglas negotiated these treaties to facilitate settlement, he was only prepared to purchase Indian land in areas where Europeans wanted to

---

[80] An analysis of the Fort Victoria treaties in relation to what is known about Songhees ethnography has been made by Wilson Duff, "The Fort Victoria Treaties," *BC Studies* 3 (1969): 52 and passim.

[81] Douglas to Barclay, 18 March 1852, HBCA, A-11/73.

[82] Douglas to Barclay, 3 September 1849, HBCA, A-11/72.

[83] The point is made by Duff, "Fort Victoria Treaties," p. 24. See also Douglas to Barclay, 16 May 1850, HBCA, A-11/72. Blanshard was aware that the Indians were paid at a 300 per cent markup (Blanshard to Grey, 18 February 1851, CO.305/3).

[84] For the texts of these treaties see Hudson's Bay Company, Land Office Victoria, "Register of Land Purchased from the Indians, 1850–1859," PABC. Edited versions are contained in British Columbia, *Papers Connected with the Indian Land Question, 1850–1875* (Victoria: R. Wolfenden, 1875) pp. 5–11. These papers were also published with a different pagination in British Columbia, Legislative Assembly, *Sessional Papers*, 2d Parl., 1st sess., 1876, pp. 161–328B.

[85] Douglas to Barclay, 16 May 1853, HBCA, A-11/74.

take up land. The Cowichan Indians wanted to sell their lands in the same way as the Songhees had done, but Douglas refused their request on the grounds that settlement was not immediately moving into that area.[86] It was a decision that was to produce major problems in the future.

Once treaties were signed, however, Douglas was determined to protect Indian land from encroachment, although this rule did have one exception to prove it. Contained within the Hudson's Bay Company land around Fort Victoria was a ten-acre Indian reserve. That is, as far as everybody was concerned in 1854 it was an Indian reserve.[87] But by the end of the decade the land had been re-allotted as the site of the government offices.[88] There is undoubtedly something symbolic about the fact that the legislative buildings of British Columbia stand on land that perhaps rightfully belongs to the Indians.[89] The exception is an interesting one, but generally Douglas did make every effort to protect Indian rights guaranteed by the treaties he made.

Douglas's concern for Indian welfare also found expression in areas other than land policy. His attitudes to the Indians were a mixture in which the knowledge of the fur trader was accompanied by the paternalistic concerns of the nineteenth-century humanitarian. His ideas about the need and means to "improve" the Indians had been adumbrated as a fur trader. Now, as governor of a settlement colony, not only was the need for philanthropy greater, but there was also much more potential for action. Like those of his contemporaries who saw any hope at all for the survival of the North American Indian, his hope was expressed in terms of the Indians becoming red-skinned Europeans. Christianity, education, and agriculture—the holy trinity of British colonial policy on aborigines—were to be the means by which the Indian could achieve this new status. Consequently Douglas's intention was both to secure for the Indians sufficient land for them to develop and maintain a livelihood based on agriculture and to encourage "schools and clergymen to superintend their moral and religious training."[90] He believed the "untutored

---

[86]Douglas to Barclay, 16 May 1850, HBCA, A-11/72.

[87]Pemberton to Barclay, 1 September 1854, Douglas to Barclay, 26 August 1854, HBCA, A-11/75.

[88]Minutes of the Council of Vancouver Island, 25 March 1859, CO.305/10; Pearse to Colonial Secretary, 1 February 1865, British Columbia, Colonial Correspondence (Inward Correspondence to the Colonial Government), PABC, file 910 (hereafter cited as CC); Day and Son, Lithographers to the Queen, *Map of Victoria and Part of Esquimalt District* (London: 1861).

[89]In his letter to Barclay of 26 August 1854, HBCA, A-11/75, Douglas reported that the Indians had offered the ten acres to him for sale, but that he had declined the offer. The possibility remains that the land was subsequently purchased from the Songhees, although I have found no evidence of such a sale.

[90]Douglas to Lytton, 14 March 1859, Great Britain, Colonial Office, Original Correspondence, British Columbia, 1858–1871, CO.60/4, UBCL (hereafter cited as CO.60).

reason of man" to be a contemptible thing and said that those fools who denied the ennobling influence of religion would be cured of their idle fancies by a few months' residence among the Indians.[91] So, whenever he could, Douglas gave encouragement and assistance to missionaries of all denominations who came to work among the Indians. He had his own plans for social reorganization as well. In 1860 he wrote that he had long cherished the hope that he would be able to organize the Indians into communities in which peace and the enforcement of laws would be facilitated by the appointment of Indian police officers and magistrates. As the only plan that promised to result in the moral elevation of the Indians, Douglas thought that its successful operation would "raise an imperishable monument to the justice and philanthropy of the Government which lends it support." He added, however, that the plan would cost money and therein lay the impediment. Douglas never found the money to put these ideas into action.[92]

Before 1849 and the arrival of the colonists there had been no need to contemplate measures for the rearrangement of Indian society. During the fur-trading period it had been unnecessary to develop policies designed to avoid hostilities with the Indians. Douglas ruled the colony autocratically; he took little advice and retained power in his own hands as much as possible, yet the settlers still influenced his policies. The mere fact of their presence demanded that new measures be taken for the regulation of race relations. Then, in spite of Douglas's predilections, the elective principle was conceded in 1856 with the establishment of a Legislative Assembly with seven members. Company men dominated the first House and the government of the colony, but their time was passing. Having established a foothold in government, the settlers were to play an increasing part in the administration of the colony. The few colonists on Vancouver Island in the 1850's were the harbingers. Besides these settlers, forerunners of a different kind also began arriving in the 1850's.

The officers of the Hudson's Bay Company were aware at least as early as 1850 that there was gold on the Queen Charlotte Islands. This kind of information could never be contained, and in 1852 gold seekers from the United States began to appear on the islands. Their presence necessitated the promulgation of laws to regulate their activities, and Douglas's responsibilities were increased when he was issued with a commission as lieutenant-governor of the Queen Charlotte Islands. The Haida were unenthusiastic about the arrival of white men come to exploit resources that the Indians regarded as theirs.

[91]Douglas to Hargrave, 5 February 1843, James Hargrave Collection, Series 1, Letters Addressed to James Hargrave, 1821–1886, PAC.

[92]Douglas to Newcastle, 7 July 1860, CO.305/14; Douglas to Lytton, 14 March 1859, CO.60/4; Douglas to Smith, 30 October 1857, HBCA, A-11/76.

Douglas knew that there was likely to be conflict since the company had already been forced to abandon its own efforts to find gold on the Queen Charlottes because of the "turbulent opposition" of the Indians.[93] The expectations of hostility were not to be disappointed, and American miners were driven off the islands by the Haida. The most famous incident was the capture and plunder of the *Susan Sturgis*. She carried a group of gold miners, and, according to Douglas, the captain, Matthew Rooney, disregarded all warnings about the disposition of the Indians and showed "a lamentable want of judgement." Fortunately, there was no loss of life. The Haida chief, Edenshaw, who had visited Victoria and presumably talked with Douglas, convinced the Indians not to take the lives of the crew of the *Susan Sturgis*.[94] But this was the kind of incident that competition between Indians and whites for resources was likely to produce, and the Queen Charlotte gold "rush" was only a prelude to the main event.

Throughout the 1850's reports and samples indicating the existence of gold in the interior of New Caledonia had dribbled into Victoria. By the summer of 1857 it was evident that there was gold in considerable quantities along the Fraser and Thompson rivers. In November Douglas wrote to the company headquarters in London and, in a consciously metaphorical manner, noted that the "prospects of the district are really becoming brilliant." Douglas also realized that, as the "auriferrous character of the country" became more apparent, an influx of "motly adventurers" from the south was likely.[95] It was a probability that caused him concern, for gold miners arriving in large numbers would not only ferment hostilities with the Indians but also disturb the company's trading relations. The Indians of the area quickly ascertained the value of gold as a trade item and had already served notice of their opposition to intruders. A group of American miners who came north looking for gold in 1857 were forcibly ejected by the Thompson River Indians, and there were reports of another group being plundered by the Okanagans.[96]

Although he was apprehensive about the consequences of gold discoveries, the letters that Douglas wrote in the winter and spring of 1857–58 show that he still thought that the company's old relationship with the Indians would

---

[93]Douglas to Barclay, 28 December 1851, HBCA, A-11/73.

[94]Douglas to Newcastle, 8 June 1853, CO.305/4. The Haida chief had a special relationship with Governor Douglas. Edenshaw was descended from the chief named Cunneah, who had exchanged names with Captain William Douglas in the early years of the maritime fur trade. Consequently, Edenshaw and the governor of Vancouver Island shared the same name (see William Henry Hills, Journal, 23 May 1853, "Journal on Board H.M.S. *Portland* and *Virago* 8 August 1852–8 July 1853," UBCL; and Meares, *Voyages*, p. 365).

[95]Douglas to Smith, 27 November 1857, HBCA, A-11/76.

[96]Douglas to Labouchere, 15 July 1857, CO.305/8; and Douglas to Smith, 26 May 1857, HBCA, A-11/76.

continue. While settlement was in the process of terminating the company's hegemony over Vancouver Island, Douglas assumed that the fur traders were still secure on the mainland. He obviously hoped that the arrangement that the company had with the Indians for trading furs could automatically be applied to the acquisition of gold. The Indians did not want outsiders extracting gold, and this disposition coincided exactly with the interests of the company. In fact, Douglas could not help admiring the wisdom and foresight of the Indians, who were inadvertently arranging things for the benefit of the Hudson's Bay Company. He instructed the servants to leave the Indians to work the gold themselves, on the assumption that they would bring it into the company posts as an article of trade.[97] A fort for the specific purpose of trading gold from the Indians was planned, and building was begun in April 1858 at the forks of the Fraser and Thompson rivers. It was reported in the same month that Chief Trader Donald McLean had obtained 130 ounces of gold dust over a period of eighteen days, and prospects for the future looked just as promising.[98] Even late in the spring of 1858 Douglas and the other company officers were arranging for the continuation of the same reciprocal relationship that they had always had with the Indians. They were unaware of the disruptive human deluge that was to flood into New Caledonia in the next few months: a surge of humanity that was to signal the end of the fur trade.

British colonial policy makers had turned the administration of the colony of Vancouver Island over to the Hudson's Bay Company in 1849 and made Douglas governor for a variety of reasons. But important among those reasons was the advantage of the fur traders' "systematic" methods of dealing with the Indians compared to the "mere caprice of ordinary settlers."[99] On the whole the Colonial Office was satisfied with Douglas's handling of Indian-European relations, and even some settlers were impressed with his efforts.[100] Historians, however, have been quick to criticize company rule for not fostering colonization. They have been less willing to recognize that by maintaining relatively peaceful relations with the Indians Douglas made a crucial contribution to the establishment of the settlement frontier. Douglas quite rightly pointed out that by establishing friendly relations with the Indians the com-

[97]Douglas to Simpson, 17 July 1857, HBCA, D-5/44.
[98]Douglas to Smith, 19 April 1858, HBCA, A-11/74.
[99]Minute by Frederick Peel on Douglas to Newcastle, 28 February 1853, CO.305/4.
[100]See, for example, Lytton to Douglas, 14 August 1858, Great Britain, Colonial Office, Despatches to Vancouver Island; W. Colquhoun Grant, "Description of Vancouver Island, by its First Colonist," *Journal of the Royal Geographical Society* 27 (1857): 320.

pany rendered the area west of the Rockies habitable for settlers.[101] Anglo-centric commentators, both in the nineteenth and twentieth centuries, have evaluated the success of the company's administration according to the size of the settler population rather than by the nature of the relations with the Indians. Even in the nascent stage of settlement the Indians were becoming of secondary importance. Before many of them had realized it, settlement had established a foothold under the auspices of the old fur-trading organization that they were so used to dealing with. On Vancouver Island in the 1850's the fur-trading and settlement frontiers had merged in a way that allowed one to engender the other.

[101]*British and American Joint Commission*, 2: 55.

4

The Image of the Indian

The prevailing idea which exists amongst the later arrivals and present population as to the character of the Indian tribes in those early days, is not, in my experience, borne out by facts. I have heard such terms as treacherous, vindictive, revengeful, and murderous applied to them; possibly some may have deserved the epithets; but taken as a whole, I submit that, with the opportunities they had, we may consider them fairly entitled to a more lenient verdict.[1] —J.R. ANDERSON

Students of race relations now recognize that images are frequently more potent determinants of behaviour than "reality" and that Europeans in contact with indigenous people act according to perceptions which are often quite different from what "actually exists." Indigenous society and behaviour is viewed through a cultural filter that distorts "reality" into an image that is more consistent with European preconceptions and purposes. The process is complete when the image becomes more real than "reality" as the basis for policy and action.

Before looking at the impact of the change from fur trade to settlement on the Indians of British Columbia, it is important, therefore, to examine the image of the Indian that had already built up in the mind of the European and the extent to which it changed with the coming of the settlers. There were, of course, as many images of the Indian as there were Europeans in British Columbia. Furthermore, it is a "well-known but elusive fact that a person can hold contradictory ideas towards the same thing at different times,"[2] and even more elusive is the ambivalence of many racial attitudes. Neither individuals nor groups were necessarily consistent in the opinions that they expressed about the Indians. Yet common attitudes do emerge from the collection of individual views, and it is the consensus that this chapter will try to isolate and describe.

In their evaluations of various Indian groups fur traders and settlers sometimes shared opinions, but the differences in their attitudes towards the Indians were more significant than the similarities. The maritime fur traders were

---

[1]Anderson, "Notes and Comments," p. 170.
[2]H. G. Barnett, *Innovation: The Basis of Cultural Change* (New York: McGraw-Hill, 1953), p. 399.

transient visitors to the coast with only limited opportunity or inclination to understand the Indians, but the land-based fur traders lived amongst the Indians for extended periods and so could be much more objective in their assessment of Indian behaviour. When the settlers arrived there was a definite change in the tone of writing about the Indians. In the sense that they had pre-conceptions about the Indians and their cultures and refused to change their opinion on the basis of new experience, the settlers as a group were more prejudiced than the fur traders. Frequently settler images were in large part the consequence of events and currents of thought in the metropolis, whereas traders' attitudes were more a product of life on the frontier. That is, generally traders reacted to what they saw, while settlers tended to react to what they expected to see.

From the first European contacts with the Indians of British Columbia layers of misunderstanding were laid down by the reports of uninterested and unskilled observers. We have no firsthand information about Indian culture before the Europeans arrived, and even the earliest visitors saw a culture that was undergoing change as a result of their presence.

Some early traders and explorers remained ignorant about Indian culture because they assumed that there was nothing worth studying. One of the first traders to come to the coast, James Strange, who led an expedition in 1786, considered that "such is the savage state of the Inhabitants" that knowledge of their social usages was unlikely to afford any edification to even the most curious reader. He was, however, prepared to broach the subject in so far as it would "admit of Entertainment."[3] Other traders had more pressing reasons for not recording their impressions of the coastal Indians. Because their activities were of dubious legality, many fur-trading captains were anxious not to leave any reports at all.

Among the early visitors, however, there were some Europeans who took a lively interest in the Indians. In an age of scientific exploration, the nations of Europe sent expeditions to the Pacific expecting them to return with a fund of information on the places that they had visited, including accounts of the "manners and customs" of the inhabitants. Spanish navigators, for example, received instructions to record the customs, political systems, religion, and barter of the northwest coast Indians. Some explorers had both a natural curiosity and many years of experience in examining the behaviour of indig-enous people. Their experience made men like James Cook acute and rela-tively dispassionate commentators on other cultures. But even those who took an interest encountered almost insurmountable obstacles. The lack of a

---

[3]James Strange, Journal, 6 July 1786, *James Strange's Journal and Narrative of the Commercial Expedition from Bombay to the North-West Coast of America . . .* (Madras: Government Press, 1929), p. 22.

common language as well as conceptual barriers meant that many aspects of Indian culture could not be enquired into. Europeans often had to rely on outward behaviour to assess inner motivation, a procedure that was bound to produce misconceptions.

Even at the time of the early voyages it was apparent to some that the evidence being used to make judgments about the nature of the Indians could easily be manipulated to conform to preconceived notions. Meares, for instance, claimed that Maquinna was a cannibal. He gave as evidence of anthropophagy the fact that he had seen the chief sucking blood from a wound in his leg and declaring it to taste good. But Peter Puget rightly pointed out that if "all Mens characters were drawn from such vague & Shallow Conclusions, . . . few would be found free from injurious slander."[4] James King, who came to the coast with Cook in 1778, noted that the superficiality of their observations meant that Europeans could come to quite contrary conclusions about the character and disposition of the Indians. Judgments were based on personal experience, and clearly the experience and reactions of individuals varied greatly. Consequently, while some concluded that the Indians were sullen, obstinate, and mistrustful, others said that they were docile, good-natured, and unsuspicious.[5] Other distortions of reality were created when assessments were based on fantasy rather than empiricism. The chronicler of Dixon's voyage was taken to task by another explorer because of his imagination which was "much disposed to be startled and take the alarm."[6] For the objective individual it was difficult enough to represent Indian culture accurately, but for the fanciful person it was virtually impossible. And for all Europeans, whatever their frame of mind, the recording of impressions of the Indian way of life was incidental to the primary concerns of exploration or trade.

Early European visitors to the coast tended to be superficial observers. Their journals make much of physical differences between Indians and Europeans. On the northern coast perhaps the most frequently emphasized feature in the trading journals was the labret worn by Indian women, while in the

---

[4]Meares, *Voyages*, p. 257; Puget, "Log of the *Chatham*," 4 May 1793, p. 45. I am not particularly concerned here with the debate about whether or not the northwest coast Indians ate human flesh. Warren Cook (*Flood Tide of Empire*, p. 190 and n. 107) has listed a number of contemporary sources in support of the contention that the Nootka, at least, were probably cannibals, although on investigation some of the references turn out to be somewhat inconclusive. It is also interesting that the Cook expedition, after a month at Nootka, could find "no certain proof" that the Indians were cannibals; Samwell, *Journal*, 3 April 1778, Beaglehole, part 2, p. 1092. However, the essential point here is not whether cannibalism actually existed, but the ease with which many Europeans assumed that it did.

[5]King, *Journal* [April 1778], Beaglehole, part 2, pp. 1406–7.

[6]Fleurieu, *A Voyage*, 1: 477.

south the practice of flattening the forehead received great attention. Descriptions of physical appearance were often accompanied by expressions of revulsion, and aversion to the Indians' physical appearance began to assume the tone of a moral judgment. Vancouver, who was less tolerant than Cook, his former captain, had been, considered the labret to be "an instance of human absurdity" that had to be seen to be believed.[7] Not only did many visitors consider the Indians to be "the nastyest race of people under the sun,"[8] but there were also strong suggestions that they barely qualified as humans at all. Comments about "that savage inhumanity which distinguishes these People from the race of Human Kind" and about individual Indians behaving "more like a brute animal than a rational Creature"[9] reveal this tendency to dehumanize the Indians.

By their lengthy physical descriptions which emphasized the ways in which the Indians differed from themselves, Europeans were exaggerating the separation of the two races. They were making the point, for their own benefit, that the Indians were something distinct and other than themselves. The Indians were not only different but inferior. Europeans always feared being reduced to the level of "savages," and so from the first contacts on the northwest coast they tended to emphasize traits that established their separateness from the Indians, rather than those that demonstrated their common humanity.

Aspects of the Indian way of life that were less clearly manifest than physical appearance were not so well documented in the journals. Apart from the fact that early visitors could not converse with the Indians in their own language, many Indians were reluctant to reveal much of their private knowledge anyway. Moreover, when Indians did divulge private information, they tended to tell the European inquirer what they thought he wanted to hear rather than what was actually true. Voyagers often found this attitude exasperating, and sometimes concluded that the Indians were a people who had little respect for the truth.[10] Several commentators noted the difficulty of investigating the political organization of the Indians.[11] When their social structure was described, it was often in terms of crude analogies to European patterns, such as comparing Indian government to the feudal system. Because

---

[7]Vancouver, *A Voyage*, 2: 280.
[8]Thomas Manby, Journal, 24 April 1792, "A Journal of Vancouver's Voyage, 1790–1793," UBCL.
[9]Bishop, *Journal*, 11 September 1795, Roe, pp. 97–98; Samwell, *Journal*, 31 March 1778, Beaglehole, part 2, p. 1090.
[10]Vancouver, *A Voyage*, 1: 269.
[11]See, for example, Cook, *Journal*, 26 April 1778, Beaglehole, part 1, p. 322; Manby, "Journal," 24 July 1792.

religious beliefs and customs also proved very difficult to investigate,[12] it was often simply assumed that the Indians lacked any concept of religion. In the area of Indian ceremonial life, Europeans stressed the distinctive and the bizarre, again demonstrating that the Indians were unlike themselves. Some Indian customs both shocked and fascinated observers and thus received much attention. Others, such as the dances of the Nootka women, so scandalized Europeans that "decency" compelled them to omit detailed descriptions.[13]

Comments about the role of Indian women in trading and in society in general are an interesting and puzzling aspect of the journals. There are frequent references to the control that Indian women had over bartering, and sometimes this fact was extended into assertions that Indian society was ruled by a "petticoat government."[14] These conclusions are too frequent for traders to be merely generalizing from a few isolated examples or reading each others' journals and repeating mistakes. Yet the statements are difficult to explain through the ethnographies. Many, although not all, of the accounts of the importance of the role of Indian women come from the northern coast where the Indians had a matrilineal social organization. But a matrilineal society is not necessarily matriarchal, and, in any case, there need be nothing in the transactions of traders to reveal the society as matrilineal. Moreover, some accounts of the crucial role of women in trading came from the south where society was organized patrilineally. The most likely explanation seems to be that the voyagers were seeing women in an unaccustomed role. Europeans were perhaps surprised by the assertiveness of Indian women, and here again they exaggerated the difference between the Indians and themselves.

It is certain that the cultural baggage that the Europeans brought with them to the northwest coast included preconceptions about Indian behaviour. Pre-eminently they expected the Indians to be both hostile and treacherous. Juan Pérez, perhaps the first European to record his impressions of the Indians of British Columbia, rejected Indian invitations to come ashore because he feared treachery. Fourteen years later Dixon was similarly suspicious when some Haida indicated that his crew would be welcome in their village, and he assumed that once ashore his men would be "instantly butchered." Even

[12]Cook, *Journal*, 26 April 1778, Beaglehole, part 1, p. 322; Malaspina, "Politico-Scientific Voyages," 2: 222; Fleurieu, *A Voyage*, 1: 403.

[13]Mozi̇̃o, *Noticias*, p. 60.

[14]"Haswell's Log of the First Voyage" [June 1789], "Hoskins' Narrative" [July and August 1791], "Boit's Log," 8 July 1791, Howay, "*Columbia*," pp. 96, 235, 372: Caamaño, "Journal," 1792, p. 205; "Journal Kept on Board the Armed Tender *Chatham*," June and September 1793, PABC; Vancouver, *A Voyage*, 2: 343; Bishop, *Journal*, 16 June 1795, Roe, p. 63.

present day historians have judged this caution to be well advised given the Haida's "subsequent record of attempting to overpower trading vessels without provocation."[15] Europeans expecting such total hostility naturally found evidence to support their prejudice. Any Indian attack, or suspected attack, was reported in the journals for others to read. Accounts of individual acts of aggression produced racial generalizations that all Indians were warlike. Even when Indians approached them in an outwardly friendly way, Europeans often believed that they were just more devious than most and were therefore especially untrustworthy. Although it was conceded that sometimes Indians were friendly and co-operative—it was said, for example, that Cook "met with remarkable sivel treatment from the natives"[16]—Europeans tended to believe the worst about the Indians. Cleveland knew when he met the Haida chief named Altatsee off Langara Island that two years earlier the Indian had been present when an American captain named Newberry had been accidentally killed. But the demeanour of Altatsee caused Cleveland to very much doubt that the death was an accident.[17] It was the pejorative rather than the complimentary that was remembered from the descriptions of the Indians, and the coastal Indians generally emerged from the initial contact period with an unenviable reputation. The familiar stereotype of the Indians as filthy, treacherous, lazy, lascivious, and dishonest was already established by the maritime fur traders. Such judgments were not always absolute: frequently the northwest coast Indians were being evaluated relatively, often in comparison with the apparently more appealing people of the Pacific Islands.

A pattern of misunderstanding had already been laid down, but it might be expected that with the shift to a land-based fur trade a more sympathetic, or at least a more impartial, picture of the Indian might emerge. The employees of the fur-trading companies had closer contact with the Indians over extended periods of time. They could, therefore, observe aspects of the Indians' way of life that ships' crews, because of their limited contact, were unable to see. The annual pattern of activities, for example, could only be documented by someone who lived among the Indians for a year. There were, of course, still obstacles in the way of factual objectivity. The Indians remained reluctant to divulge information on certain subjects, sometimes believing that the fur traders' inquiries were "directed by improper motives."[18] At times the Indians still gave answers to please the questioner and so retained their reputation for being unreliable. Nor were the traders entirely free of prejudice. In fact, their very closeness to the Indians often forced them to accentuate ideas of Indian inferiority and to make every effort to ensure that the Indians recognized

---

15Cook, *Flood Tide of Empire*, p. 60; Dixon, *A Voyage*, p. 206.
16"Haswell's Log of the First Voyage," 16 March 1789, Howay, *"Columbia,"* p. 59.
17Cleveland, *Voyages*, p. 108.
18Charles Ross to Simpson, 1 October 1842, HBCA, D-5/7.

white superiority. The first of the fur traders to cross the Rockies later recorded his opinion that it was easier "for a civilised people to deviate into the manners and customs of savage life, than for savages to rise into a state of civilisation."[19] Obliged to forego the "pleasures of polished . . . society," the traders expressed a concern that they would tend to assimilate with those whom they lived closest to, "viz—the wretched aborigines."[20] The traders were very much concerned about their own image and needed to define clearly the boundary between "civilization" and "savagery." Nevertheless, in spite of all these impediments, the land-based fur traders did record a great deal of information about the Indian that was relatively unbiased.[21]

Company traders had little truck with notions of the noble savage. That concept was a metropolitan literary convention not typically held by those in close contact with the Indians on the frontier. Yet sometimes the vision of the man on the spot was so limited that his opinions of the Indians are no more reliable than those of the European novelist. Alexander Caulfield Anderson, in an article published in 1863, cautioned that generalizations about the Indians should not be based on extreme examples. He wrote:

> Such of my readers as in the absence of other opportunity, may have formed their impressions of Indian life and character from the alluring fictions of Mr. Cooper; or those who, on the opposite hand, have imbibed well founded prejudices from communication with the wretched fish eaters of the Columbia and its neighbouring coast, will do well to pause as regards the majority, between both extremes.[22]

In a book entitled *Traits of American-Indian Life and Character*, written by "A Fur Trader," the author tried to correct certain false impressions conveyed by recent publications. He pointed out from the start the vast difference "between those who travel in pursuit of amusement or science, and men like us who only encounter these hardships for vile lucre." The implication throughout this book is that the traders were closer to frontier realities and therefore more objective. According to this particular "Fur Trader" the Indians did not possess all of the fine qualities often attributed to them in popular literature and not every Indian was a hero. But the fur traders' attitudes towards the Indians were not entirely negative. While the book contains some invec-

---

[19]Lamb, *Journals and Letters of Mackenzie*, p. 65.

[20]Tolmie, *Journal*, 10 December 1834, p. 297; see also Tod to Edward Ermatinger, 29 June 1836, Ermatinger Papers; McLean, *Notes*, 2: 261; and Saum, *The Fur Trader*, p. 5.

[21]The conclusion was also reached by Saum, *The Fur Trader*, p. 11.

[22]Alexander C. Anderson, "Notes on the Indian Tribes of British North America, and the Northwest Coast," *Historical Magazine* 7 (1863): 80.

tive, there are also many complimentary remarks.[23] Company traders, in contrast to the typical settler, were prepared, or perhaps had, to make allowances for the Indians.

Customs that outraged other Europeans were often described dispassionately by fur traders, and comparisons were sometimes made with corresponding western practices. The "indomitable passion" for gambling among some Indian groups was said, when carried to excess, to result in misery and degradation. Later, gaming was to be the subject of much anguished comment by missionaries and philanthropically-minded government officials. The "Fur Trader" observed the custom and momentarily lamented the Indians' "want of the civilised education of Europe." Yet, in the next instant, he was "humiliated by the remembrance of similar scenes in the most refined society." On observing mourners grieving at a Carrier funeral, the "Fur Trader" experienced a "gratification deep beyond measure to witness among rude beings such as these, the excitement of those pure feelings of our nature which remind us of our common origin."[24] Even the head flattening custom of the Indians of southern British Columbia that so shocked many Europeans was compared by Alexander Ross to the English women's habit of compressing their waists. "All nations, civilised as well as savage, have their peculiar prejudices," he remarked.[25] Traits that other Europeans were to find disgusting, the fur traders often recorded without judgment, although, as Lewis Saum has pointed out, the traders' tolerance was selective. Generally, "the excusable flaws in Indian nature were those that had little or no impact on the economics of trader-Indian relations."[26]

Another measure of the traders' familiarity with the Indians was that they tended to generalize less than other Europeans. While settlers were inclined to make racial generalizations about all the Indians of British Columbia, the fur traders had some awareness of individual differences[27] and an even greater consciousness of tribal differences. Not all the Indians were equally admired or disliked: therefore, many of the fur traders' judgments were not simply racist but rather the result of comparing one group of Indians with another.

23[Ogden?], *Traits*, pp. 5–6, 21, 188, and passim. In an article on the problem of the authorship of this book, F. W. Howay argues convincingly, although not with absolute finality, that the "Fur Trader" of the title page was Peter Skene Ogden ("Authorship of Traits of Indian Life," *Oregon Historical Quarterly* 35 [1934]: 42–49). For other examples of the rejection of noble savagism see Fleurieu, *Voyage*, 1: 479; Cox, *Adventures*, p. v.

24[Ogden?], *Traits*, pp. 152–53, 160.

25Alexander Ross, *Adventures of the First Settlers on the Oregon or Columbia River: . . .* (London: Smith, Elder, 1849), pp. 99–100.

26Saum, *The Fur Trader*, p. 176.

27Ibid., p. 59.

The various tribes were classified according to a definite hierarchy of merit. If the southern tip of Vancouver Island is taken as a starting point, the Indians became more attractive in the eyes of the fur traders as one travelled northward along the coast or eastward into the interior. The Indians of the northern coast were thought to be superior to those of the south, and the coastal Indians generally were regarded as inferior to those who lived inland.

The notion that the Indians of the northern coast (the Haida particularly, but also the Tsimshian) were superior was based on observable physical differences, on the opinion that they were less degraded by western contact, and on the fact that they posed a greater military threat. Traders revealed their bias by describing the northern Indians as cleaner, fairer, taller, and better built than those to the south: in short, the Haida and Tsimshian were more attractive because they were seen to be more like Europeans. Perhaps the classic exposition of this point was written by Dr. John Scouler in a communication to the Royal Geographical Society of London.

> This northern family, if we select the Queen Charlotte's Islanders as specimens, are by far the best looking, most intelligent and energetic people on the N.W. coast, and in every respect contrast favourably with the Southern Tribes of Nootka Sound and the Columbia. They are taller and stronger than the Nootkans, their limbs are better formed, and their carriage is much bolder. They permit the hair of the upper lip to grow, and their mustachios are often as strong as those of Europeans. Their complexion, when they are washed and free from paint, is as white as that of the people of the S. of Europe.[28]

These comments were not penned by a fur trader, but Scouler gleaned much of his information from conversations with traders, many of whom would have agreed with his remarks.[29] Because they were thought to be more attractive physically, the Indians of the northern coast were more often taken as wives by fur traders than Salish women.

But the perceived superiority of the Haida and Tsimshian was not just a matter of physique; they were also seen to be morally and intellectually superior. The Haida particularly were thought to be adaptable and industrious and for this reason better able to withstand the degrading influences of western civilization. But they were also more warlike. Simpson once noted that the further north one goes on the coast the more formidable the Indians become.[30] It was a maxim that most company men agreed with, and they

---

[28]Scouler, "Observations," p. 218.
[29]See, for example, Dunn, *History*, p. 283; Charles Ross to Simpson, 10 January 1844, Lamb, "Five Letters," p. 115; and Saum, *The Fur Trader*, p. 118.
[30]Simpson to Smith, 17 November 1828, Merk, p. 300.

therefore anticipated hostility when they established forts in the area. "In the north," wrote Tolmie, expecting to be posted at Fort McLoughlin, one "must be continually armed to the teeth as the Indians are dangerous."[31]

The coastal Indians, then, were not equally esteemed by the fur traders. But the Indians of the coast were definitely considered to be inferior to those of the interior. This judgment was based on observable differences in ways of life. At its most simple level the view was that hunters were superior to fishermen. It was as if the method by which an Indian tribe gathered its livelihood imprinted a certain set of traits on its nature. "Fishing" Indians lived in a different environment and had a different way of life from "hunting" Indians, and fur traders claimed that these factors largely accounted for variations between tribes. The fishermen not only lived differently, but also looked, acted, and thought differently from the hunters. The idea that there was a close correlation between environment and culture was common in the eighteenth and early nineteenth centuries, and observers of the coastal northwest saw something akin to the "tropical exuberance" that Philip Curtin has described in West Africa.[32] The coast was thought to be a luxuriant environment that yielded a livelihood with little effort on the part of the Indians. Such an environment made its inhabitants not only lazy, but also "gross, sensual, and for the most part cowardly." By contrast "those tribes, who, with nerves and sinews braced by exercise, and minds comparatively ennobled by frequent excitement live constantly amid war and the chase" were in every way more attractive.[33]

This view pervades the writings of the fur traders. Ogden, or the "Fur Trader," wrote of the "stately independence" which distinguished "the native hunter of the wilds of North America, from the more ignoble fisher of its waters."[34] Douglas noted that few of the Indians of the Cowlitz River area evinced "a desire to become hunters by courting the nobler, elevating and more arduous exercise of the chase"; while Tod catalogued the differences between the two types of Indians. To him, the fishers were mean, sneaking, thieving, and deceiving, whereas the hunters were noble and generous.[35] It was almost as if by mounting a horse the Indian transformed his whole character. In fact, Commander Charles Wilkes of the United States exploring expedition asserted in 1841 that the Indians should never be seen except on horseback. Mounted, he said, the Indians were "really men" and inspired a certain amount of respect, but dismounted they became "lazy lounging

---

[31]Tolmie, *Journal,* 9 May 1833, p. 175.
[32]Curtin, *The Image of Africa,* pp. 61ff.
[33]Anderson, "Notes," p. 80.
[34][Ogden?], *Traits,* p. 79.
[35]Douglas, Diary, 3 April 1840, James Douglas, "Diary of a Trip to the Northwest Coast, 22 April–2 October 1840," PABC; Tod, "History," p. 63.

creatures, insensible to any excitement but his low gambling propensities."[36] It was this dichotomy between hunter and fisher that accounted for the decreasing respect for the Indians as fur traders travelled westward from the mountains to the sea. By the time they had reached the mouth of the Columbia the Indians seemed quite detestable. They were, wrote Dugald Mac-Tavish, "the most miserable and wretched" of the Indians that he had seen.[37]

This feeling among fur traders that the Indians of the interior were superior to those of the coast was not entirely unrelated to some Indians' view of themselves. The upper Thompson, for instance, looked down on their lower Thompson neighbours and on the Salish, while the Indians closer to the coast feared the more warlike up-river Indians.[38]

Economic considerations played a large part in the fur traders' assessment of the various Indian tribes. To the extent that the coastal Indians were dealers rather than hunters they were not appreciated by the traders. Company men preferred Indians who captured and brought pelts directly to a fort to the apparently idle "home guards" who acted as middlemen and forced up prices. Confident of the profits to be made as middlemen, many fort Indians did not see any need to hunt for furs themselves, a conclusion that did not particularly endear them to the traders. With the arrival of settlers the economic basis for the notion that the interior Indians were superior began to disappear, and yet the attitude persisted.

Writers who described Vancouver Island and British Columbia during the settlement period constantly reiterated the point that the inland hunter was a more admirable kind of Indian. Their preference was described in much the same terms as the fur traders'. One traveller was agreeably surprised at the physique of the Indians when he reached the Thompson River, and even went as far as to speculate that the interior Indians were European and the coastal Indians mongoloid in origin.[39] Their physical superiority was the visible evidence of less tangible characteristics that distinguished the interior tribes from those of the coast. In short, the inland Indians were "in every way a nobler race."[40] Even Franz Boas had to wait for his second period of field

[36]Wilkes, *Narrative*, 4: 311.

[37]Dugald MacTavish to Mrs. MacTavish, 19 October 1839, Glazebrook, *Hargrave Correspondence*, p. 307; Saum, *The Fur Trader*, pp. 37, 115.

[38]James Teit, *The Thompson Indians of British Columbia*, Memoirs of the American Museum of Natural History, ed. Franz Boas (n.p., 1900), pp. 269–70; Wilson Duff, *The Upper Stalo Indians of the Fraser Valley, British Columbia*, Anthropology in British Columbia Memoir no. 1 (Victoria: Provincial Museum, 1952), p. 96.

[39]R. Byron Johnson, *Very Far West Indeed: A Few Rough Experiences on the North-West Pacific Coast* (London: S. Low, Marston, Low and Searle, 1872), pp. 85–86.

[40]Anderson, "Notes and Comments," p. 112.

work in British Columbia and a trip to the Kootenays before he saw his "first real Indians."[41] This kind of opinion was both widely held and widely publicized among settlers.[42] Colonists also saw the interior Indians as a greater potential threat than the coastal tribes. Readers of the *British Colonist* were told that "it is not from the miserable, fish-eating tribes on the seaboard, but from the more noble and war-like redman of the interior, who live by the chase, that real danger is to be apprehended."[43]

The feeling that interior people, who had fewer contacts with Europeans than coastal people and who were therefore less degraded, was common in other British colonies.[44] Yet, in some ways, the view is a curious one in the British Columbian context. Those settlers who thought at all about the future of the Indians usually saw it in terms of a settled agricultural existence. Presumably the coastal Indians, who already had fixed village sites, conformed more closely to this ideal than the more nomadic Indians of the interior.[45] There is an ambivalence about the settlers' disrespect for those Indians who most closely approached their supposed future status; although it is an ambivalence that ran deep in British thought about aborigines. Colonists were aware that western contact was as likely to be degrading as elevating to the Indians, and they despised those Indians who succumbed. The lingering

---

[41]Boas, Diary, 18 July 1888, Ronald P. Rohner, ed., *The Ethnography of Franz Boas: Letters and Diaries of Franz Boas Written on the Northwest Coast from 1886 to 1931* (Chicago: University of Chicago Press, 1969), p. 102.

[42]See Blanshard's testimony, Great Britain, House of Commons, *Report from the Select Committee on H.B.C.*, pp. 286, 292; Alexander Caulfield Anderson, *The Dominion at the West: A Brief Description of the Province of British Columbia, its Climate and Resources* (Victoria: R. Wolfenden, 1872), pp. 80, 98, 100; C. W. Barrett-Lennard, *Travels in British Columbia, with the Narrative of a Yacht Voyage Round Vancouver's Island* (London: Hurst and Blackett, 1862), p. 40; Robert Brown, Journal, 23 March 1866, "The Land of the Hydahs, a Spring Journey Due North . . . Spring of 1866," PABC; John Keast Lord, *The Naturalist in Vancouver Island and British Columbia* (London: R. Bentley, 1866), 2: 226ff; Mathew Macfie, *Vancouver Island and British Columbia: Their History, Resources and Prospects* (London: Longman, Green, Longman, Roberts and Green, 1865), p. 428; Mayne, *Four Years in British Columbia*, p. 242.

[43]*British Colonist*, 30 November 1869. Similar feelings were widely held in North America. A contributor to *Atlantic Monthly* claimed that the widespread idea that Indian management in Canada was superior to that in the United States could be explained by the fact that the American Indians were "bold and fierce hunters of the buffalo" and therefore difficult to deal with in comparison with the "quiet and gentle savages of a cold climate and a fish diet" (*Atlantic Monthly* 41 [1878], 385–86).

[44]See Cairns, *Prelude to Imperialism*, p. 17; and Curtin, *The Image of Africa*, pp. 408–9. At least one writer on British Columbia during the settlement period was aware of this comparison (see Macfie, *Vancouver Island*, p. 428).

[45]The fur traders also saw these least admirable Indians as the most likely candidates for civilization (see Saum, *The Fur Trader*, p. 228).

hangover of the noble savage idea meant that the settlers still had a surreptitious regard for the Indians who still roamed wild and free.

Settlers also inherited and perpetuated the fur traders' image of the Indians of the northern coast. One visitor went so far as to say that "The Hydah Indian is probably the finest savage I have ever had the pleasure of meeting."[46] Because the northern tribes seemed a much greater military threat than the Salish, some considered that no colony could be established on Vancouver Island without being rendered safe against them by a strong detachment of troops. As in other parts of the British Empire the colonists at once feared and respected aborigines who were a potential danger.[47] So the northern Indians commanded some admiration from many of the settlers, while the Songhees were despised.[48] The mixed feelings with which the northern Indians were regarded were perhaps best expressed by a resident of Puget Sound, James G. Swan, writing in the *San Francisco Evening Bulletin* in 1860. The "very intelligence" of these Indians along with their courage and determination, made them a "terror and a dread" in the United States and Victoria; they are "the only real foe we have to look out for on this frontier." And yet, at the same time, Swan believed that "if it were possible to effect an exchange and substitute the northern Indians for the lazy, 'cultus' and trifling tribes of Flatheads, the Territory would be benefited."[49]

While fur traders and settlers shared some impressions of the Indians, the differences in their attitudes were much more marked. Settlers held many opinions about the Indians that the fur traders had not adhered to, and after settlement began the general tendency was for the image of the Indian to become more disparaging and more subjective. Their writings indicate that

[46]William Downie, *Hunting for Gold: Reminiscences of Personal Experience and Research in the Early Days of the Pacific Coast* ... (San Francisco: Press of the California Publishing Co., 1893), p. 216.

[47]Rear-Admiral Phipps Hornby to J. Parker (Admiralty), 29 August 1849, HBCA, A-8/6. This attitude is clearly seen in the settlers' differing attitudes and behaviour towards the Maoris in New Zealand and the Aborigines of Australia, and T. O. Ranger has pointed out similar differences in settler opinion about the Shona and Ndebele prior to the revolts of 1896–97 in Southern Rhodesia (*Revolt in Southern Rhodesia*, ch. 1, particularly p. 36; see also Cairns, *Prelude to Imperialism*, p. 114).

[48]Robert M. Ballantyne, *Handbook to the New Gold Fields*: ...(Edinburgh: A. Strahan, 1858), p. 78; MacDonald, *British Columbia*, pp. 128–29; Mayne, *Four Years in British Columbia*, p. 73; Morison, "Reminiscences," p. 78; Doyce B. Nunis, Jr., ed., *The Golden Frontier: The Recollections of Herman Francis Reinhart, 1851–1869* (Austin: University of Texas Press, 1962), p. 143; Sproat, *Scenes and Studies*, pp. 23, 99; Wilson, *Journal*, 23 March 1859, Stanley, p. 46; Kuper to Moresby, 26 July 1852, CO.305/3.

[49]James G. Swan, *Almost out of the World: Scenes from Washington Territory the Strait of Juan de Fuca 1859–1861*, ed. William A. Katz (Tacoma: Washington State Historical Society, 1971), pp. 97–98.

many settlers had little or nothing to say in favour of the Indian way of life. Many came to British Columbia with preconceptions, and few altered their views on the basis of experience.

The 1850's and 1860's were a period when racial attitudes were hardening in Britain, the birthplace of many of the first settlers of Vancouver Island and British Columbia. It has been argued that the changes in attitudes to other races were related to changes in the social structure of Britain,[50] but there were also other, more overt, indices of the development in thinking. The heady days of the abolition of slavery and of the Select Committee on Aborigines in the 1830's had passed. Both the movement for the abolition of slavery and the Aborigines Protection Society had lost much of their earlier singlemindedness and direction. The humanitarian movement enjoyed a resurgence of official influence while Earl Grey was at the Colonial Office, but this was its last fling, and it declined after 1852. By that time permanent under-secretary James Stephen, whose connections with "Exeter Hall" had always been strong, had retired to a chair of history at Oxford. A sign of the changing times was the establishment of the colony of Vancouver Island not in a hot flash of humanitarian zeal as New Zealand had been nine years earlier, but for the more prosaic reasons of imperial strategy. Events on the fringes of the empire also had their influence on metropolitan racial attitudes. The Indian Mutiny followed by the wars in South Africa in the 1850's, the Maori-European land wars in New Zealand, and the rebellion in Jamaica in the 1860's all shocked and horrified Englishmen. These conflicts seemed to corroborate negative views of aborigines and forced racial undercurrents closer to the surface.

Events such as these were both a cause and a result of racial thought. During the 1850's the scholarly debate between the advocates of monogenesis and polygenesis, having been largely resolved in favour of the former, was dropped as attention turned to evolutionary ideas. Evolutionary theories of race were being aired before the publication of *The Origin of Species* in 1859 and seemed to be confirmed by the fate of aborigines in areas already settled by Europeans. None of the three theories on race—monogenesis, polygenesis, or evolution—changed the general British view that the races of the world were arranged in a hierarchy with themselves at the top. But in the late 1850's the notion of British superiority and aboriginal inferiority was being solidified from a generally held hypothesis into an empirically proven doctrine by

[50]Douglas Alexander Lorimer, "British Attitudes to the Negro, 1830–1870" (Ph.D. dissertation, University of British Columbia, 1972), pp. 146–47 and passim; Philip Mason, *Patterns of Dominance* (London: Oxford University Press, 1970), p. 22.

the work of scientists and pseudo-scientists.[51] The general result of this trend was to confirm the racist error that race was the principle determinant of culture.

Settlers coming to Vancouver Island and British Columbia out of such a climate of opinion often held such fixed ideas about the inferiority of the Indian that contact modified them little. Immigrants with more refined sensibilities than most—or perhaps with greater pretensions—often found their first contact with the Indians shocking. Helmcken thought the first Indians he saw on nearing Victoria to be "dirty greasy nasty-smelling creatures," while another new arrival thought they were "the most hideous beings . . . imaginable." One young lady coming into Victoria on the *Tory* found her first sight of a naked Indian so upsetting that she burst into tears.[52] Those settlers whose first and most frequent contacts were with the Indians of the Victoria area based their stereotype on what were generally agreed to be the most "degraded" Indians of the colonies. A resident of Vancouver Island once noted that his contemporaries were far too apt to judge the whole race by those Indians they saw "lounging about the towns," who were at once the most civilized and the most debased of the Indians.[53]

The proposition that civilization would bring not only degeneration but also annihilation to the Indians was one that was much more frequently expounded by settlers than it had been by fur traders. Some recognized that their impact on the Indians was different from that of the traders. Captain Grant told the Royal Geographical Society in 1857 that hitherto the Indians' relations with white men had been mostly commercial ones that had not interfered with their "ordinary pursuits." But now settlement would mean both displacement and death for the Indians.[54] In further contrast to the fur traders, many settlers, including Grant, thought that the Indian and the European could not assimilate. The reason, in the words of one of the colonists, was that "their habits and natures" were "in direct opposition."[55] So the disappearance of the Indians was regarded as inevitable as the influx of European settlers. It was widely held, both in Britain and North America, that colonization by definition involved the extermination of the "inferior" indigenous peoples. The inevitability of the Indians' doom was said by some

[51]Curtin, *The Image of Africa*, p. 29, describes pseudo-scientists as those who are "misled by a little learning into wild speculations which the best science, even in their time, would not sustain on the basis of reason and evidence."

[52]Smith, *Reminiscences of Helmcken*, p. 80; Bayley, "Early Life on Vancouver Island," p. 2.

[53]Robert Brown, Journal, 19 August 1864, "Journal of the V[ancouver] I[sland] Exploring Expedition vols. 1 to 5, 7 June to 14 September 1864," PABC.

[54]Grant, "Description," pp. 303–4.

[55]MacDonald, *British Columbia*, p. 160.

to be a law of nature.[56] At least one visitor to the Pacific northwest was prompted to ponder the question of why the Indians had been placed on the earth at all. Perhaps, he concluded, they were only meant to live a life in the wilds until "races of greater capacity were ready to occupy the soil. A succession of races, like a rotation of crops, may be necessary to turn the earth to the best possible account."[57] But whatever the reason given, many settlers looked forward to a not too distant future when the Indians would have disappeared.

Aware that their presence was tending to destroy the Indian and his way of life and sometimes even feeling guilty about it, the settlers were unlikely to see much value in the culture that they were eliminating. By disparaging Indian culture Europeans could convince themselves that little of worth would be lost if the Indian way of life was brought to an end. At the same time they reminded themselves, by comparison, of the excellence of their own institutions. With some exceptions, pioneer accounts of the Indians contained much that was contemptuous, and they were suffused with ignorance.

The tone of many reports of the Indians can be gathered from the chapter headings of books describing British Columbia. In his *British Columbia and Vancouver Island*, Duncan George Forbes MacDonald described the following as "Prominent Features in the Life and Character of the Indians—Slaves Horribly Abused—The 'Medicine Man' and the Dead—Mode of Scalping—Young Indians more Savage than Old—Horrible Modes of Torture—Barbarous Conduct of an Old Squaw—Shocking Cruelties to an Old Man and Instance of Cannibalism—Horrible Massacre of Emigrants—Cruel Custom of getting rid of the Aged—." The picture is admittedly ameliorated by one account of a "Touching Instance of Parental Affection—."[58] MacDonald wrote a good deal of drivel about the Indians, as he did about most topics that he tackled in his book, and his is an extreme example of the tendency to disparage the Indians. Nevertheless, MacDonald's caricature of Indian life demonstrated to the settler that there was little to be valued or preserved. Like many accounts, it also succeeded in treating all Indians as if they were the same and ignored the differences between the various Indian cultures of British Columbia. The fantastic and the bizarre were emphasized to make all Indians seem the same at least insofar as they were all so different from Europeans.

[56]See, for example, Sproat, *Scenes and Studies*, p. 272; MacDonald, *British Columbia*, p. 132; *British Columbian*, 2 December 1865.

[57]J. W. Boddam-Wetham, *Western Wanderings: A Record of Travel in the Evening Land* (London: R. Bentley and Son, 1874), p. 287.

[58]MacDonald, *British Columbia*, p. 125.

The image of the Indian certainly became less positive with the transition from fur trade to settlement. Some colonists, like the journalist Donald Fraser, may have found that they had "taken rather a fancy to these Indians"; but more would have agreed with John Coles, a rancher, who wrote that jailing an Indian for being a vagabond was absurd since they were "all vagabonds with a *very very few* exceptions."[59] For the prejudiced individual among the colonists every aspect of the Indians and their society seemed to confirm their inferiority. The Indian physique was described in disparaging terms.[60] "Phrenologically speaking," wrote one visitor, adding a dash of bogus science, "the development of the North American Indian is of a low order, the animal propensities preponderating greatly over the intellectual faculties."[61] Both the persons and the habitations of the Indians were said to be exceedingly filthy. Writers dismissed Indian ceremonies as "disgusting" or as "grotesque antics," accounts of which would only tax the patience of their readers.[62] The Indian mind was thought to be "full of weird strange fancies and imaginations," and the Indian to be "strangely superstitious."[63] Apart from a "few miserable superstitions, and a childish belief in omens," the Indians were believed to have no religious concepts and were regarded as "incapable of retaining any fixed idea." According to settler reports they acted more from instinct than from reason and were nearly destitute of any sense of right and wrong.[64] They were warlike, but treacherous and cunning rather than courageous. "In British Columbia," it was asserted, "the new arrival is waited for by the crafty bloodthirsty and implacable savage, who never throws away a chance, never exposes himself to the weapon of an enemy, nor misses an opportunity of slaughter and revenge."[65] The Indians were also said to be dishonest and deceitful as well as lazy and unsuited to manual labour. Perhaps one of the most revealing comments about the Indian was that he "exhibits very little deferential respect for his superiors."[66] The picture of prejudice was summed up by Grant when he concluded that "the nature of the

---

[59]*The Times*, 5 August 1858; *British Colonist*, 3 June 1859.

[60]See, for example, John Domer, *New British Gold Fields: A Guide to British Columbia and Vancouver Island* . . . (London: W. H. Angel, n.d.), p. 24.

[61]John Emmerson, *British Columbia and Vancouver Island: Voyages, Travels and Adventures* (Durham: W. Ainsley, 1865), pp. 51–52.

[62]Macfie, *Vancouver Island*, p. 431; Mayne, *Four Years in British Columbia*, pp. 258–60; MacDonald, *British Columbia*, p. 156.

[63]Newton H. Chittenden, *Official Report of the Queen Charlotte Islands for the Government of British Columbia* (Victoria: Printed by Authority of the Government, 1884), p. 19; Mayne, *Four Years in British Columbia*, p. 259.

[64]Grant, "Description," pp. 296, 308–10; Chittenden, *Official Report*, p. 18.

[65]MacDonald, *British Columbia*, p. 70; Grant, "Description," p. 296; Barrett-Lennard, *Travels*, p. 41.

[66]Chittenden, *Official Report*, p. 14.

red man is savage and perverse. He prefers war to peace, noise to quiet, dirt to cleanliness, and jugglery to religion."[67]

Like most stereotypes, the settlers' view of the Indians was nurtured by ignorance. As long as they knew little about Indian society, the settlers had no reason to doubt their assumed superiority. When he was Indian reserve commissioner in the late 1870's, Gilbert Malcolm Sproat wrote that one of the most singular experiences that he had was the impossibility of getting accurate information about the Indians from people who lived in their midst. He was amazed that Europeans who had lived among the Indians for years had such a superficial knowledge of them. For instance, Sproat was told on occasions that the Indians were incapable of building irrigation ditches "when ingeniously constructed ditches several miles in length were almost visible."[68] Sproat's difficulty in gathering reliable information is indicative of the tendency of the colonists to filter out data that did not confirm their opinions of the Indians.

One might expect that the artistry of the north coast Indians would be a point in their favour in the mind of the settlers, a sign that the Indian possessed something that might be called a culture. A few admired Indian art and some were impressed with Indian "ingenuity" and "faculty for contrivance,"[69] but for others Indian art merely provided confirmation of the depravity of Indian nature. Their carving was dismissed as "hideous" or "grossly obscene."[70] Certainly Sproat believed that many settlers were steeped in an intolerance that prevented them from having any sympathy for the people among whom they were living. Nor was Sproat alone in this opinion. Robert Brown, the leader of the Vancouver Island exploring expedition of 1864, wrote that few of the white settlers took the trouble to learn about the Indians, and even fewer really knew anything nefarious about them, although they were loud in their dogmatic denunciations.[71]

Of course, racial prejudice was not confined to the European settlers. The Indians themselves were not immune. While he was gold commissioner at Lytton, Henry Maynard Ball claimed that the Indians of the area treated the Chinese as lesser beings and that they did not miss any opportunities to com-

---

[67]W. C. Grant, "Remarks on Vancouver Island, Principally Concerning Townsites and Native Population," *Journal of the Royal Geographical Society* 31 (1861): 211.

[68]Sproat to Philip Vankoughnet, deputy superintendent general of Indian affairs, 26 November 1879, and Sproat to superintendent general of Indian affairs, 9 January, 1878, Canada, Department of Indian Affairs, Record Group 10, Black Series, Western Canada, vol. 3,612, file 3,756, and vol. 3,657, file 9,193, PAC (hereafter cited as RG10).

[69]Macfie, *Vancouver Island*, pp. 484–85.

[70]Hills, Diary, 7 May 1853.

[71]Brown, "Journal," 10 June 1864.

mit outrages against them.[72] There is also evidence that the Cowichan considered themselves superior to the blacks who came to settle on southern Vancouver Island and Saltspring Island in 1858.[73]

Although vestiges of the concept remained, settlers, like fur traders, tended to reject the noble savage idea. A few individuals remarked that they had never seen a "Fenimore Cooper" Indian.[74] But, unlike the fur traders, the colonists were too often unprepared to make allowances for the cultural differences between themselves and the Indians. Some of their aspersions were probably justified from a relative point of view—Indians' houses may well have been dirtier than European ones—but many were merely examples of cultural differences. The Indians did not have European attitudes towards work, for example: they went through periods of relative inactivity, but they also worked extremely hard when necessary. But the settlers, viewing the Indians from the vantage point of their own values and ignoring the seasonal variations in the Indians' work patterns, simply generalized that they were lazy.

In many ways this oversimplified assessment of the Indian was self-perpetuating. Settlers repeated each others' published remarks about the Indians, with or without acknowledgement.[75] Nor were the Indians unaware of the attitude of many settlers towards their cultures, and their awareness only increased their reluctance to discuss their society. When Boas came to the coast, he found that some Indians were very suspicious of his information gathering. A Cowichan Indian responded to his requests by pointing out that the "whites look upon the Indians not as humans but as dogs, and he did not wish anyone to laugh at things that were their laws, such as painted houses and articles used for celebrating their festivals."[76] Observers in the early 1860's had noticed a similar response on the part of the Indians. Sproat found it difficult to obtain knowledge of Indian religious ideas because they commonly assumed that no white man was capable of understanding such mysteries. In Sproat's case they were correct. He went on to say that little reliance could be

[72]Ball to colonial secretary, 2 May 1860, British Columbia, Gold Commissioner, Lytton, Correspondence Outward, 1859–1870, PABC; see also The Bishop of Columbia, *A Tour of British Columbia* (London: Clay Printers, 1861), p. 18.

[73]Richard Charles Mayne, Journal, 5 April 1860, "Journal of Admiral Richard Charles Mayne, 1857–1860," PABC; Robin W. Winks, *The Blacks in Canada: A History* (Montreal: Yale University Press, 1971), p. 278.

[74]Barrett-Lennard, *Travels*, pp. 44–45; Morison, "Reminiscences," p. 58.

[75]Domer, *New British Gold Fields*, p. 24; William Carewe Hazlitt, *British Columbia and Vancouver Island;* . . . (London: G. Routledge & Co., 1858), p. 187, Grant, "Description," p. 301; and MacDonald, *British Columbia*, p. 153. Grant claimed that the Indians "pass the greater portion of their time in a sort of torpid state, lying beside their fires," and the assertion was repeated by MacDonald in almost identical words.

[76]Boas, *Diary*, 6 September 1866, Rohner, p. 54.

placed on Indian explanations of religious matters because in nine out of ten cases they were full of "lies and misstatements," either aimed at mystifying the inquirer "or owing to the mental weakness of the savage on religious subjects."[77] In the absence of authentic interpretations of customs, settlers substituted their own. Carrier ceremonies associated with the cremation of the dead were the subject of much jaundiced comment by Europeans. The artist Paul Kane, for example, being unable to learn of any motive or explanation for the customs, could "only account for them in the natural selfishness, laziness and cruelty of the Indians."[78] Undoubtedly settler opinion of the Indians often operated as a self-fulfilling prophecy. It has been argued that, in a situation where one group sees another as inferior, the subordinate group will tend to act in accordance with the role allotted to it, thus confirming the opinion of the dominant group.[79]

The missionaries, as a group, exhibited much more sympathy for the plight of the Indians than did the settlers, and yet missionary publications did little to ameliorate the image of the Indian. By the middle of the nineteenth century missions were less popular in Britain than they had been in the earlier decades, but missionary publications still reached a wide audience. Indeed, since missions relied on voluntary contributions, publications were essential to their existence. Missionary magazines were intended to whip up enthusiasm for missionary work, and one of the techniques they used was to show how the unredeemed aborigine was doomed to a life of barbarism. The darker the picture of Indian savagery, the greater the need for missionaries and the more God could be glorified by the Indians' conversion. In his first report from Fort Simpson in February 1858, William Duncan describes in graphic terms the cruel murder of a slave by a Tsimshian chief.[80] His account of this event turns up again and again both in missionary publications and in secular accounts of

[77]Gilbert Malcolm Sproat, "The West Coast Indians in Vancouver Island," *Transactions of the Ethnological Society of London*, n.s. 5 (1867): 253; see also H. Spencer Palmer, *Report of a Journey from Victoria to Fort Alexandria via Bentinck Arm* (New Westminster: Royal Engineer Press, 1863), p. 7.

[78]J. Russell Harper, *Paul Kane's Frontier Including "Wanderings of an Artist among the Indians of North America" by Paul Kane* (Austin: University of Texas Press, 1971), p. 108.

[79]See Mason, *Patterns of Dominance*, p. 199: Peter Loewenberg, "The Psychology of Racism," in Gary B. Nash and Richard Weiss, eds., *The Great Fear: Race in the Mind of America* (New York: Holt, Rinehart and Winston, 1970), p. 187.

[80]Duncan, Journal, 17 February 1858, William Duncan Papers, UBCL, C.2154 (hereafter cited as WDP).

the Indians of British Columbia,[81] and the description is often used to demonstrate that such behaviour typified the Indian character.

The missionary could never deny the humanity of the Indians, for that would be to deny their capacity for salvation. Nevertheless, in their descriptions of the Indians as "miserable specimens of humanity" requiring to be rescued from a "state of heathen darkness and complete barbarism,"[82] missionary publications distorted Indian culture as much as works written by laymen.

In recent publications various scholars have examined and attempted to explain the causes of racial prejudice of the kind that existed in Vancouver Island and British Columbia. Roy Harvey Pearce in his study *The Savages of America* was one of the first to recognize the complexities of Indian-White relations. He argued that for the settler concerned to establish and defend a beachhead of civilization in the wilderness the Indian was the symbol of something that he must not allow himself to become.[83] The British colonist established a line of cleavage based on race and could not permit any crossing of that barrier by admitting that the Indian was in any way comparable to western man. So in their accounts of the Indians the settlers tended to stress those aspects of Indian life that were repellent to Europeans and thus denied their common humanity with the Indians. In Vancouver Island and British Columbia settlers were particularly uneasy about the presence of half-breeds because they blurred the racially determined distinction between "savage" and "civilized." While the children of mixed marriages played an important role on the fur-trading frontier, with the advent of settlement attitudes to both the marriages and the children became much less positive. This change in attitude was undoubtedly due, at least in part, to the arrival of European women in appreciable numbers. The fact that the governor's wife was part Indian was difficult for many of the colonists to cope with. Some found it necessary to explain Lady Douglas on the grounds that she was "not a woman of much colour."[84] Even worse than the half-breeds in the mind of the settler was the European who voluntarily assumed the way of life of the Indians. These men were a living denial of the absolute separateness of the two cultures.

---

[81]See, for example [Church Missionary Society], *Metlahkatla: Ten Years' Work Among the Tsimsheean Indians* (London: Church Missionary Society, 1869), pp. 16–17; [Eugene Stock], *Metlakahtla and the North Pacific Mission of the Church Missionary Society* (London: Church Missionary House, 1881), p. 19; and Mayne, *Four Years in British Columbia*, p. 285.

[82]*Christian Guardian*, 6 April 1859; *Church Missionary Intelligencer*, July 1856, p. 167.

[83]Roy Harvey Pearce, *The Savages of America: A Study of the Indian and the Idea of Civilization* (Baltimore: Johns Hopkins Press, 1965), pp. 4–6, 48–49.

[84]Emmerson, *British Columbia*, p. 35.

In his book *Patterns of Dominance*, Philip Mason has noted that psychological research has generally confirmed the hypothesis that there is a strong correlation between racial intolerance and insecurity.[85] Certainly the Europeans felt insecure in relation to the Indians in the early years of settlement on the northwest coast. The colonists were overwhelmingly outnumbered, and some of them at least had been told fearful stories about the Indians before they left home.[86] Mason has also observed, more specifically, that an individual who has recently risen or fallen sharply in the social scale is likely to exhibit racial intolerance.[87] The point has particular pertinence in a colonial situation. In a population where the majority have recently left the homeland in order to better themselves and are therefore experiencing a period of dislocation, the need to reassure themselves of their own "civilization" can be satisfied by emphasizing the "savagery" of the aborigines. This tendency would be further strengthened to the extent that there was a heightened consensus in the colonial society.[88] There were, therefore, numerous pressures within the settler society for the perpetuation of prejudice.

At the beginning of this chapter the assumption was made that there was a relationship between the Europeans' image of the Indians and their behaviour towards them. This relationship is a complex one. Attitudes were both a cause and a result of action. The differences between the attitudes of fur traders and settlers coincided with their intentions. When trade was the Europeans' object the Indian was seen as primitive but responsive to the advantages of co-operation rather than hostile. When permanent settlement was the intention of the Europeans and they coveted Indian land, the Indian became a hostile savage, a hinderance rather than a help to the new arrival. The things written and said about the Indians became more and more abusive. But behaviour towards the Indians also arose out of the opinions that were held about them. Therefore one might expect that if the settlers' image was largely based on prejudice and ignorance there would be little in their behaviour and policies to benefit the Indian and that, as attitudes became more abusive, so would the treatment of the Indians.

---

[85]Mason, *Patterns of Dominance*, p. 35.

[86]N. de Bertrand Lugrin, *The Pioneer Women of Vancouver Island 1843–1866* (Victoria: Women's Canadian Club, 1928), p. 77.

[87]Mason, *Patterns of Dominance*, p. 35.

[88]Louis Hartz has argued that fragment cultures "heighten consensus by shrinking the European social universe" (Hartz, "A Comparative Study of Fragment Cultures," in Hugh Davis Graham and Ted Robert Gurr, eds., *Violence in America: Historical and Comparative Perspectives* [New York: Bantam Books, 1969], p. 107). In Vancouver Island and British Columbia humanitarianism, which tended to militate against overt racism, was not as well developed as it was in the parent society; there was therefore a greater proportion of people of like mind in relation to the Indians than there was in Britain.

5

Gold Miners and Settlers

As an inferior race... we believe... [the Indians] must give way in order
to make room for a race more enlightened, and by nature and habits
better fitted to perform the task of converting what is now a wilderness
into productive fields and happy homes.[1] —BRITISH COLONIST, 1861

The events of the summer of 1858 were to end the dominance of the fur trade
in Vancouver Island and British Columbia. Although furs did not cease to
change hands between Indians and Europeans, by the end of the summer the
fur trade was being replaced as the most important factor in the relations
between the two races. The first signs came late in April. When news that the
Fraser River contained gold in substantial quantities reached California, men
began to move. On 21 April Douglas reported that four hundred miners had
arrived at Victoria and throughout the summer this trickle of hundreds became a torrent of thousands. In May Douglas wrote to the company that,
while it was impossible to stem the tide of gold miners, he still intended to try
to protect the company's interests on the mainland.[2] But the second end was
as impossible to achieve as the first.

As the influx of miners increased, the Hudson's Bay Company was losing
control of the fur-trading preserve. The men who came to the Fraser in 1858
came to make money quickly, primarily by gold mining, but if there was profit
in trading, they were not predisposed to respect the privileges of the company.
The company's exclusive licence to trade with the Indians west of the mountains that expired in 1858 had become untenable anyway. During the summer
Victoria had burgeoned from a village into a town. In contrast to the situation
only nine years earlier, when Blanshard had remarked that Victoria was
merely a fur-trading post, by "the end of 1858, Fort Victoria was an anachro-
nism."[3] On the mainland petty traders were dealing with the Indians and un-
dercutting the company's prices. Ogden's earlier prophecy, that the fur
traders were "truly a doomed race,"[4] was coming true.

[1]*British Colonist*, 19 February 1861.
[2]Douglas to Smith, 21 April 1858, HBCA, A-11/76; Douglas to Smith, 18 May
1858, ibid.
[3]Cf. Rich, *History of the H.B.C.*, 2: 761; and Ormsby, *British Columbia*, p. 130.
[4]Quoted in Archie Binns, *Peter Skene Ogden: Fur Trader* (Portland, Ore.: Binfords
and Mort, 1967), p. 337.

In 1857 the Select Committee on the Hudson's Bay Company had recommended that the company's rule on Vancouver Island should be ended. Negotiations for the transfer of power began in January 1858. Officially, the dual position of James Douglas came to an end. In May Douglas tried to protect the interests of the company by issuing a proclamation prohibiting vessels not licensed by the company from entering the Fraser River. His action drew a reprimand from the Colonial Office. Douglas was informed that he was not to use his power as governor to protect the interests of the Hudson's Bay Company and that it was contrary to law and to his instructions to attempt to exclude people from British territory.[5] On 2 August 1858 the British government passed an act establishing direct rule on the mainland, and New Caledonia became British Columbia. Douglas was offered the governorship of the new colony, but only on the condition that he sever his connections with the Hudson's Bay Company. Having fulfilled this requirement Douglas was appointed governor of British Columbia on 14 August 1858. The transitional phase was over and the fur trade was coming to an end.

The gold miners were the advance guard of the settlement frontier. These newcomers not only had a different set of attitudes from those of the fur traders, but they also made quite different demands on the Indians. The reciprocity of interest between Indians and Europeans broke down because settlers came not so much to accommodate to the frontier as to re-create the metropolis. Vancouver Island and British Columbia were changing from colonies of exploitation, which made use of indigenous manpower, to colonies of settlement, where the Indians became at best irrelevant, and at worst an obstacle, to the designs of the Europeans. Rather than economic co-operation, there was now economic rivalry between the races. An irreversible and immutable process of change began as groups of Europeans came to transform the wilderness and, with varying degrees of consciousness, to change the Indians who were seen as a part of it.

With the coming of the gold miners, Indians and Europeans were, for the first time, competing for the resources of the country. They were followed by settlers whose fundamental desire was to acquire the land that hitherto had been in the possession of the Indians. Even more deliberate acculturation occurred as the plans of the missionaries and administrators began to be implemented. The combined impact of these groups was to force the pace of cultural change and to take the initiative out of Indian hands. During the fur trade the Indians had been able to select items they wanted to incorporate into their social fabric according to their own priorities and to reject others that were not acceptable. With settlement, this freedom was lost. The Indians were

---

[5]Douglas to Stanley, 19 May 1858, CO.305/9; Lytton to Douglas, 16 July 1858, ibid.

moving from a non-directed acculturation experience to a situation in which culture change was directed from outside.

Directed culture change occurs in those situations where there is a relationship of dominance and submission between the two groups in contact.[6] Settlement brought such a relationship to Vancouver Island and British Columbia. Coercive pressures, with varying degrees of subtlety, were brought to bear on the Indians. During the period of the fur trade Europeans had been a small minority and their numbers had been fairly constant, but after the establishment of settlement the European population increased rapidly and the Indian population declined. Rather than a few select individuals who came with limited aims, there was a new population that intended fundamental change. Furthermore, the Indians now began to encounter Europeans who not only wanted to change their way of life but who also had the power to do so. Previously there had been a situation of Indian dominance; now the balance of power was tipping in favour of the Europeans. When the interests of the two races were in conflict, the settlers were increasingly in a position to force their will on the Indians; and settlement brought the clash of the two cultures in a way that the fur trade had never done.

Not all Indian groups were immediately or equally affected by these developments. Some of the coastal groups—the Haida, Kwakiutl, and Nootka especially—and the more isolated interior Indians had only limited contact with gold miners and settlers during the 1860's. But among those Indians who lived in proximity to the Europeans a process was begun that was eventually to affect all the Indian groups of British Columbia.

Conflict began with the gold miners. The men who came to the Fraser and Thompson rivers in 1858 were impelled by an excitement that is now perhaps impossible to comprehend fully. It had driven many from Europe, and some half way round the rim of the Pacific. Those who came to the two colonies brought with them the hysteria that accompanied all new strikes. One Vancouver Island settler wrote home in 1858 that "the people seems to be going mad altogether about the gold mines."[7] Hundreds of bustling miners came to get rich, and to do so quickly. They were intolerant of anything that stood in their way. They had already demonstrated in California that they would give especially short shrift to any "savages" seen as a hindrance to their activities.

---

[6]As Ralph Linton has defined it, directed culture change occurs in "those situations in which one of the groups in contact interferes actively and purposefully with the culture of the other" (see Linton, ed., *Acculturation*, p. 502). Spicer has more recently written that "the distinction which Linton saw between directed and non-directed situations remains basic to any attempt to develop generalizations in the field of acculturation." The distinction is fundamental because "it makes clear the two most general classes of contact situation" (Spicer, ed., *Perspectives*, p. 519).

[7]Annie Deans to her cousin, 4 July 1858, Deans, Correspondence Outward.

The miners imported exactly the same attitude into British Columbia, but here they encountered a different kind of Indian. As one of their number pointed out, the Indians of the Fraser and Thompson rivers were used to commercial dealings with Europeans.[8] In 1858 many Indians already understood the value of gold to whites, and many more were rapidly learning. So the Indians were unlikely to look with favour on miners who came rampaging in to take resources that they not only owned but also knew the value of. Douglas reported to his superiors that the Indians were extremely "jealous of the whites and strongly opposed to their digging the soil for gold."[9] It was a situation that was bound to produce interracial tension.

From the beginning there was violence between the miners and the Indians. Much of it undoubtedly went unreported, but the records are sufficient to indicate the tenor of the situation. A large proportion of the mining population were transients, men who had cut loose from the ties and restraints of established societies. As a consequence of the unstable conditions that they had lived under, many had become "habituated to violence."[10] As Douglas, in one of his more pompous moments, put it, "I have just been informed that a number of that class of persons commonly called 'rowdies' in California have taken up their quarters in this Colony." Douglas was concerned that the influx of Americans would lead to "difficulties" between whites and Indians.[11] Another observer described the gold mining town of Yale as a nest "whence issues the wretch who will shoot an Indian in the back when he finds one alone and unarmed."[12] Some of the miners came up from California boasting that they would "clean out all the Indians in the land,"[13] and there were instances of the kind of indiscriminate killing of Indians that was a feature of the American west. A company of miners coming north along the old Hudson's Bay Company trail destroyed the winter provisions in an unattended Indian village on the shore of Okanagan Lake. Some of the party objected to this behaviour, but the perpetrators thought that it was "great fun." The following day a group of unarmed Indians were massacred by the miners. Even the member of the party who relates the incident thought that it was "a brutal

[8]Downie, *Hunting for Gold*, p. 202.
[9]Douglas to Labouchere, 6 April 1858, CO.305/9.
[10]Matthew Begbie to Douglas, 3 February 1859, CC, file 142a.
[11]Douglas to William Brooker, British consul in San Francisco, 23 June 1858, Vancouver Island, Governor, Correspondence Outward; Douglas to Labouchere, 29 December 1857, CO.305/8.
[12]*The Times*, 25 December 1858.
[13]Nunis, *The Golden Frontier*, p. 120.

affair." Apart from a general paranoia about hostile Indians, this attack was not motivated by any particular grievance against the Okanagans.[14]

The Fraser Canyon was also the scene of interracial violence in the summer of 1858. There were individual killings of both miners and Indians, and on at least two occasions the situation threatened to escalate into serious conflict. There were some in the colonies who were quite cavalier about the possibility of an Indian war,[15] but Douglas was very worried about the possible consequences. He feared that a "sanguinary war of races" would be "the inevitable consequence of a prolonged state of misrule" and would plunge the government into difficulties.[16] In both cases of major hostilities Douglas visited the mining area. His intervention at Hill's Bar in June settled the conflict, and a potentially ugly situation at Yale had resolved itself just before his arrival late in August. The mutual antagonism between miners and Indians had been threatening to boil over. Rumours were flying, and when some dead miners were found it was assumed that they had been murdered by Indians. The miners at Yale formed themselves into volunteer companies to take reprisals against the Indians up river. There was wild talk about exterminating the Indians, but these militia units involved themselves more in bravado than in action. Incredible stories continued to circulate. On 25 August 1858 the *Daily Victoria Gazette* reported that the Indians had murdered forty-two men and had horribly mutilated the bodies of thirty-eight of them. The following day the story was retracted as untrue, for in fact friendly Indians had prevented a major clash from developing. Nevertheless, the miner who carried the so-called news to Yale had created a ferment of excitement in the town. Eventually, however, the situation began to simmer down as the miners made peace treaties with the Indians. But already a number of Indians had been killed, some villages destroyed, and an Indian prisoner nearly lynched by a crowd of angry miners.[17]

Outbreaks of violence such as these were symptomatic of a general antagonism between the two races. Large numbers of miners and Indians were working in close proximity on the gold bars. One witness said that there were

---

[14]Ibid., pp. 125–27. The party had had a skirmish with Indians before crossing the line into British territory. It would seem that Europeans were quite capable of punishing one group of Indians for the supposed crimes of another. This was the kind of misdirected retaliation that the whites accused the Indians of.

[15]When the possibility of an Indian war came to the attention of Charles Wilson of the Boundary Commission, he wrote in his diary, "hurra! for a little out of door work, & excitement, & see if Victoria Crosses can be earned in America as well as India" (Wilson, *Diary*, 30 August 1858, Stanley, p. 32).

[16]Douglas to Captain Frederick Montressor, 24 August 1858, Vancouver Island, Governor, Correspondence Outward.

[17]Accounts of these events are to be found in the *Daily Victoria Gazette*, 20, 24, 25, 26, 28 August and 1 September 1858; and Ovid Allard to Douglas, 20 August 1858, CC, file 10.

from sixty to seventy Europeans working alongside four to five hundred Indians at Hill's Bar alone in the summer of 1858.[18] Each race harboured grievances against the other. Numerous accusations of Indians killing miners, whether true or not, incensed the Europeans. Miners also complained of Indians stealing their equipment, stock, and food. Then there were the efforts of the Indians to prevent the miners from extracting any gold at all. There were reports of Indians trying to stop the miners from proceeding up the rivers and attempting to impose taxes on those working ground claimed by the Indians.[19] Large assemblies of Indians tended to make the miners uneasy, and they were apt to conclude that Indian gatherings were "for no friendly purpose."[20] Government officials reported to Victoria that all these factors made the miners apprehensive and touchy, even though they had brought much of the Indian hostility on themselves.[21] Apart from the simple objection to the presence and activities of the miners, the Indians objected to the abuses that they had to endure. They reiterated in reverse the miners' allegations of theft, complaining that miners took their stock and destroyed their crops. Indians also complained that miners abused their women[22] and were generally insulting. Indian accusations were corroborated by European observers, who wrote of the miners treating the Indians with "cowardly cruelty." One of the gold commissioners even went as far as to express the belief that it was "a fallacy" to "endeavour to enlist the good will of the American or Irish toward the Indian."[23]

The miners and their operations were a major interference with the life and livelihood of the Indians, who were, consequently, becoming very unsettled. The Fraser Canyon had been the major salmon fishing area, not just for the Indians in the immediate vicinity, but for those as far away as the Strait of Georgia. Mining operations disrupted the catching and drying of a major staple in the Indian diet. The 1858 run turned out to be a poor one for salmon anyway, but many held that the activities of the miners were responsible for depleting the fishery. Certainly one of the reasons that the Indians had opposed the entrance of the miners in the first place was the fear that the

---

[18]Ballantyne, *Handbook*, p. 18.

[19]*Daily Victoria Gazette*, 20 August 1858; Domer, *New British Gold Fields*, p. 51.

[20]*Daily Victoria Gazette*, 20 August 1858.

[21]Allard to Douglas, 20 August 1858, CC, file 10.

[22]Begbie to Douglas, 25 April 1859, CC, file 142b; Allard to Douglas, 20 August 1858, CC, file 10; *The Times*, 1 December 1858.

[23]Mayne, *Four Years in British Columbia*, p. 50; *The Times*, 1 December 1858; Richard Hicks to Douglas, 26 October 1858, CC, file 767; William Cox to W. A. G. Young, 6 April 1862, CC, file 377.

salmon would be eliminated from the rivers and streams.[24] Miners also interfered with the Indians' land holdings; village sites, fishing stations, and cultivated areas were all intruded upon.

The first winter after the arrival of the miners was a hard one for the Indians. Government officials and others wrote numerous reports of Indians being destitute and starving.[25] It was natural, and probably just, for the Indians to blame the miners for their situation. Many Europeans simply explained the Indians' lack of food as being a result of their "natural improvidence," but mining did damage the Indians' resource areas. Many Indians were caught by the mania for gold, and some probably neglected their traditional summer food-gathering, either to mine or to provide ancillary services for the white miners. Judge Matthew Begbie rightly pointed out that the willingness of the Indians to work hard for wages seemed to argue against the idea of "natural improvidence"; indeed, many Indians were able to support themselves and their families by becoming wage earners.[26] Others, however, obviously miscalculated their winter needs. The pressure of starvation forced some Indians to steal from Europeans. Also, Indians of the canyon, attracted by the possibility of trade and work, abandoned their winter villages and began to congregate around the mining towns.[27] There the Indians found less desirable characteristics. By all accounts the mining towns, particularly Yale, were unsavoury places. As Indians began to acquire liquor from white traders and Indian women became prostitutes or the temporary wives of miners, drunkenness and prostitution brought the attendant evils of degradation and disease.

Had the mining areas returned to their pre-1858 condition after the miners had departed, their impact on the Indians might have been as transitory as their presence. Most of the miners left the canyon area during the winter, and as one field became exhausted, they moved on to fresher ones. Gradually most

[24]*Daily Victoria Gazette,* 26 August 1858; Arthur Thomas Bushby, Journal, 22 March 1859, Dorothy Blakey Smith, ed., "The Journal of Arthur Thomas Bushby, 1858–1859," *BCHQ* 21 (1957–1958): 150; J. Despard Pemberton, *Facts and Figures Relating to Vancouver Island and British Columbia* ... (London: Longman, Green, Longman and Roberts, 1860), p. 132; Douglas to Labouchere, 15 July 1857, CO.305/8.

[25]Allard to Douglas, 26 August 1858, CC, file 10; Matthew B. Begbie, "Journey into the Interior of British Columbia," *Journal of the Royal Geographical Society* 31 (1861): 243; Cox to Brew, 6 April 1859, in F. W. Howay, ed., *Early History of the Fraser River Mines,* Archives of British Columbia Memoir no. 6 (Victoria: C. F. Banfield, 1926), p. 101; Mayne to Captain G. H. Richards, 7 July 1859, CO.60/5; Douglas to Lytton, 25 April 1859, CO.60/4; William Manson, Journal, 20 March 1860, "Fort Kamloops, Journal, January 1859–November 1862," PABC.

[26]Begbie to Douglas, 25 April 1859, CC, file 142b; Henry Ball to colonial secretary, 12 May 1860, CC, file 95.

[27]Duff, *The Upper Stalo,* p. 41.

of the mining population moved north. By the early 1860's the Cariboo was the centre of attention, and in the early 1870's there were gold strikes on the Skeena and Omineca rivers. To the east there was a strike at Rock Creek and brief excitements in the Kootenays and in the Big Bend country. But as the miners departed, their place was taken by other Europeans who were to have an even more profound influence on the Indians. At the time of the establishment of the new colony of British Columbia, hopes were expressed in Britain that a more permanent population would be added to the gold seekers, and in Victoria Douglas had already recommended "that the whole country be immediately thrown open for settlement."[28] These hopes were not disappointed. Permanent settlers arrived in increasing numbers, and they began to have an impact on the Indians that was to be equally as permanent.

Settlers, like gold miners, showed little of the circumspection that characterized the fur traders' dealings with the Indians. Many were high-handed in their treatment of the Indians. One observer claimed that in many instances the white man considered himself "entitled to demand their wives or their sisters, and if such demand is disputed, to proceed to acts of violence to gain their object."[29] Often when Indians complained about mistreatment, they were simply treated with abuse, and sometimes they responded in kind. Many of the "outrages" perpetrated by Indians on the Europeans could be attributed, according to Matthew Macfie, "to some wanton violation of the personal or domestic rights of the Indians on the part of the whites." Attacks on Europeans which appeared to be without provocation were perhaps a consequence of the fact that "some of the tribes have held the presence of our race to be practically an invasion."[30]

The quintessential conflict between the settlers and the Indians was over land. Land was as crucial to the continuation of Indian culture as it was to the aims of the settlers. The overwhelming desire that brought the settlers so far from home was for "advancement," both economic and social, and for many the acquisition of land was the primary means of achieving their goal. For the speculator, land was the means of making a profit, and for the settler with a little capital, it was the means of rising above the level of the "mere labourer."[31] Land meant either money or status or both to the colonist. He had come

---

[28]Great Britain, *Hansard's Parliamentary Debates*, 3d ser., 151 (1858): 1099. The hope was expressed by Edward Bulwer Lytton, who had recently retired as secretary of state for the colonies. Douglas to Stanley, 10 June 1858, CO.60/1.

[29]H. Richards to Baynes, 26 August 1859, CC, file 1,212a; see also Cox to Young, 16 February 1861, CC, file 375; Peter O'Reilly to Young, 28 June 1862, CC, file 1,281.

[30]Brown, "Journal," 24 July 1864; Macfie, *Vancouver Island*, pp. 461–62.

[31]See Sproat, *Scenes and Studies*, p. 281.

to the colonies to acquire the land that could be no longer obtained in Britain, and he was in no mood to take the claims of the Indians into account.

As far as the Indians were concerned, the land was theirs, as it had been from time immemorial. Concepts of ownership varied from one tribe to another, but traditionally the Indian identified strongly with his locale. Settlers were sometimes surprised at the number of geographic features and places that the Indians had names for. Grant noted that in Sooke Harbour "every little point to which a white man would not dream of giving a name has its separate appellation."[32] Many Indian groups possessed myths that explained the existence of the topographic features in their locality. Most commonly in Indian societies house sites and food-gathering places were owned by the kinship group, and most groups had definite notions of territoriality and trespass. But the Indians' relationship with the land was spiritual as well as material. Some groups believed that just as all growing things had a soul, so also did the rocks and the water, since they had all been people during the mythological age. The "land mysteries" were a part of the religious beliefs of many interior Indians.[33] The land, as well as sustaining life, was life. When he was working as reserve commissioner among the Shuswap in the 1870's, Sproat wrote in a letter to Ottawa that "I do not exaggerate in saying that some of these Indians die if they lose their land: they take it so much to heart."[34] To relieve the Indian of his land was to deprive him of the place of his ancestors and to take away part of his identity.

Naturally the Indians' attitude to, and use of, the land was not unchanging. It is probable that the fur trade resulted in a sharpening of notions of territoriality among some groups, and it is certain that as the Indians lost land they placed a greater value on what they retained. European contact had also induced some tribes to turn from a purely hunting and gathering economy to the cultivation of increasing areas of their land and, particularly in the interior, to running growing herds of horses and cattle. But either way the Indians were in competition with the settlers. If the Indians farmed, either for subsistence or for profit, they competed directly with the Europeans. If they retained their traditional economy, the rivalry was even greater, for the two ways of using the land were mutually exclusive. It was difficult for the Indians to hunt or pick berries on land that had been ripped up by the farmer's plough. The conflict was simple and inevitable: the Indians had the land and the settlers wanted it.

[32]Grant, "Description," p. 287.
[33]James Teit, *The Shuswap*, Memoir of the American Museum of Natural History, ed. Franz Boas (New York: G. E. Stechert, 1909), p. 598; and Teit, *The Thompson*, pp. 338, 357.
[34]Sproat to superintendent general of Indian affairs, 18 April 1879, RG10, vol. 3,668, file 10,345.

Europeans had never lacked justification for dispossessing aborigines of their land. There were biblical injunctions that could be cited in support of their actions. Perhaps the first Englishman to comment on the subject was Sir Thomas More. The people of More's *Utopia* considered that the most just cause for war was "when any people holdeth a piece of ground void and vacant to no good nor profitable use, keeping others from the use and possession of it which notwithstanding by the law of nature ought thereof to be nourished and relieved." John Locke, in his *Second Treatise of Government*, implies that an agricultural people might justly force a hunting population to alter its economy.[35] Perhaps the authority that was most frequently referred to in North America was the Swiss jurist, Vattel, who held that people who do not settle and cultivate the land cannot have a true and legal possession of it. In his *The Law of Nations*, first published in 1760 and republished in 1834, Vattel concluded that people in North America had "not deviated from the view of Nature" by depriving the Indians of some of their land.[36]

Among those settlers who thought that deeply about the question, Vattel's view prevailed. The *British Columbian* held that "according to the strict rule of international law territory occupied by a barbarous or wholly uncivilized people may be rightfully appropriated by a civilized or Christian nation."[37] Sproat discussed the same question with some of his fellow colonists soon after their arrival in the Alberni area in 1860. They agreed that the dispossession of the Indians was legitimate on the grounds that all the land was "lying waste without prospect of improvement."[38] Europeans generally thought that hunters and gatherers made incomplete use of the land, and it was even asserted that the Indians placed no value on their land because they never cultivated it.[39] Settlers were either unwilling or unable to understand Indian concepts of land tenure and, instead, made the easier assumption that the land was lying "waste." They thought it "a great pity to see this beautiful country so well adapted to the wants of man, lying waste, when so many Englishmen and Scotchmen would be glad to come here and till the soil."[40] Another, more portentous, way of justifying possession of their land was to deny the human-

---

[35][Thomas More], *More's Utopia and a Dialogue of Comfort* (London: Everyman's Library, 1955), p. 70; John Locke, *Two Treatises of Civil Government* (London: Everyman's Library, 1966), pp. 129–41.

[36]M. de Vattel, *The Law of Nations; or Principles of the Law of Nature Applied to the Conduct and Affairs of Nations and Sovereigns* (London: Newbery, 1760), Book 1, p. 91.

[37]*British Columbian*, 1 June 1869.

[38]Sproat, *Scenes and Studies*, pp. 7–8.

[39]William Banfield to colonial secretary, 23 February 1860, CC, file 107.

[40]W. Downie, "Explorations in Jarvis Inlet and Desolation Sound, British Columbia," *Journal of the Royal Geographical Society* 31 (1861): 254. Ironically, Downie was writing about the Babine Lake area.

ity of the aboriginal inhabitants. That current of thought was seldom far below the surface of the settlers' writings on the Indians. Whatever the reason or the rationalization, nearly all the settlers agreed that the "indolent, contented, savage, must give place to the busteling [sic] sons of civilization & Toil."[41]

In British Columbia and Vancouver Island there were some local factors that intensified interracial conflict over land. Europeans and Indians tended to select land for the same reasons; they both wanted land that was fertile and productive. While the total land area of the two colonies was large, only a small proportion was suitable for cultivation. The facts of geography therefore focused the tension on comparatively small pockets of fertile river valley land. Prior to the arrival of the settlers, very little of the land was "waste" in the sense that it was unowned. Consequently, if one tribe was displaced by European settlers, it could not move to another place without intruding on the territory of another group. Unlike Australia there was no vast unused interior that the aborigines could retreat to, so the land question could not be deferred for long; it had to be settled on the spot. The activities of speculators added to the pressure on Indian land.[42] When land was bought by Europeans for the purposes of speculation, it was withheld from those who wanted to farm it, so that even more Indian land was needed to satisfy the needs of farming settlers. A further factor adding to the intensity of the clash was that the more settler pressure there was on Indian land, the more the Indians valued the land that they had left and the more reluctant they became to give it up.

Given the growing numbers of settlers arriving in British Columbia and the increasing imbalance in the power relationship, it was perhaps inevitable that the Indians should be the losers in the struggle for the land. As had happened, and would happen, all over North America, the Indians lost large amounts of their territory. In areas where pressure from Europeans was particularly intense, even Indian village sites and cultivated fields were intruded upon.[43] Those Indians who initially thought that the Europeans only wanted the use of the land soon came to realize that they intended total possession. When

[41]Bell to John Thompson, 27 February 1859, James Bell, Correspondence Outward, 1859, PABC.

[42]Observers claimed that there was considerable land speculation in the two colonies (see, for example, Downie, *Hunting for Gold*, p. 263; MacDonald, *British Columbia*, p. 66). The Victoria *Daily Press*, 17 March 1862, wrote that four-fifths of pre-empted land was held in violation of the pre-emption regulations.

[43]Douglas to Frederick Seymour, 9 May 1864, CO.60/22; A. C. Elliott to Arthur N. Birch, 15 July 1864, CC, file 515; W. H. Franklyn to colonial secretary, 24 June 1864, CC, file 599; J. B. Launders to colonial secretary, 3 June 1865, CC, file 969; Richard Clement Moody to Crease, 22 October 1863, Sir Henry P. P. Crease Papers, PABC.

Europeans owned land, they fenced it in and often became irate when the Indians or their stock trespassed on it. European ownership of land also had a destructive aspect. Settlers failed to realize that the Indians had developed an economy that was finely tuned to the environment. Europeans, by contrast, tended to dominate their environment and extracted the minerals and fertility from the soil. This is what the European meant when he talked about "improving" the land. Gradually, the ecological balance that the Indian way of life was based on was being eroded. All the Indians of British Columbia did not lose their land at the same rate. Some coastal groups, such as the Kwakiutl and Haida, were little affected. But the developing Indian dissatisfaction over the land question was indicative that most of the Indians were very annoyed by the dispossession they were experiencing.

When the Indians lost their land, it was not only their means of subsistence that was removed. They were also deprived of a major part of their social and spiritual identity. It has been argued, with considerable validity, that "next to introducing epidemics and firing bullets into their bodies, the most effective way to destroy natives is to take away their lands." The extent to which an indigenous people have retained their land is the best single criterion on which to judge their survival. It has been shown in other parts of the world that there is a close correlation between losing land, depopulation, and social disorganization among indigenous peoples.[44] Certainly in British Columbia the Indians experienced both depopulation and major social disruption during the period in which the settlers were moving onto their land. The exact causal relationship between loss of land and the declining Indian population of the 1860's may be difficult to establish, but there was a quite direct relationship between the Indians' removal from their land and the loss of control over their society. Not just because they were deprived of their livelihood, but also because legislating the Indians off their land required a degree of political control over them on the part of the settlers. In order to dispossess the Indians, the settlers had to curtail their freedom of action in many ways. When, for example, the Indians violently protested the taking of their land, the settlers demanded that coercion be used against them by government forces.

There were many minor incidents of Indians either threatening or actually attacking settlers whom they felt were stealing their property. In 1864 there

[44]Douglas L. Oliver, *The Pacific Islands* (Cambridge, Mass.: Harvard University Press, 1961), p. 157; M. P. K. Sorrenson has demonstrated, for example, that loss of land and not defeat in wars was the major cause of Maori depopulation (Sorrenson, "Land Purchase Methods and their Effect on Maori Population, 1865–1901," *Journal of the Polynesian Society* 65 [1956]: 184 and passim).

was a dispute between the Canoe Creek Indians and a settler named R.P. Ritchie. The Indians claimed that Ritchie had taken their cultivated lands and deprived them of access to water. Some of the Indians wanted to kill the settler but "wiser counsels" prevailed.[45] In the same year the Cowichan objected to the presence of a settler who had fenced in part of their reserve, and they questioned a Roman Catholic priest about the advisability of killing the man. On a number of occasions Europeans conducting mining operations in Skidegate Inlet asked for protection from the government against the Indians. Early in 1870 it was reported that there was much excitement among the Fraser Valley Indians over their loss of land and that the peace of the area was endangered.[46] Some attacks on settlers were too easily attributed to the Indians. On 3 May 1863 the *British Colonist* carried the story, under the headline "Another Indian Outrage," of the house of a Hornby Island settler being destroyed by fire. The newspaper, however, cited no evidence that the Indians were responsible other than the claim that they had been "troublesome and insolent" to settlers in the past.[47]

These niggling incidents were comparatively minor affairs, but in 1864 there was a more major assault. Early in the morning of 30 April a group of Indians attacked a road party that was working on the Homathko River, and thirteen white men were killed.[48] The motivation behind this attack was complex, and it is now impossible to isolate the overriding cause. Though there were undoubtedly a number of personal grievances that arose out of the treatment of the Indians employed by the road party,[49] one of the underlying causes was the Indians' dislike of European intrusion into their territory. The road party was in the employ of Alfred Waddington, who had surveyed a townsite at the head of Bute Inlet, had pre-empted land there, and was now trying to form a road link with the Cariboo gold mines. Waddington was the epitome of the colonial developer, and the Indians were not a part of his calculations. Until the early 1860's the Indians of the Chilcotin country and the Homathco Valley had been relatively isolated from European contact, although they no doubt realized that the Waddington road would provide

---

[45]Elliott to Birch, 15 July 1864, CC, file 515.

[46]Brown, "Journal," 24 July 1864; A. R. Green and E. C. Waddington to Young, 7 March 1864, CC, file 321; Herbert Gaston to Young, 5 May 1868, and Gaston to Hankin, 30 August 1870, CC, file 637; Holbrook to Musgrave, 7 January 1870, CC, file 778(2).

[47]*British Colonist*, 5 May 1863.

[48]It was subsequently discovered that a ferryman named Tim Smith, stationed further down river, had been killed the previous day.

[49]Chartres Brew to colonial secretary, 23 May 1864, CC, file 193; Morison, "Reminiscences," pp. 10–11.

access for European influence and would lead to further alienation of land. The attack on the road workers was to some extent an attempt to exclude settlement and land development. After the murders on the Homathko, the Indians moved deeper into Chilcotin territory where they attacked a pack train and also killed a settler named William Manning who had established himself near Puntzi Lake. Apparently Manning had usurped an Indian "camping site" near a spring and had driven the Indians off. When the Indians attacked Manning, they "even went to the trouble of breaking up the ploughs and other agricultural implements."[50] By attacking settlers and the lines of communication that maintained their existence, these Indians were recording their protest against the invasion of their land by Europeans.

The reaction of the colonists to these killings, particularly in Victoria, was immediate and noisy. At first settlers could scarcely believe that a party of "strong robust fearless" white men could be nearly all murdered by a dozen "cowardly savages."[51] But as the facts of the matter were established, the settlers made it clear that they were not going to treat lightly any threat to their presence in the colonies. The murders were a flash point in the history of race relations that revealed the attitudes of many of the settlers to Indians who might impede development. Throughout May 1864 the Victoria newspapers clamoured for retribution against the murderers. The killings were described as "fiendish" and as having been committed without provocation by cowardly and treacherous Indians.[52] Some demanded that justice be done, while others simply called for revenge. By the beginning of June Victorians were highly dissatisfied with the apparent lack of action by the government in the face of continuing reports of murders of Europeans in the Chilcotin country. On June 1 the *British Colonist* described the killing of the packers, noted the folly of waiting for the tardy actions of the authorities, and called for citizens to take matters into their own hands. There were, pointed out the editorialist, hundreds of men who would volunteer and who would not rest until "every member of the rascally murderous tribe is suspended to the trees of their own forests."[53] That evening, in a manner typical of the American west, the people of Victoria held a public meeting at which 129 men volunteered to take up arms against the Indians responsible for the killings. Men such as Amor De Cosmos revealed publicly their "antipathy and hatred" for the Indians. De Cosmos said that "he had lived among the Indians and knew their treachery." One man, C.B. Young, did remind the audience that justice should be even-handed and that the fencing off of Indian potato patches by Europeans was

[50]Begbie to Seymour, 30 September 1864, CC, file 142g; Seymour to Cardwell, 9 September 1864, CO.60/19.
[51]*British Colonist*, 13 May 1864.
[52]Ibid., 12 May 1864.
[53]Ibid., 1 June 1864.

Plate 1. The Haida village of Skidegate, 1884. Clinging to narrow beaches, Haida villages in the late nineteenth century were described as being a forest of totem poles.

Plate 2. The Kwakiutl village of Newitty was photographed in the late 1870's when it was visited by Indian Superintendent Dr. I. W. Powell. Many years earlier Newitty had been a major centre of the maritime fur trade.

Plate 3. Many citizens of Victoria resented the Songhees village being located on the Inner Harbour. They considered the presence of a large Indian population undesirable and saw the potential value of the land as real estate. Arrangements were completed to move the reserve to Esquimalt in 1910.

Plate 4. By the time this photograph was taken c. 1884 the Nootka Sound Indians had lost their pre-eminence as fur traders and had experienced a severe decline in wealth. With settlement, vessels of the Royal Navy were used to keep the coast Indians under control.

Plate 5. The Koskimo were a Kwakiutl group living on Quatsino Sound. They sustained heavy losses in warfare with the Newitty in the 1850's, which may account for the lack of men in this group. It has also been suggested that the small number of children in such group photographs is indicative of a declining population.

Plate 6. Quamichan village. The Quamichan were a Coast Salish group living in the Cowichan area. Both house and canoe styles were quite different from those of the northern coast.

Plate 7. This group of Interior Salish, probably Shuswap, was photographed by Frederick Dally at Blue Tent on the upper Fraser River c. 1868.

Plate 8. Doctor Bob, a Stalo shaman of the Yakweakwioose reserve near Sardis, was reputed to be 106 years old when this photograph was taken at the turn of the century. Earlier he had worked as a runner for the Hudson's Bay Company.

Plate 9. Lokah, Cowichan chief. Both governme officials and missionaries presented uniforms an insignia of office to co-operative Indian leaders. Lokah was presented with a medal by the Gover General of Canada for helping to prevent interra violence when reserves were being laid out in th Cowichan area.

Plate 10. This group of upper Fraser River Indians are probably Thompson. Many Europeans, both fur traders and settlers, thought that the Indians of this area were superior in every way to those of the southern coast.

Plate 11. This group of lower Fraser River Indians photographed at New Westminster, otherwise known as "stump city" in the 1860's, show in their dress signs of extended contact with Europeans.

Plate 12. Thomas Crosby's Methodist mission village at Port Simpson in 1884. Like most missionary villages, the church was the dominating building at Port Simpson.

Plate 13. This group of Indians and half-breeds at Fort Rupert was photographed by the geologist George M. Dawson in 1885. After its establishment in 1849, Fort Rupert, like other coastal forts, attracted Indians from a number of villages. The Indian population at Fort Rupert was thus an amalgam of several Kwakiutl groups.

Plate 14. In the late nineteenth century Alert Bay, on Cormorant Island, superseded Fort Rupert as a centre of Kwakiutl population. With the injection of new wealth into Indian society after European contact, potlatches like this one increased both in size and frequency.

Plate 15. The Kwakiutl village of Tsanwati, Knight Inlet, photographed by Edward Dossetter in the 1870's.

Plate 16. Members of the Metlakatla community outside the imposing, although alien, church built under the direction of William Duncan.

Plate 17. Indian women spinning wool at Metlakatla. Like most missionaries in British Columbia, William Duncan not only worked to convert the Indians to Christianity, but he also wanted to teach his followers the "useful arts" of Western civilization.

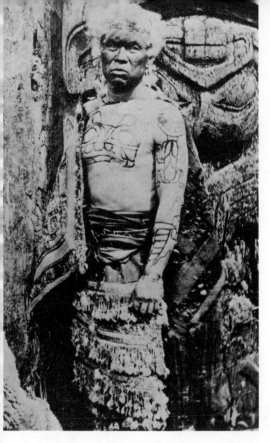

Plate 18. This Haida shaman was photographed in the late 1870's. The following decade, with the coming of missionaries to the Queen Charlotte Islands, the role of the shaman was undermined.

Plate 19. Roman Catholic missionaries were particularly active among the Indians of the Lower Fraser Valley. This photograph of a devotional service led by Roman Catholic priests was taken near Saint Mary's mission c. 1868.

Plate 20. The Reverend J. B. Good was particularly impressed with these Thompson Indians from the Lytton area, and at their request he began a mission among them in 1867. The Lytton Indians were also at the centre of the Indian self-improvement committee which so greatly alarmed the settlers in 1879.

Plate 21. The Fraser Canyon was a major fishing location for Indians as far away as the Strait of Georgia. Having been caught, the salmon were laid out to dry on racks. This traditional food resource of the Fraser River Indians was disrupted with the coming of the gold miners in 1858.

Plate 22. Encampment of Thompson Indians. The Indians of the interior were more mobile than those of the coast, particularly during the food-gathering months of summer.

Plate 23. Indian group at Lytton.

Plate 24. Isadore (standing centre) and Kootenay Indians, c. 1887. Some European observers, including Sam Steele, were deeply impressed with the Kootenay in general and Isadore's capacity for leadership in particular. This impression did not, however, translate into reasonable treatment of the Kootenay when their reserves were laid out.

Plate 25. Indian encampment at Arrow Lake. Note the distinctive style of canoe.

not justice, nor was it justice when a cricket pitch was taken out of the Indian reserve at Nanaimo. But most Victorians at the meeting were not interested in such logic, and the proposal that the Indians responsible for the murders should be hanged on the spot was greeted with "general cheers."[54] This meeting contained all the elements of vigilantism, an aberration often assumed to have been absent from the history of the Canadian west.

John Tod was somewhat amused at all these frantic preparations, and the old fur trader reminded a former comrade of how the Indians used to be kept in "complete subjection" by "a mere handful of Fur Traders." Apparently some settlers were amazed that such small numbers of fur traders could have survived amongst a large and "lawless" Indian population.[55] The offer of volunteers was declined by the authorities, although the leaders of the Indians held responsible for the murders were later captured, tried, and hanged. Their fate was a signal to the Indians that it was not advisable to object to the presence of Europeans with violence and that vigorous punitive measures would be taken against those who attacked settlers.

Besides an enforced loss of land, economic opportunities for the Indians were being reduced in other ways by the presence of the settlers. The Indian began to face competition from the European for the resources of the water as well. During his stay on Vancouver Island in the early 1850's, Captain Grant had foreseen that fishing rights were likely to cause friction between Indian and European, "as all the tribes are singularly jealous of their fishing privileges, and guard their rights with the strictness of a manorial preserve."[56] This prophecy became a reality during the 1860's as commercial fishing began to develop, first on the Fraser River and then on the rivers and inlets to the north. As early as 1859 when the salmon stopped running in the Lytton area, the supposed reason was that a fishing company had placed a net across the river.[57] Increasingly the Indians were to feel the restrictions that European fishermen placed on their traditional freedom to harvest the rivers and the sea.

Prior to settlement the Indians had provided the essential manpower for the fur trade economy, but now Indian labour was only of marginal significance in the economic concerns of the Europeans. Farming was not particularly labour intensive, and in the interior ranching used very little manpower in proportion to land. Although from the beginning of settlement on Vancouver Island some Indians were employed by European farmers, it was

---

[54]Ibid., 2 June 1864; Bute Inlet Massacre, "Programme, Minutes and Volunteers Roll of Public Meeting Victoria, 1864," PABC; cf. Nanaimo chief to Arthur Kennedy, 31 May 1864, CC, file 594.
[55]Tod to Edward Ermatinger, 1 June 1864, Ermatinger Papers.
[56]Grant, "Description," p. 304.
[57]Thomas Elwyn to Young, 13 August 1859, CC, file 524.

usually only on a seasonal or piecework basis, so the income was neither steady nor permanent. Whereas during the fur trade period any Indian could bring furs to a fort and sell them, now Indians could gain employment only at the pleasure of the whites. Indians of the interior earned money packing for the Europeans, but one official reported that they faced starvation when they could not obtain the work that they had become accustomed to.[58]

There were other reports of Indians not being paid for their labour. John Muir, an old resident of the Sooke area, was apparently in the habit of giving the Indians he employed promissory notes which they were subsequently unable to redeem. It was claimed that Waddington and his men did the same thing to Indians who had been employed on the Bute Inlet road party.[59] When they were paid, Indians seldom received as much as Europeans did. Of course, many settlers thought that the Indians were unsatisfactory as labourers; that they were naturally lazy, that they had to be constantly supervised, and that they could not persevere at a job for any length of time. Indians were useful as hewers of wood and drawers of water, commented one observer, but were not "always to be trusted with what may be termed the more delicate and refined portions of household service, such as, for instance, the washing up of dishes."[60] Other settler spokesmen strongly objected to employing Indian workers on principle. The editor of the *British Colonist* considered that to bring Indian labour into competition with European immigration would be highly detrimental to the country's best interests. Indian labour was not the kind that was required to develop the colonies, rather "it is Caucasian-Anglo-Saxon bone, muscle, and intellect that we want."[61] The same newspaper had expressed the opinion a few months earlier

> that it would be much more to our advantage if we were to encourage a thrifty white population, who would buy town lots, build cottages, bring their families hither, and pay taxes, rather than a horde of redskins, who spend their money for whiskey, and never contribute a dollar towards the public treasury.[62]

These words were probably written by De Cosmos, and they certainly reflect his particularly rabid brand of racism. The love of Amor De Cosmos, rather

---

[58]John Boles Gaggin to Young, 11 January 1861, CC, file 620.

[59]Richard Golledge to acting colonial secretary, 18 August 1864, CC, file 647; see also J. D. B. Ogilvy to Seymour, 6 February 1865, CC, file 1,267; Morison, "Reminiscences," p. 10.

[60]R. C. Lundin Brown, *Klatsassan, and Other Reminiscences of Missionary Life in British Columbia* (London: Society for Promoting Christian Knowledge, 1873), p. 172.

[61]*British Colonist*, 19 February 1861.

[62]Ibid., 26 October 1860.

than being cosmic, had distinct limitations, and it was not extended to include the Indians. Many settlers would, however, have agreed with his view that the Indians should be spectators rather than participants in the development of the colony.

By depriving the Indians of land and making only limited use of Indian labour, the effect of the settlement frontier was to diminish Indian wealth. Particularly on the coast, the Indians had traditionally placed great emphasis on wealth and property as the bases of power and strength in their society. The ability to acquire wealth was the major measure of the vitality of an Indian tribe, and an individual without property lacked the means to establish his status. The fur trade had stimulated Indian culture by adding to Indian wealth and therefore to the scope of Indian creativity. Settlement, on the other hand, often had the effect of subtracting from Indian wealth and thus tended to stultify their culture.

A large number of Indians tried to alleviate the decline in their fortunes by moving to live, either permanently or temporarily, near European towns. But they were not made very welcome by the settlers, many of whom did not want to live in close proximity to groups of Indians. At Fort Hope there was pressure to remove the Indians from a reservation close to the town, although Begbie advised against the move on the grounds that the Indians provided trade and could earn more by working in the town than they could by farming.[63] Governor Douglas received quite different advice from one of his officials in Yale. There the medical officer, Dr. M.W. Fifer, wrote that the town council had given consideration to the question of moving the Indian reserve away from the town. It was unnecessary, he said, to detail the evils that resulted from the presence of the Indians "to the detriment of the morals of the white Inhabitants." Fifer was particularly concerned about the settlers' children. The townspeople wished to banish vice from the daily sight of their offspring. As with most requests for Indian removal, there was also a professed concern for the Indians. It was said that the town was harmful to the Indians: that the women became depraved and diseased and that all the Indians became addicted to alcohol. The people of Yale thought that these undoubted social problems would be solved if the Indians were removed further away from the town and restricted from entering it after certain hours of the day.[64]

In both New Westminster and Victoria there was similar pressure for Indian removal. The *British Columbian* complained that "decent people" in New Westminster were being subjected "to the intolerable nuisance of having

---

[63]Begbie to Douglas, 11 April 1860, CC, file 142c.
[64]Fifer to Douglas, 25 August 1860, CC, file 558.

filthy, degraded, debauched Indians as neighbours."[65] In Victoria, where the numbers of Indians and Europeans were greater, white agitation for Indian removal was even more vociferous. By the end of the 1850's most of the Songhees had moved to a reserve on the opposite side of the harbour from the old fort. Following the gold rush boom in Victoria, increasing numbers of Indians from the northern coast came to spend the summer in the town. In April 1859 the *Victoria Gazette* estimated the population of the various Indian groups at Victoria to be 2,835, and the following year Douglas reported to London that 2,000 Indians from the north were living near the town. Douglas wrote that these Indians were of value to the town as labourers and consumers.[66] The Indians came to trade furs and handicrafts, and they provided the townspeople with a supply of fish, game, and produce. Apparently some Indians felt that the Europeans were gullible traders and thought that they could make large profits in Victoria.[67]

The Indians who came to Victoria undoubtedly benefited economically, but socially the effects were not so beneficial. With considerable numbers of Indians of various tribes living in close quarters, disputes were bound to occur. During the summer of 1860 there was a major feud between the Haida and other groups which produced several outbreaks of violence. Such hostilities were exacerbated by the large quantities of illegal, and therefore impure, liquor that the Indians were able to acquire and consume. In spite of every effort by the authorities, it proved impossible to prevent the sale of "ardent spirits" to the Indians. In 1860 an act was passed to prohibit the sale or gift of intoxicating liquors to the Indians,[68] but it was extremely difficult to police. Frederick Whymper, an artist who visited the northwest coast in 1864, claimed that there were 336 cases and 240 convictions involving Europeans selling liquor to the Indians between 1858 and 1864.[69] Presumably there would have been many more convictions but for the impediment that whiskey sellers could not be convicted on Indian evidence alone. All this activity in the courts seemed to make little impact on the liquor trade; in fact, it was claimed in 1860 that selling liquor to the Indians had become one of the most profitable businesses in Victoria.[70] Indian drinking was associated with other crime.

[65]*British Columbian*, 20 January 1864.

[66]*Victoria Gazette*, 28 April 1859; Douglas to Newcastle, 7 July 1860, CO.305/14.

[67]*Victoria Gazette*, 22 March 1859.

[68]Vancouver Island, *A Collection of the Public General Statutes of the Colony of Vancouver Island Passed in the Years 1859, 1860, 1861, 1862 and 1863* (Victoria: Evening Press, 1864), p. 37. The act replaced an earlier one passed by the Legislative Council of Vancouver Island on 3 August 1854.

[69]Frederick Whymper, *Travel and Adventure in the Territory of Alaska . . . and in Various Other Parts of the North Pacific* (London: J. Murray, 1868), p. 36n.

[70]*British Colonist*, 8 March 1860.

There was a considerable amount of theft, and there were numerous cases of assault in Victoria involving Indians, either as perpetrators or victims. Murders were also fairly common, and Indians were responsible for some of them, although there was a tendency for Victoria newspapers to attribute unsolved murders to Indians without real evidence.[71]

Prostitution was another problem. The coming of the settlers meant changes in the relationships between European men and Indian women. An Indian wife was a positive advantage to a fur trader but not to a settler. Some settlers did form temporary liaisons with Indian women, but more commonly they provided merely a temporary satisfaction of desires. The term "squaw," with all its pejorative connotations, was virtually unknown on the early fur-trading frontier but was widely used after the arrival of the settlers. Large numbers of Indian women from the north came to Victoria annually to earn money by prostitution. Apparently some were able to raise their husband's social position with the wealth that they acquired in this way. Women could earn twice as much as prostitutes in Victoria as they could further up the coast. So-called "squaw dance houses," brothels, and Indian women "dressed up as fine as 'White Soiled Doves' do in California" were all features of certain streets in Victoria in the early 1860's.[72]

In the minds of many of the colonists social ills such as these were associated with the presence of the Indians rather than with the sudden influx of a large and unstable European population. As a consequence, there was constant pressure in the early years of settlement, both from the colonists and from their representatives in the legislature, to have the Indians removed from the vicinity of Victoria, and especially to have the Songhees' reserve relocated. It was felt that no matter how appropriate the presence of the Indians might have been to the needs of the Hudson's Bay Company, these circumstances had passed and policies must now be changed to meet present and future exigencies.[73]

As with many public issues in Victoria, the *British Colonist* led the fray. The newspaper once expressed the opinion "that the rascally redskins who refused to subscribe to the *Colonist*, have got to make room for white men who will."[74] The editors were probably only half joking, and they did have reasons besides boosting the circulation of their paper for advocating the removal of the Indians. On 8 January and 26 February 1859 the *Colonist* pub-

---

[71]See, for example, *Victoria Gazette*, 25 June 1858.

[72]Francis Poole, *Queen Charlotte Islands: A Narrative of Discovery and Adventure in the North Pacific* (London: Hurst and Blackett, 1872), p. 313; Sproat, *Scenes and Studies*, p. 92; Nunis, *The Golden Frontier*, p. 143.

[73]*Victoria Gazette*, 24 February 1859.

[74]*British Colonist*, 6 September 1861.

lished unsigned letters demanding that the Indians be moved from Victoria. "How much longer," a letter writer asked, "are we to be inflicted with the intolerable nuisance of having hundreds upon hundreds of hideous, half-naked, drunken savages in our midst?" How terrible was the example to our children, to our sisters and daughters, to have the streets "teeming with droves of these disgusting objects, reeling about and shouting."[75] Settlers seemed to be particularly concerned about the possibility of "insults to female modesty," and one of them hinted darkly that "with such disgusting sights before the young, who can tell that the foundation is not gradually being laid of wickednesses too fearful to mention." Settler outrage at the possibility of miscegenation was only thinly disguised by such remarks. Letters like these written by its subscribers were supported editorially by the *British Colonist.*[76]

Social problems and offence to settler sensibilities were two reasons for the demands for the relocation of the Indians, but a third, and probably more important, reason was that with the growth of Victoria the Songhees reserve had become a valuable piece of real estate. Colonial developers would have preferred to see the land turned to a profit by themselves, than to have it occupied by the Indians. Attempts were made by the settlers to buy the land from the Songhees, but Douglas forestalled that move by placing a notice in the *Victoria Gazette* to the effect that the reserve was the property of the Crown and that the Indians could not convey legal title to it.[77] But there was also agitation in the House of Assembly to have the Indians removed by official action. James Yates, a tavern owner and government critic, introduced the question of removing the Indian reserve from across the harbour at several meetings of the assembly during January and February 1859. On 25 January he moved to ask the governor if they had the power to remove the Indians, and if not, why not. In a letter dated 5 February 1859, Douglas informed the Speaker and the members of the assembly that he was not prepared to see the Indians moved because the government was pledged by treaties that he had made not to disturb their occupation of the land. Douglas added, however, that he was prepared to allow the leasing out of parts of the reserve.[78] But this action was not enough for those who wanted removal, and Yates continued to agitate in the assembly. On the 15 February he introduced another resolution to have the Indians moved and one for a committee to be established to enquire into the circumstances of the Indians coming into the area so that His Excellency could be fully informed. The debate which ensued was not carried

---

75Ibid., 26 February 1859.
76Ibid., 8 January and 5 February 1859.
77Douglas to Lytton, 9 February 1859, CO.305/10.
78Vancouver Island, House of Assembly, Minutes, 25 January 1859; Douglas to Speaker and gentlemen of the House of Assembly, 5 February 1859, CO.305/10.

on "entirely within the rules of good breeding and parliamentary usage." Yates had made it clear that he wanted to see the reserve purchased from the Indians, divided into town lots, and sold to the highest bidder. He argued that Douglas's proposal to lease the land was absurd, since the income would be enormous and would give the Indians such an inflated idea of the value of the property that it would be impossible to purchase it from them in the future. Anyway, Yates added, nothing could be done to improve the condition of the Indians while they remained where they were with liquor so easy to obtain. Joseph Despard Pemberton pertinently pointed out that it was only since their lands had become valuable that the Indians were found to be a nuisance and, taking a swipe at Yates, remarked that if liquor was a problem then the grog shops should be closed. Both of Yates's resolutions were lost, but the assembly continued to raise objections to the idea of leasing the land.[79] Although Douglas resisted the efforts to have the Indians removed, it was clear that the settlers did not want them living near Victoria any more than they wanted them occupying valuable land.

A further consequence of the large numbers of Indians visiting and living in Victoria was that disease increased and spread among them. Indians who came to Victoria for the summer carried diseases when they returned home, spreading ailments more rapidly than if the population had remained stationary. Venereal disease, for example, was contracted by Indian women in Victoria and then carried up the coast where it caused death and infertility. The most striking instance of the transmission of disease in this way was the smallpox outbreak of 1862. During March of that year smallpox was brought to Victoria, probably by a sailor coming from San Francisco, and it soon took hold among the Indians. In the middle of the nineteenth century little was known about the mechanism by which smallpox was spread. Newspapers in Victoria were advising citizens to clean up any refuse that was likely to cause miasma,[80] and the ultimate method used to try to control the disease among the Indians was the worst one possible. As it became apparent that more and more Indians were infected with smallpox, Victorians began to agitate to have them removed from the vicinity of the town. Finally the authorities evicted the Indians and burned down their houses.[81] Rather than being contained at its source, the highly contagious disease was allowed to spread up the coast as the northern Indians returned home, infecting others wherever they made a landfall. From the coast the disease also began to spread into the interior,

[79]Vancouver Island, House of Assembly, Minutes, 8 and 15 February and 3 March 1859; *Victoria Gazette*, 17 February 1859.

[80]Victoria *Daily Press*, 26 March 1862.

[81]*British Colonist*, 1 and 14 May 1862.

until the Indians of a large part of the two colonies were in contact with it. This increased incidence of smallpox produced considerable excitement and hysteria among the settlers. For some the impact of the disease confirmed their expectation that the Indians were soon to die out. Contemporary remarks about smallpox converting Indian "camps into graveyards" should therefore be treated with some caution, as should statements by more recent commentators that the epidemic beginning in 1862 reduced the Indian population by one-third.[82] During 1862 thousands of Indians were vaccinated,[83] and by that time there must have been a degree of built-up immunity as a result of previous contact with the disease. Nonetheless, there can be no doubt that large numbers of Indians died.

In many respects the 1862 smallpox outbreak was representative of the kind of change that the Indians faced with the arrival of the settlers. Just as the Indians had been introduced to smallpox before 1862, their culture had been changed as a result of the European presence prior to the coming of the settlers; but now the pace of change outstripped the Indian ability to cope with it. The old cures for illnesses proved ineffective against smallpox, and traditional social forms were inadequate to cope with the crisis that settlement brought to Indian culture. During the fur trade change had been gradual enough for the Indians to accommodate, but in the years following 1858 a great range of major disruptions were introduced too quickly for the Indians to adapt easily.

Indians realized that their way of life was being seriously disrupted. They objected to the interference, and yet they could do little about it. In 1860 when

---

[82]R. C. L. Brown to Douglas, 18 February 1863, CC, file 214; Duff, *Indian History of B.C.*, p. 43. Such assessments of the impact of smallpox are based on estimates of the pre-1862 population which could be inaccurate. It is interesting to note that in one area where there was a count of the Indian population that "seems quite remarkable in its accuracy and detail" before 1862 the population decline was much lower than one-third. The rate of decline among the Stalo for the years 1839–1879 was 17.2 per cent, although the figure is given with the proviso that it is probably too low (see Duff, *The Upper Stalo*, pp. 28–29).

[83]In the following references to Indians having been vaccinated, the numbers mentioned are given in brackets. *British Colonist*, 26 April 1862 (200); *British Columbian*, 14 May 1862 (3,000); Victoria *Daily Press*, 27 March and 27 April 1862 (30 and 500); Ball to colonial secretary, 6 June 1862, CC, file 96 (1,790); Elliott to Young, 10 December 1862, CC, file 513 (considerable number); Manson, Journal, 4, 5, 6 and 7 August 1862 (large numbers); Moffatt to H.B.C. board, Victoria, 19 August 1862, Hamilton Moffatt, "Letterbook, Fort Rupert, Fort Simpson and Fort Kamloops, 1857–1867," PABC (more than 100); Robson, Diary, 7, 8, and 11 April 1862, Ebenezer Robson Papers, PABC (77, 35, and 50); Hills (bishop of Columbia), Diary, 23 June 1862 (30 or 40); [Society for the Propagation of the Gospel], *Report of the Incorporated Society for the Propagation of the Gospel in Foreign Parts, 1863* (London: Society for the Propagation of the Gospel, 1863), p. 57 (100's).

Sproat arrived at Alberni Canal to supervise the establishment of a sawmill, he announced to the Indians that they must move their village as he had bought all the surrounding land from the Queen and wished to occupy the site of the village. The Indians must have been astonished at the odd behaviour of this white man, but they proceeded to negotiate a sale. It became apparent, however, that the Indians were unwilling to move themselves from their village. One of the tribal elders later said prophetically,

> We see your ships, and hear things that make our hearts grow faint. They say that more King-George-men will soon be here, and will take our land, our firewood, our fishing grounds; that we shall be placed on a little spot, and shall have to do everything according to the fancies of the King-George-men.

The old man added that "we do not want the white man. He steals what we have. We wish to live as we are." But the opposition was futile. The Alberni Indians prepared to resist the intrusion of Sproat's party by force, but the European's vessels were equipped with cannon, and after the use of these was demonstrated, the Indians "saw that resistance would be inexpedient, and began to move from the spot."[84] The scene was one that was repeated in many places in the two colonies. Indians everywhere were trying to convince the settlers that they had no business being there because the land belonged to them.[85] But by 1858 it was already too late to turn back the settlers, and in any case their societies were too fragmented for the Indians to provide serious opposition. Neither the Salish nor the Shuswap, nor even the Chilcotin, could prevent the advance of settlement on their own, and the Indians had never acted together before. Hitherto there had been no reason for united action. Recalling his arrival in Alberni some time later, Sproat said that the clattering of ships' cables had not been heard before by the Indians of the area, but it was a noise "that might well be remembered by the people, for their land really passed into the unrelaxing English grip as our anchors sank to the bottom."[86]

Some Indians, as individuals or groups, tried to oppose the penetration of the whites, while others merely retreated from a situation that they felt was beyond their control. Sproat told the Ethnological Society of London that, after having spent some time among the Indians, he noticed that a large number of them "no longer visited the settlement in their former free independent way, but lived listlessly in their villages, brooding seemingly over heavy thoughts." These Indians gradually shrank from association with the Euro-

---

[84]Sproat, *Scenes and Studies*, pp. 3–4.
[85]Mayne, "Journal," 5 April 1860.
[86]Sproat, "The West Coast Indians," p. 244.

peans. Sproat's not implausible explanation for this behaviour was that the Indians had begun to mistrust their old habits and traditions and yet were stunned and confused by the technical achievements and vitality of western culture. Sproat also noticed that illness had increased among the Indians for no immediately apparent reason; he claimed that it was not caused by excessive drinking or sexual contact with the whites but that it was the result of despondency produced by contact with western culture.[87] Another official reported an increase in the suicide rate among the Indians of the Douglas area.[88] Certainly if Sproat's description is at all accurate, these Indians were experiencing an acute cultural crisis.

The settlement frontier, then, was bringing major disruptions to the cultures of those Indians in constant contact with the whites. Some groups still remained fairly isolated from settlement during the 1860's and in some cases were still vigorously asserting their own culture. Not all Indians experienced the anomie which Sproat describes. Some coast Indians were still developing and asserting Indian cultural forms. Helen Codere has shown that among the Kwakiutl winter ritual and potlatching were increasing in the years after the establishment of settlement,[89] and the Haida were still developing their art forms to such an extent that their villages appeared from a distance as a forest of totem poles.[90] Because of their relative isolation, these groups had yet to experience the full impact of the settlement frontier, but nonetheless the developments in Kwakiutl ritual and Haida art can be seen as assertions of Indian culture in response to the malaise brought about by the white man's pressure.[91]

During the 1860's many Indians in British Columbia were experiencing what, eventually, all would experience: a disruption of their culture. It was a disturbance that the Indians could tolerate or object to but, in the long term, could not really resist. The attitudes and actions of the settlers meant that options were closing off for the Indians, and their freedom of action was being limited. But miners and settlers were not the only agents of cultural change at work among the Indians after 1858.

---

[87]Ibid., p. 254.

[88]Gaggin to Young, 28 January 1860, CC, file 619.

[89]Codere, *Fighting with Property*, 4 and passim.

[90]Lady Dufferin, Journal, 31 August 1876, *My Canadian Journal 1872–1878*, ed. Gladys Chantler Walker (Don Mills, Ont.: Longmans Canada, 1969), p. 209.

[91]I am particularly indebted to Wilson Duff for this insight. He pointed out that his own work on Haida art and the research of Susan Reid on Kwakiutl winter ritual and potlatching lend support to the interpretation that these groups were responding through the medium of their own cultural forms to the presence of Europeans.

6

The Missionaries

... they saw that Christianity meant nothing less than the subversion of
every evil work and no compromise.[1] —WILLIAM DUNCAN, 1875

The presence of settlers and gold miners radically altered Indian society, but these changes were the by-products of other European objectives. Settlers did not come to British Columbia with a specific policy of transforming Indian culture; they simply expected the Indians to give way before their demands. So the changes brought by settlers were, to a degree, inadvertent, although the effect on the Indians was no less profound for that reason. The missionaries, however, had developed quite deliberately and consciously thought out plans of acculturation for the Indians. They were a part of the settlement frontier because they demanded major concessions from the Indians, even though they desired changes of a different kind and for different reasons than the settlers.

Missionaries had been operative in the area that was to become British Columbia before the establishment of the settlement frontier, but their efforts had met with little success. Protestant missions to the northwest coast during the fur-trading period were few and short-lived. In 1829 Jonathan Green, representing the American Board of Commissioners for Foreign Missions, made a trip from the Sandwich Islands to the northwest coast to investigate the possibility of establishing a mission. Green visited several points on the northern coast, including Kaigani, the Nass River, and Skidegate, and wrote a report advocating that missionary attention should be paid to that part of the world.[2] But apparently the American board did not follow up his suggestion, at least not north of the forty-ninth parallel. Seven years later another Protestant missionary came to the coast. The Reverend Herbert Beaver arrived at Fort Vancouver in September 1836, having been sent out by the

---

[1]Duncan to Honorable David Laird, May 1875, Church Missionary Society Archives, C.2/0, UBCL (hereafter cited as CMSA).

[2]Jonathan S. Green, *Journal of a Tour on the North West Coast of America in the Year 1829* ... (New York: C. F. Heartman, 1915), p. 103.

Hudson's Bay Company as a chaplain and a missionary to the Indians. Beaver may, as Ogden once remarked, have been suited by name to the fur trade,[3] but it is difficult to imagine a man less suited by nature to that environment. He completely lacked the toleration required to survive on the fur-trading frontier.

Missionaries did not leave Europe to accommodate themselves to the frontier; they came with plans to alter Indian society totally. They were, therefore, misfits within the fur-trading environment. The fur traders knew that the missionaries could destroy the fur trade by converting the Indians to a new way of life. Nevertheless, the traders' attitude to most missionaries was one of uneasy toleration. Men like Beaver, however, infuriated them. The Reverend Beaver seemed unwilling to make any concessions to the milieu he was trying to work in. He was overly concerned with maintaining "the dignity of my station."[4] He complained about the accommodation that he was provided with at the fort; he protested that his allowance of food and wine was insufficient for a man of his position; and when he began to work as a teacher and a minister, he was prepared to make absolutely no allowance for the fact that most of his pupils and congregation were Roman Catholic. McLoughlin wanted Beaver to teach a non-denominational form of Christianity that would be appropriate to the catholic character of the company's staff, but Beaver would teach only the doctrines of the Church of England. He was astonished at the strong hold of "Popery" in the fort and, even worse, that it was "defended and sustained by the head of the establishment himself."[5] But the issue that really enraged Beaver was the marital status of the officers and men of the company. Many of the marriages of company men and Indian or half-breed women were unions made in the "manner of the country" rather than formalized according to church ritual. A situation that the fur traders took so much for granted horrified the missionary. In his letters Beaver raved about "unhallowed connections" and women "living in a state of concubinage." He demanded that if a married chaplain was to dwell within the fort, all those whose marriages were not solemnized before God should be made to live outside the

[3]Ogden to McLeod, 25 February 1837, "Old Letters from Hudson's Bay Company Officials and Employees from 1829–1840," *Washington Historical Quarterly* 2 (1908): 260.
[4]Beaver to Benjamin Harrison, 27 March 1838, Jessett, *Reports and Letters*, p. 102.
[5]McLoughlin to governor, deputy governor and committee, 15 November 1836, Rich, *McLoughlin's Letters, First Series*, p. 162; Beaver to Church of England Protestant Magazine, 1 February 1841, in Herbert Beaver, "Experiences of a Chaplain at Fort Vancouver, 1836–1838," ed. R. C. Clark, *Oregon Historical Quarterly* 39 (1938): 23.

walls. As far as the traders were concerned, this suggestion was ridiculous. The crisis on this matter came when Beaver, in a letter to the company, referred to McLoughlin's wife as a "female of notoriously loose character" and as "the kept Mistress of the highest personage in your service at this station."[6] When he read these remarks, McLoughlin was incensed. The unfortunate Beaver learned something of the McLoughlin temper when he was severely beaten in the quadrangle of the fort by the chief factor. Soon after this incident McLoughlin left on furlough, and before he returned Beaver had departed from Fort Vancouver. The missionary had been utterly unable to cope with conditions inside the fort let alone begin work among the Indians.

Beaver's behaviour might be put down to personal eccentricity were it not for the fact that his attitudes were typical of the evangelical missionary. Some years earlier Simpson had written prophetically that if a missionary was to be sent to work in a fur-trading area he

> ought to be cool and temperate in his habits and of a Mild and conciliatory disposition even tempered and not too much disposed to find fault severely with any little laxity of Morals he may discover at the Coy's. Establishment otherwise 'tis to be feared he would find his situation uncomfortable and it might even interfere with the objects of his Mission.[7]

After the Beaver interlude at Fort Vancouver, Douglas also commented that a clergyman in the fur-trading country should be devoted to the support of principles rather than forms, shun discord and avoid uncharitable feelings, and temper zeal with discretion.[8] But these were characteristics that were seldom found in a Protestant missionary of the nineteenth century. Men like Beaver were zealous and determined, doctrinaire and obdurate. They saw themselves waging a war, often vainly, against an "irresistable torrent of iniquity,"[9] and they were not disposed to make concessions to the enemy.

The first Roman Catholic missionaries to come into contact with the Indians of the northwest coast were the friars who came with the early Spanish voyagers. Some of the Spaniards were very sanguine about the possibility of converting the Indians. Francisco de Eliza, the Spanish commandant at Nootka, thought in 1792 that if the settlement were maintained for a few years, there would be very few Indians remaining unconverted.[10] But these

---

[6][Beaver], "The Natives of the North West Coast," p. 138; Beaver to governor and committee (of the Hudson's Bay Company), 10 October 1837, HBCA, B-223/b/19.

[7]Simpson, *Journal*, 1824, Merk, p. 108.

[8]Douglas to governor, deputy governor and committee, 5 October 1838, HBCA, B-223/b/21.

[9]Beaver, "Experiences," p. 30.

[10]Eliza to conde de Revillagigedo, 7 July 1792, Elizabeth Daylton, trans., "Official Documents Relating to Spanish and Mexican Voyages of Navigation, Exploration and Discovery . . . ," UBCL.

hopes were not to be realized. After the departure of the Spanish from Noot-ka, it was many years before Roman Catholic missionaries came again to the Indians of the area. During the Hudson's Bay Company years a number of Roman Catholic missionaries stationed to the south made forays into New Caledonia. In 1838, the same year that Beaver ended his ministry, the first Roman Catholic priests arrived at Fort Vancouver. Fathers Francis N. Blanchet and Modeste Demers were sent out by the bishop of Quebec to begin a mission in Oregon. In 1841 Demers travelled to Fort Langley, and in the following year he joined Ogden's brigade which left Fort Vancouver to supply the posts of New Caledonia. Demers went as far north as Stuart Lake, passed the winter at Fort Alexandria, and returned to Fort Vancouver in April 1843. During the mid-1840's the Jesuit priest Father Pierre De Smet was travelling among the Kootenay and Okanagan Indians, while Father John Nobili S.J. was operating in northern New Caledonia. When Douglas made a journey of reconnaissance to the southern tip of Vancouver Island in 1843, he was accompanied by Father Jean-Baptiste Bolduc, who spent some time working among the Coast Salish. Following the establishment of the colony of Van-couver Island, Demers, who had been consecrated bishop of Vancouver Island, and Father Honoré Timothy Lempfrit both laboured among the Indians, particularly in the Victoria and Cowichan areas.

Yet all these efforts by Roman Catholic missionaries had only a minimal effect. The first of them to travel among the Indians of New Caledonia made only fleeting contact with each group. In spite of liberal sprinklings of bap-tismal water and the use of visual aids such as the Catholic ladder, the impact of these missionaries was superficial. As a later Oblate missionary to British Columbia put it, these early visits "were but skirmishes."[11] Hundreds were baptized with little or no preparation, and under these circumstances baptism obviously did not mean conversion to Christianity.[12] Many Indians who received "God's water" then felt secure and simply returned to their old way of life.[13] As they conceived it, they had propitiated the new god and no real change in life-style was required. Even when the missionaries tried to establish themselves more permanently, they met with little success. In 1852 Douglas had to ask Lempfrit to abandon his mission to the Cowichan. The Indians had attacked the missionary's property and had treated him with contempt,

[11]Morice, *History of the Northern Interior*, p. 234.
[12]Cf. Ormsby, *British Columbia*, p. 168.
[13]A. G. Morice, *History of the Catholic Church in Western Canada, from Lake Superior to the Pacific, 1659–1895* (Toronto: Musson, 1910), 2:298.

proving to Douglas that they were not prepared to benefit from religious teaching and that for Lempfrit to remain in the area would endanger the peace of the colony. Douglas wrote to the Colonial Office that, as a result of this situation, he intended to discourage missionaries from working among the Indians except within the boundaries of the settlement where they could be protected and supported.[14]

During the fur-trading period some Indians had also imbibed rudimentary notions of Christianity in an informal way from traders. William Tolmie noted in his journal at Fort Nisqually that on occasions he had endeavoured to acquaint the Indians "with the existence of a Supreme Being, his creation of the world and Commandments to Man."[15] Both of the fur-trading companies active on the Pacific slope employed French Canadians and Roman Catholic Iroquois who conveyed aspects of Christianity to the local Indians. Sometimes Christian concepts spread among the Indians with startling rapidity. In 1829 two young Indians, one a Spokan and the other a Kutenai, returned to their homes after having been educated and baptized at Red River. One of the men, Spokan Garry, began preaching the white man's religion to Indian groups, and his message was spread over great distances. John McLean, as far away as Fort Saint James, reported that a brand of Christianity taught by these two young men had spread with amazing rapidity to Fort Alexandria and then to the Stuart Lake area.[16]

Indians on the fur-trading frontier were introduced to Christianity from a variety of sources, but their disposition towards western religion was the same as it was towards other aspects of European culture: they were free to select and reject as they pleased. Some did reject Christianity altogether. Others simply added the Christian god to the existing pantheon as a kind of insurance policy. Still others developed syncretistic cults that were a fusion of Indian and European elements. These prophet movements are particularly interesting examples of the kind of selective adaptation that was possible for the Indians during the fur-trading period. It is questionable whether the prophet dance, for example, had its roots in the aboriginal beliefs of the people or whether it was a post-contact phenomenon. But it is certain that Christian elements were increasingly added to the prophet cults after missionaries

[14]Douglas to Lempfrit, 26 May 1852, Vancouver Island, Governor, Correspondence Outward; Douglas to Grey, 28 March 1852, CO.305/3.

[15]Tolmie, *Journal*, 10 November 1833, p. 249.

[16]McLean, *Notes*, 1:263. For an account of Spokan Garry and Kutenai Pelly see Alvin M. Josephy, Jr., *The Nez Percé Indians and the Opening of the Northwest* (New Haven and London: Yale University Press, 1965), pp. 85–87.

had been active in a given area.[17] These Indian prophets prepared the way for later missionaries. Yet it was not until after the coming of settlement that the missionaries were sufficiently well organized to bring major change to Indian culture and the Indians were faced with more compelling reasons to adopt Christianity in its entirety.

The last years of the 1850's, the years that saw the permanent establishment of settlement, also marked the beginning of effective missionary work among the Indians. In June 1857 William Duncan, the best known missionary sent to British Columbia by the Anglican Church Missionary Society, arrived in Victoria. The following year the Oblates of Mary Immaculate established a centre for their operations at Esquimalt, and 1858 was also the year in which the sisters of Saint Ann arrived. In 1859 the first Methodist missionaries arrived from Canada to begin work on the west coast, and representatives of the Society for the Propagation of the Gospel in Foreign Parts came to British Columbia. It was no accident that the establishment of effective missions to the Indians coincided with the beginning of settlement. As long as their traditional way of life remained intact, the Indians had no reason to adopt a new value system such as Christianity. It was only after the disruptive impact of settlement seemed to render old truths ineffectual that the Indians needed to turn to new ones. Acceptance of missionary teaching by Indians was a sign that they sensed that their culture was undergoing major change and that they needed new knowledge to cope with their new situation.

The aims of the missionaries were at one with the general impact of the settlement frontier in the sense that the missionaries demanded total cultural capitulation from the Indians. No matter how much missionary societies might debate the question of whether civilization should precede or follow evangelization, in effect the two were inextricably intertwined. The missionaries brought a new set of religious beliefs to the Indians, beliefs which were to cleanse them "from the awful superstitions in which they were now sunk."[18] But they also assumed that the "improvement" of the heathen was an essential part of their becoming Christian, and for the European of the nineteenth

---

[17]See, for example, Wayne Suttles, "The Plateau Prophet Dance among the Coast Salish," *Southwestern Journal of Anthropology* 13 (1957): 388; Diamond Jenness, *The Carrier Indians of the Bulkley River: Their Social and Religious Life*, Smithsonian Institution Bureau of American Ethnology Anthropology Paper no. 25 (Washington, 1943), p. 547; Morice, *History of the Northern Interior*, p. 234. For a discussion of the literature of the prophet dance and of the question of whether it was an indigenous cult or the consequence of acculturation, see Hilary Eileen Rumley, "Reactions of Contact and Colonization: An Interpretation of Religious and Social Change among the Indians of British Columbia" (M.A. thesis, University of British Columbia, 1973), pp. 30ff.

[18]George Hills, *A Sermon, Preached at the Farewell Service Celebrated in St. James Church, Piccadilly, on Wednesday, Nov. 16, 1859...* (London: Rivingtons, 1859), p. 8.

century "improvement" meant westernization. The missionaries were aggressively confident about the superiority of their own culture and therefore had no qualms about interfering with the customs of the Indians. Unlike those of the trader, the demands of the missionaries could not be incorporated into existing Indian society; their teaching and their example had to be either accepted or rejected, and acceptance meant virtually a total cultural change for the proselyte. Nor did the missionaries simply demand a transformation in outward behaviour from their converts; they also required that, in the words of John Wesley, they be "born again of the spirit." Outward change was to be accompanied by a conversion of the heart and mind so that the Christian Indian became a completely new being.

William Duncan, the most successful of the Protestant missionaries to work in British Columbia, was in many ways typical of the rest, and so his mission to the Tsimshian will be examined in some detail. Of humble origins, Duncan had struggled to rise above his birth, and by his own efforts he had elevated himself into the ranks of the lower middle class.[19] This upward mobility was common among young men who were converted to the missionary life,[20] and for some the decision to work as a missionary was an extension of their drive for success in the secular world. As a missionary in a foreign land Duncan could achieve the respectability and position of leadership that he had striven for in Britain. Duncan's desire to become a missionary also arose out of an intensely felt religious fervour. As a young man Duncan experienced two conversions, the first of which was to evangelical Christianity. The doctrinal position of the evangelicals was a product of the spiritual revolution in Britain associated with the names of John Wesley and George Whitefield. It was a belief that took the convert from the depths of despair at his own unworthiness to the heights of joy when he contemplated God's mercy to him.[21] Like many others Duncan tended to exaggerate his shortcomings, and the intense experience of sin made possible a heightened experience of salvation. The Wesleyan doctrine of salvation by grace was essentially a doctrine for sinners. Duncan once wrote in his journal "I resolve & resolve and plan & pray—but all is unavailing. I go back to my sin as a dog returns to

---

[19]For the details of Duncan's early life see Usher, *William Duncan*, pp. 3–10.

[20]Morris Zaslow claims that Duncan's humble origins and lack of formal education made him an atypical candidate for the C.M.S. (Zaslow, "The Missionary as Social Reformer: The Case of William Duncan," *Journal of the Canadian Church Historical Society* 8 [1966]: 52). In fact, many of the C.M.S. missionaries came from such a background (see W. N. Gunson, "Evangelical Missionaries in the South Seas, 1797–1860" [Ph.D. dissertation, Australian National University, 1959], pp. 12ff; and Judith Binney, *The Legacy of Guilt: A Life of Thomas Kendall* [Auckland: Auckland-Oxford University Press, 1968], p. 2).

[21]See, for example, Duncan, Journal, 27 November 1853 and 15 October 1854, WDP, C.2,154.

his vomit. I am indeed a lost sinner." The realization of his sinfulness awakened in Duncan the desire to be converted into a new creature. Out of this religious experience came Duncan's second conversion to the missionary vocation. Among the evangelicals the experience of personal rebirth often developed into a desire to be instrumental in the salvation of others. Duncan "pitied the poor heathen and felt exceedingly desirous of the salvation of all men."[22]

The evangelical believed that natural man, that is, man without God, was utterly depraved. He considered the phrase "noble savage" a contradiction in terms and substituted in its place a picture of a degraded brute, who could be rescued from eternal damnation only by concerted missionary activity. The evangelical missionaries of the nineteenth century believed in the equality of man, since before God all souls were equal; but they also believed that it was only through the work of missionaries that the heathen could be saved from his depraved natural state and his potential equality could be converted into real equality.

His desire to save the "perishing" heathen led Duncan to present himself as a candidate for the mission field, and in 1854 he began his training at the Church Missionary Society's Highbury College in London. He was still at Highbury in 1857 when the call came to work among the Indians of the northwest coast. Captain James Prevost of the Royal Navy had written to the C.M.S. pointing out that the Indians of the coast remained "in a state of heathen darkness and complete barbarism" in spite of manifesting "a great desire and aptitude to acquire the knowledge and arts of civilized life." Prevost suggested that the Indians were mentally and physically equal, if not superior, to the Maoris of New Zealand,[23] among whom agents of the C.M.S. had been labouring for so many years. So it was decided to send a missionary to the northwest coast, and Duncan was chosen.

Duncan arrived in Vancouver Island conscious of his personal inadequacies and yet confident that his mission was divinely ordained. He had seen the signs that providence was on his side. At Valpariso he had gone ashore and nearly missed his ship when it departed, but he had made it back in time. This experience he "set down as a *direct* mercy from and a special interposition of God on my account." He was to recall later that, as he began his mission to the Indians, he "never doubted for a moment that I should be able to subvert heathenism, and triumph over ignorance."[24]

[22]Duncan, Journal, 9 March 1873, WDP, C.2,155; ibid, 4 October and 26 April 1854, WDP, C.2,154.

[23]Letter of James Prevost, *Church Missionary Intelligencer*, July 1856, pp. 167–68.

[24]Duncan, Journal, 15 April 1857, WDP, C.2,154; speech of Duncan to a missionary meeting, Victoria *Evening Express*, 10 June 1863.

But Duncan was not just the emissary of mid-Victorian evangelical Christianity, he was also the representative of mid-Victorian civilization. His work towards the conversion of the heathen was to be combined with an attack on Indian social practices. Before his arrival at Fort Simpson Duncan saw much to convince him that it would not be easy to eradicate the "abominations" of the Indians. On observing the noise and confusion of the Songhees village at Victoria, he longed for the time when "these dens of darkness & iniquity would be illuminated by the Gospel light." Among the "atrocities" and the "superstitions" of the Fort Rupert Indians he saw practices that were "overwhelmingly shocking to behold." There was much that required "improvement," and Duncan almost despaired at the enormity of the task ahead of him.[25] He arrived at Fort Simpson on 1 October 1857, and from that day he began his assault on Tsimshian culture.

During the first months among the Tsimshian, Duncan found some things about the Indians to admire and much to abhor. One of his positive impressions of the Tsimshian was that they were "a fine intelligent race." He noted a "conscious superiority both in numbers and ability" which distinguished the Tsimshian from the Indians of the southern coast. He was astonished at "their skill in both the useful and the fine arts," and he observed that the ability to work metal or carve wood seemed to be intuitive among the northern Indians. Duncan was obliged to demonstrate that the Indians had a capacity for improvement; after all, if the Tsimshian were completely unregenerate, his mission would be pointless. But as well as the admirable, there were also many aspects of Tsimshian culture that appalled and horrified the young missionary, and therein lay another justification for his work. Duncan could not "describe the condition of this people better than by saying that it was just what might be expected in savage heathen life."[26]

He had arrived at Fort Simpson at the beginning of the "season in which the deep heathenism and darkness of this people is manifested,"[27] that is, the period of winter dancing and ceremonial. It was the time of year when the whole tenor of Indian life changed, when secular matters were put in the background while the religious and mystical aspects of existence were explored and celebrated. It was natural enough that the missionary should find this part of Tsimshian culture particularly objectionable, since he was there to inculcate an entirely new religion. The ritual of the winter season was described by Duncan as a "horrid fabrication of lies";[28] he thought that the role

[25]Duncan, Journal, 3 and 29 September 1857, WDP, C.2,154.

[26]Ibid., 7 October and 30 November 1857 and 14 January 1858, WDP, C.2,154; and Duncan to Venn, 6 October 1857, CMSA.

[27]Duncan, Journal, 12 October 1858, *The Church Missionary Record*, June 1859, p. 181.

[28]Ibid., 16 November 1859, CMSA.

of the shaman was sinister, the winter dances frivolous, and the potlatch wasteful. He realized the importance of these customs within Tsimshian society, but the realization only increased the importance of stopping what was heathenish and idolatrous. The incidence of drunkenness and violence in the Tsimshian village adjacent to the fort appalled the missionary, as did the widespread prostitution of Indian women. He perceived many aspects of the Indian personality that seemed to confirm their savagery. The most pronounced trait of the Tsimshian was pride, he wrote in his journal, although "they have many other corruptions in a deplorable measure" such as the dishonesty and trickery for which they are notorious, their jealousies and feuds, and their abominable custom "of revenging crime on anyone who belonged to the same tribe as the culprit." He later recalled that

> To attempt to describe the condition of these tribes on my arrival would be but to produce a dark and revolting picture of human depravity. The dark mantle of degrading superstition enveloped them all, and their savage spirits, swayed by pride, jealousy and revenge were ever hurrying them to deeds of blood. Thus their history was little else than a chapter of crime and misery.

Duncan was some months recovering from the initial "depressing sensation which the sight of their state has awakened," but these impressions only increased his evangelical zeal. "O dreadful, dreadful, to see one's fellow creatures like this when the blessed Gospel has been 1,000 years in the world," he thought.[29]

Duncan was particularly impressed that the example of Fort Simpson had apparently had no impact on the Indians. The fort had clean, orderly premises with a large, well-cultivated garden, "an oasis in the desert," and yet the Indians, who had imitated none of these things, lived in dingy, smoky houses in which, to Duncan, filth and discomfort were the most striking features. Yet the missionary did not see the fur traders' lack of influence as a cause for despondency. How was it, he asked himself, that the Indians could have mixed with a group of Europeans for twenty years and yet have remained in their savage state? It was simply that the right means of acculturation had not been tried. Civilization without Christianity lacked the vitality to effect real cultural change: "Civilization appeals to the eye & to the hand but not to the heart." Apart from Christianity, civilization was not "a fit instrument for awakening the long slumbering offspring of Adam."[30]

Perceiving "a great mountain of heathenism"[31] before him, Duncan began

[29]Ibid., 17 February 1858, 16 October 1857, 14 January 1858, WDP, C.2,154; Duncan to Laird, May 1875, CMSA.
[30]Duncan, Journal, 17 February 1858, WDP, C.2,154.
[31]Speech of Duncan to missionary meeting, Victoria *Evening Express*, 10 June 1863.

working to remove it. The task of learning the Tsimshian language, begun while he was in Victoria, Duncan continued during his first winter at Fort Simpson. The fact that he was not satisfied with the Chinook jargon as a means of communicating his ideas indicated that he aspired to a different kind of influence over the Tsimshian than the fur traders had. His investment in learning Tsimshian was not to preserve what was an essential part of the culture but to facilitate the introduction of cultural change among the Indians. Duncan's work on the language began to bear fruit in May 1858 when he translated the first "truths of the gospel" into Tsimshian. The following month he preached for the first time in the houses of the Indians in their own language. When the missionary addressed the Indians, he laid great emphasis on sin and its consequences, on showing to the Tsimshian "the evil of their doings" and "illustrating from their own customs" their need for a saviour.[32]

The other means of instruction besides preaching was teaching. During the first month at Fort Simpson Duncan founded a school inside the fort. Then in the summer of 1858 work was started on building a school outside the walls, and instruction was begun there in November 1859. The students were taught reading, writing, counting, singing, and religious knowledge. As in most C.M.S. missions, Duncan's school at Fort Simpson was an important agent of acculturation; it gave the missionary daily opportunity to teach the Indians systematically about the new way of life he hoped to introduce among them.

During the time that Duncan worked out of Fort Simpson his mission met with some success. He claimed to detect a quickening of interest in his teaching and perceived a stirring of opinion against the "heathenish winter customs." During 1861 and 1862 there was even more tangible evidence that the Tsimshian were responding to his message. By July 1862 fifty-eight Indians had been baptized or accepted as candidates for baptism.[33] But Duncan was becoming increasingly convinced that Fort Simpson was not a conducive environment for achieving the kind of thoroughgoing reformation among the Indians that he was aiming for.

As early as 1859 Duncan was toying with the idea of moving away from Fort Simpson to a place where his neophytes could be isolated from those influences that militated against his work. He was exercising his mind on the problem of what was becoming of the young people under his instruction when "temporal necessities" compelled them to leave his school. "If they are permitted to slip away from me into the gulf of vice and misery which everywhere surrounds them," Duncan felt that all his efforts would be wasted.[34]

[32]Duncan, Journal, 17 May and 13 June 1858, WDP, C.2,154; Duncan to Cridge, 7 February 1860, CC, file 395.

[33]Duncan, Journal, 19 November 1859, [Church Missionary Society], *Metlahkatla*, p. 39; Baptismal Register, 1861–1862, WDP, C.2,159.

[34]Duncan, Journal, 1 July 1859, [Church Missionary Society], *Metlahkatla*, p. 53.

The solution was to move the Christian Indians to a place where a much more controlled environment could be established. Duncan wanted to move his followers away from the baneful influence of European civilization, from Fort Simpson and from the fatal attraction of Victoria, and also from those unrepentant Indians who refused to accept the Christian way of life. He concluded that the only way to "stem the tide of dissipation and ruin" that he saw around him was to take his "little band of catechumens out of the reeking camp—in a sense, indeed, to beat a retreat, but only for the purpose of gathering up our strength, securing our position, and thus the more successfully to confront and assail the evils around us."[35] In consultation with the Indians, Metlakatla, the old village site of the Tsimshian tribes, was selected as the location for a completely new kind of Indian village. In May 1862 Duncan and a small group of Tsimshian followers left Fort Simpson to establish a new society.

There were many reasons why a significant number of Tsimshian should be willing to make such a radical break in their pattern of life and follow a missionary from another land to establish a model village based on the standards of another culture. Important among the reasons for the move was the disruptive influence that the settlement frontier had had on Tsimshian society. Towards the end of the 1850's the traders at Fort Simpson noted a change among the Tsimshian: drunkenness was increasing to the point where it threatened to disrupt the trade seriously. An entry in the Fort Simpson journal noted that "we now have immense trouble with our Indians and in a few years I have some doubts if an establishment can be kept up at this place."[36] After 1858 more and more Tsimshian made the summer trip to Victoria, and Tsimshian leaders were becoming concerned about the debilitating effects of these excursions. An old Indian told Duncan that "they had seen nothing among the first whites who came among them to unsettle them in their old habits"[37] but now that the Tsimshian were faced with serious and unsettling social problems. The disruption of their society in the late 1850's and early 1860's was not, as one historian has claimed, a consequence of the absence of any means of social control among the Tsimshian,[38] but rather a result of new and disturbing influences that impinged from outside Indian society. Indian solutions to social problems were no longer effective, and many Tsimshian felt that they were losing control of their situation. Duncan sensed that, particularly among the young, the presence of the Europeans and the visits to

[35]Duncan to Laird, May 1875, CMSA.

[36]Fort Simpson, Journal, 5 June 1859 and following entries, and 11 October 1856, HBCA, B-201/9.

[37]Duncan to Douglas, 25 October 1860, CC, file 498; Duncan to C.M.S., 25 July 1864, CMSA.

[38]See Zaslow, "The Missionary as Social Reformer," p. 54.

Victoria had shaken Indian confidence in the old knowledge and had awakened a spirit of inquiry. He wrote in his journal that "there is generally a belief among them that the whites do possess some grand secret about eternal things and they are grasping to know it."[39] The timing of Duncan's arrival among the Tsimshian was propitious: he was there to provide an answer at a time when the Indians were being forced to ask fundamental questions.

That old Tsimshian beliefs were being called into question was dramatically highlighted at the time of the move to Metlakatla. Two days after Duncan and his followers left Fort Simpson the smallpox, brought north from Victoria, struck among the Indians. The effect of the disease provided an important object lesson for Duncan and for those Indians who were considering joining his new community. At Fort Simpson "the heathen sought refuge in their charms & lying vanities . . . they sang their heathen songs and kept the rattle of the conjurers almost perpetually going." But many hundreds were stricken with the disease, whereas at Metlakatla only five of those who had originally left with Duncan died. The Tsimshian shaman was confronted with a situation that was alien to his experience and with which he was unable to cope. All the "deceits" of the "conjurers" proved to be of no avail; it was clearly a victory for the white man's god.[40]

Another student of Duncan's mission to the Tsimshian has contended that his successes were in part the result of his ability to accommodate to Indian ways. It has also been claimed that Duncan was particularly influenced by the ideas of Henry Venn, the secretary of the C.M.S. from 1841 to 1872. Venn advocated a degree of toleration of native customs and thought that the major objective of the C.M.S. should be the establishment of "Native Chusches" run by the indigenous population.[41] But it was not Venn who went to work among the Tsimshian, and it is crucial in studying the cultural impact of any C.M.S. missionary on an indigenous population to look, not at the current missionary theory being advocated in London, but at what the individual agent actually did on the spot. There is an inherent contradiction in the argument

[39]Duncan, Journal, 14 January 1858, WDP, C.2,154.

[40]Duncan reckoned that 500 of the Fort Simpson Tsimshian caught smallpox (Duncan to C.M.S., 6 March 1863, CMSA; Duncan to Douglas, 6 March 1863, CC, file 498).

[41]See Usher, *William Duncan*, pp. 17ff; Jean Usher, "Duncan of Metlakatla: The Victorian Origins of a Model Indian Community," in W. L. Morton, ed., *The Shield of Achilles: Aspects of Canada in the Victorian Age* (Toronto and Montreal: McClelland and Stewart, 1968), pp. 293–97. Usher does not, however, provide any evidence that Duncan was particularly influenced by Venn's theories apart from the general point that Venn was secretary of the C.M.S. while Duncan was training at Highbury, nor is there any evidence in Duncan's early journals that Venn was his mentor.

that Duncan was a Victorian missionary whose "cultural reference was always London"[42] and the claim that he acted in response to Tsimshian culture. There is very little evidence that Duncan, in his dealing with the Tsimshian, was particularly tolerant of Indian customs; in fact, the evidence is overwhelmingly to the contrary. Like most missionaries, Duncan came among the Indians essentially to teach rather than to learn and to convert rather than to conserve. It was, for instance, true that Duncan was prepared to close his school to allow the Indians to participate in the spring fishing. Clearly, Indians who came to school starving would not make particularly receptive pupils. Duncan was, however, adamantly determined not to close the school when Tsimshian leaders claimed that it interfered with the winter ceremonial. This was the kind of rigid policy that, by provoking the hostility of Tsimshian leaders, very nearly led to disaster. It is also very dificult to see that "Duncan was at great pains" to treat the Tsimshian chiefs "as they were treated by their own people,"[43] when he was making every effort to destroy the potlatch that was the major basis of their authority. It was impossible to attack the ritual that validated chieftainship and not lower the authority of the chiefs.

Duncan did make minor concessions to Tsimshian culture while he was at Fort Simpson and his position among the Indians was tenuous, but the move to Metlakatla was an emphatic assertion of his desire to disengage his followers from Indian culture. The object was to draw the Indians "out of the miasma of heathen life, and away from the deadening and enthralling influence of heathen customs."[44] The point of moving to Metlakatla was to isolate converts from Indian customs, not to foster their continued existence. Metlakatla was to be a community that was to be in contrast with, not similar to, other Indian villages. One only has to look at the rules that Duncan laid down for residents at Metlakatla to see just how radical the break with the Indian past was. Duncan required his followers

1)   To give up their *Ahlied* or Indian devilry.
2)   To cease calling in conjurers when sick.
3)   To cease gambling.
4)   To cease giving away their property for display.
5)   To cease painting their faces.
6)   To cease drinking intoxicating liquor.
7)   To rest on the Sabbath.
8)   To attend religious instruction.
9)   To send their children to school.

[42]Usher, "Duncan of Metlakatla," Morton, p. 307.
[43]See Duncan, Journal, 14 December 1858, CMSA; and cf. Usher, *William Duncan*, p. 53.
[44]Duncan to Laird, May 1875, CMSA.

10) To be cleanly.
11) To be industrious.
12) To be peaceful.
13) To be liberal and honest in trade.
14) To build neat houses.
15) To pay the village tax.

Here was the essence of the change that not only Duncan, but most of the missionaries in British Columbia, hoped to bring about among the Indians. Five regulations prohibited traditional Tsimshian customs integral to the Indians' old way of life, and ten more were designed to establish a new one. And these were only the minimal requirements that Duncan expected of those who joined him. He knew very well that obeying these injunctions meant giving up the customs that were "most *dear* to the heathen Indians" and that for many Indians to surrender to his regulations was "like the cutting off the right hand & plucking out the right eye."[45] Christianity at Metlakatla was to mean the subversion of every "evil" Indian custom, and according to Duncan there was to be no compromise. This was not the kind of gradual change that Venn had advocated.[46]

Duncan was quite consciously trying to replace the Indian past with a future based on the precepts of Victorian England. The site of Metlakatla may have been Indian, but the village itself was Victorian. Duncan did concede minor points to the Indians. In the first houses that were built at Metlakatla Duncan permitted more than one nuclear family to live in each dwelling, although in different rooms. This kind of compromise does not, however, deny the thoroughness of the social changes that he made. To many observers the houses at Metlakatla still seemed to be "similar to labourers cottages at home," and inside those homes Duncan himself wanted to see the Indians surrounded by all the Victorian trappings.[47] The houses were arranged according to the European manner, in streets running at right angles to the coast, rather than in a single line facing the water. Metlakatla was a model of Victorian order and regularity. Dominating the village was the massive church; not built according to any Indian pattern, but with arched windows, crenellations, flying buttresses, and all the features of the European mason's craft assiduously carpentered into northwest coast cedar.

In the organization of the village there were apparent concessions to the

[45]Duncan to C.M.S., 28 April 1862 and 6 March 1863, CMSA.
[46]Duncan to Laird, May 1875, CMSA; see also Usher, "Duncan of Metlakatla," Morton, p. 296.
[47]Usher, "Duncan of Metlakatla," Morton, p. 303; Robert Doolan to C.M.S., 14 July 1864, and Rev. Edward Cridge to C.M.S., 27 September 1867, CMSA; Duncan, Journal, 17 November 1863, WDP, C.2,155.

Indians that were not really concessions at all. Duncan refused to permit certain Christian rituals to be celebrated at Metlakatla, not just because he thought that they would be misunderstood by the Indians, but also because his refusal to accept ordination disqualified him from conducting the sacraments of the Church of England.[48] Law and order was maintained at Metlakatla by a group of twenty uniformed constables, but the fact that Duncan selected Indians for these positions would seem to be not so much the result of "remarkable insight"[49] as of the simple reality that there was no one else around to carry out these duties. Discipline at Metlakatla was strict and rigorously administered, with a severity that some missionaries objected to.[50] The government of village affairs was nominally in the hands of a native council of twelve, but effectively Duncan was the ruler. Clan divisions and obligations were not recognized at Metlakatla, polygamy was disallowed, and patrilineal inheritance replaced the old matrilineal Tsimshian system.

According to missionary propaganda, Metlakatla elevated the Tsimshian from being "savages of the most degraded and ferocious kind" to "decent orderly Christians," who were now to be seen "clothed and in their right mind, and sitting at the feet of Jesus."[51] Both Indians and Europeans were impressed with the contrast between the Christian Indians and those of the surrounding tribes, and none more so than Admiral Arthur Cochrane, who visited Metlakatla in 1873 and on observing the Indians at work was prompted to exclaim "I say these men are not Indians, they are white men."[52]

At Metlakatla Duncan was the source of all authority, both religious and secular, and in this respect he deviated from the missionary theory of Henry Venn. For Venn the most important function of the C.M.S. missionary was to train members of the indigenous population as pastors so that they could take over the missionaries' role. Venn believed that the missionary who did not educate an indigenous ministry to replace himself was building on an insecure foundation. The missionary should, therefore, avoid putting himself before the people as a leader. According to Venn, "prompting to self-action is more

[48]Cf. LaViolette, *Struggle for Survival*, p. 27; and Usher, *William Duncan*, p. 111.
[49]Usher, "Duncan of Metlakatla," Morton, p. 306.
[50]Owen to C.M.S., 9 October 1867, CMSA.
[51]*Church Missionary Intelligencer*, May 1872, p. 153; Columbia Mission, *Report of the Columbia Mission . . . 1866* (London: Rivingtons, 1866), p. 34.
[52]Doolan, Journal, 29 January 1866, and Doolan to C.M.S., 14 July 1864, CMSA; Seymour to Buckingham, 27 September 1867, CO.60/29; speech of Dufferin delivered at Victoria, 20 September 1876, in Henry Milton, ed., *Speeches and Addresses of the Right Honourable Frederick Temple Hamilton Earl of Dufferin* (London: John Murray, 1882), p. 211; Lady Dufferin, *Journal*, 29 August 1876, p. 206; George Davis, *Metlakahtla: A True Narrative of the Red Man* (Chicago: Ram's Horn Company, 1904), p. 75; Duncan to C.M.S., 29 January 1874, CMSA.

important than inducing men to follow a leader."[53] These concepts, which Venn developed in response to the specific problems faced by C.M.S. missionaries in East Africa, were not applied by Duncan at Metlakatla. Duncan was a proud, determined man who could tolerate no limitation on his leadership, either by a European or an Indian. He was a man who enjoyed the praise of others. In his early journals he reprimands himself for his pride and his enjoyment of the admiration of the other students at Highbury. As a missionary on the northwest coast Duncan relished the notoriety and acclaim that his work brought him among the European population as much as the adulation that he received from his Tsimshian followers.[54] He was not willing to share these advantages of leadership with anyone. At Metlakatla Duncan's rule was absolute. The Tsimshian may have chosen the site, but it was Duncan who ran the village. As one of the misionaries who tried to work with Duncan complained, "even the most trivial and private matter is known to & controlled by Mr. Duncan from whose decision there is no appeal."[55]

Contrary to Venn's exhortation that the missionary should not become indispensable to his followers, Duncan led the people of Metlakatla in all things. Duncan's authority as religious leader of the settlement was augmented by secular power when he was appointed justice of the peace in 1863. This position made Duncan a representative of British law on the coast and enabled him to call on the assistance of the Royal Navy. At least one governor felt that Duncan was "a little too fanatical to be trusted with the direction of the proceedings of a ship of war 500 or 600 miles from Head Quarters,"[56] but the fact that he could call on vessels of war to buttress his authority greatly enhanced his power over the Indians. Yet another role that Duncan assumed was the control of the commercial dealings of the settlement. Duncan described his position in the village this way.

> I saw it to be necessary that I should for a time be everything to this settlement & the Indians naturally & confidently look to me to be everything to them;—thus I have placed myself at the head of their trade,—I am appointed their magistrate,—they pay their taxes to me,—I carry on their public works, as well as attend to the duties which properly belong to my sphere.[57]

[53]*Church Missionary Intelligencer*, April 1860, p. 90; see also Jean Usher, "Apostles and Aborigines: The Social Theory of the Church Missionary Society," *Social History* 7 (1971): 42ff; Henry Venn, *Retrospect and Prospect of the Operations of the Church Missionary Society* (London: Seeley, Jackson and Halliday, 1865), p. 5.

[54]Duncan, Journal, 18 November 1853, 21 March 1854 and 25 June 1857, WDP, C.2,154; *British Colonist*, 9 June 1863; Duncan to C.M.S., 4 December 1870, CMSA.

[55]Owen to C.M.S., 9 October 1867, CMSA.

[56]Seymour to Buckingham, 30 November 1868, CO.60/33.

[57]Duncan to C.M.S., 23 January 1864, CMSA.

The trouble with positions of leadership like this is that they tend to become self-perpetuating. Outside observers felt that Duncan ran his mission in an autocratic and patriarchal manner, and A.C. Anderson was probably correct when he wrote that the weakness of the Metlakatla system was that if Duncan died, "the whole edifice which he has founded with so much pains, would probably crumble to the ground." Nor was Anderson alone in that opinion. Joseph Trutch also thought that if the mission was deprived of Duncan's presence then much of the good work would be undone.[58] Moreover, Duncan could tolerate no one who might threaten to usurp his position. No Tsimshian pastors were ordained during the thirty years that he worked among them. None of the other missionaries that the C.M.S. sent out to work with him, either ordained or lay, stayed at Metlakatla for long. Some of them departed for other reasons, but many left because they found Duncan impossible to work with. Similar factors lay behind Duncan's disagreement with Bishop William Ridley in the 1880's and his final rift with the C.M.S. If, as Venn had advocated, the first object of the mission was to train Indians to take over the leadership, then it would not have mattered whether Duncan or Ridley was the pre-eminent representative of the C.M.S. at Metlakatla.

Many missionaries in British Columbia, of various denominations, followed Duncan's example: both the specific example of Metlakatla and the general example of trying to introduce a new way of life to the Indians. Few, however, were able to emulate Duncan's success. Other missionaries lacked Duncan's drive and determination and were unable to isolate their followers so completely from outside influences. Moreover, other Indian groups proved to be less tractable than the Tsimshian. For example, the Roman Catholic missionaries who worked for over ten years at Fort Rupert made very little impression on the Kwakiutl.

There were C.M.S. missionaries who spent some time at Metlakatla before moving to establish missions of their own. The first of these offshoot missions was established at Kincolith on the Nass River. Work among the Nishga was begun by the Reverend Robert Doolan in 1864, and three years later the mission was taken over by the Reverend Robert Tomlinson. It was Tomlinson's objective to change the Nishga "from ignorant bloodthirsty cruel savages into quiet useful subjects of our Gracious Queen," and to this end he founded the

---

[58]Clement Cornwall to superintendent general of Indian affairs, 8 December 1887, RG10, vol. 3,776, file 37,373-2; Morison, "Reminiscences," p. 28; Oskar Teichmann, ed., *A Journey to Alaska in the Year 1868: Being a Diary of the Late Emil Teichmann* (New York: Argosy-Antiquarian, 1963), p. 118; Anderson, *Dominion at the West*, pp. 95–96; Trutch to the officer administering the government, 22 June 1869, CC, file 954; see also I. W. Powell to superintendent general of Indian affairs, 26 August 1879, Canada, Department of the Interior, "Annual Report . . . 1879," Canada, *Sessional Papers*, 4th Parl., 2d sess., 1880, no. 4, p. 117.

mission village at Kincolith on the same principles as Metlakatla.[59] Further expansion occurred in the 1870's. The Haida had frequently visited Metlakatla in order to trade; they had observed the mission there and often asked for a missionary to come and work amongst them on the Queen Charlotte Islands. In response to these requests the Reverend W.H. Collison established himself at Massett in 1876. Two years later the Reverend A.J. Hall began work at Fort Rupert, which had been abandoned by the Roman Catholics. Later he moved his mission to Alert Bay. In 1883 Aiyansh was established up the Nass River and placed in the charge of the Reverend J.B. McCullagh, who also modelled his village on Metlakatla.

In 1860 the newly arrived Bishop of Columbia, George Hills, went on a tour to inspect his new diocese. Crossing over from Victoria to New Westminster, he travelled up the Fraser River as far north as Lillooet. In the following few years Anglican missionaries, under the auspices of the Society for the Propagation of the Gospel in Foreign Parts, began to work among the Indians at many places that the bishop had visited. By the end of the decade the society's missionaries were active in Victoria, Cowichan, Saanich, Nanaimo, Comox, Alberni, New Westminster, Yale, Hope, Lytton, the Cariboo, and Kincolith.[60]

Perhaps the most successful of these missionaries was the Reverend J.B. Good, who was stationed first at Nanaimo and then at Yale. While he was at Yale, Good received a request from the Lytton Indians to go and work amongst them. Good thought that the upper Thompson, who lived a "free independent life on horseback," were Indians "of a superior order."[61] So in 1867 he moved north and began a mission amongst the once warlike Lytton Indians. Before he went to work with them Good had pointed out to the Lytton people "all their manifold hypocrisy, uncleanness, and idleness, and many other sins and evil practices," and he had warned them that things would have to change. Accordingly, Good began his mission by attacking such customs as shamanism and polygamy as well as teaching Christianity. In an effort to reduce disease he advocated new methods of sanitation, and he tried to direct the Indians towards "the formation of habits of steady industry, economy and sobriety." In the first months of his mission he started a boys' school to instil "habits of instant obedience." Within a few years Good had acquired a piece of land a small distance from the "evil influences" of Lytton township. He built a church on the site, and Saint Paul's became the centre of

---

[59]Tomlinson to Trutch, 25 January 1870, Tomlinson to Archdeacon Woods, 31 October 1871, CMSA.

[60]*Report of the Columbia Mission . . . 1869* (London: Rivingtons, 1869), p. 79.

[61]John Booth Good, "The Utmost Bounds: Pioneer Jottings of Forty Years Missionary Reminiscences of the Out West Pacific Coast, 1861–1900," PABC, unpaginated; *Report of the Columbia Mission . . . 1867* (London: Rivingtons, 1867), pp. 67, 80; *Report of the Columbia Mission . . . 1868* (London: Rivingtons, 1868), p. 35; *Report of the Columbia Mission . . . 1874* (London: Rivingtons, 1874), p. 13.

his mission. In the Indian villages of the surrounding area he worked to secure the allegiance of the chiefs, and he appointed Indians as watchmen to observe and report on the behaviour of community members. Good was less authoritarian than Duncan, but these measures are reminiscent of the Metlakatla system, and, like Duncan's, Good's aim was to "carry out a perfect code of social and domestic reform."

Roman Catholic missionaries also spread out from southern Vancouver Island over the mainland during the 1860's, beginning the "grand task" of converting and "civilizing" the Indians.[62] From the centre in Esquimalt the Oblate Vicar of Missions to Oregon, Father Louis D'Herbomez, directed the work of his order in British Columbia. The first mainland station was established in 1859 when Father Charles Pandosy was sent to work among the Okanagan Indians. Other stations were established at Kamloops and Williams Lake, but it was in the lower Fraser Valley that their influence was strongest. In 1861 Father Leon Forquet established Saint Mary's mission near the site of the present Mission City, and it became an important centre for disseminating Roman Catholicism among the Salish. The Indian schools at Saint Mary's placed particular emphasis on industrial education, and some government officials were impressed with the results achieved.[63] These schools were organized along lines that were advocated as the most effective for re-educating Indians. Day schools were held to be unsatisfactory because they only allowed temporary contact with the pupils. What was felt necessary were industrial and agricultural schools, "where the children are lodged, boarded and clothed" and where they could "spend several years in acquiring regular habits of order and discipline and a taste and liking for work."[64] By removing Indian children from traditional influences, such schools were designed to be a primary means of acculturation, as were the Christian communities that the Roman Catholics developed among the Sechelt Indians during the 1860's.

These communities were not dissimilar from the pattern at Metlakatla. Indians who joined villages established according to the Oblates' "system" were required to build new houses after the European pattern, and in each community the dominating building was the church. Like Duncan, the priests required their followers to adhere to a set of rules which demanded that the Indians give up old customs such as dancing, gambling, potlatching, and patronizing the shaman, and they also had to pledge to abstain from intoxi-

[62]*Missions de la Congregation des Missionaires Oblats de Marie Immaculée* (Paris: A. Hennuyer, 1862), 1: 101.

[63]Rev. Leon Fouquet to Douglas, 11 April 1864, CC, file 584; Birch to Carnarvon, 25 October 1866, CO.60/25.

[64]A. Louis to the Honourable H. L. Langevin, 29 September 1871, Canada, Parliament, *British Columbia Report of the Hon. H. L. Langevin, C.B., Minister of Public Works* (Ottawa: J. B. Taylor, 1872), p. 159; see also Fouquet to Douglas, 11 April, 1864, CC, file 584.

cating liquor. Control of each village was in the hands of a few "chiefs," often appointed by the missionaries. Other Indians were designated to police the rules of the community. These "watchmen" reported on the conduct of the village people, a system of "spying on other Indians" that some observers found objectionable.[65] The Roman Catholic Church had centuries of missionary experience behind it, and its missionaries were usually more tolerant of traditional Indian customs than were the Protestants, so there was probably a greater degree of syncretism in Roman Catholic villages than there was at Metlakatla. Nevertheless, the "system" had considerable cultural impact on the Indians. In 1871 the sacrament of confirmation was administered to all the Sechelt Indians, and observers also reported considerable change in the secular culture of the Indians.[66]

The third major denomination whose missionaries were active among the Indians of British Columbia in the 1860's was the Methodist. In February 1859 the Reverends Ephraim Evans, Arthur Browning, Ebenezer Robson, and Edward White arrived in Victoria, the first Methodist missionaries to begin work among the Indians. These men divided their time between the Indians and the European population, and this practice limited their influence among the Indians. It was the young, enthusiastic Thomas Crosby who developed the Indian mission as a separate entity, and he was to be instrumental in plucking many "brands from the burning." Working first as a lay missionary but later ordained, Crosby began his missionary career at Nanaimo in 1863, then he moved to the Chilliwack area, and in 1873 he established a mission at Port Simpson. In the course of his career Crosby waged a total war against Indian customs. At Nanaimo the chiefs tried to extract concessions from Crosby. If they could be allowed to continue their dances, they promised to attend church and send their children to school. Dancing was not very evil, they said, and they ought to be able "to keep up a little of what their fathers told them." But Crosby was obdurate. He told the Indian leaders he could have nothing to do with the old way, "the dance, the potlatch etc., it is all bad." The Indians whispered among themselves that the missionary was as immovable as a post.[67] Crosby, like other Methodist missionaries, placed a great emphasis on itinerant preaching and camp meetings as a means of evan-

---

[65]Sproat to the minister of the interior, 7 December 1876, RG10, vol. 3,611, file 3,356(5). For accounts of the Roman Catholic "system" see Duff, *Indian History of B.C.*, p. 91; Morice, *History of the Catholic Church*, pp. 351–52; and Edwin M. Lemert, "The Life and Death of an Indian State," *Human Organization* 13 (1954): pp. 23–27. For some criticisms of Lemert's article see Jacqueline Judith Kennedy, "Roman Catholic Missionary Effort and Indian Acculturation in the Fraser Valley 1860–1900" (B. A. essay, University of British Columbia, 1969), pp. 79–86.

[66]See Lemert, "The Life and Death of an Indian State," pp. 23, 25.

[67]Thomas Crosby, *Among the An-ko-me-nums or Flathead Tribes of Indians of the Pacific Coast* (Toronto: W. Briggs, 1907), pp. 104–5.

gelization. But his village at Port Simpson was in some respects modelled on Metlakatla. Once again the buildings were European in style, a code of laws banning many Indian customs was drawn up, and a council was established to administer them.[68]

The many missionaries working in British Columbia met with varying degrees of success. In some places the Indians remained aloof or were even hostile to missionary teaching. Missionaries made little impression on the boisterous, unredeemed Kwakiutl. Many Indians felt that the missionaries required them to give up too many of their old customs. This feeling was particularly strong among those who had more of an investment in the continuance of the traditional Indian way of life. So older people and Indian leaders frequently resisted the efforts of missionaries. When the C.M.S.'s Nass mission was established and the Nishga chiefs remained unmoved by Doolan's preaching, Duncan concluded that the reason must be that these leaders, realizing that on becoming Christian they would have to forgo many of the benefits of their present position, were unprepared to make the sacrifice.[69]

Unconverted Indians sometimes made efforts to reassert traditional culture against the inroads of the missionaries. Duncan wrote home of attempts among the Tsimshian to revive "heathenism." Within that group and others the effect of the missionary presence was to divide the Indians into pro- and anti-missionary factions. The consequent hostilities between the two groups produced further fragmentation in Indian society.

As well as attempts to reassert traditional Indian culture, there were also some syncretistic movements among the Indians. Good recalled one such phenomenon that had occurred during the time that he was stationed at Lytton. An Indian prophet on the lower mainland had acquired, through a vision from heaven, a secret medicine that rendered the user invulnerable from bullets or any other weapon. He also taught his adherents a kind of military drill which he claimed would make them triumphant over any foe. This prophet travelled up the Fraser River gathering followers as he went. According to Good, he was animated by a ferocious hatred of the white man and urged his followers to combine to throw the Europeans from the country. Evidently this movement fizzled out when the prophet was killed by poisoning,[70] but the appearance of such mystical religious sects is a common reaction of indigenous people to the intrusion of Europeans. A mixture of Christianity and autochthonous elements, these millenarian movements looked forward to the time when the Europeans would be driven from the land and the things

---

[68]Thomas Crosby, *Up and Down the North Pacific Coast by Canoe and Mission Ship* (Toronto: Missionary Society of the Methodist Church, 1914), pp. 65–66.

[69]Duncan to C.M.S., 12 July 1865, CMSA; see also W. H. Collison, *In the Wake of the War Canoe* . . . (London: E. P. Dutton, 1915), pp. 108–11.

[70]Good, "Utmost Bounds."

that they had usurped would be returned to their rightful owners. Many of these movements had in common the belief that their faith and ritual would preserve them from the bullets of the Europeans. Typically these sects arose at a time of cultural dislocation. They were the product of a limited acquaintance with missionary teaching, and often they indicated that the Europeans had become so dominant that more rational means of resistance were seen to be ineffectual.

Other Indians undoubtedly observed the forms, but not the substance, of the new religion. Bishop Hills noted that Indians would give their attention for a time to anyone who went amongst them with any appearance of authority. Secular observers claimed the Indians parroted the liturgy but attached no great significance to the new ceremonies and continued to indulge in their favourite vices after they had left the church.[71] Attracted by novelty or motivated by a desire for the goods and the technical abilities that the missionaries brought with them, some Indians observed the requisite formalities without necessarily being "born again." They modified some of their behaviour but not their way of thinking.

Indians might become Christian for reasons that were quite different from those that the missionaries thought were prompting them. When Crosby began baptizing large numbers of Indians at Port Simpson, Duncan wrote that the Methodist missionary "did not know (perhaps he did *not* care to know) that the poor Indians were seeking baptism from his hands *to act as a charm* for their bodily preservation."[72] Presumably Indians at Metlakatla could also have been similarly motivated.

Some parts of British Columbia, particularly in the interior, were still covered only by itinerant missionaries. These men scarcely remained in one place long enough to induce the Indians "to adopt the habits of civilization."[73] Other missionaries dissipated much of their energy fighting the influence of other denominations. Thus, they operated against each other. Feeling was particularly strong between the Protestants and Roman Catholics at times. The C.M.S. held that "Romanised heathenism is far more difficult to deal with than the same element in its original state." For some Protestants converting Indians from Roman Catholicism seemed as important as converting them from paganism.[74]

Notwithstanding the limitations on their effectiveness and the variations in their impact, there is no doubt that the missionaries introduced consider-

[71]Hills, Diary, 7 June 1861; Barrett-Lennard, *Travels*, pp. 149–50; Boddam-Wetham, *Western Wanderings*, pp. 304–5.

[72]Duncan to C.M.S., 29 March 1876, CMSA.

[73]Ball to colonial secretary, 28 December 1869, CC, file 101(a).

[74]*Church Missionary Intelligencer*, November 1858, p. 245; C. Bryant to Robson, 4 October 1870, Robson Papers.

able social change to many groups of British Columbia Indians. Numerous non-missionaries commented on the reformation that the missionaries had wrought among those Indians who were receptive to their teaching. When anthropologists began making field trips to British Columbia in the 1880's, they sometimes made implied criticisms of the missionaries' role as social innovators. Franz Boas said of the Lytton Indians that they "unfortunately have been Christians for a long time, and that stands very much in my way. I hear very little about olden times."[75]

At the same time then, about the end of the 1850's, the settler and the missionary began to impose major social change on Indian society. The missionaries worked within the framework of governmental coercion established by the settlement frontier. Indeed, many officials saw their programme of social renovation as the Indians' only hope for the future. Governor Douglas expressed the opinion that Duncan's work "gives rise to the gratifying hope that the Natives will yet, through God's blessing be rescued from ignorance, and assume a respectable position in British Columbia." Eight years later one of his successors, Governor Frederick Seymour, agreed with him.[76]

There was, however, a vast difference between the changes introduced by the settlers and those that the missionaries planned for the Indians. The Indians were largely irrelevant to the settlers' concerns, and in any case it was thought that they were shortly destined for extinction. So, as far as many of the settlers were concerned, the Indians had no future. To the missionaries, however, the Indians very definitely had a future; although it was seen in terms of them ceasing to be Indians and closely imitating the whites. The belief that the Indians would soon die out, which some settlers used as an excuse to ignore their problems, was, for the missionary, a spur to immediate action.[77] The missionaries thought that the Indians could be saved from extinction if they could be turned, as quickly as possible, into red-skinned replicas of the Europeans. The missionaries were the representatives in British Columbia of the optimistic, humanitarian view that European colonization need not necessarily be an unmitigated disaster for the Indians. They believed that with appropriate action and legislation the Indians could be saved, even though their culture would be destroyed. Both settler and missionary believed that the Indian was degraded by contact with "civilization," but the missionary thought that, given the right conditions, the process could be arrested. The matter was, however, extremely urgent. Duncan thought that, unless some-

---

[75]Boas, *Diary*, 13 July 1888, Rohner, p. 100; see also Krause, *The Tlingit*, p. 215.

[76]Douglas to Newcastle, 18 October 1859, CO.60/5; Seymour to Buckingham, 27 September 1867, CO.60/29.

[77]See, for example, *Report of the Columbia Mission . . . 1863* (London: Rivingtons, 1863), p. 18.

thing was done for the Indians of the Victoria area, in five or ten years they "will have passed into the jaws of the insatiable destroyer."[78] In order to avert such a catastrophe, the missionaries planned for an Indian future in a way that many settlers thought was unnecessary.

The differing approaches of the settler and the missionary were clearly exemplified in their attitude to the Indians who lived on the reserve across the harbour from Victoria. To the settlers these Indians were irredeemable reprobates who ought to be removed from the vicinity of the town. The missionaries, on the other hand, planned for the "improvement" of the Songhees. Often they too advocated the removal of the Indians from the debilitating influence of the Europeans, but missionaries wanted removal in order to begin positive plans for social change, and not simply as a negative deferral of the issue of the Indians' survival. During the summer of 1860 Duncan spent some time in Victoria and concerned himself with the plight of the Indians there. He gave Governor Douglas a great deal of advice on how to ameliorate conditions on the Songhees reserve and outlined a plan for setting up an organized community that would have been very similar to Metlakatla had it been established.[79] The Reverend A.C. Garrett was also prominent in efforts to organize the future of the Victoria Indians. He opened a school among the Songhees and was active on an Indian improvement committee in the early 1860's. Both of these men registered their strong objections to settler opinion either that a passive policy should be adopted towards the Indians, leaving them alone to meet their fate, or that their eventual doom should be hastened by a policy of extermination. At a missionary meeting in Victoria Duncan said that the colonists would be judged by generations to come on their treatment of the Indians, either to their disgrace or their honour. Presumably the former was the case, for Duncan was disappointed in the lack of effort on the part of the government to improve the condition of the Songhees.[80]

Because of their differing conceptions of the Indians' future, missionaries and settlers sometimes clashed. Many settlers thought that the missionaries were simply wasting their time. De Cosmos wrote in the *Colonist* that the populace had "heard too much about educating Indians." He claimed that one "might as well try to turn the waters of the Fraser from their course, as to

---

[78]Duncan to C.M.S., 14 May 1861, CMSA.

[79]Memorandum of Duncan, 22 June 1860, and Duncan to Douglas, 25 October 1860, CC, file 498; Duncan to C.M.S., 24 August 1860, CMSA.

[80]Speech of Duncan to a missionary meeting, *British Colonist*, 9 June 1863 and Victoria *Evening Express*, 10 June 1863; A. C. Garrett, "Reminiscences," PABC, p. 16; Duncan to C.M.S., 14 May 1861 and 8 February 1871, CMSA.

think of reforming the older savages." The editor did concede some hope for the younger generation, providing they were removed from the influence of the Europeans.[81] In many ways the movement to protect the Indians conflicted with the chief preoccupation of the settlers. While Duncan thought that posterity would judge the colonists on the basis of their treatment of the Indians, most settlers thought that the truest test of their civilization lay in the development of roads, towns, farms, and trade. The Indians were not an important factor in any of these considerations. Most missionaries realized that any effort to secure a future for the Indians had to be based on a sound economic foundation and that culture change and economic development must go hand in hand. For them this conclusion meant that the Indians had to have sufficient land to develop an agricultural way of life. So missionaries often became advocates of the Indians' right to fair treatment over the land question. Acting as spokesmen for the Indians, they often aroused anger among the European settlers. At Metlakatla Duncan aimed to put his community on a secure economic footing by developing the village as a trading post. By vigorously developing trade at his mission station, Duncan earned the disapproval of many of the white inhabitants of the coast.[82] Often the aims of philanthropy could not be reconciled with those of colonization. Given such differences of purpose, it is ironic that the more successful the missionaries were, the more they tended to encourage settlement. To the extent that they convinced the Indians to abide by British law, they reduced the threat of violence and thus made the colony more attractive to settlers.

The missionaries aimed for a different kind of impact on the Indians than the fur traders had done. George Blenkinsop once criticized them for not following the example of the officers of the Hudson's Bay Company who confined themselves to their "legitimate business" and did not interfere in the internal disputes of Indian society. The missionaries, of course, could not agree. Duncan upbraided the fur traders for their alleged lack of concern for the bodies and souls of the Indians, and as far as he was concerned it was most definitely the "legitimate business" of the missionary to interfere with all aspects of the Indians' way of life in order to rescue them from barbarism and bring them to salvation.[83] The demands of the fur traders had been easily incorporated into Indian society, their activities being quite comprehensible to the Indians. But the missionaries were a part of the settlement frontier and required major social change of the Indians. Because the missionaries did not separate western Christianity and western civilization, they approached

---

[81]*British Colonist*, 13 March 1860.

[82]Boas to his parents, 31 October 1886, Rohner, p. 51; Whymper, *Travels and Adventures*, p. 40.

[83]Duncan to Seymour, 10 September 1868, CC, file 498; Duncan, Journal, 7 October 1857, WDP, C.2,154.

Indian culture as a whole and demanded a total transformation of the Indian proselyte. Their aim was the complete destruction of the traditional integrated Indian way of life. The missionaries demanded even more far-reaching transformation than the settlers, and they pushed it more aggressively than any other group of whites.

7

Government Administrators

The Indians really have no right to the lands they claim, nor are they of any actual value or utility to them; . . .

It seems to me, therefore, both just and politic that they should be confirmed in the possession of such extents of land only as are sufficient for their probable requirements for purposes of cultivation and pasturage, and that the remainder of the land now shut up in these reserves should be thrown open to pre-emption.[1] —JOSEPH TRUTCH, 1867

The third major acculturative agent at work among the British Columbia Indians after the establishment of the settlement frontier was the government official. Sometimes these administrators supported the efforts of the missionaries; mostly they represented the demands of the settlers; and only seldom did they advocate the interests of the Indians. The single most important exception was James Douglas. As long as he was governor of the two colonies, the Indians did have a sympathetic advocate who stood between them and the unrestrained pressure of settlement. Within the limitations of the means at his disposal, Douglas tried to protect the Indians from the worst effects of the settlement frontier. With his departure from public office, however, this restraint was removed and the Indians began to feel the full brunt of a settler-oriented set of government policies.

During the transitional years Douglas had tried to act as a mediator between the needs of the Indians and the demands of the settlers, and he continued to fulfil this role after 1858. As governor, Douglas tended to be autocratic. He often acted singlehandedly and with a minimum of consultation. Colonials, anxious to gain access to power, naturally resented Douglas's lack of enthusiasm about devolving governmental authority. For the Indians, who would be unrepresented in a settler-dominated administration, there were advantages in having a governor whose position was not dependent on the popular will and who was prepared to act in their interests.

At the time of the arrival of the gold miners the Colonial Office had urged Douglas to consider "the best and most humane means of dealing with the Native Indians." The secretary of state for the colonies, Sir Edward Bulwer Lytton, left the details of policy to the governor's "knowledge and experience"

---

[1]Trutch, Report on the Lower Fraser Indian Reserves, 28 August 1867, B.C., *Papers Connected with Indian Land*, p. 42.

but warned him that the "feelings of this country would be strongly opposed to the adoption of any arbitrary or oppressive measures towards them." In reply to this exhortation, Douglas made the same commitment to the Colonial Office that he had to his House of Assembly three years earlier: that he would make every effort to ensure that all the "civil and agrarian rights" of the Indians were protected.[2] Douglas's expectations for the Indians were well expressed in his hope that Duncan's mission to the Tsimshian would have the effect of raising the Indians to "a respectable position in British Columbia."[3] He wanted to see the Indians treated as much as possible on a level of equality with the whites, with the eventual objective being assimilation into settler society. Douglas thought that as friends and allies the Indians could render valuable assistance to the colony, and he knew that their enmity would lead to much suffering among the settlers and would retard the development of the colony.[4]

Concerned about the "numberless evils" that would flow from Indian hostility, Douglas agreed with the need to treat them with "liberality and justice."[5] It was on this premise that he acted in his efforts to establish law and order in the gold fields. He was determined to impress upon the minds of the miners "the great point that the law will protect the Indians equally with the white man."[6] Using the Australasian example, Douglas appointed gold commissioners, who also acted as policemen, magistrates, and Indian agents in the gold fields. When selecting these officers Douglas looked for men who had some knowledge of the Indian character and who could administer the laws with "propriety and discretion," although the shortage of good candidates in the new colony meant that these ideals were not always lived up to. Douglas advised the Indians to seek redress through these representatives of British law rather than through the traditional modes of retaliation.[7] Douglas's personal capacity for settling disputes was strikingly demonstrated during the conflict at Hill's Bar in 1858. Strong words were said to each side. The miners were told that the law would protect the Indians no less than the white man, and Douglas took one of the Indians involved in the affray into the government service. Douglas wrote that the man was "an Indian highly connected in

---

[2]Lytton to Douglas, 31 July 1858, Great Britain, Colonial Office, Despatches to Vancouver Island; Douglas to Lytton, 11 October 1858, CO.60/1; Douglas, address to House of Assembly, 12 August 1856, Vancouver Island, House of Assembly, Minutes.

[3]Douglas to Newcastle, 18 October 1859, CO.60/5.

[4]Douglas to Lytton, 14 March 1859, CO.60/4.

[5]Ibid.; and Carnarvon to Douglas, 11 April 1859, Great Britain, Colonial Office, Despatches to British Columbia, 1859–1871, PABC.

[6]Douglas to Lytton, 11 October 1858, CO.60/1.

[7]Douglas to Newcastle, 22 March 1860, CO.60/7; Douglas to Stanley, 15 June 1858, CO.60/1; Douglas to Newcastle, 9 October 1860, CO.60/8.

their way, and of great influence, resolution and energy of character" and that he proved to be "exceedingly useful in settling other Indian difficulties."[8]

Douglas was determined that disputes between Indians and miners were to be treated with caution. Subordinates who dealt circumspectly with disagreements between the races were praised, while those who interfered hastily were reprimanded. Douglas expressed his approval of an official who made no attempt to punish the Indians for offences merely alleged to have been committed during a quarrel with miners. Such action would have been tantamount to waging war on the Indians who were, to all intents and purposes, Her Majesty's subjects and entitled to the protection of the law.[9]

Douglas wanted to be judicious, and yet he was firm on the need to maintain law and order. His placement of government officials at likely trouble spots usually had the desired effect. An Indian agent in the Oregon Territory, noting that in British Columbia treatment of the Indians was more conducive to peace between the races, argued that the colony's system of government placed greater restraint on the lawless class in society. He explained that while there was more individual freedom in the United States, in the gold mining areas of British Columbia the government official's tenure was not dependent on the mood of the populace.[10] As a consequence, vigilantism, the American response to the absence of effective law enforcement on the frontier, did not flourish in British Columbia, and the Indians were afforded a greater degree of protection.

Douglas also continued efforts to keep peace on the coast, but again his intention was that the law should protect the Indians as much as the whites. Both in Victoria and up the coast, Douglas used the vessels and men of the Royal Navy to settle disputes between Indians and Europeans and, increasingly, to intervene in intertribal hostility. In Victoria the colonists were still apprehensive about the possibility of an attack on the settlement by the northern Indians, and many fabricated reports of Indian attacks were circulating.[11] While acknowledging that there were isolated incidents of violence, Douglas thought that there was no real cause for alarm. When there was a real need to do so he intervened. In 1859 there was a conflict between the Tsimshian and Haida at Victoria, and he assembled a military force and interceded to prevent any threat to the town. The Colonial Office approved of this action, but

[8]Douglas to Stanley, 15 June 1858, CO.60/1.

[9]Douglas to Colonel Hawkins, 1 July 1861, Vancouver Island, Governor, Correspondence Outward, 27 May 1859–9 January 1864, Private Official Letterbook, PABC.

[10]T. W. Davenport, "Recollections of an Indian Agent," *Quarterly of the Oregon Historical Society* 8 (1907): 355.

[11]Douglas to Newcastle, 21 May 1863, CO.305/20.

at the same time cautioned Douglas that military force should be used only when absolutely necessary and then only with great caution. Further up the coast Indians were receiving lectures from naval officers on the desirability of ending intertribal warfare, and in 1860 Rear-Admiral R.L. Baynes advised Douglas that magistrates should be placed on the coast to maintain law and order and to protect the Indian against the white man.[12]

In pursuance of that objective Douglas instituted proceedings even in questions involving his former employers. In 1859 naval officers reported that there had been a dispute between Hudson's Bay Company men and the Indians at Nanaimo over the theft of the key to the company store. When the Indians were not sufficiently forthcoming on the matter, two of them were beaten up—one was flogged insensible and the other was found by a naval surgeon to have had his "arm broken and head badly damaged." Douglas set an investigation of the incident in motion, but in the end he was unable to bring charges for lack of evidence.[13]

Douglas was not able to bring justice to all Indians of this "turbulent frontier." The Indians of the west coast of Vancouver Island were particularly obstreperous, and naval vessels were frequently sent to pacify them. The first and only exclusively Indian agent appointed by Douglas, William Banfield, was also sent to this area in 1859. Banfield was instructed to stop the sale of spirits to Indians, to prevent disturbances arising among the Indians and between Indians and white men, and, if possible, to induce the Indians to abandon "their revolting and savage customs" and live "in accordance with civilised usages."[14] This was a great deal to ask of one man among a population of unruly Indians. In 1862 Banfield disappeared, and it was assumed in Victoria that he had been killed by the Indians of Barkley Sound.[15]

On the periphery it was difficult to arrange fair trials in matters involving Indians. When an Indian was shot by a European at Alberni, Gilbert Malcolm Sproat, as local magistrate, arranged an *ad hoc* inquest into the cause of death. The jury of white men first brought down a verdict that the victim had been "worried by a dog" and then after retiring to reconsider, that he "fell over

[12]Newcastle to Douglas, 22 July 1859, Great Britain, Colonial Office, Despatches to Vancouver Island; Prevost to Baynes, 18 July 1860, Richards to Baynes, 7 August 1860, Baynes to secretary of the Admiralty, 10 September 1860, Great Britain, Admiralty Correspondence, vol. 2, 1858–1860, PABC.

[13]Richards to Baynes, 31 August 1859, CC, file 1,212a; Douglas to Baynes, 1 November 1859, George Cary to acting colonial secretary, 1 November 1859, Great Britain, Admiralty Correspondence, vol. 2.

[14]Douglas to Banfield, 27 April 1859, Vancouver Island, Governor, Correspondence Outward.

[15]J. W. Pike to Rear-Admiral Denman, 27 September 1864, CC, file 1,210; *British Colonist*, 4 March 1864.

a cliff."[16] Even at the centre in Victoria the court trials of Indians involved many pitfalls. In 1860 Alfred Waddington published a four page broadsheet entitled *Judicial Murder* in which he complained that a Tsimshian Indian had been hanged on evidence obtained through an interpreter who spoke Chinook but who was not competent in either Tsimshian or English.[17] It was often difficult for the courts to decide whether Indians were providing true information or merely using the British judicial process to settle old scores. The Indian tried for murdering Banfield was acquitted on the strong suspicion that the man who gave evidence against him wanted to eliminate the accused as a dangerous member of the community. Other Indians in similar situations were less fortunate and were hanged on the basis of testimony given by individuals seeking vengence.[18] Even where there were the best of intentions on the part of officials, frontier justice was often rough and ready in its handling of Indians.

Even more than discrepancies in legal procedure, it was policy on the crucial land question, the issue that was so vital to the interests of each race, that most clearly shows the attitude of the various colonial administrations to the Indians. In this important and indicative matter Douglas attempted to treat the Indians fairly and, as in other areas, to defend their interests against the encroachment of settlers. Douglas was not opposed to the influx of agricultural settlers; on the contrary he positively encouraged it. He thought that without "the farmers aid, British Columbia must forever remain a desert," and accordingly he gave consideration to governmental measures to encourage settlement. It was particularly important to Douglas that colonization should be fostered in a way that would result in a preponderance of the "English element."[19] But he was also determined that the Indians should not be swept aside as the settlers scrambled to possess the land. Douglas was told by the Colonial Office that there were already too many instances where colonists had forgotten the claims of the Indians, and so he was instructed that when settlement began to impinge on Indian land in Vancouver Island and British Columbia, "measures of liberality and justice" should be adopted to compensate them for the surrender of their territory. This directive from Downing Street seemed fairly straightforward, but the following month a qualification was added. Douglas was cautioned to avoid laying out Indian

---

[16]Sproat, *Scenes and Studies*, p. 76.

[17][Alfred Waddington], *Judicial Murder* [Victoria, 1860], p. 1.

[18]T. L. Wood to acting colonial secretary, 24 November 1864, CC, file 54; *British Colonist*, 3 July 1863.

[19]Douglas to Newcastle, 18 October 1859, CO.60/5; Douglas to Merivale, 29 October 1858, Vancouver Island, Governor, Correspondence Outward; Douglas to Lytton, 19 February 1859, CO.60/4.

reserves that might check the progress of white settlers in the future.[20] Even the governor's instructions created a tension between the demands of the settlers and the rights of the Indians that was difficult to resolve. This tension was fundamental to the increasing inadequacy of Indian land policy during the colonial period.

Douglas's policy until 1859 was to compensate the Indians for the surrender of their land[21] and to lay out reserves in the areas that settlers were beginning to move into. He rejected the American system of removing the Indians from their traditional homes and relocating them on large, amalgamated reserves. Rightly concluding that this policy produced hostility rather than settlement, Douglas advocated that Indian reserves should always include the Indians' cultivated fields and village sites "for which from habit and association they invariably conceive a strong attachment, and prize more, for that reason, than for the extent or value of the land."[22] Having established reserves according to these principles, Douglas was equally concerned that they should not be reduced, either by the inroads of individuals or the collective action of the House of Assembly of Vancouver Island. This determination was demonstrated by his responses to efforts to have the Songhees removed from their Victoria reserve. In 1858 the secretary of state for the colonies declared that "I highly approve of the steps which you have taken, . . . with regard to the Indians."[23]

There were, however, new factors beginning to place limitations on Douglas's freedom to act according to his own precepts. Following his appointment as governor of the gold colony in 1858 and the consequent severance of his ties with the Hudson's Bay Company, Douglas could no longer dip into the company stores for the goods that he had given to the Indians as compensation for the surrender of their land. At the same time, the Indians were becoming more aware of the value of their land, and the cost of extinguishing their title was increasing. A new source of cash was required, but none proved

[20]Lytton to Douglas, 11 April 1859, CO.305/10; Lytton to Douglas, 20 May 1859, B.C., *Papers Connected with Indian Land*, p. 18.

[21]There would appear to be some discrepancy between Douglas's claim that he continued the practice of purchasing Indian land until 1859 (Douglas to Newcastle, 25 March 1861, B.C., *Papers Connected with Indian Land*, p. 19) and the fact that the last of the treaties was made at Nanaimo in 1854. His reference to 1859, however, probably related to a land purchase made by William Banfield, a government Indian agent, from the Indians of Barclay Sound (see deed of land purchase, 6 July 1859, Hudson's Bay Company, "Register of Land").

[22]Douglas to Lytton, 14 March 1859, B.C., *Papers Connected with Indian Land*, p. 17.

[23]Lytton to Douglas, 24 August 1858, Great Britain, Colonial Office, Despatches to British Columbia.

available. This problem was made abundantly apparent when settlers began moving into the Cowichan-Chemainus district of Vancouver Island. During his expedition to the Cowichan area to apprehend the Indian who had attacked Thomas Williams in 1856, Douglas had been impressed by the valley and the prospects that it held for settlers. Within three years settlers were moving into the area, the Cowichan were becoming uneasy about the activities of survey parties, and even some colonists were demanding that, in their own interests, Indian title to the area be extinguished. In 1850 the Cowichan had offered to sell their land and Douglas had turned them down, but now the Indians were divided over the question of selling. One party was in favour of a sale while another, including mostly young men, was opposed. Douglas anticipated trouble in "adjusting" these differences between the Indians,[24] but the real trouble was to come from elsewhere.

"Want of funds" rather than Indian intransigence was to prevent the extinguishing of Indian title to the Cowichan-Chemainus district. In 1860 the colonial estimates included the provision of £2,000 to purchase Indian title to the Chemainus district. Most members of the Vancouver Island House of Assembly felt that it was the responsibility of the imperial government to provide funds for the purpose, and at a meeting on 3 July 1860 the item was stricken out of the estimates.[25] In 1861, bearing in mind "that from the dawn of modern colonisation until the present day, wars with aborigines have mainly arisen from disputes about land,"[26] the assembly petitioned the British government to provide a loan of £3,000 to extinguish Indian title to the Cowichan-Chemainus area. In London the request was placed on the bureaucratic merry-go-round. The Treasury argued that, as the Vancouver Island House of Assembly had asserted the liability of the imperial government, it was actually asking for a grant and not a loan. It was also felt at the Treasury that only land required immediately for settlement needed to be purchased and therefore that £3,000 was an excessive amount to grant.[27] In short, it was not prepared to pay. Newcastle replied to Douglas that, while he was "fully sensible of the great importance of purchasing without loss of time the native title to the soil of Vancouver Island," the acquisition of title was a purely colonial matter and the British taxpayer could not be burdened with the

[24]Douglas to Tolmie, 6 September 1856, Fort Victoria, Correspondence Outward, 1850–1858, Letters Signed by James Douglas (Unbound Letters), PABC; Douglas to Lytton, 25 May 1859, CO.305/10; *British Colonist*, 4 July 1859.

[25]*British Colonist*, 30 June and 5 July 1860; Vancouver Island, House of Assembly, Minutes, 28 June and 3 July 1860.

[26]Petition of House of Assembly to Newcastle, enclosure in Douglas to Newcastle, 25 March 1861, CO.305/17.

[27]Treasury to Sir Frederick Rogers, 25 September 1861, CO.305/18.

expense. The Colonial Office simply handed the matter back to the local legislature, saying that it should give Douglas the power to raise the loan locally.[28]

In spite of their pretensions, neither the imperial government nor the colonial authorities were prepared to allocate money to buy out Indian title to Vancouver Island. The administrators of a post-Corn Law empire were unwilling to spend money on the colonies, while the colonial legislature considered itself unable to raise the funds. Caught in the centre, the Indians of the two colonies received no compensation for the alienation of their land after 1859. The governments of Great Britain and Vancouver Island both recognized aboriginal title, but from this time reserves were laid out without treaties extinguishing their title to the land.[29]

Although he was unable to compensate the Indians for the loss of their land, Douglas continued to advocate the protection of their rights. The realities of the situation were accurately expressed when he wrote to the Colonial Office that "the Native Indian tribes are protected in all their interests to the utmost extent of our present means."[30] The chronic shortage of funds was a constant limitation on the implementation of Indian land policy. In 1862, for example, Douglas could not grant the request of the chief commissioner of lands and works for £35 to defray the costs of staking out Indian reserves.[31] Financial restrictions severely circumscribed his freedom of action, but within these limits Douglas tried to treat the Indians with favour.

When issuing instructions to those laying out Indian reserves, Douglas made it clear that the Indians were to have as much land as they wanted. In the interior reserves were laid out by the gold commissioners. Many were established by William Cox, the gold commissioner at Rock Creek in the early 1860's, whose sympathy for the Indians was evidenced by the fact that his land allocations to them were substantial by later standards. He staked out reserves in the Okanagan and on the South Thompson and Bonaparte rivers, following Douglas's orders that the Indians were to have whatever land they

---

[28]Newcastle to Douglas, 19 October 1861, B.C., *Papers Connected with Indian Land*, p. 20. This suggestion was made in spite of the fact that the Emigration Office had pointed out to the Colonial Office that without an Imperial guarantee a loan could only be raised on "disadvantageous terms" (F. W. Murdock to Rogers, 12 June 1861, CO.305/18).

[29]With the exception of treaty no. 8, initially made by the federal government in 1899 and extended in 1900 to include the Beaver and in 1910 to include the Slave, both groups occupying the northeastern corner of the province (Canada, *Indian Treaties and Surrenders* [Ottawa: Queen's Printer, 1912], 3: 290–300; Duff, *The Indian History of B.C.*, pp. 70–71).

[30]Douglas to Lytton, 5 November 1858, CO.60/1.

[31]Young to Richard Clement Moody, 9 June 1862, B.C., *Papers Connected with Indian Land*, p. 24.

asked for. At Kamloops, for example, Cox laid out a reserve extending approximately six miles up the North Thompson, twelve miles along the South Thompson and running back to the mountains.[32]

The instruction that reserves were to be established "as they may be several-ly pointed out by the Indians themselves" was so frequently repeated that there is no room for doubt that this was Douglas's policy. This instruction was to be followed by all those officials laying out Indian reserves, and where the area required by the Indians appeared to be insufficient for their needs, additional areas were to be laid off.[33] On at least one occasion after a reserve had been laid out, Indian protestations that the area was not sufficient got back to Douglas, and his response was to ensure that their grievance was met. In a letter to Colonel R.C. Moody, the chief commissioner of lands and works in the mainland colony, his views were clearly expressed.

> Notwithstanding my particular instructions to you, that in laying out Indian Reserves the wishes of the Natives themselves, with respect to the boundaries, should in all cases be complied with, I hear very general complaints of the smallness of the areas set apart for their use.[34]

This observation was followed by instructions to Moody to investigate the complaints and to enlarge the reserves sufficiently to remove all cause for objection by the Indians. In response to the criticism, Moody claimed that the "interests of the Indian population are scrupulously, I may say jealously regarded by myself and every officer and man under my command."[35] But there had been other dissatisfaction expressed about Moody's department. Settlers claimed that land had been reserved by the lands and works depart-ment and subsequently thrown open to pre-emption without sufficient notice, so that only members of the department could benefit. There were also sug-gestions that rather too many pieces of land were recorded in the names of government servants, particularly those in the lands and works department.[36] Douglas sometimes had difficulties with his local officials, and he felt that Moody in particular was inclined to be insubordinate. In this case the gover-nor ordered that all government and Indian reserves should be publicized so that it was quite clear what land was available for pre-emption.

---

[32]Cox to Moody, 31 October 1862, ibid., p. 26.

[33]See, for example, Moody to Cox, 6 March 1861, Good to Moody, 5 March 1861, Parsons to Turnbull, 1 May 1861, ibid., pp. 21–22; Young to chief commissioner of lands and works, 11 May 1863, CC, file 331.

[34]Douglas to Moody, 27 April 1863, B.C., *Papers Connected with Indian Land*, p. 27.

[35]Moody to Douglas, 28 April 1863, CC, file 935.

[36]Circular letter from colonial secretary, 5 April 1861, CC, file 326.

Confusion over what land was free to be pre-empted sometimes encouraged settlers to lay claims to parts of Indian reserves. But, having established reserves in accordance with the wishes of the Indians, Douglas was equally concerned that these areas were not to be reduced by the encroachment of settlers. Europeans who took land permanently occupied by Indians in the hope that the government would later validate their claim were to be disappointed.[37] Colonists were informed that they would not be permitted to settle on Indian reserves and that the village and cultivated sites of the Indians could not be legally pre-empted. The obvious probability that the settlers would take advantage of the Indians was the reason why Douglas did not grant the Indians title to their reserves, but instead retained it in the hands of the Crown.[38] In 1858 Peter O'Reilly was supervising the survey of Hope township and, in order to facilitate matters, advised the governor that the Indian reserve adjacent to the town should be moved "to some more suitable locality." O'Reilly thought that the move could be easily accomplished "by making a trifling remuneration to the Chiefs," but a note pencilled on his letter by Douglas simply stated that "the Indians must not be disturbed."[39] While Douglas was governor of the two colonies, the Indians were on occasion permitted to add to their reserves when they wanted to re-locate a village. A reserve laid out for the Indians on the Coquitlam River later proved to be "altogether insufficient to raise vegetables enough for their own use," and Douglas had the area increased. At Langley, when the Indians wanted to re-establish their village on the other side of the river opposite the fort, they were granted a new reserve of 160 acres.[40]

During the Douglas regime the reserved lands of the Indians remained secure, and other methods of acquiring land were also open to them. In May 1862 Moody wrote to Douglas that a Squamish Indian desired to purchase a suburban lot near New Westminster. He pointed out that the lot was "at some distance from the town, so that it cannot prove an annoyance," and he requested instructions on the matter. Douglas replied to the effect that Indians could both pre-empt land and purchase town lots under similar conditions to anyone else in the colony: that is, providing they resided on the claim, built a

---

[37]Moody to Crease, 22 October 1862, British Columbia, Colonial Secretary, Correspondence Outward 1860–1870, vol. 4, PABC.

[38]Young to Cox, 6 October 1862, ibid.; Proclamation of James Douglas, 4 January 1860, British Columbia, *List of Proclamations 1858, 1859, 1860, 1861, 1862, 1863, and 1864* (n.p., n.d.), unpaginated; Ball to McLean, 21 March 1860, British Columbia, Gold Commissioner, Lytton, Correspondence Outward; Douglas to Newcastle, 18 February 1860, CO.60/7.

[39]O'Reilly to Moody, 8 December 1859, and O'Reilly to Young, 24 December 1859, CC, file 1,277.

[40]Douglas to Moody, 27 April 1863, B.C., *Papers Connected with Indian Land*, p. 27; Young to chief commissioner of lands and works, 26 June 1862, CC, file 328.

dwelling, and cleared and cultivated a certain amount of land. His immediate response to Moody's letter had been that as the Indians "are in point of law regarded as British subjects," they "are fully entitled to the rights and privileges of subjects."[41] Implicit in the decision to allow the Indians to purchase and pre-empt land was the view that culture was not racially determined and that Indians had the capacity for social "improvement" and could assimilate into white society.

Near the end of his term of office, Douglas outlined his Indian land policy to the colonists. He claimed that his policy of reserving the "village sites, cultivated fields, and favourite places of resort" of the Indians and securing them against encroachment by settlers had been "productive of the happiest effects on the minds of the Natives."[42] It would seem that his remark had some validity. Many Europeans were impressed with the positive influence that Douglas's personality and policies had on the Indians. Helmcken recalled that the Indians always felt certain of receiving "favour and justice" from Douglas, while the Reverend Edward Cridge said that Douglas's treatment of the Indians gave him "unbounded Influence" among them. After he relinquished the governorship, while many objected to other policies, most settlers agreed that his handling of the Indians had been "of vast benefit to the colony." In retrospect at least, the Indians of the two colonies were also satisfied with the treatment they had received under Douglas. More than ten years after he left office Indians still recalled and praised the manner in which he had dealt with them.[43] Yet, in spite of all this favourable reaction, nearly every aspect of Douglas's Indian policy was drastically altered after his retirement.

As long as Douglas remained in office, his strength was that he could intercede personally on behalf of the Indians and, within certain limits, protect them from the worst effects of settlement. The weakness of his policy was that it was too dependent on his own personal magnanimity and that it was never codified in any legislative enactment. The effect of the failure to establish a self-perpetuating policy soon became apparent. Because his land policy had not been established by statute, it was subject to misinterpretation and manip-

[41]Moody to colonial secretary, 27 May 1862, including memo by Douglas, CC, file 931; Young to Moody, 18 June and 2 July 1862, B.C., *Papers Connected with Indian Land*, pp. 24–25.

[42]Minutes of the meeting of the Legislative Council, 21 January 1864, British Columbia, *Journals of the Legislative Council of British Columbia* (New Westminster: R. Wolfenden, 1864), p. 2.

[43]Smith, *Reminiscences of Helmcken*, p. 199; Cridge, "Characteristics of James Douglas"; Prevost to Baynes, 31 August 1858, CO.60/2; Victoria *Evening Express*, 10 March 1864; James Lenihan to superintendent general of Indian affairs, 7 November 1875, Canada, Department of the Interior, "Annual Report ... 1875," Canada, *Sessional Papers*, 3d Parl., 3d sess., 1876, no. 9, p. 54.

ulation when men less favourably disposed towards the Indians came to power.

Many colonists found Douglas's method of government objectionable and were not particularly sorry when he left office. Although the populace also quickly tired of the new governors, in 1864 there was a hope that they would introduce a new age in the colonies. The last of the fur traders was gone from official life. In Vancouver Island the settlers were said to be delighted, "at the contrast between the *quondam* fur-trapper and his gentlemanly successor," and in British Columbia editorialists expressed the hope that the new governor would inaugurate an "enlightened" Indian policy.[44] The Indians, with good reason, were not quite so confident about the future.

Douglas was succeeded by two men, neither of whom had his interest or influence in Indian affairs. Frederick Seymour, in British Columbia, and Arthur Kennedy, in Vancouver Island, were both less substantial figures than Douglas. Of the two, Kennedy was probably more able, but his rule in Vancouver Island was only an interlude of two years in the middle of the six other governorships he occupied in various colonies. Unlike Chief Factor Douglas, both Seymour and Kennedy came as career governors, and both suffered from a malady that was not uncommon among men who moved about from post to post on the periphery of empire. It was often assumed that all "natives" were about the same and, therefore, that experience with the aborigines of one colony somehow equipped an administrator for dealing with those of another. Kennedy had already held two governorships—in Sierra Leone and Western Australia—before he came to Vancouver Island, and by virtue of that experience he felt quite competent to govern the Indians. Kennedy announced to the Indians soon after his arrival that, "I have had experience in the government of native tribes in various parts of Her Majesty's dominions and I can therefore the more easily appreciate your character."[45] Seymour, whose most recent post had been as lieutenant-governor of British Honduras, was also confident of his ability to deal with native races. Early in his governorship of British Columbia he gained local popularity and Colonial Office praise for his firm handling of the Indians responsible for the killings at Bute Inlet in 1864. This commendation seems to have upset his judgment somewhat, and he earned a rebuke from the Colonial Office when he noted in a despatch that, in the event of a real emergency, "I may find myself compelled to follow in the footsteps of the Governor of Colorado . . . and invite every white man to shoot each Indian he may meet."[46]

The policies of both governors differed in fundamental ways from those of

[44]Macfie, *Vancouver Island*, p. 322; *British Columbian*, 21 May 1864.
[45]Kennedy to Cardwell, 23 August 1864, CO.305/23.
[46]Seymour to Cardwell, 4 October 1864, CO.60/19.

Douglas. Kennedy was prepared to permit settlers to occupy parts of Indian reserves, provided it did "not involve trouble with the Indians."[47] Kennedy also thought that it was a mistake to allow an Indian reserve to exist near Victoria, thus allowing the two races to mix together "to the great degradation of one, and the demoralisation of both." He therefore advocated removal. Having been a fur trader, Douglas did not think in terms of the separation of the two races, so he had no objection to the existence of the Victoria reserve. Nor did he lay out other reserves with separate development in mind. Rather, he aimed to provide the Indians with a base from which they could establish a position within colonial society. The notion that races could be separated, as was being proved in other parts of the empire, was chimerical anyway. But Kennedy knew all about dealing with "natives," and it was his considered opinion that the Indian policy of the two colonies, while it "may have been at one time expedient," is "certainly no longer necessary or possible."[48]

Efforts to suppress violence apart, Seymour operated more on the level of fatuous generalities than of establishing a sound Indian policy.[49] His professed concern for the Indians of British Columbia mostly involved dispensing largesse rather than protecting their interests. Soon after his arrival, Seymour became aware that the Indians felt that they had lost a protector and a friend with the departure of Douglas from official life. The new governor determined to demonstrate to the Indians that he had "succeeded to all the powers of my predecessor and to his solicitude for their welfare." His method of making this point clear was to extend an invitation to the Indians to come to Government House in New Westminster and celebrate the Queen's birthday. On the first of these occasions, in 1864, a luncheon was provided at the expense of the government; but the guests were informed that the rewards "to all good Indian Chiefs" would be greater next time.[50] Accordingly, Seymour requested the colony's agents in London to forward "one hundred small cheap canes with silver gilt tops of an inexpensive kind, also one hundred small cheap English flags suitable to canoes 20 to 30 feet long." Seymour's innovation in Indian policy was to introduce a "practice which worked very successfully in Honduras, of presenting a staff of office to the chief of each friendly tribe." Understandably, some Indians were not impressed by this nonsense and ridiculed those who attended future Queen's birthday celebrations at Government House.[51]

---

[47]Memo of Kennedy on John Companion to Kennedy, July 1865, CC, file 343.

[48]Kennedy to Cardwell, 1 October 1864, CO.305/23.

[49]See address of Seymour to the Legislative Council of British Columbia, 12 December 1864, B.C., *Journals of the Legislative Council*, pp. 4–5.

[50]Seymour to Cardwell, 31 August 1864, and enclosure, CO.60/19.

[51]Seymour to Cardwell, 23 September 1864, CO.60/19; Seymour to Cardwell, 7 June 1865, CO.60/22.

These gatherings did, however, provide some Indian leaders with an opportunity to express their opinion on matters that concerned them more acutely than free luncheons and gilt canes. On at least three occasions the Indians present at the celebrations petitioned Seymour to protect their reserves.[52] The first time his reply was clear "you shall not be disturbed in your reserves." Three years later the reply was a little more equivocal, as the Indians were assured that their reserves would not be reduced without Seymour's personal inspection.[53] The actual wording of the replies is, however, immaterial. While Seymour was making reassuring gestures at Queen's birthday celebrations, his chief commissioner of lands and works was carrying out a reallocation of reserves that involved a considerable reduction in size, and there is no evidence that Seymour visited any of the reserves concerned. In relation to the Indians' land, Seymour's professed "solicitude for their welfare" was verbal rather than real.

The imperial authorities, who had been so concerned about the treatment of the Indians in 1858, took less interest in their welfare after 1864. British Columbia was established during a period of downturn in enthusiasm for empire. Moreover, British Columbia and Vancouver Island were never among the most crucial concerns of the imperial authorities, and other colonies demanded, and got, more attention.[54] When the British government refused to help pay the cost of suppressing the Chilcotin Indians in 1864, local newspapers did not miss the point that the mother country was currently financing a war against the Maoris in New Zealand.[55] But the imperial government remained unwilling to spend money on a colony "which has been forced into existence by its gold discoveries."[56] Just as it was unwilling to pay the expenses of the colony, the Colonial Office did not pay much attention to British Columbia's Indian policy. It is quite untrue to say that "the land policy of the Imperial Government effectively restrained the actions of the colonials and their local officials" in British Columbia.[57] Britain's mild commitment to

---

[52]Enclosures in Seymour to Cardwell, 31 August 1864 and 7 June 1865, CO.60/19 and 21; Seymour to Carnarvon, 19 February 1867, CO.60/27.

[53]Enclosure in Seymour to Cardwell, 31 August 1864, CO.60/19; Seymour to Carnarvon, 19 February 1867, CO.60/27.

[54]Nor have the two colonies been given much attention by imperial historians. In *The Cambridge History of the British Empire*, for instance, the history of British Columbia before 1871 is dealt with in three pages.

[55]*British Columbian*, 21 December 1864.

[56]Lytton to Douglas, 29 May 1859, Great Britain, Colonial Office, Despatches to British Columbia.

[57]LaViolette, *The Struggle for Survival*, p. 101. Unfortunately, LaViolette does not cite any of the "several historical studies" which he claims have established this point; and he introduces an element of confusion by saying (p. 101) that the land policy of the imperial government effectively restrained local officials but then (p. 104) that "the Colonial Office . . . was quite powerless to exercise local control."

fair treatment of aborigines was of little help to the British Columbia Indians. It was the men on the spot who formulated and executed Indian land policy in the colony after 1864.

Policy-makers in the colonies were not a third party acting as an arbitrator between Indian and European but men who were deeply involved in the society of settlers. They were dealing with matters that intensely affected their own lives and so were hardly likely to be objective. The humanitarians in Britain had long advocated that native policy should be added to the four other areas that Durham's report had recommended as being imperial responsibilities. They assumed that settlers would, if given the opportunity, oppress the aborigine and therefore urged that Indian affairs should not be controlled by colonists. During the debate in the British House of Commons on the establishment of the colony of British Columbia, Henry Labouchere, once a secretary of state for the colonies, also advocated the need for a strong executive to prevent white settlers from molesting the Indians. When Douglas had been appointed governor of Vancouver Island, it was partly because, as a fur trader, he would protect the Indians from the "mere caprice of ordinary settlers," but now Indian policy was firmly in the hands of those capricious settlers.[58]

The restraining presence of Douglas had been removed; Seymour and Kennedy were less concerned than their predecessor about Indian rights regarding land; and the Colonial Office ceased to be a moderating influence after 1864. The person who stepped in to fill this vacuum was Joseph William Trutch, who was appointed chief commissioner of lands and works for British Columbia in 1864. For the next seven years he was to have more influence on Indian land policy than any other individual. He was recommended for the post by Douglas because he was a competent surveyor and engineer,[59] not because of any ability to deal with Indian affairs. But in the absence of any other effective authority, Indian policy devolved to him.

Trutch was very much a part of settler society. He epitomized the developmental mentality which so many men brought to the colonies. He arrived in British Columbia in 1859 with eight years' experience behind him in the United States as a surveyor and farmer. After working for five years in British Columbia as a surveyor and engineer, he succeeded Colonel Moody as chief commissioner of lands and works. Trutch's interest in the gold colony in the early years was in building roads and bridges, in surveying townships and establishing farms, and in amassing a personal fortune. To him, the colony was an area of land requiring development and consequently anything, or

---

[58]Great Britain, *Hansard's Parliamentary Debates*, 3d ser., 151 (1858): 1108; Minute by Peel on Douglas to Newcastle, 28 February 1853, CO.305/4.

[59]Douglas to Newcastle, 14 September 1863, CO.60/16.

more importantly anyone, who stood in the way of that development had to be moved.

Trutch was also very much a product of imperial Britain's confidence in the superiority of her own civilization. Other races came somewhat lower on the scale of human existence than the British, and in the racial hierarchy the Indian was scarcely human at all. In a reference to the Indians of the Oregon Territory Trutch used revealing terminology. "I think they are the ugliest & laziest creatures I ever saw, & we shod. as soon think of being afraid of our dogs as of them."[60] He tended to see the indigenous American as bestial rather than human, and his view was essentially unmodified by continued contact with the Indians. Between 1859 and 1864 he employed Indians on his public works projects in British Columbia, and as chief commissioner of lands and works he visited Indian villages in many parts of the colony. Yet he continued to see the Indians as uncivilized savages. In 1872 he told the prime minister of Canada that most of the Indians of British Columbia were "utter savages living along the coast, frequently committing murder amongst themselves, one tribe upon another, and on white people who go amongst them for the purpose of trade."[61] Trutch had stereotyped the Indians as lawless and violent, and was frequently preoccupied with the need to suppress them by a show of force. Killings amongst the Indians themselves were bad enough, but an attack against Europeans was the ultimate breakdown of the colonial situation. What was needed in such cases, thought Trutch, was a theatrical demonstration of European power. The dispatch of warships to coastal trouble spots, for example, would produce "a salutary impression" on the Indians.[62] Whereas Douglas had wanted the law to operate "with the least possible effect on the character and temper of the Indians," Trutch insisted that British law must be "enforced among them at whatever cost."[63]

Douglas had mostly referred to the "Native Indians," but Trutch seldom called them anything other than savages, and he was sceptical about their capacity for "improvement." After twenty years on the northwest coast, and even a visit to Metlakatla, he was to remark that "I have not yet met with a

---

[60]Trutch to Charlotte Trutch, 23 June 1850, Joseph Trutch Papers, UBCL, folder A1.b.

[61]Trutch to Macdonald, 14 October 1872, Sir John A. Macdonald Papers, PAC, vol. 278.

[62]Trutch to secretary of state for the provinces, 16 November 1871, British Columbia, Lieutenant-Governor, Despatches to Ottawa, 14 August 1871 to 26 July 1875, PABC.

[63]Douglas to Colonel Hawkins, 1 July 1861, Vancouver Island, Governor, Correspondence Outward, Private Official Letterbook; British Columbia, *Report and Journal by the Honourable the Chief Commissioner of Lands and Works, of . . . the Visit of His Excellency the Late Governor Seymour to the North-West Coast . . .* (Victoria: Government Printing Office, 1869), p. 3.

single Indian of pure blood whom I consider to have attained even the most glimmering perception of the christian creed." The reason for this situation, according to Trutch, was that "the idiosyncrasy of the Indians of this country appears to incapacitate them from appreciating any abstract idea, nor do their languages contain words by which such a conception could be expressed."[64] There is no evidence that Trutch was particularly fluent in any of the Indian languages or that he had made any study of Indian religion, poetry, or art.

It was this archetypal colonialist who made Indian land policy from 1864 to 1871. His views regarding colonial development and the absolute inferiority of the Indian coalesced to produce something of an obsession with the idea that the Indians were standing in the way of the development of the colony by Europeans. In the minds of men like Trutch, the Indians had to be relieved of as much land as possible so that it could be "properly" and "efficiently" used by European farmers. Trutch believed British Columbia's future lay in agriculture. Therefore, the colony's development had to be fostered by "large and liberal" land grants to settlers,[65] and Indian land claims could not be allowed to hinder this development. As governor, Douglas had also been an advocate of colonial development through European settlement, but he had not allowed this view to override his concern for Indian rights. In contrast to Douglas, who wanted to protect the Indians from the progress of settlement, Trutch wanted to move them out of the way so that settlement could progress.

Under Trutch much of the land the Indians had acquired under Douglas was taken away from them. The process of whittling away the reserves began in 1865 when Philip Nind, the gold commissioner at Lytton, reported on Indian land claims in the Thompson River area. The main point of his letter to the colonial secretary was that the Indians were claiming "thousands of acres of good arable and pasture land" and that these claims had "the effect of putting a stop to settlement in these parts."[66] The areas referred to as "claims" in Nind's letter were the reserves that Cox had laid out earlier. Governor Seymour referred and deferred to Trutch on this matter, and Trutch was quite

> satisfied from my own observations that the claims of the Indians over tracts of land, on which they assume to exercise ownership, but of which

---

[64]Trutch to secretary of state for the provinces, 26 September 1871, B.C., *Papers Connected with Indian Land*, p. 101.

[65]Letter by "British Columbian," *Victoria Gazette*, 16 January 1860. A letter to his brother indicates that the one in the *Gazette* was written by Trutch (see Trutch to John Trutch, 20 January 1860, Trutch Papers, folder Al.f).

[66]Nind to colonial secretary, 17 July 1865, B.C., *Papers Connected with Indian Land*, p. 29.

they make no real use, operate very materially to prevent settlement and cultivation, in many instances beside that to which attention has been directed by Mr. Nind, and I should advise that these claims be as soon as practicable enquired into and defined.[67]

Colonists were wanting to acquire the area of the Thompson River that had been reserved for the Indians, and clearly a settler government could not allow settlement to be impeded. In a letter to Trutch the officer administering the government in Seymour's absence, Arthur N. Birch, felt that it was too late in the year to carry out a general reduction of reserves, but he noted that the governor was very desirous of reducing the Thompson River reserves and requested that Walter Moberly, the assistant surveyor general of the colony, inquire into the matter. On the basis of Moberly's report,[68] Trutch informed Birch that the reserved land was "entirely disproportionate to the numbers or requirements of the Indian tribes" and that it was "very desirable, from a public point of view, that it should be placed in possession of white settlers as soon as practicable."[69] Trutch had never taken a census of the Indians of the area, and so he could not know what their numbers were, and naturally these requirements were as Trutch, and not the Indians, assessed them. But the land was valuable, and, therefore, even though it had been reserved for them, the Indians had to make way for settlement. In October 1866 a notice appeared in the *Government Gazette* indicating that the reserves of the Kamloops and Shuswap Indians had been redefined. The so-called "adjustment" meant that out of a forty-mile stretch of the Thompson River the Indians were left with three reserves, each of between three and four square miles. The remainder of the land hitherto reserved for them was to be thrown open to pre-emption from 1 January 1867.[70]

The reallocation carried out in the Kamloops area provided a precedent when Trutch carried out a second series of reductions involving Indian reserves in the Lower Fraser area. Pressure for these cut-backs came from the settlers. In February 1867 John Robson moved in the British Columbia Legis-

[67]Trutch to colonial secretary, 20 September 1865, ibid., p. 30.

[68]Good to Trutch, 26 September 1865, British Columbia, Colonial Secretary, Outward Correspondence, September 1860–May 1872, Letters to Lands and Works Department, PABC. Seymour was absent from the colony on a trip to England from September 1865 to November 1866. Moberly to Trutch, 22 December 1865, B.C., *Papers Connected with Indian Land*, p. 33.

[69]Trutch to colonial secretary, 17 January 1866, B.C., *Papers Connected with Indian Land*, pp. 32–33.

[70]*Government Gazette*, 6 October 1866. There is no indication of how far back from the river the original reserves went, although at Kamloops Cox's original description of the reserve noted that it extended back to the mountains (see Cox to Moody, 31 October 1862, B.C., *Papers Connected with Indian Land*, p. 26).

lative Council that the governor be informed of the desirability of having the Lower Fraser reserves "reduced to what is necessary for the actual use of the Natives."[71] Again it seems that Seymour referred the matter to Trutch for a report, and once again Trutch advocated reductions. His reasoning was similar to that adumbrated in the Kamloops case. The Indians were holding good land that they were not using in a productive way; therefore, it ought to be made available to settlers. Trutch also concluded that, as in the case of the Kamloops and Shuswap reserves, there was no great need to compensate the Indians for the land that they lost. After all, wrote Trutch,

> The Indians really have no right to the lands they claim, nor are they of any actual value or utility to them; and I cannot see why they should either retain these lands to the prejudice of the general interests of the Colony, or be allowed to make a market of them either to Government *or to individuals.*[72]

Having denied the Lower Fraser Indians the right to retain even the lands that had been reserved for them under Douglas and, therefore, to compensation for land that they were relieved of, Trutch initiated the policy of "adjustment." Seymour, ignoring his promises to the Indians, authorized and approved of the action.[73] It is difficult to discover precisely how much land the Indians lost, although there can be little doubt that a considerable area was involved. The report of one of the surveyors who marked out the reserves noted that the new boundaries would open 40,000 acres for settlement.[74]

In carrying out these reductions, Trutch had changed Douglas's Indian land policy to make it fit more closely the priorities of a settlement colony. In attempting to validate his actions, Trutch, with some help from the colonial secretary, W.A.G. Young, deliberately misrepresented the nature of Douglas's instructions to his officers. Trutch also adopted the tactic of claiming, quite wrongly, that those responsible for laying out the original reserves had either exceeded or misunderstood their instructions. The consequence was that Trutch reduced reserves that Douglas considered quite satisfactory in their original form.[75]

The alterations made by Trutch were also indicative of a fundamental

---

[71]Minutes of the meeting of the Legislative Council, 11 February 1867, B.C., *Journals of the Legislative Council,* p. 16.

[72]Trutch, Report on the Lower Fraser Indian Reserves, 28 August 1867, B.C., *Papers Connected with Indian Land,* p. 42.

[73]Young to Trutch, 6 November 1867, ibid., p. 45.

[74]B. W. Pearse to Trutch, 21 October 1868, ibid., p. 53.

[75]For a more detailed discussion of these points see Robin Fisher, "Joseph Trutch and Indian Land Policy," *BC Studies* 12 (1971–72): 12–18.

change in attitude towards the position of the Indian in the colony. Men like Trutch thought that the Indians would play only a very minimal role in the future of British Columbia and therefore that they required only a minimal amount of land. Indian pre-emption of land, proposed by Douglas as the means by which the Indian could integrate into settler society, was virtually denied them in 1866. A land ordinance of that year prevented the Indians from pre-empting land without the written permission of the governor, and by 1875 there was only a single case of an Indian pre-empting land under this condition. It was Trutch's opinion that to allow Indians to pre-empt land would create an "embarrassing precedent."[76] At the same time as he was reducing Indian reserves to a minimum, Trutch was advocating measures that would increase the amount of land that a settler could acquire. His suggestion that a European, in addition to a pre-emption of 160 acres, be allowed to purchase up to 480 acres was incorporated in the 1865 land ordinance.[77] Meanwhile, he was requiring that an Indian family exist on ten acres, an area that was not only insufficient for many Indian families to subsist on but which also failed to take into account the differences in the economies of the various Indian groups.

Trutch's view that Indian reserves should be reallocated on the basis of ten acres per family was another basic change from Douglas's policy. Douglas had included in his directions to those laying out reserves in British Columbia the provision that if the area demanded by the Indians did not equal ten acres per family then the reserves were to be enlarged to that extent.[78] Instead of using ten acres as a minimum as Douglas had intended, Trutch used it as a maximum figure. When instructing O'Reilly to re-allocate the Bonaparte reserve, for example, Trutch wrote that "as a general rule it is considered that an allotment of about ten acres of good land should be made to each family in the tribe.[79] Such was never the intention of Douglas. His opinion was clear enough in his instructions at the time, but he outlined them with even greater clarity some years later. "It was never ... intended that they should be restricted or limited to the possession of 10 acres of land, on the contrary, we were prepared, if such had been their wish, to have made for their use much more extensive grants." The letter containing this statement was written by Douglas in 1874 in response to a request for information by I.W. Powell, the pro-

---

[76]British Columbia, *Appendix to the Revised Statutes of British Columbia, 1871 ,* ... (Victoria: R. Wolfenden, 1871), pp. 93–94; "Report of the Government of British Columbia on the Subject of Indian Reserves," 17 August 1875, B.C., *Papers Connected with Indian Land*, appendix, p. 4; Trutch to acting colonial secretary, 22 October 1866, CC, file 947.

[77]B.C., *Appendix to the Revised Statutes*, p. 87.

[78]Brew to McColl, 6 April 1864, B.C., *Papers Connected with Indian Land*, p. 43.

[79]Trutch to O'Reilly, 5 August 1868, ibid., p. 50.

vincial commissioner of Indian affairs. Powell had asked Douglas if during his administration there had been any particular acreage used as a basis for establishing Indian reserves. Douglas answered the specific question, but he also commented more generally that his surveying officers had instructions to meet the wishes of the Indians in every particular. "This was done with the object of securing to each community their natural or acquired rights; of removing all cause for complaint on the ground of unjust deprivation."[80] This letter in which Douglas recapitulates his policy indicates the extent to which Trutch brought radical change to the colony's dealings with the Indians and their land and makes nonsense of the claim that in laying out reserves officials throughout the colonial period followed Douglas's example.[81]

While Trutch's Indian land policies were not in harmony with those of Douglas, they were very much in tune with settler demands. To the extent that it is possible to assess the attitudes of the settlers, they coincided with Trutch's. The newspapers certainly approved the reduction policy. The *British Columbian* reported on the good service that had been done for the colony by reclaiming "a most valuable and extensive tract of land improperly given to the Indians, under a previous administration." The editor of the *British Columbian*, who claimed to be a constant defender of Indian rights, hastened to add that those rights did not include the right "to hold large tracts of valuable agricultural and pastoral land which they do not and cannot use."[82] One could always rely on De Cosmos to be forthright on Indian matters. Readers of the *Colonist* were told in 1863 that they could no more talk of Indian right to the land "than we can prate of the natural right of a he-panther or a she-bear to the soil." To the editor both the problem and its solution were simple:

> shall we allow a few vagrants to prevent forever industrious settlers from settling on the unoccupied lands? Not at all . . . . Locate reservations for them on which to earn their own living, and if they trespass on white settlers punish them severely. A few lessons would soon enable them to form a correct estimation of their own inferiority, and settle the Indian title too.[83]

Colonial newspapers also disapproved of the idea of allowing Indians to pre-empt land. The *British Columbian* was horrified at the thought of Indians

---

[80]Douglas to Powell, 14 October 1874, Sir James Douglas, Correspondence Outward, 1874, PABC. Douglas added that "This letter may be regarded and treated as an official communication."

[81]Cf. LaViolette, *The Struggle for Survival*, p .16.

[82]*British Columbian*, 24 October 1866 and 2 December 1865.

[83]*British Colonist*, 21 March 1863 and 8 March 1861.

being able to locate on land wherever they pleased and urged that they be absolutely confined to their reserves. White men, wrote the editor, would be hardly likely to want to settle where there was the possibility of having Indian neighbours on every side.[84]

These newspapers undoubtedly reflected the opinions of a good many of their subscribers. After all, one of them reminded its readers, the farming pioneers of a new country cannot be expected to have "that sentimental regard for the 'poor Indian' which certain members of the Legislative Council" have exhibited.[85]

That comment notwithstanding, the representative assemblies in both colonies reflected settler opinion on Indian land, and much of the pressure for removing the Indians from their land came from these institutions. In Victoria there were the efforts of the assembly to remove the Songhees from their reserve, and there were similar pressures on the mainland where the Legislative Council urged the reduction of reserves. One member of the British Columbia Legislative Council even felt that ten acres of land per family was unnecessarily large for the Indians.[86] Although most government members advocated the interests of the settlers, it was perhaps Trutch's own official position that most clearly pinpoints their influence on government. That the chief commissioner of lands and works should also control Indian land policy goes a long way towards explaining why it so closely mirrored the aspirations of the colonists. Because the same person was responsible for allocating land to Europeans and Indians, he could not reflect the interests of both; and because that person was Trutch, Indian rights were not considered important. British policy, and to a lesser extent Canadian policy, was formulated by men who were not so closely involved in the process of settlement.

The Indians had no constitutional body which could represent their views, but it is clear that they were unhappy about the new policies. Trutch had informed Seymour that there would be no difficulty in reducing the reserves "with the full concurrence of the Indians themselves."[87] This assurance was quite misleading. Trutch had failed to perceive, or completely ignored, Indian objections to his policy. One of the many petitions on the question forwarded to Seymour demonstrates that the Indians saw with great clarity what was happening to their land, and they did not like what they saw.

[84]*British Columbian*, 28 June 1862.

[85]*British Colonist*, 19 May 1869.

[86]Resolution by the Honorable Mr. R. T. Smith, 3 May 1864, B.C., *Journals of the Legislative Council*, p. 41.

[87]Trutch to Young, 19 November 1867, B.C., *Papers Connected with Indian Land*, p. 46.

Governor Douglas did send, some years ago his men amongst us to measure our Reserve and although they gave us only a small patch of land in comparison to what they allowed to a white man our neighbour, we were resigned to our lot . . . .

Some days ago came new men who told us that by order of their Chief they have to curtail our small reservation, and so they did to our greater grief; not only they shortened our land but by their new paper they set aside our best land, some of our gardens, and gave us in place, some hilly and sandy land, where it is next to impossible to raise any potatoes: our hearts are full of grief day and night.[88]

The petitioners went on to express their confident belief that such a measure could not have been approved by the representative of the Queen, who was "so gracious and so well disposed towards her children of the forest." Unfortunately, their confidence in Seymour was misplaced. This petition was representative of numerous protests being made by Indians about their treatment over the land question. In the late 1860's Indians from many parts of the colony were objecting to the way in which the settlers had taken their land.

Indian dissatisfaction over settler behaviour towards them made them restless and sometimes led to violence. In the absence of a satisfactory Indian policy, the government had to use coercion to contain Indian discontent. On the coast, warships continued to be used against recalcitrant Indians. Some naval officers believed that in conflicts "between the White Population and the Indians the fault is more generally on the part of the former than the latter."[89] Yet the retribution that was taken by the navy against the Indians was often harsh. When the trading vessel *Kingfisher* was captured and its crew murdered by the Indians of Clayoquot Sound, the naval vessels *Sutlej* and *Devastation* were sent to seek vengeance. In the course of trying to capture the culprits nine Indian villages and sixty-four canoes were destroyed by shelling, and thirteen Indians were killed. It probably would have been of little consolation to the Clayoquot Indians if they had read in the *Colonist* the report which noted that this action "was conducted according to the strict rules of civilized warfare."[90] The navy was not supposed to be waging a war,

---

[88]Petition from the Lower Fraser chiefs, enclosure in Fr. P. Durieu to Seymour, 6 December 1868, CC, file 503.

[89]Baynes to Douglas, 4 September 1860, Great Britain, Admiralty Correspondence, vol. 2; Richards to Baynes, 31 August 1859, CC, file 1212a.

[90]Victoria *Evening Express*, 11 October 1864. This action was authorized by Rear-Admiral Denman and approved by Governor Kennedy (see Kennedy to Cardwell, 14 October 1864 and enclosures, CO.305/23; *British Colonist*, 17 October 1864).

but conducting a police action. The shelling and destruction of Indian villages on the coast by naval vessels was not uncommon during the colonial period.

Policing interracial contact in the interior was more difficult, but the dissidents of the Chilcotin country learned in 1864 that they were not immune from British law. Governor Seymour organized two parties of men to go into the Chilcotin country to capture the murderers of the Bute Inlet road workers. One party under Cox was made up of volunteers from the gold fields and approached from Alexandria, while another under Chartres Brew advanced from Bentinck Arm. Seymour himself accompanied the latter expedition. Settlers in the interior expected harsh measures to be taken against the Chilcotin, and some believed that the government forces should exterminate the tribe.[91] Cox's force was composed mostly of Americans who were "not much disposed to relish the restraint" which the governor placed on them while carrying out the operation.[92] Seymour said that he had joined the expedition to ensure that the Indians were treated with moderation. Eventually, Klatsassin and some of the others involved in the murders were misled, either intentionally or unintentionally, into surrendering to Cox's party and were subsequently tried and executed. Other Chilcotin Indians also suffered as a result of the action taken against the killers. Because they were involved in these operations during the hunting and fishing seasons, a number of Chilcotin died of starvation during the winter of 1864–65. The Colonial Office, while warning Seymour about the danger of taking any action that might result in warfare with the Indians, was pleased with his handling of this affair.[93]

The colonial authorities were not, however, always so impressed with the vigour with which Seymour responded to disputes involving Indians. When three Metlakatla Indians were murdered by some Nass people, Seymour twice sent the gun-vessel *Sparrowhawk* to the area, but, because the conflict involved Indians only, the naval officers refused to make any arrests. In response to Seymour's claim that the matter was now taken out of his hands, · the Colonial Office had to point out to the governor that his present inaction "contrasts strongly with the stirring and expensive operations" that he took against the Chilcotin when they committed outrages against Europeans. Seymour was reminded that Indians who had "placed themselves under what

---

[91]Baxter to his brother, 10 June 1864, Sutcliffe Baxter, Correspondence Outward, PABC.

[92]Seymour to Cardwell, 9 September 1864, CO.60/19.

[93]Begbie to Seymour, 30 September 1864, CC, file 142g; Seymour to Cardwell, 8 June 1865, CO.60/22; Cardwell to Seymour, 16 July 1864, Great Britain, Colonial Office, Despatches to British Columbia.

they suppose to be the protection of British Law" were as much entitled to rely on the government for redress as any settler.[94] Seymour was finally goaded into action by the rebuke and went north on the *Sparrowhawk* himself to settle the matter. Shortly after leaving Metlakatla in June 1869, Seymour died on board ship.

Generally it had been Seymour's policy to interfere in crimes involving Indians. Early in his governorship when an Indian murdered a woman "in accordance with Indian custom," Seymour had the man arrested and tried. Presuming that Douglas had made no effort to capture Indians who killed other Indians, Seymour commented that much as he wished "to follow the Indian policy of my predecessor, I cannot sanction murder being committed in our most settled districts."[95]

Apart from taking their land and suppressing violence, the colonial government's policy towards the Indians was largely one of neglect. At least twice towards the end of the colonial period the government's Indian policy was attacked as being hopelessly inadequate by those with a humanitarian concern for the Indians. The Reverend William Sebright Green, in a letter to the Aborigines Protection Society, and the Reverend George Hills, bishop of Columbia, in a letter to the secretary of state for the colonies, criticized British Columbia's Indian policy. In both cases Trutch was called upon to defend colonial action, or rather inaction. He had already revealed his basic belief about the Indian policy of the colony at a meeting of the Legislative Council in February 1869, where he is reported to have maintained that

> Our system of treatment of the Indians was more humane than in any other country. Our laws entitled them to all the rights and privileges of the white man; they have thriven under them and had vastly improved in every respect by contact with the white man. The laws when applied to the Indians were always strained in his favour.[96]

This statement was erroneous on every point, but subsequent defences of policy were merely an elaboration of this fundamental attitude.

The burden of Green's criticism was that the government of British Columbia had neither policy nor concern for the Indians. Governor Anthony Musgrave, who made no real contribution to Indian policy, requested Trutch to comment on these criticisms and afterwards agreed with his opinions.[97] Part

---

[94]Seymour to Buckingham, 30 November 1868, CO.60/33; Granville to Seymour, 7 March 1869, Great Britain, Colonial Office, Despatches to British Columbia.

[95]Seymour to Cardwell, 8 May 1865, CO.60/21.

[96]*British Colonist*, 12 February 1869.

[97]Musgrave to Granville, 29 January 1870, B.C., *Papers Connected with Indian Land*, appendix, p. 10.

of Trutch's reply was that the government had "striven to the extent of its power to protect and befriend the Native race." In fact, he continued, "its declared policy was that the Indians should in all respects be on the same footing as Europeans." It has been shown how, under Trutch, the government's idea of equality worked in relation to the important land question. As Trutch explained it, the Indians were given such lands "as were deemed proportionate to, and amply sufficient for, the requirements of each tribe."[98] The settlers were treated equally because they were allowed what was sufficient for their requirements.

Nor were the Indians equally protected by the law. In some instances Indians who brought cases of their cultivated areas being trampled by settler's cattle before the courts failed to secure convictions, whereas Indian defendants in similar cases were found guilty. A government official pointed out that magistrates had no power by legislation to eject settlers who encroached on Indian reserves. In some places white settlers were even granted pre-emption certificates for areas of land that included potato patches belonging to Indians.[99] No doubt the Indians concerned in such cases would have been intrigued with Trutch's claim that they were equal with the European before the law.

In his memorandum written in response to Green's criticisms, Trutch also took the opportunity to claim that British Columbia had always denied the idea of aboriginal title. He wrote that "the title of the Indians in fee of the public lands, or any portion thereof, has never been acknowledged by Government, but, on the contrary, is distinctly denied." Trutch does not, however, explain why the Vancouver Island House of Assembly should ask the imperial government in 1861 for £3,000 to extinguish an Indian title that they did not recognize the existence of. He also argued that the treaties that Douglas made with the Indians of Vancouver Island were "not in acknowledgement of any general title of the Indians to the lands they occupy" but were simply "for the purpose of securing friendly relations between those Indians and the settlement of Victoria."[100] This was definitely not the interpretation of those most closely involved in the signing of the Fort Victoria treaties. Douglas clearly considered that he was purchasing Indian land,[101] and the Indians

[98]Trutch, memorandum, enclosure in Musgrave to Granville, 29 January 1870, ibid., appendix, pp. 10–13.

[99]*British Columbian*, 9 July 1864; Powell to attorney-general, 12 January 1874, and Powell to Trutch, 21 June 1873, B.C., *Papers Connected with Indian Land*, pp. 126, 116; Ball to Crease, 18 August 1868, Crease Papers.

[100]Trutch, memorandum, enclosure in Musgrave to Granville, 29 January 1870, B.C., *Papers Connected with Indian Land*, appendix, p. 11.

[101]Douglas to Newcastle, 25 March 1861, ibid., p. 19.

themselves, although they had yet to comprehend European concepts of land ownership, knew that the paper that they were signing involved more than a declaration of friendship.

In his letter, the bishop of Columbia was concerned about the paucity of government spending on Indians. This point may have proved a little difficult for Trutch to refute, for the colonial estimates indicate that allocations for Indians were miserable; and often only a fraction of the amount included in the estimates appeared in the end-of-year statement of actual expenditure. Trutch did concede that "from the pecuniary inability of the Colony in the past no such appropriations have been made as could have been wished."[102] He did, however, neglect to mention the allocation of money collected by leasing Indian reserve land. Douglas had intended that rents from the leasing of the Victoria reserve were to be used for the benefit of the Indians. Early in 1873 the newly appointed superintendent of Indian affairs was having difficulty in discovering what had happened to the sum of $1,984.82 that had been handed to Trutch in 1869 by the commissioners of the Songhees reserve. The reply was that, instead of being spent on Indian needs, the sum "formed part of the assets of the Colony at the date of Confederation."[103] In spite of the fact that he had misappropriated Indian money, Trutch apparently had no conscience about describing British Columbia's Indian policy "as a well considered system, ably devised by experienced men specially interested in favour of the Indians."[104]

Trutch did, however, have some other arguments to offer on the question of parsimony with funds. While British Columbia had not spent as much as she might have done directly on the Indians, the bishop of Columbia was forgetting that the Indians were partaking of "the advantages of civilization which we have brought to them." For example, the Indians could now use roads and trails without even having to pay the tolls that were often imposed on white people. Europeans had also brought to the Indians implements "of husbandry and agriculture, the chase and fishing etc., which before they were without." Trutch does not explain how the Indians had survived in the northwest coast environment without developing some very sophisticated equipment for gathering food. Another of the benefits of civilization mentioned was one that was particularly close to his heart:

[102]Trutch to secretary of state for the provinces, 26 September 1871, ibid., p. 100.

[103]Powell to provincial secretary, 4 February 1873, and John Ash to Powell, 5 February 1873, ibid., p. 112.

[104]Trutch to secretary of state for the provinces, 26 September 1871, ibid., pp. 99–101.

the blessings which result from the preservation of law and order throughout the country, instead of those scenes of bloodshed and robbery which prevailed formerly among them, and amidst which their lives were passed in a state of constant dread and uncertainty of life and property.

With arguments such as these, Trutch had little difficulty in convincing himself that Indian policy in British Columbia had been "essentially benevolent towards the Indians."[105]

Trutch's facile attempts to defend it actually revealed how emaciated colonial Indian policy was. With a government so blatantly pro-settler, the advantages that accrued to the Indians from the "blessings of civilization" were bound to be outweighed by the disadvantages. The freedom to use roads and bridges hardly compensated the Indians for the dispossession of their land.

Even being subject to British law and order was a blessing in disguise. One of the results was that Indian leaders were losing their authority. Traditionally, leadership in Indian society was based on respect rather than authority. Government officials assumed that Indian leaders had far more authority to make decisions affecting their people than was actually the case. Indian leaders were not absolute governors, but, having made the mistake, whites often held chiefs responsible when other Indians refused to abide by arrangements made between Indian leaders and government officials.

Chiefs were manipulated to serve the ends of the settler government. If one individual proved difficult to deal with, a more pliant personality was sometimes elevated to "chieftainship" by government administrators. A new kind of Indian leader emerged: one who was not necessarily qualified according to the traditional standards but who fulfilled the role of mediator with the whites. These spokesmen were often invested with symbols of office in order to bolster their authority among the Indians. This was the beginning of a development which resulted in the title "chief" meaning to many Indians a man appointed by a government official to conduct the affairs of the reserve.[106]

It has been said that probably "the most significant turning point in the

---

[105]Ibid.
[106]Seymour to Cardwell, 23 September 1864, CO.60/19; The Bishop of Columbia, *A Tour of British Columbia*, p. 23; Duff, *The Upper Stalo Indians*, p. 81.

acculturative history of an Indian tribe was the loss of political autonomy."[107]
This was exactly the experience of many British Columbia Indians during the
1860's. They were losing their freedom of choice within the contact situation.
They could no longer adapt selectively to the alien culture, and they could not
destroy its representatives without severe retribution. They were losing control of their own destiny as it was increasingly directed from the outside by a
government that ignored Indian needs in order to satisfy settler demands.

[107]Robert F. Berkhofer, Jr., *Salvation and the Savage: An Analysis of Protestant
Missions and American Indian Response, 1787–1862* (Lexington: University of
Kentucky Press, 1965), p. x.

8

The Consolidation of Settlement: The 1870's and 1880's

Everybody says, "sure what the devil is the good of a Government that
can't put a few siwashes off a man's land."[1] —ARCHIBALD DODDS, 1874

British Columbia's confederation with Canada was perhaps the last chance
that the Indians had of policy towards them undergoing any significant
change. But the chance was lost. The 1870's and 1880's simply saw the continuation and consolidation of policies designed by settlers to meet their own
requirements, while Indian needs continued to be ignored by government.

Knowing that Canada's Indian policy was somewhat different from British
Columbia's, the Indians hoped that a new system would be adopted towards
them after Confederation.[2] They thought that the changes in the white man's
world might bring them a better deal, particularly over land. Throughout
the 1870's the Canadian authorities were making treaties with the prairie
Indians to extinguish their title to the land. These treaties were indicative of a
policy that was different from British Columbia's in a number of ways. The
prairie Indians had none of the freedom of choice implied by the word
"treaty," for the numbered treaties were imposed on the Indians rather than
negotiated with them.[3] Nevertheless, these treaties were a recognition of the
principle that the Indians had rights to the land that ought to be extinguished

[1]Archibald Dodds to attorney general, 11 June 1874, B.C., *Papers Connected with
Indian Land*, p. 133.

[2]Trutch to Macdonald, 16 July 1872, Macdonald Papers, vol. 278; I. W. Powell
to superintendent general of Indian affairs, 4 February 1875, Canada, Department of
the Interior, "Annual Report . . . 1874," Canada, *Sessional Papers*, 3d Parl., 2d sess.,
1875, no. 8, p. 64; "Petition of the chiefs of Douglas Portage, of the Lower Fraser,
and other tribes of the mainland to Bute Inlet," 14 July 1874, B.C., *Papers Connected
with Indian Land*, p. 137.

[3]The first of the numbered treaties was signed at Lower Fort Garry on 3 August
1871 (see Peter A. Cumming and Neil H. Mickenberg, eds., *Native Rights in Canada*
[Toronto: the Indian-Eskimo Association of Canada, 1972], pp. 121ff). For some
account of the "negotiations" that preceded the signing of some of the subsequent
treaties see Alexander Morris, *The Treaties of Canada with the Indians of Manitoba
and North-West Territories . . .* (Toronto: Belfords, Clark & Co., 1880), passim.

before settlers moved in.[4] The minimum of 160 acres per family was a much larger allocation of reserve land than British Columbia had given, and in addition there was provision in the treaties for initial payments followed by annuities and other forms of assistance. The formality of a treaty involved a limited recognition of Indian rights and needs such as had not occurred in British Columbia since 1859, and after Confederation the Indians hoped that this policy might be extended across the Rockies.

But they were to be disappointed. The Indians were totally unrepresented in the negotiations that preceded Confederation, and their concerns were given virtually no consideration in the business deal that established the union with Canada. The majority of British Columbians were non-participants in Confederation. During the debate on union in British Columbia there was only minor discussion of Indian affairs. A motion for the protection of the Indians during the change of government was lost twenty to one and another, advocating the extension of Canadian Indian policy to the new province, was withdrawn. Consequently, the Terms of Union proposed by the governor-in-council of British Columbia contained no reference to the Indians.[5] Presumably clause thirteen of the final terms, the one that deals with Indians, was added in Ottawa, and as Trutch was the only person closely involved with colonial Indian policy who was present at those discussions, he can be fairly attributed with responsibility for the clause.[6]

Clause thirteen of the Terms of Union states that:

> The charge of the Indians, and the trusteeship and management of the lands reserved for their use and benefit, shall be assumed by the Dominion Government, and a policy as liberal as that hitherto pursued by the British Columbia Government shall be continued by the Dominion Government after the union.

[4]This policy had not, however, been followed consistently in all the areas that became the Dominion of Canada in 1867. The numbered treaties on the prairies were based on the Robinson-Huron and Robinson-Superior treaties of Upper Canada signed in 1850 (see Cumming and Mickenberg, *Native Rights in Canada,* p. 124). But Indian title to parts of Upper Canada and all of Lower Canada and the Maritime colonies had not been extinguished by treaty.

[5]British Columbia, Legislative Council, *Debate on the Subject of Confederation with Canada, Reprinted from the Government Gazette Extraordinary of March, 1870* (Victoria: R. Wolfenden, 1870), pp. 146–47, 157–59. The mover of the second motion, John Robson, was particularly concerned to see that the Canadian system of appointing Indian agents to consider Indian interests should be extended to British Columbia. By doing this, said Robson, "we should set the Indian mind at rest and let them see that confederation will be a greater boon to them than the white population."

[6]Another student of the subject has come to the same conclusion on the basis of the similarity between clause thirteen and Trutch's memorandum of 1870 (see Cail, *Land, Man, and the Law,* p. 186).

To carry out such a policy, tracts of land of such an extent as it has hitherto been the practice of the British Columbia Government to appropriate for that purpose, shall from time to time be conveyed by the Local Government to the Dominion Government in trust for the use and benefit of the Indians, on application of the Dominion Government; and in case of disagreement between the two Governments respecting the quantity of such tracts of land to be so granted, the matter shall be referred for the decision of the Secretary of State for the Colonies.[7]

The wording of this clause is very curious indeed, particularly the stipulation that "a policy as liberal as that hitherto pursued by the British Columbia Government shall be continued by the Dominion after the union." A variety of words could be used to describe colonial policy prior to union, but "liberal" is not one of them. Certainly, if Canadian policy was to be the criterion, the colony's policy was considerably less than liberal. Trutch must have been aware of this fact, and even if he really believed that British Columbia's was a liberal policy, clause thirteen was deliberately misleading. Subsequently David Laird, the Canadian minister of the interior from 1873 to 1876, thought that the framers of the clause "could hardly have been aware of the marked contrast between the Indian policies which had, up to that time, prevailed in Canada and British Columbia respectively."[8] Unfortunately, it is more likely that the British Columbia representatives were aware of the discrepancy in policies but wanted to camouflage it. Certainly Trutch was quite satisfied that "as to Indian policy . . . the wisest course would be to continue the system that has prevailed hitherto."[9] Maintenance of the status quo was precisely what the British Columbians hoped to achieve by agreeing to give the dominion government only as much land for Indian reserves as had "hitherto been the practice of the British Columbia Government to appropriate for that purpose."

Clause thirteen was aptly numbered. It was unlucky for the Indians because it meant that some time was to elapse before the federal authorities realized just how illiberal the colony's treatment of them had been. The province meanwhile was determined to stand by the letter of the law. In the years following Confederation, federal officials trying to extract concessions on the land question from the province on behalf of the Indians were notified that "all that it is 'reasonable and just' to demand of the Provincial Government is

---

[7]British Columbia, *British North America Act, 1867, Terms of Union with Canada, Rules and Orders of the Legislative Assembly* . . . (Victoria: R. Wolfenden, 1881), p. 66.

[8]Memo of David Laird, 2 November 1874, B.C., *Papers Connected with Indian Land*, p. 152.

[9]Trutch to Macdonald, 14 October 1872, Macdonald Papers, vol. 278.

that the 13th Section of the Terms of Union should be faithfully observed."[10] Naturally, in interpreting the clause, the province took the policy "hitherto pursued by British Columbia" to mean Trutch's policy and not Douglas's.

Just as they were excluded from the debate on Confederation, the Indians were prevented from having any role in government after 1871. Responsible government came to British Columbia after Confederation and increased the settler's power over the Indians. Although it was a great boost to settler ego, responsible government held no advantage for the Indians. No one in government was responsible to them, and so they had no way of influencing policy. There was no thought of giving the Indians of British Columbia the vote. Quite the contrary, in 1872 and 1875 legislation was passed which specifically excluded Indians from voting purely on the grounds of race.[11] Even the new De Cosmos newspaper, the *Victoria Daily Standard*, was editorially opposed to such racist legislation.[12] As was being proved in other parts of the British Empire, protecting native interests was incompatible with granting self-government to colonists.

Because they were excluded from the political process, the only way that the Indians could ameliorate their condition was by self-help. But even this road was often blocked by the settlers. In 1879 there was a meeting of a large number of the tribes of the southern interior at Lytton. Indians from the Fraser and Thompson rivers, the Nicola Valley, and the Similkameen area gathered to discuss their problems. Gilbert Sproat, the Indian reserve commissioner, was present at the meeting, and he reported on the measures that were taken. The Indians agreed on a set of regulations designed to foster the education of their children, to improve sanitary and medical facilities in the villages, to subdivide arable land on an individual basis, to reduce the number of non-working days, to abolish the potlatch, and to levy fines for drunkenness and gambling. A head chief, a Spuzzum Indian named Michael, and a council of thirteen were elected to administer these ordinances.[13] This meeting was a promising attempt by the Indians to adapt to the settlement frontier and to compete with the Europeans. In nearly every respect the measures proposed by the Indians at Lytton paralleled those advocated by European philanthropists. Sproat remarked in a letter to Ottawa that the Lytton meet-

[10]John Ash, provincial secretary, to James Lenihan, 12 October 1874, Canada, Department of Indian Affairs, British Columbia Early Correspondence, 1873–1876, RG10, vol. 1,001; see also Lord Dufferin to Carnarvon, 4 December 1874, Great Britain, Colonial Office, Original Correspondence, Canada, CO.42/730, PAC (hereafter cited as CO.42).

[11]British Columbia, *Journals of the Legislative Assembly of the Province of British Columbia . . .* (Victoria: R. Wolfenden, 1872, 1875), pp. 65, 44–45.

[12]*Victoria Daily Standard*, 21 April 1875.

[13]Sproat to superintendent general, 26 July 1879, RG10, vol. 3,669, file 15,136.

ing demonstrated "the laudable desire of the Indians to make efforts, at their own cost principally, to improve the physical condition and the minds of their children and to train themselves for citizenship."[14]

The settlers, however, were horrified at this development. They were not so much interested in Indians improving their physical and social conditions as in the threat that any "confederation" of tribes might pose to their security. Apparently only Europeans were to be permitted to confederate to benefit themselves. In the preceding years there had been rumours of an Indian outbreak in the interior, and the Lytton meeting provoked a recurrence of settler fears. Many objected strongly and loudly to the Indians' attempt to organize. Both in his newspaper and in a letter to the prime minister, De Cosmos emphasized the danger to white security posed by this development. He thought that the Indians should not be allowed to combine for any purpose in case they might endeavour "to obtain some privilege or concession antagonistic to white interests." He considered the Lytton gathering to be "in every way objectionable," and he hoped that the head chief would not be recognized and that the regulations would not be confirmed. Many other settlers wrote of the supposed danger of any effort by Indians to organize, and their opinions were supported by the Indian superintendent in Victoria and the department in Ottawa.[15]

Sproat, on the other hand, felt that many of these objections arose out of a simple ignorance of the Indians and their problems. According to him, many settlers, "whose notion of Indian management is terrorism," seemed to have had their racial prejudice "stirred to the depths" by these elementary proposals by the Indians to improve their conditions.[16] Certainly the settlers were more interested in keeping the Indians under control than in listening to their grievances, and the way to ensure their subjugation was to keep them divided. Hence the settlers feared and discouraged any attempt by the Indians to co-operate to advance their own interests. The Reverend J.B. Good, who had worked as a missionary among the Lytton Indians for more than ten years, noted that there was a ready chorus in the province against any action either for, or by, the Indians, however sensible it might be.[17] The settlers

---

[14]Sproat to superintendent general, 10 November 1879, ibid., file 10,691.

[15]*Victoria Daily Standard*, 26 November 1879; De Cosmos to Macdonald, 29 September 1879, Macdonald Papers, vol. 293; A. C. Anderson, William Duncan, Roderick Finlayson, William J. MacDonald, J. W. McKay, Archibald McKinlay, W. F. Tolmie, Charles Vernon, Captain James Prevost to George A. Walkem, 25 September 1879, Powell to superintendent general, 28 September 1879, Phillip Vankoughnet, deputy superintendent of Indian affairs, to Macdonald, 22 September 1879, RG10, vol. 3,669, file 10,691.

[16]Sproat to superintendent general, 5 and 10 September 1879, RG10, vol. 3,669, file 10,691.

[17]Enclosure in Sproat to superintendent general, 18 October 1879, ibid.

intended to maintain their position of dominance, and so they did not want to foster Indian development, even paternalistically, towards a distant future when the Indians would be able to act independently. The Indians were wards of the Crown and should be treated as such.

As far as the settler government was concerned, the Indians were a population to be administered rather than listened to. Decisions were made to be imposed not discussed. The Indians remained irrelevant to the major concern of the settlers: the development of the resources of the province. Neglect, and even hostility, on the part of the settlers meant that Indian administration in British Columbia in the two decades after Confederation was a shambles.

The federal government appointed two men to be responsible for the administration of Indian affairs in the province during the 1870's. Dr. Israel Wood Powell was appointed Indian superintendent in 1872 and was based in Victoria, and in 1874 James Lenihan was appointed as second superintendent centred in New Westminster. Powell was the senior superintendent with particular responsibility for the coastal Indians, while Lenihan was expected to concentrate on the interior tribes. Neither man, however, was entirely suited to the position he held.

The appointment of Powell was foisted on John A. Macdonald by pressure from the British Columbia members of Parliament, even though the prime minister thought that the appointee "ought to have known more about the Indians."[18] Others were also unimpressed by Powell's qualifications for the position. Writing in private to his daughter, Douglas indicated that he was somewhat less than enthusiastic about the appointment of Powell as Indian superintendent. Sproat thought that Powell knew little about Indian ways, and, nine years later, Franz Boas thought so too.[19] Apart from Powell's personal inadequacies, Sproat observed that to try to administer Indian affairs from an office in Victoria was "an absurdity."[20] Powell also continued to practise medicine in Victoria at a time when the management of Indian affairs should have been a full-time occupation.

The selection of Lenihan as the second superintendent is even more difficult to understand. At the time of his appointment he was in business in Toronto, and there is no evidence that he was particularly familiar with the Indians or the province to which he was sent. Furthermore, it was apparent to some at

[18]Macdonald to Trutch, 30 October 1872, Joseph Trutch, Correspondence with Sir John A. Macdonald, 1871–1891, PABC.

[19]Douglas to Martha Douglas, 28 September 1872, Douglas, Private Papers; Sproat to minister of the interior, 27 August 1877, RG10, vol. 3,653, file 8,702; Boas to his parents, 2 November 1886, Rohner, p. 51.

[20]Sproat to E. A. Meredith, deputy minister of the interior, 9 April 1877, RG10, vol. 3,641, file 7,567.

the time of his arrival that he was mentally inadequate for his task, and by the end of the 1870's it was obvious to most. Lenihan was, in the parlance of the day, going "soft in the head." It was evident to Sproat in 1877 that Lenihan felt uncomfortable in the presence of Indians and, in conferences, succeeded only in offending them. Lenihan's incompetence nearly resulted in disaster in the tense situation that existed in the Kamloops area in the summer of 1877. By 1880 Powell had to admit to his superiors in Ottawa what was common knowledge in British Columbia, that Lenihan was "too weak in the mind to talk five minutes with Indians." The Indians were shrewd negotiators, and whenever Lenihan tried to deal with them he was "at once made the unfortunate subject of ridicule."[21]

Indian administration in British Columbia was chaotic because, in addition to the personal inadequacies of the officials, nearly every action that they tried to take was impeded by the deliberately obstructionist tactics of the provincial authorities. Constant wrangling between the provincial government and federally appointed officials frequently paralyzed Indian policy. The province was unwilling to make any concessions to the Indians and certainly did not want to see the federal government make any significant changes to the settler-dominated policies that had operated before Confederation. British Columbia strongly resented Ottawa's "interference" in Indian matters. As one provincial premier wrote to Sproat, the Canadian minister of the interior was thousands of miles from the scene and knew nothing of the facts or merits of provincial policy. Andrew C. Elliott said that the provincial government wanted to treat the Indians justly, but that justice also required that the interests of the settlers should not be sacrificed.[22] He was merely restating, and not reconciling, the old incompatible opposites. Most members of the provincial government were either farming settlers or involved in land speculation, and they fostered their own, and not Indian, interests. Sproat was amused at the dogmatism of those government members who had spent all their time in Victoria and perhaps knew enough Chinook to ask an Indian to blacken their boots, but who gave the appearance of understanding the wishes, requirements, and social condition of a large and widespread Indian population.[23] Out of ignorance or antipathy the provincial government did little for the Indians and then blamed the federal government when things went wrong.

[21]Sproat to minister of the interior, 27 August 1877, RG10, vol. 3,653, file 8,702; Sproat to superintendent general, 30 October 1877, RG10, vol. 3,612, file 3,756(22); Powell to Macdonald, 28 January 1880, Macdonald Papers, vol. 364.

[22]Elliott to Sproat, 27 September 1877, RG10, vol. 3,651, file 8,540.

[23]Sproat to Vankoughnet, 27 November 1878, RG10, vol. 3,670, file 10,776.

Initially the federal government's plan was to establish a three-man board to manage Indian affairs in the province. The board was to be comprised of the two Indian superintendents and the lieutenant-governor. But the newly appointed lieutenant-governor was Joseph Trutch, and he was determined to defend colonial policy, his policy, against differing ideas held in Ottawa. He had been opposed to Powell's appointment in 1872, not because he had any criticism of his professional or business ability, but because he thought that the lieutenant-governor should control Indian affairs. According to Trutch, Dr. Powell "might perform the duties of the office well enough if acting under the ultimate direction and advice of someone of more experience here."[24] That "someone of experience" was, of course, Trutch himself. If he retained control of Indian policy, he would ensure that things remained as they were. So when the three-man board of management was established in 1874, Trutch was not interested in serving on it unless he directed its actions, and he was prepared to hinder its work if he was not given a controlling position. Powell was preparing to visit Kamloops in the summer of 1874 to discuss the land question with the Indians, and Trutch objected to the trip on the grounds that Powell was acting too independently. The lieutenant-governor did not want Powell to make any promises to the Indians that would interfere with any future action of the board. He told the minister of the interior that he was prepared to act on the board only if he had the authority to direct the management of Indian affairs in the province.[25] By now, however, the federal government was becoming aware of some of the elements of the situation in British Columbia: an awareness that was reflected in Laird's reply. Trutch was told that "I very much doubt . . . whether the Government would be prepared to delegate to any person in British Columbia the general control of Indian affairs in the Province."[26]

Trutch's was not the only attempt to frustrate Powell's work. After his appointment, Powell quickly ascertained that the land question was still the most crucial and, therefore, the most troublesome issue. Just as quickly he realized that it was going to be extremely difficult to extract concessions from provincial officials or even to obtain their co-operation. The federal authorities were faced with a running battle over the acreage question in the early 1870's. In 1873 Ottawa suggested that Indian reserves should be allocated on

[24]Trutch to Macdonald, 14 October 1872, Macdonald Papers, vol. 278.

[25]Powell to minister of Indian affairs, 27 July 1874, CO.42/730; Trutch to Laird, 30 January 1874, Peter O'Reilly Papers, PABC.

[26]Laird to Trutch, 8 July 1874, O'Reilly Papers. It is also worth noting that the board of management was originally suggested by Macdonald, who frequently corresponded with Trutch. But by 1874 the Liberals were in office in Ottawa, and the change in government partly accounts for the change in attitude towards the management of British Columbia's Indian policy.

the basis of eighty acres per family, but British Columbia countered with an offer of ten. Powell managed to gain a short-lived agreement on twenty acres, but with the collapse of that accord no further bids were taken. The final stage of these negotiations was the acceptance in 1875 of a suggestion by William Duncan that no specific acreage be allocated, but rather that individual situations be examined by a commission and a decision reached on the basis of the local knowledge of the then non-existent Indian agents.[27]

But these intergovernmental negotiations only exposed the surface of the problem, and at the local level there was even more confusion. In 1874 Powell completed a survey of the Musqueam reserve which indicated that, although the band included 70 families, they had only 314 acres reserved for them, 114 of which, in Powell's opinion, were quite useless.[28] Evidently the band had not received ten acres per family, and on the basis of twenty acres they required 1,400. The chief commissioner of lands and works, Robert Beaven, whom Sproat described as "a narrow, stubborn man," replied to Powell's request that an appropriate amount of land be surveyed for the Indians with a series of petty questions designed to obstruct the survey.[29] The provincial government demonstrated that it was still more concerned with reducing Indian reserves than with any just settlement of the matter. Beaven informed Powell that he was unable to grant extensions to present reserves unless the superintendent would guarantee, on behalf of the dominion government, that the Indians would agree quietly to reductions.[30] In 1875 Powell again applied to the provincial government for lands to make up the deficiency in reserves that had been surveyed. This time the reply was that the basis of twenty acres agreed to only applied to future reserves and not to those already in existence. As some reservations amounted to only two acres per family, Powell felt that he could do little else than terminate surveys until the question was settled.[31]

Powell made this decision in spite of the growing urgency of the problem. He knew that Indians from all over the province were becoming increasingly dissatisfied as a result of the government's dilatory policy. Powell felt that visiting the Indians, particularly in the interior, when he could bring no finality on the land question did more harm than good to race relations. From the coast and the interior, wherever whites had settled or looked likely to settle, Indian complaints poured in about the treatment that they had received.

---

[27]"Report of the Government of British Columbia on the Subject of Indian Reserves," 17 August 1875, B.C., *Papers Connected with Indian Land*, appendix, p. 9.
[28]Powell to Beaven, 31 July 1874, ibid., p. 134.
[29]Sproat to Vankoughnet, 9 April 1879, RG10, vol. 3,684, file 12,836; B.C., *Papers Connected with Indian Land*, pp. 134–35.
[30]Beaven to Powell, 10 August 1875, B.C., *Papers Connected with Indian Land*, p. 135.
[31]Powell to superintendent general, 4 February 1875, Canada, Department of the Interior, "Annual Report . . . 1874," p. 64.

When Lenihan opened his office in New Westminster, he was inundated with Indian protests, and the paramount concern was land.[32] Lenihan also discontinued visits to Indian groups because he was unable to answer satisfactorily their questions about land policy.

A petition sent to Powell by 110 Indian leaders of the Lower Fraser area in 1874 was representative of many complaints he received from Indians of the coast and Lower Mainland. They protested the arbitrary way in which the British Columbia government had located and divided their reserves and the fact that their cultivated land was not protected against encroachment by whites. These Indians said that they had attempted to adopt the white man's ways. "We are not a lazy and roaming-about people, as we used to be," they told the Indian superintendent. They had tried to develop agriculture and animal husbandry, but they were discouraged and depressed. Having made their dissatisfaction known to government officials on many occasions, they had received no redress. Now, they told Powell, they felt "like men trampled on, and are commencing to believe that the aim of the white man is to exterminate us as soon as they can."[33] The leaders of the Nanaimo Indians told Trutch that their men were "getting old and grey" waiting for the promises of the government to be fulfilled.[34]

Sometimes the provincial government refused even to listen to these complaints. When Alexis, the chief at Cheam, wrote to Lenihan complaining about the inadequacy of his reserve, his letter was duly passed on to the provincial secretary. Alexis had pointed out that the reserve had been laid out without consultation with the Indians and that even twenty acres per family "was a mockery, was destruction to the Indian race." The provincial secretary, however, also discovered that the chief's letter contained language "disrespectful to her Majesty" and threats of violence against white settlers. He therefore informed Lenihan that he did "not consider it within the scope of my duty to submit to the Lieutenant-Governor in Council any such offensive document."[35]

In the interior similar grievances were similarly expressed. The Chilcotin, for example, were continuing their hostility to the intrusion of whites, main-

[32]Powell to superintendent general, 1 October 1875, and Lenihan to superintendent general, 7 November 1875, Canada, Department of the Interior, "Annual Report . . . 1875," pp. 44, 53.

[33]"Petition of chiefs of Douglas Portage, of Lower Fraser, and other tribes of the mainland to Bute Inlet," 14 July 1874, B.C., *Papers Connected with Indian Land*, p. 137.

[34]Nanaimo Chiefs to Trutch, May 1872, British Columbia, Provincial Secretary, Correspondence, 1872–1890, PABC.

[35]Alexis to Lenihan, 15 May 1875, Ash to Lenihan, 26 May 1875, Canada, Department of Indian Affairs, British Columbia, Early Correspondence, RG10, vol. 1,001.

taining that the land was theirs and objecting to settlers living on it. Apparently the Chilcotin thought that the Europeans were going to appropriate their land without compensation and that they would be confined to limited reserves. Oddly, given that this had been his precise policy in the past, Trutch described the Chilcotin fear as a "misapprehension" in a letter to Ottawa.[36] It was in the Kamloops area, where Trutch first carried out his reduction programme, that discontent was really simmering. The grievances are familiar. As the Oblate missionary, Father C.J. Grandidier, wrote:

> The whites came, took land, fenced it in, and little by little hemmed the Indians in their small reservations . . . . Many of these reservations have been surveyed without their consent, and sometimes without having received any notice of it, so they could not expose their needs and their wishes. Their reserves have been repeatedly cut off smaller for the benefit of the whites, and the best and most useful part of them taken away till some tribes are coralled on a small piece of land, as at Canoe Creek or elsewhere, or even have not an inch of ground, as at Williams Lake. The natives have protested against those spoliations, from the beginning. They have complained bitterly of that treatment, but they have not obtained any redress.[37]

The Shuswap and related Indians of the southern interior had become so suspicious of government officials that the bands of Nicola and Okanagan lakes refused to accept presents from Powell, "lest, by doing so, they should be thought to waive their claim for compensation for the injustice done them in relation to the Land Grants."[38] In 1874 Powell visited Kamloops and heard the complaints of the Indians. They told him that they had insufficient land for their large and growing herds of cattle and horses, while white settlers around them were able to pre-empt and lease thousands of acreas of land and then often treated the Indians with cruelty.[39]

Powell returned from his visit to the interior convinced that the Indians had valid grievances that ought to be rectified. He also realized that many of the problems arose out of the reductions carried out by Trutch. He had written to Douglas to ascertain the nature of his land policy and concluded that it was the actions of his successors, in response to settler demands, that had

[36]Trutch to secretary of state for the provinces, 24 June 1872, British Columbia, Lieutenant-Governor, Despatches to Ottawa.
[37]Father C. J. Grandidier to the editor of the *Victoria Standard*, 28 August 1874, B.C., *Papers Connected with Indian Land*, pp. 145–46.
[38]Memo of Laird, 2 November 1874, ibid., p. 153.
[39]Powell to minister of Indian affairs, 27 July 1874, CO.42/730.

engendered most of the discontent.[40] And now the situation was becoming even more acute. The Indians were learning the value of their land at the same time as they realized that they were rapidly being hemmed in on their limited reserves. The government had appeared before many of the Indians only as an official wanting to "adjust" their land, so they could be forgiven for thinking that the only policy that the government had towards them was to take their land. As some interior Indians put it "first one chief had come, then another and another, all saying the same thing and all afterwards cutting and carving their lands." Powell was of the opinion that there had not been an Indian war in British Columbia "not because there has been no injustice to the Indians, but because the Indians have not been sufficiently united."[41]

Other people, both inside and outside the province, were also becoming aware of the inequity of the government's Indian land policy. Lord Dufferin, the governor general, wrote to the Colonial Office drawing attention to the fact that since 1864 British Columbia had carried out land appropriations without "reference to the consent or wishes of the original occupants." All the Indian grievances were repeated, and Dufferin urged the colonial secretary to intervene, since Canada's reputation for "just and Humane" dealings with the Indians depended on a proper settlement of the dispute.[42] Two years later when Dufferin visited British Columbia, he pointed out to the government that its actions since Douglas left office had produced an "unsatisfactory feeling amongst the Indian population" and that it was time that their rights were recognized.[43] The government was also under pressure from some editorial writers to change its attitude. Newspapers in the east were reporting on the "high handed injustice" with which British Columbia treated its Indians, and even locally there were editorial calls for the government to stop behaving in a way that was bringing disgrace to the province.[44]

But the government still blandly argued that the colonial government had done its best for the Indians, and Premier George Walkem even claimed that the Indians had been satisfied under the old land system. Walkem had signed a memorandum in 1875 that highly praised pre-Confederation Indian policy, and Sproat, who was living with the premier at the time, was, in his ignorance, impressed with the document. Subsequent investigation of the facts, however,

[40]Powell to superintendent general of Indian affairs, 4 February 1875, Canada, Department of the Interior, "Annual Report . . . 1874," pp. 63–64.

[41]Reserve commissioners to superintendent general, 23 February 1877, Canada, Indian Reserve Commission, Correspondence, Memorandums etc., 1877–1878, PABC; memo of Laird, 2 November 1874, B.C., *Papers Connected with Indian Land*, p. 153.

[42]Dufferin to Carnarvon, 4 December 1874, CO.42/730.

[43]Speech of Dufferin at Government House, Victoria, 20 September 1876, Milton, pp. 209–11.

[44]*British Colonist*, 27 April and 24 December 1875.

disclosed the truth to Sproat.[45] The government meanwhile continued to act as if the Indians did not exist. In 1874 the province passed a new land act that consolidated all previous legislation. The act was disallowed by the federal government because it included no reference to Indian title or rights to land and failed to make any provision for the establishment and protection of Indian reserves. In spite of federal objections, the act was allowed to come into effect after some inconsequential amendments had been made.

The provincial government remained under some pressure to change its views, and in 1875 it appointed a committee to investigate Indian lands and reserves. To assist the work of this committee the government also published the *Papers Connected with the Indian Land Question, 1850-1875*. These papers were made public with understandable reluctance. For some time the premier refused to table the papers; then there was some delay at the printers when it was discovered that he had "mistakenly" laid bogus material before the House.[46] The papers collectively constitute an indictment of British Columbia's Indian land policy. The committee of investigation accordingly advocated the acceptance of the memorandum of the Canadian minister of the interior of the previous November. In this memorandum David Laird had established the inadequacies of past policies and the corollary that adhering to the thirteenth clause of the Terms of Union would not be sufficient to "satisfy the fair and reasonable demands of the Indians." He therefore recommended that the province should be required to take necessary steps to redress Indian grievances.[47]

As soon as the Walkem government realized that its own committee was taking the federal line, it began to filibuster the tabling of its report. Walkem and Beaven, who as members of the committee had refused to attend any of its meetings, now argued in the House that the report was invalid because some members of the committee had not taken part in the deliberations. Walkem added that the Indians already had more than enough land because in laying out the original reserves Cox had thrown pieces of paper into the air on a windy day and the spots where they landed marked the boundaries of the reserve. The remark drew the appropriate laughter from his colleagues. For the premier the Indian land question was something to joke about, but apparently federal Indian policy was no laughing matter. At the meeting of the

---

[45]*Victoria Daily Standard*, 21 April 1875; "Report of the Government of British Columbia on Indian Reserves," 17 August 1875, B.C., *Papers Connected with Indian Land*, appendix, pp. 1–9; Sproat to Vankoughnet, 9 April 1879, RG10, vol. 3,684, file 12,836.

[46]*British Colonist*, 9 May 1875.

[47]Memo of Laird, 2 November 1874, B.C., *Papers Connected with Indian Land*, pp. 151–55.

House on 20 April 1975, the report was referred back to the committee so that the government could put "the Committee in possession of any information it might possess bearing upon the subject."[48] Yet the two ministers still refused to attend any meetings, apart from dropping in to browbeat the other committee members into forgetting about the report altogether. On 21 April it was announced that the House would be prorogued at 2:30 the following day. For the first time in history Trutch arrived on time and, as lieutenant-governor, declared the session closed before the committee's report could be tabled.[49] The Walkem government was clearly not of a mind to listen to any advice on its handling of Indian affairs.

It might be expected that the subtleties of the government's manipulation of the House would pass unnoticed by the Indians, but, as Sproat reported, the Indians of the province were "wide awake" and knew exactly what was going on in Victoria. The government's handling of the committee of inquiry was fully reported in the *Colonist*, and half-breeds in Victoria read the newspapers to Indians who in turn transmitted the news from tribe to tribe "with a rapidity that outstrips the mail." The missionaries also provided the Indians with information about government policies towards them.[50] Many Indians were thus able to keep abreast of all the subtle variations in provincial Indian policy.

In 1876 the province came to an agreement of sorts with the federal government on the Indian land question. The basis of this accord was William Duncan's suggestion that Indian lands should be examined by a commission and then allocated according to individual situations rather than a set acreage. The dominion government had apparently given up any idea of extinguishing Indian title, partly because of the expense that would be involved and partly because Ottawa already had troubles enough with the "spoilt child of Confederation." As long as the Indians remained "contented," the federal government was not disposed to raise the question of their rights to the soil. Now that there was an area of agreement, some were hopeful that the vexed land question was on the way towards a satisfactory solution. But there had been no change of government in British Columbia and no real change in governmental attitudes. It was portentous that the province deleted the words "speedy" and "final" adjustment of the question from their version of the terms of the commission.[51]

---

[48]B.C., *Journals of the Legislative Assembly, 1875*, p. 44.

[49]See *British Colonist*, 21 and 28 April and 9 May 1875; Powell to Laird, 26 April 1875, RG10, vol. 3,621, file 4,825.

[50]Sproat to Laird, 30 September 1876, RG10, vol. 3,637, file 7,131.

[51]David Mills to Sproat, 3 August 1877, Canada, Indian Reserve Commission Correspondence; G. E. Shankel, "The Development of Indian Policy in British Columbia" (Ph.D. dissertation, University of Washington, 1945), pp. 124–25.

In 1876 two commissioners, one to represent the Dominion and another representing the province, were appointed, and after some delay by the local government, the third, joint commissioner was selected. Two old Hudson's Bay Company men, A.C. Anderson and Archibald McKinlay, were chosen to represent Canada and British Columbia respectively. Anderson, however, was constrained to address the provincial government "pointedly" on a number of occasions about the appointment of the third member of the commission,[52] and the summer, the best time for field work, had passed before a decision was taken. Finally agreement was reached on the appointment of Gilbert Sproat.

Sproat was the pivotal and most energetic member of the joint commission. He had returned to British Columbia in 1874 after an absence of nine years. His earlier writings, in which he records his experiences during his residence at Alberni in the early 1860's, reveal him as a thoughtful observer of the Indians and their reactions to the presence of the European. Now, as reserve commissioner, Sproat proved to be long-winded and opinionated, sending a blizzard of letters to Ottawa. Other officials found Sproat's lengthy letters and reports rather tedious. The Department of the Interior, for example, was impressed with Sproat's ability but thought him to be "somewhat prolix" when he sent "a *volume* as his first report." In British Columbia Walkem huffed that Sproat was "wholly unfit for anything but verbose, voluminous, tiresome correspondence."[53] The judgment of the province's first minister notwithstanding, Sproat's letters to Ottawa provide a detailed and generally accurate account of the working of the joint commission and the considerable problems that it encountered. They also reveal Sproat's tendency to become more and more sympathetic with the predicament of the Indians and correspondingly critical of the provincial government's dealings with them. In fact, he defended his lengthy reports on the grounds "that *great evils* have been caused in the past by loose and curtailed records of many transactions of the government with the Indians."[54] It is also evident that Sproat was a great admirer of Douglas and his Indian policy; and he concluded, along with many others, that the reversal of Douglas's policies was at the root of the current Indian dissatisfaction.

From the beginning it seemed that the provincial government intended to hinder every action taken by the joint commission. After delays on the appointment of personnel, Victoria began to procrastinate on the question of

---

[52]Anderson to minister of the interior, 17 August 1876, RG10, vol. 3,633, file 6,425(1).

[53]Meredith to Powell, 18 October 1876, Israel Wood Powell Papers, PABC; Walkem to Macdonald, 1 March 1879, Macdonald Papers, vol. 293.

[54]Sproat to minister of the interior, 22 March 1877, RG10, vol. 3,645, file 7,937.

expenses. Because it considered Indian affairs to be a purely federal matter, British Columbia was initially unwilling to contribute anything towards the cost of the reserve commission, but the argument did move on to become one over the relative share to be borne by each government. Because of these delays, the commission was not able to start work among the troubled tribes of the interior during 1876 and had to confine its activities to the Lower Mainland and Vancouver Island. The commissioners realized the urgency of their task and felt that these delays would produce a "pernicious effect" among the Indians. But Sproat was hopeful that the work that the commission did on the coast during the winter of 1876–77 would begin to allay the fears of the interior Indians. He understood that whatever they did on the coast would be known by the inland tribes.[55]

The reserve commission began its work with an examination of the Musqueam reserve on Point Grey. Here, as at each place they visited, a census was taken so that, for the first time, reserves were based on some knowledge of the Indian population in the locality. Existing reserves were confirmed and in many places extended, and new reserves were also established. Indians were told that the commission would not interfere with land legally held by settlers, but it did try to arbitrate in places where the rights of settlers and Indians clashed. The Indians of the coast were also informed that they would not be given land to lie idle, even though the day after McKinlay had made this point to the Musqueam, he recorded in his diary that it was a great pity to see so much fine farming land unused because it was in the hands of white speculators. McKinlay, as provincial representative on the commission, was particularly prone to delivering homilies to the Indians on how the white man had improved the land and on the benefits of following the settlers' example.[56] However, the commissioners had been especially instructed not to make any attempt to alter the habits of the Indians radically "or to divert them from any legitimate pursuits or occupations."[57] Within their terms of reference the members of the joint commission did try to treat the Indians of the lower coast with a modicum of liberality and justice.

Meanwhile, in the southern interior the Indians were growing more and more angry. The delays in the visit of the commission had only increased their discontent. They had expected the commission in the summer of 1876 and were exasperated when it failed to appear. It was late in June 1877 before the

[55]Anderson to minister of the interior, 29 September 1876, RG10, vol. 3,633, file 6,425(1); Sproat to Laird, 30 September and 27 November 1876, RG10, vol. 3,637, file 7,131 and vol. 3,611, file 3,756(1).

[56]Archibald McKinlay, Diary, 9, 10, and 20 November 1876, Diary, 1876–1877, PABC.

[57]Canada, Department of the Interior, "Annual Report . . . 1876," Canada, *Sessional Papers*, 3d Parl., 4th sess., 1877, no. 11, p. xvi.

commissioners arrived in Kamloops. Already the provincial government was agitating to have the commission abolished. The province complained that the joint commission was an excessively expensive way of settling land disputes with Indians and that in any case only those Indians presently in contact with settlers needed to have reserves allocated. Throughout the greater part, of the province, wrote the provincial secretary, the Indians were likely to remain completely isolated from intercourse with the whites. Even if this were true, it was evident that experience had still not taught the province that the land question should be dealt with before it became a problem. The province suggested that in future reserves should be allocated by the Indian superintendents, subject to the approval of the chief commissioner of lands and works. But, as Sproat rightly observed, if decisions were dependent on the approval of the chief commissioner of lands and works, not a single reserve would be laid out.[58]

Early in June the commission's trip to the interior was still being delayed by discussions between Victoria and Ottawa. Then, suddenly, there was a demand for action. A member of the provincial government came to the commissioners' office in Victoria urging them to leave at once for the interior. After their enforced inactivity, the members of the commission found this sudden impetus for action surprising. It later transpired that the government was responding to settlers' fears of an Indian uprising.[59]

The evidence on whether the Indians were actually planning militant action against the settlers of the southern interior in the summer of 1877 is conflicting. Many settlers were quite sure that the Indians were organizing an uprising, while others thought that there was no cause for alarm. The Upper Thompson, Shuswap, and Okanagan Indians had always been seen as a greater threat to the settlers than most groups, so some of those who predicted an outbreak were undoubtedly apprehensive. But other, quite level-headed individuals, who were careful to point out that they were not alarmists, thought that there was serious cause for concern.[60] Growing dissatisfaction about land certainly reached a peak among the Shuswap and Okanagan during 1877. In their exasperation some Indians argued to councils that armed force was the only way to extract concessions from an unresponsive government. There was talk that the Indians were contemplating linking up with Nez Percé insurgents in the United States. Indians among the Shuswap claimed to have recently come from Chief Joseph's camp, and they gave

---

[58]Elliott to minister of the interior, 27 January 1877, Sproat to superintendent general, 13 October 1877, RG10, vol. 3,641, file 7,567.

[59]Sproat to superintendent general, 30 June 1877, RG10, vol. 3,650, file 8,497.

[60]See, for example, John Tait and J. A. Mara to Indian commissioners, 15 July 1877, RG10, vol. 3,651, file 8,540.

accounts of the battles that the Nez Percés had fought. Other Indians were said to be in contact with a Spokan sect which advocated complete withdrawal from any kind of contact with the European.[61] There was a meeting of Indians to discuss problems and tactics at the head of Okanagan Lake in late June or early July. This council was an attempt to confederate the Shuswap and Okanagan Indians, although it is doubtful if it produced absolute unanimity. An Okanagan chief known to Anderson for many years told him that the young men at the meeting were eager to fight but that the older chiefs advocated caution.[62] What does seem to have come out of the meeting was a determination to present a united front to the reserve commissioners who were expected in the area.

When the commissioners finally arrived at Kamloops, they were expecting to have to deal with Indian dissatisfaction, but they were not prepared for the depth of disaffection that they encountered. On their arrival at Kamloops, the commissioners found the Indian village to be nearly empty since most of the inhabitants were away at the Okanagan meeting. Sproat, who said that he preferred to gather his own evidence rather than to rely on the judgment of others in Indian matters, concluded that those officials who felt that there was no cause for alarm were mistaken. He thought that settlers often did not know what was going on right under their noses among the Indians and that, if an attack were being planned, the Indians would hardly be likely to inform local officials of their intentions.[63] While some settlers underestimated the gravity of the situation, the reserve commissioners were sufficiently impressed to send a desperate telegram to Ottawa claiming "Indian situation very grave from Kamloops to American border—general dissatisfaction—outbreak possible."[64]

It was Sproat's opinion that any outbreak that occurred would be the logical outcome of provincial policies. An Indian rising "would not be a revolt against authority, but the despairing action of men suffering intolerable wrong, which the Provincial Government will take no steps to remedy." Ottawa concurred. "It is obvious," wrote the minister of the interior, "that the discontent of the Indians is wholly due to the policy which has been pursued towards them by the local authorities." And he added that in the event of an Indian war "the people of Canada generally would not sustain a policy

---

[61]McKinlay, Diary, 17 August 1877; Sproat to superintendent general, 27 August 1877, RG10, vol. 3,653, file 8,701.

[62]Anderson to Meredith, 21 July 1877, RG10, vol. 3,651, file 8,540.

[63]Report of Reserve Commission, 16 July 1877, B.C., Provincial Secretary, Correspondence; Sproat to superintendent general, 27 August 1877, RG10, vol. 3,653, file 8,701.

[64]Sproat and Anderson to minister of the interior, 13 July 1877, Canada, Indian Reserve Commission, Correspondence.

towards the Indians of that Province which is, in my opinion, not only unwise and unjust, but also illegal."[65]

Peace in the interior was tenuous for a time, but eventually the reserve commissioners were able to cool the situation off. Sproat tried to calm the Indians by telling them not to brood over the past but to prepare themselves for the future. Before leaving Victoria, he had spoken to Douglas, who recalled that he had always been very careful to keep the Shuswap and Okanagan Indians in a good humour.[66] The commission therefore gave the Indians time to express all their complaints in their own way. The commissioners realized that the Indians had different concepts of time and methods of negotiating, and they felt that there was a marked contrast between the attention that they gave to the Indians and the abrupt manner in which they were treated by the colonial government.[67]

But the ultimate tactic of the reserve commission was to divide the Shuswap leaders, thus breaking up the nascent "confederation." The Roman Catholic missionary Father C.J. Grandidier had persuaded the Adams Lake band not to attend the council at the head of Okanagan Lake but to meet with the commission instead. So while the Kamloops Indians were away at the meeting, a settlement was reached at Adams Lake and with another group on the North Thompson River. These northern bands had always been among the most isolated of the Shuswap Indians.[68] When Louis, the Kamloops leader, returned, he was furious with these Indians for settling, but other chiefs were beginning to waver. Messages were constantly passing between the different bands, and a settlement in one place facilitated negotiations in another. Within some bands there were divisions between young and old. Young Indians were said to have fewer bitter memories and were less inclined to argue about the past. At Spallumcheen north of Okanagan Lake, the prestige of an old chief was destroyed when his views on the land question were rejected by other Indians negotiating with the commission. By playing off the old against the young, agreement could often be reached in situations which appeared impossible. But Sproat cautioned that while land grievances might be settled, memories of brutal and unjust treatment could not be easily erased.[69]

---

[65]Sproat to Vankoughnet, 26 November 1879, RG10, vol. 3,612, file 3,756(2); Mills to Sproat, 3 August 1877, Canada, Indian Reserve Commission, Correspondence.

[66]Report of Sproat, 1 December 1877, RG10, vol. 3,612, file 3,756(16).

[67]Sproat to superintendent general, 27 August 1877, RG10, vol. 3,611, file 3,756(12).

[68]See James Teit, *The Shuswap*, pp. 467–68.

[69]Sproat to minister of the interior, 16 July 1877, RG10, vol. 3,651, file 8,540; Reserve Commission, Journal, 23 August 1877, Canada, Department of Indian Affairs, "Journal of Proceedings of the Commission for the Settlement of the Indian Reserves in the Province of British Columbia," RG10, vol. 1,284; Sproat to superintendent general, 27 August 1877, RG10, vol. 3,611, file 3,756(12).

Leaving Kamloops, the commissioners proceeded to Shuswap Lake and then through the Okanagan Valley and into the Similkameen area before winter caught up with them. The summer of 1877 was the last in which the joint commisssion was active. In 1878 pressure from the provincial government led to the dissolution of the three-man commission, and Sproat carried on alone until 1880. Many Indians wondered if yet another change in the manner of dealing with them meant that once again their needs were to be trifled with. But as sole commissioner Sproat continued to try to achieve a reasonable settlement of the land question.

Sproat felt bound to speak for the Indians because they had great difficulty in making even their most reasonable wishes known "through an atmosphere thick with prejudice and injustice."[70] He took a great interest in the Indian way of life and argued strongly that their "manners and customs" had to be understood before reserves could be satisfactorily assigned to them. He pointed out that different parts of tribal land were frequented at different times of the year and were "linked to the hearts of the people by many associations." It was therefore impossible to open the country for settlement without interfering with the Indian mode of life. Sproat thought that this point had not been appreciated by the rulers of British Columbia since Douglas left office. The Indians of the interior were constantly on the move, and Sproat knew that it would be dangerous to try to confine them to limited reserves. They liked to gallop about to visit friends and to fish and hunt where they pleased. Sproat concluded the reserves could not be allocated as though assigning land to Ontario farmers: giving so many acres to each individual. Many interior Indians were not so much interested in acreage and good arable land as in the "old 'places of fun' up in the mountains or some places of fishing . . . where, at certain seasons, they assemble to fish, dig roots and race their horses." Sproat sometimes had Indians beseeching him that, if she could not give them good soil, would the Queen at least give them the rocks and stones of the "old loved localities" now possessed by the whites.[71]

While he did not want to alter radically the Indians' traditional way of life, it was also evident to Sproat that many were changing anyway. Among the Shuswap, for example, there had been great changes since 1865 when Nind reported that they "do nothing more with their land than cultivate a few small patches of potatoes here and there." Now they had large herds of stock, and

[70]Sproat to superintendent general, 10 November 1879, RG10, vol. 3,669, file 10,691.
[71]Sproat to superintendent general, 26 October 1878, RG10, vol. 3,612, file 3,756(1); Sproat to Mills, 27 August 1877, RG10, vol. 3,653, file 8,705.

grain and root crops were grown on most reserves.[72] As a result of Nind's report, the Indians were deprived of land, but now that their stock numbers were increasing they required more, particularly as overstocking in the interior was already destroying the natural bunch grass and replacing it with sage brush.[73] Sproat also pointed out frequently that in the arid interior land without water was useless. While provincial legislation laid down minimal Indian rights to land, there was no mention of water rights. There were desultory attempts to deal with the land question, but nothing was done to ensure that the Indians had access to water.

Even as Sproat was working to solve some of these problems, his time was running out. Public opinion was rapidly building up against the reserve commission. Many settlers, both on the coast and in the interior, thought that the commission was being too liberal. Sproat had told Indians that it was not possible to turn the country "topsy turvy" to settle land disputes. Instead, compromises had to be reached.[74] But the settlers appeared to be unwilling to compromise. Although Indians were never given as much land by the commission as they could have pre-empted if they were white, many settlers complained that Indians were being treated too generously. In the interior Sproat had tried not to interfere with the interests of the settlers, but they still protested bitterly when Indian reserves were established adjacent to their land. One group of South Thompson river settlers objected to Indian neighbours as being "a constant source of annoyance" because of their trespassing stock and "the well known thieving proclivities of the Indians themselves." Furthermore, they wrote, the roads "will be constantly haunted with hooting savages yelping curs and other frightful objects, rendering traffic on it either dangerous or impossible." In a petition to the government these settlers said that the result of having an Indian reserve adjacent to their land would be that their property "on the improvement of which we have expended upwards of a decade of our most vigorous manhood, will be confiscated, for property with such surroundings will be utterly valueless in market."[75]

Other settlers protested about Indians trespassing on their land. A man

---

[72]Nind to colonial secretary, 17 July 1865, B.C., *Papers Connected with Indian Land*, p. 29. Sproat, perhaps a little ingenuously, assumed that Nind's earlier description was accurate at the time (enclosure in Sproat to superintendent general, 6 February 1878, RG10, vol. 3,657, file 9,360).

[73]Sproat to superintendent general, 16 November 1879, RG10, vol. 3,703, file 17,626(2).

[74]Sproat to superintendent general, 26 October 1878, RG10, vol. 3,612, file 3,756.

[75]Petition in A. M. Bryan to chief commissioner of lands and works, 29 September 1877, RG10, vol. 3,668, file 10,344(2); Petition of Whitfield Chase, Alexander McBryan, D. G. MacPherson, and C. E. Williams, 24 January 1878, British Columbia, *Sessional Papers*, 2d Parl., 3d sess., and 3d Parl., 1st sess., 1878, p. 451.

named William Smith who lived near the mouth of the Fraser wrote to the Indian superintendent that

> their is some Indians settled on my Preemption and I can not get them off also their dogs are a bothering my Stock and Stealing ever thing they can get hold of and the Indians are tramping down my dykes and when I say any thing to them they call me all the mean names they can think of so I think it is time they was moved off with strick orders not to come back on the place any more.[76]

Other, more literate, complaints were received. Archibald Dodds, a Cowichan settler, concluded that "there is no law or justice here for a white man, the Indian has everything his way," and some wag in the Okanagan said that the object of the reserve commission was to put the whites on reserves.[77]

Sproat realized that there was bound to be some opposition of interest between stock-raising settlers and stock-raising Indians if the lands of the latter were to be defined. But he felt that objections like those of the South Thompson settlers were "the angry utterance of men steeped in prejudice."[78] Many settlers treated the Indians well, but when there was tension between the interests of the two races, the settlers all took a similar position. They forgot the "obligation of regarding the Indians as equal before the law, in practice, as well as theory." When settlers thought that they had been badly treated by the commission, they began to abuse it. They stirred up the newspapers, and, because most of its members were "farming settlers with the prejudices of their class," settlers had a great influence on government. Sproat began "to think that people here believe that the Indians have no rights, and that they cannot acquire them."[79]

Sproat's assessment of the mood of the settlers was generally accurate. Some disagreed with the majority opinion. The *Inland Sentinel*'s sentiments were more admirable than its spelling when it urged that "it is far better to deal fairly with those whom the creator first gave possession of the Great Loan Land."[80] But most settlers put their own interests ahead of those of the Indians, and they most assuredly had the ear of the government.

Both the Elliott administration, which held office from February 1876 to

[76]Smith to Powell, 22 May 1875, Canada, Department of Indian Affairs, British Columbia, Early Correspondence, RG10, vol. 1,001.

[77]Letter of Dodds, enclosure in Morley to provincial secretary, 23 May 1877, B.C., Provincial Secretary, Correspondence; Sproat to superintendent general, 3 October 1877, RG10, vol. 3,612, file 3,756(2).

[78]Sproat to superintendent general, 9 January 1878, RG10, vol. 3,657, file 9,193.

[79]Sproat to superintendent general, 30 October 1877, RG10, vol. 3,612, file 3,756(22); Sproat to superintendent general, 26 November 1878, RG10, vol. 3,670, file 10,769.

[80]*Inland Sentinel*, 10 June 1880.

June 1878, and Walkem's governments, which preceded and followed Elliott's, were well tuned to the demands of settlers. The votes of settlers in the interior could often be crucial to these governments with their small majorities. As Sproat asked rhetorically, "would a member of a minister, himself a settler, disregard angry and prejudiced messages from his neighbours, merely for the sake of the Indians."[81] Elliott's chief commissioner of lands and works, Forbes George Vernon, told Sproat that he agreed with the commissioner's views on the land question in the Okanagan but that, owing to the approach of his election in the district, he could take no action.[82] As far as Sproat was concerned, there was little to choose between the two administrations on Indian land policy. Walkem had made the original agreement to establish the reserve commission, and so Elliott campaigned on the idea that Walkem had made an extravagant and expensive concession. What the Indians thought about the commission or the actual cost of its operations were irrelevant, since neither the commissioners nor the Indians were consulted. It was the old story said Sproat, "anything will do for the Indians."[83]

The attitude and inaction of the settler government in Victoria was a continuing impediment to the commission's work. To meet with the approval of the provincial government, Indian reserves had to conform to every letter of the law, at the same time as all kinds of laxity were permitted with settlers' pre-emptions. For instance, the commission was informed in 1879 that the government would not recognize reserves that had not been surveyed according to the regulations laid down in the Land Amendment Act of that year. Adhering to the provisions of this act would result in greatly increased expenditure by the commission, and the act was also to apply to reserves that were already established. In the end, not a single reserve laid out by the reserve commission was approved by the provincial chief commissioner of lands and works.[84] In some places all the good land had been taken up by settlers before the commission arrived, making it difficult to find land for the Indians. In other places the provincial government allowed settlers to purchase land after it had been reserved for the Indians by the commission, and in the interior whites continued to run their cattle on winter range land set aside for the

[81] Sproat to superintendent general, 13 October 1877, RG10, vol. 3,641, file 7,567.

[82] Sproat to superintendent general, 26 November 1878, RG10, vol. 3,670, file 10,769.

[83] Sproat to Meredith, 9 April 1877, RG10, vol. 3,641, file 7,567.

[84] Edward Mohun to chief commissioner of lands and works, 23 June 1879, British Columbia, Lands Department, Correspondence, 1872–1890, PABC; see also British Columbia, *Sessional Papers*, 4th Parl., 3d sess., 1885, pp. 392–402.

Indians.[85] When Sproat wrote to government officials about such cases, they simply ignored his correspondence, although they always paid prompt attention to any letter containing the complaint of a settler. One government official told Sproat that drawing Walkem's attention to a letter on Indian business "was like calling his attention to the presence of a rattlesnake."[86] When the reserve commissioner wrote to the provincial secretary regarding the land fiasco in the Cowichan area, his letter was annotated with finely reasoned comments such as "impertinence" and "presumptuous assurance."[87] It gradually dawned on Sproat that "no government of the province will effectually recognize that the Indians have any rights to land. If it is possible to deprive them of their land, or prevent them from getting a bit of land, it will be done." Under these conditions it must have been very difficult for him to convey to the Indians the professed "anxious desire of the Provincial Government to deal justly and reasonably with them."[88]

Sproat had told Ottawa that basically there was little difference between the two governments, but at the same time he advised the Dominion that it would be wise to settle all Indian matters while Elliott was in office. He warned that once Walkem and his two cronies, Ash and Beaven, got back into power, the situation would once again become impossible. They "will do anything to embarrass and defeat the Commission," wrote Sproat prophetically.[89] Walkem was called upon to form a government in June 1878 as public pressure continued to mount against the reserve commission. Sproat noticed that the criticism of him was becoming more bitter. The member of Parliament for Yale, Francis James Barnard, said in the House of Commons that the reserve commissioner "seemed to think all he had to do was give the Indians whatever land they fancied." De Cosmos wrote to John A. Macdonald advising him that the services of Sproat ought to be dispensed with. Finally Sproat resigned under pressure early in 1880. James Fell, a Victoria businessman, wrote to congratulate Macdonald, saying that "it was high time that G.M. Sproat was brought to book and put in his proper place, and you have just

---

[85]Sproat to superintendent general, 1 May 1879, RG10, vol. 3,686, file 13,253; Powell to superintendent general, 5 November 1886, Canada, Department of Indian Affairs, "Annual Report . . . 1886," Canada, *Sessional Papers*, 6th Parl., 1st sess., 1887, no. 6, p. 96; Sproat to superintendent general, 16 November 1879, RG10, vol. 3,703, file 17,626(2).

[86]Sproat to Vankoughnet, 9 April 1879, RG10, vol. 3,684, file 12,836.

[87]Pencil notes on Sproat to provincial secretary, 7 May 1878, B.C., Provincial Secretary, Correspondence.

[88]Sproat to Vankoughnet, 9 April 1879, RG10, vol. 3,684, file 12,836; Sproat to minister of interior, 26 October 1876, RG10, vol. 3,633, file 6,465(1).

[89]Sproat to Laird, 30 September 1876, RG10, vol. 3,637, file 7,131.

done the right thing, one head is all that is required."[90] Sproat had paid the price of allowing British Columbia's Indian land policy to lapse into fair treatment of the Indians.

By 1880, not only had Sproat been eliminated from any role in Indian policy, but a number of the old gang of the early 1870's were back in office. Macdonald was prime minister again and now had the additional portfolio of minister of the interior, which included responsibility for Indian affairs. Walkem was back as premier, and even Trutch had returned to official life, having been appointed dominion agent in British Columbia on railway matters. Trutch was also to "take an advisory interest in Indian matters in British Columbia."[91] Accordingly, Macdonald asked him to suggest a replacement for Sproat, and Trutch replied that his brother-in-law would make a good reserve commissioner. So Peter O'Reilly was duly appointed.

Some old attitudes were also being expressed. Trutch agreed with those who had opposed Sproat's actions. He still did not "consider it of special moment to secure extensive tracts of land for the Indians" and thought that many Indian reserves established by Sproat were "unreasonably large," or, as Trutch was so fond of saying, "out of all proportion to the actual or prospective requirements of the Indians." Trutch later told the prime minister that the reserves laid out since 1871 had never been used by the Indians except as hunting grounds and that they were not likely to be used. Therefore Trutch advised Macdonald that in future the decisions of the reserve commissioner should be subject to confirmation by the Indian superintendent and the chief commissioner of lands and works, and this suggestion was accepted by the Department of Indian Affairs.[92]

O'Reilly was appointed Indian reserve commissioner in spite of, or perhaps because of, the fact that the Indians had made strong complaints about nearly every reserve that he laid out as a magistrate during the colonial period. The Nicola Valley reserves were a case in point. These reserves were first established by O'Reilly under instructions from Trutch in 1868. Immediately, one of the Nicola chiefs complained to the Reverend J.B. Good at Lytton that O'Reilly had ignored his expressed wishes and excluded his favourite living place, with its burial sites, water courses, and potato patches, from the

[90]Canada, Parliament, *Parliamentary Debates*, 9 (1880): 1633; De Cosmos to Macdonald, 29 September 1879, Fell to Macdonald, 25 January 1880, Macdonald Papers, vols. 293, 364.

[91]Vankoughnet to Trutch, 11 February 1880, RG10, vol. 3,710, file 17,514(2).

[92]Trutch to Macdonald, 6 November 1880, 15 January 1884, 19 May 1880, Macdonald Papers, vols. 279, 280, and RG10, vol. 3,711, file 19,581; Vankoughnet to Walkem, 22 July 1880, B.C., Lands Department, Correspondence.

reserve. Governor Musgrave was petitioned on the case, and he consulted O'Reilly, who claimed that when he established the reserve he had been directed to deal liberally with the Indians. In fact there was no instruction to this effect in Trutch's original letter. O'Reilly also argued, again quite erroneously, that, as he had never been to Nicola Lake, Good was in no position to comment on the matter. In short, O'Reilly saw no reason to change his original opinion about the adequacy of the reserves that he had established for the Nicola Indians. Having laid out their reserves in violation of their wishes, as magistrate O'Reilly then levied heavy fines against them when their cattle wandered on to a settler's unfenced field of grain.[93]

With this man as reserve commissioner the allotment of land to the Indians once again reflected settler demands or, as Trutch and O'Reilly put it, "the public interest." At a meeting of the Legislative Assembly on 14 January 1884 a resolution was passed recommending to the dominion government that it rearrange Indian reserves so that unused agricultural or timber lands could be thrown open to settlers.[94] Premier William Smithe said that the previous commissioners had allocated reserves with "reckless extravagance."[95] O'Reilly, who was personally involved in a number of ranching ventures in the province, agreed with these opinions. He spent a large amount of his time revising Sproat's work. Reserves were reduced, and the commonages that Sproat had established in the interior for the Indians to run stock on were now taken away from them. O'Reilly had two reasons for relieving the Indians of these commonages: first, that they made no use of such areas for stock raising, and, second, that the Indians' horses had eaten out these ranges to such an extent that they were destroying the grasslands.[96] When he allocated new reserves,

[93]Good to Musgrave, 19 December 1870, Trutch to O'Reilly, 5 August 1868 (the general advice in this letter was to allocate ten acres per family), O'Reilly to colonial secretary, 4 March and 12 January 1871, cf. Good to colonial secretary, 3 February 1871, B.C., *Papers Connected with Indian Land*, pp. 86–87, 50, 91, 88, 89–90; Powell to provincial secretary, 3 September 1877, B.C., Provincial Secretary, Correspondence.

[94]B.C., *Journals of the Legislative Assembly, 1884*, p. 31.

[95]Smithe to O'Reilly, 29 November 1884, B.C., *Sessional Papers*, 4th Parl., 3d sess., 1885 (Return of Indian Lands), p. xvi.

[96]O'Reilly to superintendent general, 23 November 1889 and 5 December 1888, O'Reilly to chief commissioner of lands and works, 12 November 1889, Canada, Department of Indian Affairs, Indian Reserve Commission, Outgoing Correspondence, 1876–1892, RG10, vol. 1,274.

O'Reilly's procedures were in marked contrast to the meticulous care with which Sproat worked. It was a return to the earlier method of rushing into an area, making a decision with little or no consultation, imposing it on the Indians, and then wondering why they were dissatisfied. At Soda Creek, for example, a reluctant chief was told that he had better take what land was offered to him as the commissioner had to leave the following day. It was proving particularly difficult to establish reserves in this part of the Cariboo since all the good land had already been taken up by settlers. At Alkali Lake O'Reilly gave the Indians some land that had been left by settlers because it was impossible to irrigate.[97] With decisions like these, it is not surprising that the provincial chief commissioner of lands and works now felt that he could approve the reserves allocated by the reserve commissioner, and the premier was able to write to O'Reilly that since he had assumed the position, "a much fairer and more accurate appreciation of the duties and responsibilities of the office has been displayed."[98]

Apart from the fact that Indian land policy was now back to normal, there were other indications of the settlers' dominance in the 1880's. Sometime during the decade the Indians were outnumbered by the non-Indian population of the province. During the 1880's the Indian population had declined to about 25,000. According to the census of 1880, the Indians were still the majority of a total population of 49,459, but by 1891 the Indians constituted less than one-third of a total of 98,173. The changed ratio of the population was the result not only of the near doubling of the non-Indian population during the 1880's but also of the continuing decline of the Indian population. The reversal of the population balance had implications for the power relationship between the races. In many areas of the province, the whites no longer had any fear of an Indian uprising threatening their presence, and they were correspondingly less concerned about conciliating the Indians.

[97]O'Reilly to superintendent general, 22 September 1881, Canada, Department of Indian Affairs, "Annual Report . . . 1881," Canada, *Sessional Papers*, 4th Parl., 4th sess., 1882, no. 6, p. 181; McKinlay to Tolmie, 22 May 1881, Archibald McKinlay, Correspondence Outward, 1871–1885, PABC.

[98]B.C., *Sessional Papers*, 4th Parl., 3d sess., 1885, pp. 403–10; Smithe to O'Reilly, 29 November 1884, ibid., p. xvi.

THE INDIAN PROPORTION OF THE POPULATION
OF BRITISH COLUMBIA, 1881, 1891 and 1901

Year	Indian	Total
1881	25,661[a]	49,459[b]
1891	35,202(?)[c]	98,173[d]
1901	25,488[e]	178,657[e]

a. Canada, *Census of Canada*, 1881, 4:11. This figure is probably more accurate than others of the period as it reflects the careful enumerations of the Indian reserve commission in some places and the counts taken by the newly appointed Indian agents.
b. Ibid., 4:3.
c. Canada, Department of Indian Affairs, "Annual report . . . 1891," Canada, *Sessional Papers*, 7th Parl., 2d sess., 1892, no. 14, part 1, p. 253. The census of Canada for 1891 gives no figure for the Indian population of British Columbia. This figure is based partly on estimates and, like most estimates, is probably too high. In 1873 Powell had reckoned the Indian population of the Province to be 28,500 but thought that his estimate was probably too large. See Powell to chief commissioner of lands and works, 19 April 1873, B.C., *Papers Connected with Indian Land*, p. 115.
d. Canada, *Census*, 1891, 1:366.
e. Canada, *Census*, 1901, 1:285,2. In 1894 the Department of Indian Affairs had revised its estimate of the Indian population downwards to 25,618 (Canada, Department of Indian Affairs, "Annual Report . . . 1894," Canada, *Sessional Papers*, 7th Parl., 5th sess., 1895, no. 14, part 2, p. 311), and by 1901 its estimate of 24,576 was much closer to the census figure (Canada, Department of Indian Affairs, "Annual Report . . . 1901," Canada, *Sessional Papers*, 9th Parl., 2d sess., 1902, no. 27, part 2, p. 182).

The railway, the real link with Canada, was completed in 1886 and helped to consolidate the settlers' grasp on the country. A number of Indians found temporary employment on the railway gangs, but railway workers also subjected the Indians to some of the more unsavoury aspects of Western civilization, bringing drunkenness and prostitution to those areas in which they worked. The railway and railway land also introduced a new ingredient into the Indian land confusion. The Canadian Pacific Railway ran through Indian land in a number of places without any compensation being given to the occupiers by the provincial government. By 1885 white property owners had been paid compensation for land taken up by the railway, but the rights of the Indians to similar treatment had not been conceded.[99]

By the 1880's settlers were beginning to probe the farthest corners of the province. In the far north whites were moving into the Cassiar district, and there were reports of encroachment on Indian land and mistreatment of the

[99]Sproat to superintendent general, 24 May 1879 and 3 December 1878, RG10, vol. 3,692, file 14,171, and vol. 3,670, file 10,831; Canada, Department of Indian Affairs, "Annual Report . . . 1885," Canada, *Sessional Papers*, 5th Parl., 4th sess., 1886, no. 4, p. xvi; Powell to superintendent general, 2 November 1885, ibid., p. 117.

inhabitants,[100] while in the southeastern corner the Kootenay were losing large parts of their range to settlers. The Upper Kootenay lived adjacent to the border with the North West Territories, and they had traditionally crossed the Rockies for the annual buffalo hunt. Because of their knowledge of the prairies, the Kootenay, perhaps more than any other Indians in British Columbia, could appreciate the differences between federal and provincial Indian policies, particularly after their transmontane neighbours, the Blackfeet, signed a treaty in 1877. Like the plains Indians, the Kootenay had suffered from a loss of food supply with the decline of the buffalo. By 1880 their hunting trips across the mountains were unsuccessful.[101] So the Kootenay were turning increasingly to cattle raising at the same time as settlers were beginning to covet their land. By 1884 it was apparent to the Indian administrators that reserves should be allocated to the Kootenay, and the reserve commissioner was sent out.

O'Reilly laid out the Kootenay reserves with his customary clumsiness. He was unable to take a census and so was not in a position to assess accurately the needs of the Indians. The Kootenay chief, Isadore, refused to accept O'Reilly's allocations and was most dissatisfied when the commissioner left the area, for several favourite camping spots had been excluded from the reserves.[102] Local settlers, however, complained that the Indians had been treated too generously, and William Smithe, the chief commissioner of lands and works, wrote to O'Reilly that "I cannot but think that in Kootenay you have overestimated the requirements of the Indians and underestimated those of the whites." But Lawrence Herchmer, the commissioner of the North West Mounted Police, visited the Kootenays in 1887 and concluded that the reserves established by O'Reilly were "altogether inadequate."[103] The loss of land was at the heart of Kootenay discontent.

In 1887 Isadore's followers expressed their displeasure with the authorities when one of their number, named Kapula, was arrested on suspicion of killing two miners. Two years earlier their bodies had been found near Deadman's

---

[100]*Victoria Daily Standard*, 24 January 1880.

[101]William Fernie to Powell, 30 June 1880, RG10, vol. 3,719, file 22,673. Apparently this development affected the Kootenay in the late 1870's because Powell reported in 1873 that they were still obtaining buffalo meat from the prairies (Powell to minister of the interior, 3 November 1873, RG10, vol. 3,738, file 20,013[1]).

[102]O'Reilly to chief commissioner of lands and works, 10 December 1884, Canada, Indian Reserve Commission, Outgoing Correspondence; Powell to superintendent general, 18 November 1886, RG10, vol. 3,738, file 28,013(1A); Colonel James Baker to attorney-general, 27 April 1887, Macdonald Papers, vol. 325.

[103]Smithe to O'Reilly, 29 November 1884, B.C., *Sessional Papers*, 4th Parl., 3d sess., 1885, (Return of Indian Lands), p. xvi; Herchmer to Thomas White, 5 July 1887, Macdonald Papers, vol. 325.

Creek, and it was assumed, on very little evidence, that they had been murdered by Indians. Isadore's response to the arrest of Kapula was to use force to release him from jail, although a local resident felt that the Kootenay were more concerned about their land than the arrest.[104] An *ad hoc* commission was sent to the Kootenays by the provincial government to treat with the Indians, and a detachment of North West Mounted Police from Lethbridge was sent in under Inspector Sam Steele. Later Steele was to recall that the Kootenay were generally a law-abiding and disciplined group, and he was especially impressed by Isadore's capacity for leadership. The provincial commission consisting of Powell, O'Reilly, and Forbes George Vernon came to deal with the fundamental land dispute. But these men had learned nothing from experience. Though Isadore and his band were away when the commission arrived, the reserves were revised. The commission confirmed O'Reilly's earlier decision that the part of Joseph Prairie occupied by Isadore's band had to be relinquished to Colonel James Baker, a local rancher and member of the Legislative Assembly. Steele was instructed to acquaint Isadore and his Indians with these decisions.[105] The commission also left a message for Isadore telling him that he had failed in his "duty" by allowing his men to free the murder suspect and that "when a chief does not do his duty, another chief is put in his place."[106] On his return Isadore was not pleased, either with the decision of the commission or with the sentiments expressed in their message.

This kind of shabby treatment of the Indians and their land was continuing in other parts of the province. On the northern coast the Tsimshian were also complaining bitterly. O'Reilly laid out reserves for the coastal Tsimshian and the Nishga during the 1880's. Again he did not allow time for the Indians to consider and express their needs or for himself to unravel the complexities of Tsimshian land tenure.[107] His allocations therefore created more problems than they solved. It is sometimes argued that because the coast Indians lived

---

[104]Arthur Fenwick to Powell, 15 March 1887, RG10, vol. 3,738, file 28,013(1A).

[105]Colonel S. B. Steele, *Forty Years in Canada: Reminiscences of the Great Northwest* . . . (Toronto: McClelland, Goodchild, Stewart, 1918), pp. 250–51.

[106]F. G. Vernon, Powell, and O'Reilly to Isadore, 10 October 1887, Canada, Department of Indian Affairs, "Annual Report . . . 1887," Canada, *Sessional Papers*, 6th Parl., 2d sess., 1888, no. 15, p. xcv.

[107]British Columbia, *Metlakatla Inquiry, 1884, Report of the Commissioners, together with the Evidence* (Victoria: R. Wolfenden, 1885), p. xxvi; "Report of Commissioners to Northwest Coast Indians," 30 November 1887, Port Simpson Indians to members of the land commission, 8 October 1887, British Columbia, "Papers Relating to the Commission Appointed to Enquire into the State and Condition of the Indians of the Northwest Coast of British Columbia," *Sessional Papers*, 5th Parl., 2d sess., 1888, pp. 426–59, 462, passim; Garfield, *Tsimshian Clan and Society*, p. 176.

largely off the sea they were less concerned about the land question. But the Tsimshian and the Nishga were certainly worried about the loss of hunting lands and fishing sites. They also raised the much more fundamental question of Indian title to the land. For the Metlakatla Indians the land question was also tied in with the conflict between Duncan and his followers and the C.M.S. One reason for the move to New Metlakatla in Alaska in 1887 was Indian dissatisfaction over land.[108] When the Tsimshian obstructed attempts to survey their land, the ringleaders of the opposition were repeatedly jailed. Finally in 1887 a dominion-provincial commission was sent up the coast to hear the Indians' grievances.

The Tsimshian hoped that at last there would be some action taken, but the commissioners, Clement F. Cornwall representing the Dominion and Joseph P. Planta representing the province, were empowered only to hear and report the Indians' complaints. The commissioners felt constrained to "combat and deny" the notion of Indian title "by stating the law on the subject."[109] Cornwall's opinion was that the "Indian in his wild state has no idea of property in or title to land." He has no concept of definite boundaries, said Cornwall, and his ideas regarding territory are extremely vague. In fact, "the beasts of the field have as much ownership in the land as he has." The commissioner thought that it was important to make the Tsimshian understand that the government would give absolutely no consideration to the idea of Indian title "but at the same time to humour and smooth them down and show the interest taken in them by the Government."[110] But the Tsimshian were not to be humoured. They told the commissioners that they were not ignorant people and that they knew the value of their land. Nor were they impressed when they were told that the land belonged to the Queen. "We nearly fainted when we heard that this land was claimed by the Queen," said a Kincolith chief, and at Nass Harbour an old man wanted to hear the name of the chief who had given the land to the Queen. In response to vigorous assertions of Indian title, the commissioners said that the Indians' words would be reported to the provincial government but that there would be no recognition of their title to the land. A Kincolith man retorted that they had heard government promises often enough before; this time they had hoped that the commissioners had come empowered to do something.[111]

The coastal Indians were also concerned about European inroads on their

---

[108]David Leask to William Sebright Green, 11 December 1886, F. W. Chesson Papers, 1869–1905, Glenbow Historical Library and Archives, Calgary.

[109]"Report of Commissioners to the Northwest Coast Indians," p. 418.

[110]Cornwall to superintendent general, 8 December 1887, RG10, vol. 3,776, file 37,373(2).

[111]"Report of the Commissioners to the Northwest Coast Indians," pp. 434, 439–40.

fishing privileges. Commercial fishing and canning operations increased during the 1870's and 1880's and with them Indian worries that their favourite fishing grounds would be depleted. For the coast Indians protection of their fishing rights was as important as the reservation of grazing and arable land was to the interior Indians, and the lack of effective action had made the coastal Indians equally suspicious of government officials. When O'Reilly went to lay out reserves for the Seymour Inlet Indians, they were very reluctant to point out their fishing places because they felt that once any white man knew about them, others would inevitably come to exploit them. From the Fraser to the Nass, the development of canning operations meant that traditional Indian fishing sites were sought after by Whites.[112]

The 1887 commission to the Indians of the northwest coast also uncovered another difficulty. Many Tsimshian were so dissatisfied with the government that they refused to accept the newly appointed Indian agent. The commissioners, for their part, concluded that one reason for the trouble with the Tsimshian was that they had remained isolated from government regulations and control.[113] Earlier the federal government, perhaps following Trutch's advice to Macdonald, had decided to divide British Columbia into Indian agencies, and by 1881 six agents had been appointed.[114] These men were supposed to advise the Indians and protect their interests, but they were also important agents of acculturation. The Cowichan agent was hopeful that he would soon be able to break down the old customs that hindered Indian "improvement," and the West Coast agent lectured the Indians freely "on their foolishness and ignorance."[115]

The Indian custom that Indian agents were most anxious to eradicate was the potlatch. They felt that the potlatch was a "foolish, wasteful and demoralizing custom,"[116] and their opinions were shared by the missionaries. For the missionary the potlatch was the essence of heathenism, and nearly all of them would have agreed with Duncan when he held that the potlatch was "by far

[112]O'Reilly to superintendent general, 29 October 1882, Canada, Department of Indian Affairs, "Annual Report . . . 1882," Canada, *Sessional Papers*, 5th Parl., 1st sess., 1883, no. 5, p. 109; Sproat to W. Buckingham, deputy minister of the interior, 6 November 1878, RG10, vol. 3,662, file 9,756(1); Powell to superintendent general, 21 September 1881, RG10, vol. 3,766, file 32,876.

[113]"Report of the Commissioners to the Northwest Coast Indians," pp. 420–25.

[114]Trutch to Macdonald, 6 July 1880, RG10, vol. 3,701, file 17,514(2); Canada, Department of Indian Affairs, "Annual Report . . . 1881," p. lxi. The six agencies were Cowichan, West Coast, Kwaw-kewlth, Fraser River, Kamloops, and Okanagan. In 1883 two more were added: Lillooet and Northwest Coast.

[115]Canada, Department of Indian Affairs, "Annual Report . . . 1881," p. 160, and Canada, Department of Indian Affairs, "Annual Report . . . 1883," Canada, *Sessional Papers*, 5th Parl., 2d sess., 1884, no. 4, p. 44.

[116]W. H. Lomas to Powell, 27 February 1884, RG10, vol. 3,628, file 6,244(1).

the most formidable of all obstacles in the way of the Indians becoming Christian, or even civilized."[117] Pressure from Indian agents and missionaries in British Columbia finally prompted the federal government to pass a law prohibiting potlatching. The third clause of the 1884 act amending the 1880 Indian Act stated that "every Indian or other person who engages in or assists in celebrating the Indian festival known as the 'Potlatch' or in the Indian dance known as the 'Tamanawas' is guilty of a misdemeanor and shall be liable to imprisonment."[118]

The potlatch was such an integral part of northwest coast Indian society that to eliminate it would almost be to destroy traditional Indian culture. In the event, the law prohibiting the potlatch proved virtually impossible to enforce. Indian agents could not single-handedly apprehend all the Indians who took part in the ceremony, although there were occasional arrests. In 1889 the Alert Bay agent, R.H. Pidcock, had a Kwakiutl chief named Hemasak convicted under the act and sentenced to six months' imprisonment. But Chief Justice Begbie, who heard the appeal, discharged the Indian on a technicality and noted in his judgment that the law banning the potlatch was imprecise. He pointed out that if the legislature "desired to create an offence previously unknown to the law there ought to be a definition of it in the statute."[119]

As soon as the anti-potlatch law was passed, many Indians began to protest vigorously, while others quietly determined to continue their potlatches in defiance of the law. Older people particularly resented this attempt to interfere with their traditional customs. The Cowichan petitioned the prime minister to repeal the law, while the Kwakiutl defied it by ignoring every exhortation by the Indian agent to give up the custom.[120] When Boas visited the Newitty in 1886, he had to assure them that he was not a government agent before they would accept him. Once they were sure of his intentions, however, they made it clear that they would not follow the orders to give up potlatching and that they despised the Indian administration, from Powell down, for giving such instructions.[121] It would have been degrading and economically disastrous for many chiefs to stop potlatching while they still owed obligations. Then, apart from its ceremonial and festive functions, the potlatch was a

[117]Duncan to Laird, May 1875, CMSA.

[118]Canada, *Statutes*, "An Act Further to Amend 'The Indian Act, 1880,' " 47 Vict. c. 27, *Statutes of Canada*, 1884.

[119]Enclosure in H. Moffatt to superintendent general, 30 August 1889, RG10, vol. 3,628, file 6,244(1); see also LaViolette, *The Struggle for Survival*, pp. 59–63.

[120]Enclosure in Powell to superintendent general, 26 February 1887, Pidcock to Powell, 13 September 1886, RG10, vol. 3,628, file 6,244(1); Codere, *Fighting with Property*, p. 86ff.

[121]Boas to his parents, 7 October 1886, Rohner, pp. 33–36.

means of redistributing wealth. As a Kwakiutl group pointed out, to cease pot-latching would mean that many people would not have enough to eat.[122] But most of all the ceremony was fundamental to the social organization of the coast Indians, and they could see no valid reason why it should be suppressed.

Although the potlatch law was virtually unenforceable in the 1880's, its existence was a blatant expression of the settler belief that Indian culture could be legislated out of existence. Because of their efforts to eliminate the potlatch, the Indian agents were often seen as policemen rather than as advisers by the Indians, but the agents only reflected the view of many settlers. Trutch had told the Kitkatla people some years earlier that "the days are past when your heathenish ideas and customs can any longer be tolerated in this land."[123] During the 1880's this point was being demonstrated in many ways. In 1888 there was an incident near the forks of the Skeena River which indicated the trend. The Gitksan had been restive for a number of years, and there had been more than one clash with Europeans. In 1888 a Kitwancool man killed another Indian in accordance with Indian custom. The murdered man was a sorcerer who was said to have been responsible for the deaths of a number of people. So Kitwancool Jim killed him, and Jim's brother married the widow. According to Jim's father, "it was all settled." Apparently the Indian agent in the area at first said that he would take no action, but then Jim was asked to come down to the village of Kitwanga where, through a misun-derstanding, he was shot by a special constable. The Indians were incensed, and for a time it was thought that they might attack the whites in the area. An account of this affair appeared in a local newspaper under the headline "Brit-ish Not Indian Law Must Prevail in Future."[124]

Another important measure of the nature of race relations in a multiracial society is the extent to which sexual relations between the races are legitimized by marriage. In British Columbia the pattern was indicative of settler domi-nance. Marriages with Indian women were less frequent than sexual exploita-tion or concubinage over an extended period. Around the coastal towns the prostitution of Indian women was still common, and in the interior settlers often lived with Indian women for long periods without formalizing their relationship. There were continual Indian complaints about whites molesting their women, and even after a relationship had become more permanent, the

---

[122]Petition of the Indians of Mamalilacala to Lieutenant-Governor Hugh Nelson, 10 August 1889, RG10, vol. 3,628, file 6,244(1).

[123]Kithrahtla (Kitkatla) Indians before lieutenant-governor, 3 August 1872, O'Reilly Papers.

[124]Wee-tuck-ah-yets (father of Kitwancool Jim) to provincial secretary, enclosure in A. E. Green to provincial secretary, 18 July 1888, B.C., Provincial Secretary, Correspondence; clipping enclosed in report of a committee of the Executive Council, 18 October 1888, RG10, vol. 3,802, file 49,774.

Indian women often had no security. In the interior it was not uncommon for *de facto* Indian wives to be cast aside by settlers in favour of European brides. Indian women and their half-breed children were frequently left unprovided for after the death or marriage of a settler with whom they had lived for several years.[125] The Indian reserve commission reported a case at the head of Okanagan Lake where the Indians complained about a settler named Nelson who had asked an Indian couple for their daughter in marriage. He cohabited with the girl for a number of years and had several children by her, but he did not marry her. Finally she was cast out of the settler's home, and when her father remonstrated with Nelson, he was beaten up so severely that he died of the wounds.[126] The Indians had no redress in such situations. Settlers treated the taking and deserting of Indian concubines with jocular good humour.[127]

By the end of the 1880's the "pattern of dominance" was firmly established. Perhaps the two most important examples were land and the potlatch. The possession of land was fundamental to the cultural survival of almost all the Indians of British Columbia, and the potlatch pervaded nearly every aspect of the life of the coast Indians. During the fur-trading period, both had become increasingly significant aspects of Indian culture. The possibility of Indians profiting from selling furs increased the value of their hunting lands and probably sharpened the Indians' notion of territoriality. The wealth brought by the fur trade had facilitated an increase in the number and size of potlatches. But now, with settlement, there were attempts to deprive the Indians of both land and the potlatch ritual. To the settler, Indian improvidence was epitomized by their use of the land, just as to the missionary Indian improvidence was epitomized by the potlatch. So settlers and missionaries pressured the government to enact legislation that would wean the Indians from these aspects of their traditional way of life.

Naturally some Indians resisted all these efforts to extinguish their traditions, and as long as they did, vestiges of Indian culture remained. The Kwakiutl in particular still clung "with remarkable tenacity to their customs and old mode of life."[128] But this was essentially a rearguard action, for by the 1880's the European had the initiative. The culture of many Indian groups had already been seriously dislocated, and eventually all Indians would experience to some degree the disruptive impact of the settlement frontier.

Some Indians attempted to adapt to the new situation. In their dealings

---

[125]Memo of Begbie enclosed in Powell to secretary of state for the provinces, 8 March 1873, RG10, vol. 3,599, file 1,520.

[126]Canada, Department of Indian Affairs, Reserve Commission Journal, 12 September 1877, RG10, vol. 1,284.

[127]See Crease to O'Reilly, [1868], O'Reilly Papers.

[128]Franz Boas, "Census and Reservations of the Kwakiutl Nation," *Bulletin of the American Geographical Society* 19 (1887): 232.

with the 1887 commission to the northwest coast, the Tsimshian had taken the first steps in political action. But the Indians of the province remained too divided for this to be an effective development. Other Indians made efforts to adapt to the changed economic situation. Around Burrard Inlet some Indians were employed as longshoremen; while along the coast others were employed by the canning companies, some as fishermen and others in occupations in the often unhealthy conditions of the canneries.[129] Frequently such employment was only temporary, and these marginal occupations were hardly adequate compensation for the loss of land and fishing areas.

With the transition from the fur trade and the consolidation of settlement, the Indian had been reduced from an integral to a peripheral role in British Columbia's economy, and this development largely explains the corrosion of traditional Indian cultures after 1858. During the fur-trading period Indians and Europeans were mutually interdependent. Economically each race depended on, and benefited from, the presence and activities of the other. The fur trade nurtured and stimulated Indian culture to such an extent that some anthropologists claim that the climax of Indian culture, particularly on the coast, was reached after the arrival of the white man.[130] The Indians of British Columbia met the fur trade, grappled with it, and turned it to serve their own ends. The economic reciprocity of the two races resulted in a mingling of the two cultures. Because their way of life was not under any serious threat from the fur traders, the Indians felt free to borrow adaptively from the alien culture.

Throughout the 1850's, almost imperceptibly at first, but with gathering momentum, the influence of the fur traders waned as newly arrived settlers began to assert themselves. During these transitional years, instead of a continuing community of interest, there was a growing separation of the two races. Different Europeans were arriving, and their different intentions were reflected in different attitudes towards the Indians. Settlers came to take up land and to develop the frontier in a way that would not involve the Indians. So the European image of the Indian changed. From a primitive partner the Indian became a savage opponent in the mind of the white man. Both the settler economy and the settler view of the Indians reinforced the separateness of "savage" and "civilized" man.

In 1858, with unexpected suddenness, the fur trade was ended and the settlement frontier was founded. The tendencies of the 1850's were confirmed as the old relationship between the races was terminated and the white man

[129]H. Moffatt to provincial secretary, 3 June 1889, B.C., Provincial Secretary, Correspondence.
[130]See, for example, Duff, *Indian History of B.C.*, p. 53.

became an imposition on the Indians. The combined, though different, impacts of gold miners, settlers, missionaries, and government officials began to disrupt traditional Indian cultures. The Indians were largely irrelevant to the aims of the settlers, and settler views were reflected in government policy. Many settlers thought that the Indians were doomed and that it was therefore unnecessary to be concerned about their future. The missionaries strove to eliminate traditional Indian culture and to replace it with a way of life based on European values. The Indians had been able to mould the fur trade to their benefit, but settlement was not malleable: it was unyielding and aggressive. It imposed its demands on the Indians without compromise. Because the Indians were either irrelevant or a hindrance to them, the settlers had no regrets about the dislocation or elimination of Indian cultures. As the whites became more aggressive towards Indian cultures, many Indians found that they could not cope with the pace of change. Realizing that their way of life was under attack, Indians became defensive and determined to conserve what they could of their culture rather than to borrow from the European. But the whites were relentless.

During the 1870's and 1880's the settlement frontier was firmly entrenched. The developments of the 1860's were consolidated as more and more Indian groups came into constant contact with Europeans. Indian objections to the treatment that they received were ignored, and even Indian attempts to organize to help themselves were discouraged. The separation of the races was continued. Isolated in confined rural ghettos, most Indians were unwelcome in the society of settlers. Nor did the settler governments welcome attempts to have Indian rights recognized or Indian needs satisfied. The actions of the provincial government constituted an attack on traditional Indian society and did nothing to replace it with a new way of life.

The history of Indian and European relations after 1890, at least until the Indian resurgence of the middle of the twentieth century, was simply a reassertion of what had already been established by the consolidation of settlement. The Indians continued to find the white man's political system unresponsive. Their current needs were ignored while the old cultures were eroded away. Until about 1930 the Indian population continued to decline. Future commissions and committees on the land question simply involved a repetition of the non-negotiations that had already taken place. The potlatch law was later to be enforced more vigorously than it had been in the 1880's. The Indians continued to be inconsequential in the mainstream of the province's development. By the late 1880's British Columbia was on the threshold of its second development boom, but "the Great Potlatch" was not one to which the Indians would be invited.

Bibliography

A. Primary

1. Manuscript Sources

Anderson, Alexander Caulfield. Correspondence Outward, 1868–1871. MS. PABC.
———. "Diary as an Indian Reserve Commissioner, 3 November-10 December 1876." MS. PABC.
———. "History of the Northwest Coast." TS. UBCL.
Anderson, James Robert. "Notes and Comments on Early Days and Events in British Columbia, Washington and Oregon. . . ." TS. PABC.
Ball, Henry Maynard. Journal, 18 August 1864–27 October 1865. MS. PABC.
Barkley, Charles William. "A Journal of the Proceedings on Board the *Loudoun* [*Imperial Eagle*], Charles William Barkley Esqur. Commander, 24 November 1786–11 June 1787." MS. PABC.
Barkley, Francis. Reminiscences, 1836. MS. PABC.
Bartlett, John. "Remarks on Board the Ship *Massachusetts* Capt. Joab Prince from Boston, towards Canton." TS. UBCL.
Baxter, Sutcliffe. Correspondence Outward, 10 June 1864. MS. PABC.
Bayley, Charles Alfred. "Early Life on Vancouver Island." TS. PABC.
Boit, John. "The Journal of a Voyage Round the Globe, 1795 and 1796 [in the *Union*]." photocopy. UBCL.
British Columbia. Colonial Correspondence (Inward Correspondence to the Colonial Government). MS. PABC.
———. Colonial Secretary. Correspondence Outward 1860–1870. MS. PABC.
———. ———. Correspondence re. Indian Reserves, 1861–1865, 1868–1869, 1874–1877. MS. PABC.
———. ———. Outward Correspondence, September 1860–May 1872. Letters to the Lands and Works Department. MS. PABC.
———. Gold Commissioner. Lillooet. Correspondence Outward, 1862–1868. MS. PABC.
———. ———. Lytton. Correspondence Outward, 1859–1870. MS. PABC.
———. ———. Rock Creek. Correspondence Outward, 1861–1862. MS. PABC.
———. Lands Department. Correspondence, 1872–1890. MS. PABC.
———. Lands and Works Department. Correspondence Outward, 1861–1871. MS. PABC.
———. Legislative Council. Minute Book, 24 January 1864–1 May 1868. MS. PABC.
———. Lieutenant-Governor. Correspondence Outward, 1871–1876. MS. PABC.
———. ———. Despatches to Ottawa, 14 August 1871–26 July 1875. MS. PABC.
———. Provincial Secretary. Correspondence, 1872–1890. MS. PABC.
———. Supreme Court. Notes of Proceedings, 2 May 1864–5 May 1864, by Judge Begbie. MS. PABC.
Brown, Robert. "Journal of the V[ancouver] I[sland] Exploring Expedition, vols. 1 to 5, 7 June to 14 September 1864." MS. PABC.
[Brown, Robert]. "The Land of the Hydahs, a Spring Journey due North . . . Spring of 1866." MS. PABC.
Burney, James. "Journal of the Proceedings of His Majesty's Sloop *Discovery*–Chas. Clerke, Commander, 1776–1779." photocopy. PABC.

Bute Inlet Massacre. "Programme, Minutes and Volunteers Roll of Public Meeting Victoria, 1864." MS. PABC.

Campbell, Robert. Reminiscences. TS. PABC.

Canada. Department of Indian Affairs. Black Series. Western Canada, Record Group 10. MS. PAC.

————. Indian Reserve Commission. Correspondence, Memorandums etc., 1877–1878. MS. PABC.

Chatham, H. M. Ship. "Journal Kept on Board the Armed Tender *Chatham*." TS. PABC.

Chesson, F. W. Papers, 1869–1905. xerox copies. Glenbow Historical Archives and Library, Calgary.

Church Missionary Society. Archives. C.–2/0. North Pacific Mission. British Columbia. Original Letters, Journals, and Papers, Incoming, 1857–1880. microfilm. UBCL.

Cleveland, R. J. "Log Kept by Capt. Richard Cleveland, 10 January 1799 to 4 May 1804." MS. UBCL.

Colnett, J. "Journal of the *Prince of Wales*, 16 October 1786–7 November 1788." microfilm. University of Washington Library.

Connolly, William. Correspondence Outward. TS. PABC.

Cornwall, Clement F. "Diaries of Clement F. Cornwall, 1862–1871." TS. PABC.

Cornwall, Henry P. "Diary of Henry P. Cornwall, Ashcroft, B.C., 10 December 1864–13 June 1865." TS. PABC.

Crease, Sir Henry P. P. Papers. MS. PABC.

Cridge, Edward. "Characteristics of James Douglas Written for H. H. Bancroft in 1878." photocopy. PABC.

Dawson, W. "Doings of ye Trincomalee." microfilm. UBCL.

Daylton, Elizabeth, trans. "Official Documents Relating to Spanish and Mexican Voyages of Navigation, Exploration, and Discovery, Made in North America in the 18th Century," W.P.A. Project no. 2799, Seattle. microfilm. UBCL.

Deans, Annie. Correspondence Outward, 1853–1868. MS. PABC.

Dorr, Ebenezer. Dorr Marine Collection, 1795–1820. MS. PABC.

Douglas, James. Correspondence Outward, 1874. MS. PABC.

————. "Diary of a Trip to the Northwest Coast, 22 April–2 October 1840." MS. PABC.

————. Private Papers, 1835–1877. MS and TS. PABC.

Duncan, William. Papers. microfilm. UBCL.

[*Eliza*]. "Journal of the *Eliza*, February–May 1799." photocopy. UBCL.

[*Eliza*]. "Remarks on the Voyage of the *Eliza*, 1789–1799." photocopy. UBCL.

Ermatinger, Edward. Ermatinger Papers. TS. UBCL.

————. "Letters of Edward Ermatinger from John Work, William Tod, Jane Klyne McDonald and Archibald McDonald, 2 January 1828–14 November 1856." TS. PABC.

[Espinosa y Tello, José]. "Narrative of a Voyage made by the Schooners *Sutil* and *Mexicana* in the Year 1792 to Reconnoiter the Strait of Fuca. . . ." TS. UBCL.

Fort Nisqually. Correspondence Outward, 1850–1859, Letters Signed by W. F. Tolmie. MS. PABC.

Fort Simpson. Correspondence Outward, 6 September 1841–11 October 1844, Letters Signed by John Work, Letters Addressed to John McLoughlin. MS. PABC.

————. Correspondence Outward, 20 November 1851–2 November 1855. MS. PABC.

————. Journal, 12 May 1842–22 June 1843, John Work, Roderick Finlayson. MS. PABC.

————. Journal, 15 September 1859–31 December 1862, Hamilton Moffatt, William McNeill. MS. PABC.

Fort Vancouver. Correspondence Inward, 1840, Signed by James Douglas. MS. PABC.

————. Correspondence Outward. MS. PABC.

Fort Victoria. Correspondence Inward, 1849–1859, from the Hudson's Bay Company, London to James Douglas. MS. PABC.
———. Correspondence Outward, 1850–1858, Letters Signed by James Douglas (Unbound Letters). MS. PABC.
———. Correspondence Outward, 21 December 1856–25 January 1858, Letters Signed by James Douglas (Country Letterbook). MS. PABC.
———. Correspondence to the Hudson's Bay Company on the Affairs of Vancouver Island Colony, 16 May 1850–6 November 1855, 11 December 1855–3 March 1859, Letters Signed by James Douglas. MS. PABC.
Fraser, Paul. "Thompson's River Journal, 17 August 1850–10 June 1855." TS. PABC.
Garrett, A. C. "Reminiscences." TS. PABC.
Gilbert, George. "A Journal of the Third and Last Voyage of Captain James Cook." TS. UBCL.
Good, John Booth. "The Utmost Bounds: Pioneer Jottings of Forty Years Missionary Reminiscences of the Out West Pacific Coast, 1861–1890." TS. PABC.
Great Britain. Admiralty Correspondence, 6 vols., 1848–1860 and 1866–1898. MS. PABC.
———. Colonial Office. Despatches to British Columbia, 1859–1871. MS. PABC.
———. ———. Despatches to Vancouver Island, 1849–1867. MS. PABC.
———. ———. Original Correspondence. British Columbia, 1858–1871, CO.60/1–44. microfilm. UBCL.
———. ———. Original Correspondence. Canada, 1874, CO.42/729–734. microfilm. PAC.
———. ———. Original Correspondence. Vancouver Island, 1846–1867, CO.305/1–30. microfilm. UBCL.
Hargrave, James. Hargrave Collection, Series 1, Letters Addressed to James Hargrave, 1821–1886. MS. PAC.
Helmcken, John Sebastian. Papers. MS. PABC.
Hills, George. Diaries, 1860–1887. MS. Archives of the Vancouver School of Theology.
Hills, William Henry. "Journal on Board H.M.S. *Portland* and *Virago* 8 August 1852–8 July 1853." microfilm. UBCL.
Hudson's Bay Company. Archives. microfilm. PAC.
A-8/6-10. London. Correspondence with the Colonial Office, 1849–1863.
A-11/72-84. London. Inward Correspondence from HBC Posts. Victoria, 1845–1869.
A-7. London. Locked Private Letterbook, 1823–1860.
B-5/a. Fort Alexandria, Post Journal, 1824–1867.
B-5/e. Fort Alexandria, Report on District, 1827–1828.
B-11/a. Babine (Ft. Kilmaurs). Post Journal, 1822–1852.
B-37/a. Chilcotin. Post Journal, 1837–1840.
B-113/a. Fort Langley. Post Journal, 1827–1830.
B-119/a. McLeod Lake. Post Journal, 1823–1824.
B-120/a. Fort McLoughlin. Post Journal, 1833.
B-185/a. Fort Rupert. Post Journal, 1849–1850.
B-188/a. Fort St. James. Post Journal, 1820–1856.
B-188/b. Fort St. James. Correspondence Books, 1821–1833.
B-201/a. Fort Simpson (Nass). Post Journal, 1832–1866.
B-209/a. Stikine. Post Journal, 1840–1842.
B-223/b. Fort Vancouver. Correspondence Books, 1825–1860.
B-223/c. Fort Vancouver. Correspondence Inward, 1826–1860.
B-226/a. Fort Victoria. Post Journal, 1846–1850.
B-226/b. Fort Victoria. Correspondence Books, 1844–1860.
B-226/c. Fort Victoria. Correspondence Inward, 1848–1869.
D-4/1–43. Governor George Simpson. Correspondence Outward, 1821–1851.

D-5/1–52. Governor George Simpson. Correspondence Inward, 1821–1860.
————. Land Office. Victoria. Correspondence Outward 1851–1858, Signed by J. D. Pemberton. MS. PABC.
————. ————. ————. "Register of Land Purchases from the Indians, 1850–1859." MS. PABC.
McLeod's Lake Post. Journal, 1845–1848. MS. Glenbow Historical Library and Archives, Calgary.
McDonald, Archibald. Correspondence Outward, 1830–1849. MS. PABC.
Macdonald, Sir John A. Papers. MS. PAC.
Macdonald, Ranald. Correspondence Outward, 1874. MS. PABC.
McKenzie, Kenneth. Papers. MS. PABC.
McKinlay, Archibald. Correspondence Outward, 1871–1885. MS and TS. PABC.
————. Diary, 1876–1877. MS. PABC.
————. "Narrative of a Chief Factor of the Hudson's Bay Company, 1878." TS. PABC.
McLeod, John. Correspondence Inward, July 1826–February 1837, Letterbook. TS. PABC.
————. "Journals and Correspondence of John McLeod, Senior Chief Trader, Hudson's Bay Company, who was one of the Earliest Pioneers in the Oregon Territory from 1812–1844." TS. PABC.
McMillan, James, and McDonald, Archibald. "Fort Langley Journal, 27 June 1827–30 July 1830." MS. PABC.
[Magee, Bernard]. "Log of the *Jefferson*." photocopy. UBCL.
Malaspina, Alessandro. "Politico-Scientific Voyages Around the World . . . from 1789–1794." Translated by Carl Robinson. TS. UBCL.
Manby, Thomas. "A Journal of Vancouver's Voyage, 1790–1793." photocopy. UBCL.
Manson, William. "Fort Kamloops Journal, January 1859—November 1862." TS. PABC.
Martinez, Don Estevan Josef. "Diary of the Voyage which I, Ensign of the Royal Navy, Don Estevan Josef Martinez, am going to Make to the Port of San Lorenzo de Nuca . . . in the Present Year 1789." Translated by William L. Schurz. TS. UBCL.
Mayne, Richard Charles. "Journal of Admiral Richard Charles Mayne, 1857–1860." MS. PABC.
Moffatt, Hamilton. "Letterbook, Fort Rupert, Fort Simpson, and Fort Kamloops, 1857–1867." MS. PABC.
Morison, Charles Frederic. "Reminiscences of the Early Days in British Columbia 1862–1876 by a Pioneer of the North West Coast." TS. PABC.
Muir, Andrew. "Private Diary, Commencing 9 November 1848 to 5 August 1850." MS. PABC.
[Oblates of Mary Immaculate]. "Records of the Oblate Missions of British Columbia from Oblate Historical Archives St. Peter's Province Holy Rosary Scholasticate, Ottawa." microfilm. UBCL.
O'Reilly, Peter. Papers. MS. PABC.
Pemberton, Augustus F. "Diary of Augustus F. Pemberton 15 January 1856–3 August 1858." MS. PABC.
Pidcock, R. H. "Adventures in Vancouver Island, being an Account of 6 Years Residence, and of Hunting and Fishing Excursions with some Account of the Indians Inhabiting the Islands." MS. PABC.
Powell, Israel Wood. Papers. MS. PABC.
Puget, Peter. "A Log of the Proceedings of His Majesty's Armed Tender *Chatham* Lieutenant Peter Puget Acting Commander Commencing 12 Day of January 1793." microfilm. UBCL.
————. "A Log of the Proceedings of His Majesty's Ship *Discovery* George Van-

couver Esqre. Commander Kept by Peter Puget from the 4th day of January 1791 to the 14 Day of January 1793." microfilm. UBCL.

Quadra, Don Juan Francisco de la Bogeda y. "Voyage to the N.W. Coast of North America by Don Juan Francisco de la Bogeda y Quadra . . . in the Year 1792." Translated by V. D. Webb. TS. UBCL.

Robson, Ebenezer. Papers. MS. PABC.

Ross, Donald. Papers. MS. PABC.

[Sproat, G. M.]. "Sir Joseph William Trutch K.C.M.G." TS. PABC.

Stuart, John. "Journal at the Rocky Mountain December the Twentieth 1805 [to 28 February 1806]." photocopy. PABC.

Swaine, Spellman. "A Log of His Majesty's Sloop *Discovery* Commanded by George Vancouver Esquire, 26 September 1792–2 July 1795." microfilm. UBCL.

Tate, Charles. "Life and Missionary Activities of Rev. Charles Montgomery Tate, 1852–1933." TS. PABC.

Tod, John. "Fort Kamloops Journal, 3 August 1841–19 December 1843." MS. PABC.

———. "History of New Caledonia and the Northwest Coast." photocopy. PABC.

Torrens, Robert William. "Report of Explorations and Proceedings at Clayoquot Sound, 1865." MS. PABC.

Trutch, Joseph. Correspondence with Sir John A. Macdonald, 1871–1891. MS. PABC.

———. Diaries, 1859–1870. MS. PABC.

———. Papers. MS and TS. UBCL.

United States. Despatches from United States Consuls in Victoria, 1862–1890. microfilm. UBCL.

Vancouver Island. Colonial Surveyor. "Correspondence and Papers Relating to Indian Reserves Chemainus District and W. A. Scott, 1850–1864." MS. PABC.

———. Governor (Blanshard). Correspondence Outward, 1849–1851. MS. PABC.

———. Governor. Correspondence Outward, 1850–1859. MS. PABC.

———. ———. Correspondence Outward, 27 May 1859–9 January 1864, Private Official Letterbook. MS. PABC.

———. ———. Despatches to Her Majesty's Principal Secretary of State for the Colonies, 1851–1859. MS. PABC.

———. House of Assembly. Minutes, 1856–1866. MS. PABC.

Waddington, Alfred. Papers. TS. UBCL.

Work, John. Correspondence Outward, 1828–1849. MS. PABC.

———. "Diary of a Trip of Chief Factor John Work in 1851 from Fort Simpson to Queen Charlotte Islands." MS. UBCL.

———. Journals, 1823–1851. MS. PABC.

2. *Published Sources*

Addresses and Memorials Together with Articles, Reports etc. etc. from the Public Journals upon the Occasion of the Retirement of Sir James Douglas, K.C.B., from the Governorship of the Colonies of Vancouver Island and British Columbia. Victoria: Edward Hayward, 1864.

Anderson, Alexander Caulfield. *The Dominion at the West: A Brief Description of the Province of British Columbia, its Climate and Resources.* Victoria: R. Wolfenden, 1872.

———. "Notes on the Indian Tribes of British North America, and the Northwest Coast." *Historical Magazine* 7 (1863): 73–81.

Bagley, Clarence C., ed. "Attitude of the Hudson's Bay Company during the Indian War of 1855–1856." *Washington Historical Quarterly* 8 (1917): 291–307.

Baker, A. J., trans. "Fray Benito de la Sierra's Account of the Hezeta Expedition to the Northwest Coast in 1775." *Quarterly of the California Historical Society* 9 (1930): 201–42.

Ballantyne, Robert M. *Handbook to the New Gold Fields....* Edinburgh: A. Strahan, 1858.

Barker, Burt Brown, ed. *Letters of Dr. John McLoughlin Written at Fort Vancouver, 1829–1832.* Portland: Binfords and Mort, 1948.

Barrett-Lennard, C. E. *Travels in British Columbia, with the Narrative of a Yacht Voyage Round Vancouver's Island.* London: Hurst and Blackett, 1862.

Beaglehole, J. C., ed. *The Journals of Captain James Cook on his Voyages of Discovery; the Voyage of the "Resolution" and "Discovery," 1776–1780.* Parts 1 and 2. Cambridge: Hakluyt Society, 1967.

Beaver, Herbert. "Experiences of a Chaplain at Fort Vancouver, 1836–1838." Edited by R. C. Clark. *Oregon Historical Quarterly* 39 (1938): 22–38.

[————]. "The Natives of the North West Coast of America." *Extracts from the Papers and Proceedings of the Aborigines Protection Society* 2 (1841): 131–44.

Begbie, Matthew B. "Journey into the Interior of British Columbia." *Journal of the Royal Geographical Society* 31 (1861): 237–48.

Belcher, Edward. *Narrative of a Voyage Round the World Performed in Her Majesty's Ship "Sulpher," during the Years 1836–1842....* 2 vols. London: H. Colburn, 1843.

The Bishop of Columbia. *A Tour of British Columbia.* London: Clay Printers, 1861.

Boddam-Wetham, J. W. *Western Wanderings: A Record of Travel in the Evening Land.* London: R. Bentley and Son, 1874.

British and American Joint Commission for the Settlement of the Claims of the Hudson's Bay Company and Puget's Sound Agricultural Companies. 14 vols. Montreal: J. Lovell; Washington, D.C.: Government Printer, 1865–1869.

British Columbia. *Appendix to the Revised Statutes of British Columbia, 1871;....* Victoria: R. Wolfenden, 1871.

————. *British North America Act, 1867, Terms of Union with Canada, Rules and Orders of the Legislative Assembly....* Victoria: R. Wolfenden, 1881.

————. *Journals of the Legislative Assembly of the Province of British Columbia....* Victoria: R. Wolfenden, 1872–1890.

————. *Journals of the Legislative Council of British Columbia.* New Westminster and Victoria: R. Wolfenden, 1864–1871.

————. *The Laws of British Columbia Consisting of the Acts, Ordinances, and Proclamations of the Formerly Separate Colonies of Vancouver Island and British Columbia, and of the United Colony of British Columbia....* Victoria: R. Wolfenden, 1871.

————. *List of Proclamations 1858, 1859, 1860, 1861, 1862, 1863, and 1864.* N.p., n.d.

————. *Metlakatla Inquiry, 1884, Report of the Commissioners, together with the Evidence.* Victoria: R. Wolfenden, 1885.

————. *Papers Connected with the Indian Land Question, 1850–1875.* Victoria: R. Wolfenden, 1875.

————. *Report and Journal by the Honourable the Chief Commissioner of Lands and Works, of the Proceedings in Connection with the Visit of His Excellency the Late Governor Seymour to the North-West Coast, in His Majesty's Ship "Sparrowhawk."* Victoria: Government Printing Office, 1869.

————. *Report of the Royal Commission on Indian Affairs for the Province of British Columbia.* 4 vols. Victoria: Acme Press, 1916.

————. *Sessional Papers.* Victoria: R. Wolfenden, 1872–1890.

————. Legislative Council. *Debate on the Subject of Confederation with Canada,*

Reprinted from the Government Gazette Extraordinary of March, 1870. Victoria: R. Wolfenden, 1870.

Broughton, William Robert. *A Voyage of Discovery to the North Pacific Ocean: . . . Performed in His Majesty's Ship "Providence," and Tender, in the Years 1795, 1796, 1797, 1798.* London: T. Cadell and W. Davis, 1804.

Brown, R. C. Lundin. *Klatsassan, and other Reminiscences of Missionary Life in British Columbia.* London: Society for Promoting Christian Knowledge, 1873.

Caamaño, Jacinto. "The Journal of Jacinto Caamaño." *British Columbia Historical Quarterly* 2 (1938): 189–222, 265–301.

Campa, Miguel de la fray. *A Journal of Explorations Northward along the Coast from Monteray in the Year 1775.* Edited by John Gavin. San Francisco: J. Howell, 1964.

Canada. *Census of Canada, 1881, 1891, and 1901.* Ottawa: Queen's Printer, 1882, 1893, and 1902.

——. *Indian Treaties and Surrenders.* 3 vols. Ottawa: Queen's Printer, 1891 and 1912.

——. Parliament. *British Columbia, Report of the Hon. H. L. Langevin, C.B., Minister of Public Works.* Ottawa: J. B. Taylor, 1872.

——. ——. *Sessional Papers,* 1872–1875.

——. ——. House of Commons. *Official Report of the Debates,* 1880 and 1885.

——. ——. Senate. *Journals,* 16th Parl., 1st sess., 1926–27. Appendix to the Journals of the Senate . . . Special Joint Commission of the Senate and House of Commons Appointed to Inquire into the Claims of the Allied Indian Tribes of British Columbia, . . . *Report and Evidence.* Ottawa: F. A. Acland, King's Printer, 1927.

Champness, W. "To Cariboo and Back." *The Leisure Hour* 14 (8, 15, 22, and 29 April 1865), pp. 215–19, 231–34, 246–50, and 257–60.

Chittenden, Newton H. *Official Report of the Queen Charlotte Islands for the Government of British Columbia.* Victoria: Printed by Authority of the Government, 1884.

[Church Missionary Society]. *Metlahkatla: Ten Years' Work among the Tsimsheean Indians.* London: Church Missionary Society, 1869.

Cleveland, R. J. "The Log of the *Caroline* (1799)." *Pacific Northwest Quarterly* 29 (1938): 61–84, 167–200.

Cleveland, Richard J. *Voyages and Commercial Enterprises of the Sons of New England.* New York: Leavitt and Allan, 1855.

Collison, W. H. *In the Wake of the War Canoe. . . .* London: E. P. Dutton, 1915.

Columbia Mission. *Occasional Paper.* London: James Wyld, 1860.

[——]. *Reports of the Columbia Mission.* London: Rivingtons, 1861–1880.

Cook, James, and King, James. *A Voyage to the Pacific Ocean . . . Performed Under the Direction of Captains Cook, Clerke and Gore, in His Majesty's Ships the "Resolution" and the "Discovery." In the Years 1776, 1777, 1778, 1779, and 1780.* 3 vols. London: G. Nicol and T. Cadell, 1784.

Corney, Peter. *Voyages in the Northern Pacific, Narrative of Several Trading Voyages from 1813 to 1818, between the Northwest Coast of America, the Hawaiian Islands and China. . . .* Honolulu: H.I.T.G. Thrum, 1896.

Cornwallis, Kinahan. *The New El Dorado; or British Columbia.* London: T. C. Newby, 1858.

Cox, Ross. *Adventures on the Columbia River. . . .* New York: J. & J. Harper, 1832.

Crosby, Thomas. *Among the An-ko-me-nums or Flathead Tribes of Indians of the Pacific Coast.* Toronto: W. Briggs, 1907.

——. *Up and Down the North Pacific Coast by Canoe and Mission Ship.* Toronto: Missionary Society of the Methodist Church, 1914.

Davenport, T. W. "Recollections of an Indian Agent." *Quarterly of the Oregon Historical Society* 8 (1907): 1–41, 95–128, 231–64, 353–74.

Dawson, George M. *Report on the Queen Charlotte Islands 1878.* Geological Survey of Canada. Montreal: Dawson Brothers, 1880.

De Groot, Henry. *British Columbia; its Condition and Prospects, Soil, Climate and Mineral Resources, Considered.* San Francisco: Alta California job office, 1859.

de Kiewiet, C. W., and Underhill, F. W., eds. *Dufferin-Carnarvon Correspondence, 1874–1878.* Toronto: Champlain Society, 1955.

Dixon, George. *A Voyage Round the World; but more Particularly to the North-West Coast of America: Performed in 1785, 1786, 1787 and 1788 in the "King George" and the "Queen Charlotte," Captains Portlock and Dixon.* London: G. Goulding, 1789.

Domer, John. *New British Gold Fields: A Guide to British Columbia and Vancouver Island. . . .* London: W. H. Angel, n.d.

Douglas, David. *Journal Kept by David Douglas during his Travels in North America 1823–1827. . . .* New York: Antiquarian Press, 1959.

Douglas, James. "Report of a Canoe Expedition along the Coast of Vancouver Island." *Journal of the Royal Geographical Society* 24 (1854): 245–56.

Downie, W. "Explorations in Jarvis Inlet and Desolation Sound, British Columbia." *Journal of the Royal Geographical Society* 31 (1861): 249–56.

Downie, William. *Hunting for Gold: Reminiscences of Personal Experience and Research in the Early Days of the Pacific Coast. . . .* San Francisco: Press of the California Publishing Co., 1893.

Dufferin, Lady. *My Canadian Journal 1872–1878.* Edited by Gladys Chantler Walker. Don Mills, Ont.: Longmans Canada, 1969.

[Duncan, William, and Tomlinson, Robert]. *Metlakatahla and the Church Missionary Society.* Victoria: Miller, 1887.

Dunn, John. *History of the Oregon Territory and British North American Fur Trade. . . .* London: Edwards and Hughes, 1844.

D'Wolf, John. *Voyage to the North Pacific and a Journey through Siberia more than Half a Century Ago.* Cambridge: Welch, Bigelow and Company, 1861.

Eardley-Wilmot, S. *Our Journal in the Pacific. By the Officers of H.M.S. "Zealous."* London: Longmans, Green, and Co., 1873.

Ellis, W. *An Authentic Narrative of a Voyage Performed by Captain Cook and Captain Clerke in His Majesty's Ships "Resolution" and "Discovery" during the Years 1776, 1777, 1778, 1779 and 1780. . . .* Vol. 1. London: G. Robinson, J. Sewell and J. Debrett, 1782.

Emmerson, John. *British Columbia and Vancouver Island: Voyages, Travels and Adventures.* Durham: W. Ainsley, 1865.

Ermatinger, Frank. "Earliest Expedition against Puget Sound Indians." *Washington Historical Quarterly* 1 (1907): 16–29.

[Finlayson, Roderick]. *Biography of Roderick Finlayson.* [Victoria, 1913].

———. *History of Vancouver Island and the Northwest Coast.* Saint Louis University Studies, Series B. Saint Louis: Saint Louis University Press, 1945.

Fitzgerald, James Edward. *An Examination of the Charter and Proceedings of the Hudson's Bay Company, with Reference to the Grant of Vancouver's Island.* London: T. Saunders, 1849.

Fleming, R. Harvey, ed. *Minutes of Council Northern Department of Rupert Land, 1821–1831.* Toronto: Hudson's Bay Record Society, 1940.

Fleurieu, C. P. Claret. *A Voyage Round the World, Performed during the Years 1790, 1791, and 1792, by Etienne Marchand. . . .* 2 vols. London: T. N. Longman and O. Rees, 1801.

Glazebrook, G. P. de T., ed. *The Hargrave Correspondence 1821–1843.* Toronto: Champlain Society, 1938.

Glover, Richard, ed. *David Thompson's Narrative 1784–1812.* Toronto: Champlain Society, 1962.

Grant, George M. *Ocean to Ocean: Sandford Fleming's Expedition through Canada in 1872.* . . . London: S. Low, Marston, Low, and Searle, 1873.

Grant, W. Colquhoun. "Description of Vancouver Island, by its First Colonist." *Journal of the Royal Geographical Society* 27 (1857): 268–320.

———. "Remarks on Vancouver Island, Principally Concerning Townsites and Native Population." *Journal of the Royal Geographical Society* 31 (1861): 208–13.

Great Britain. Parliament. *Hansard's Parliamentary Debates.* 3d ser. Vols. 101, 106, 151. London: G. Woodfall and Son, 1848, 1849; Cornelius Buck, 1858.

———. ———. *Papers Relative to the Affairs of British Columbia.* Parts 1-4. London: Printed by George Edward Eyre and William Spottiswoode . . . for Her Majesty's Stationary Office, 1859–62.

———. ———. House of Commons. *Report from the Select Committee on the Hudson's Bay Company; together with the Proceedings of the Committee, Minutes of Evidence, Appendix and Evidence.* [London, 1857].

Green, Jonathan S. *Journal of a Tour on the North West Coast of America in the Year 1829.* . . . New York: C. F. Heartman, 1915.

Griffin, Geo. Butler, ed. *Documents from the Sutro Collection.* Publications of the Historical Society of Southern California. Vol. 2, part 1. Los Angeles: Franklin Printing Co., 1891.

Harper, J. Russell. *Paul Kane's Frontier Including "Wanderings of an Artist among the Indians of North America" by Paul Kane.* Austin: University of Texas Press, 1971.

Harrison, Charles. *Ancient Warriors of the North Pacific; the Haidas, their Laws, Customs and Legends, with some Historical Account of the Queen Charlotte Islands.* London: H. F. and G. Witherby, 1925.

———. *The Hydah Mission Queen Charlotte Islands.* . . . London: Church Missionary House, n.d.

Hazlitt, William Carewe. *British Columbia and Vancouver Island;* . . . London: G. Routledge & Co., 1858.

Hills, George. *A Sermon, Preached at the Farewell Service Celebrated in St. James Church, Piccadilly, on Wednesday, Nov. 16, 1859.* . . . London: Rivingtons, 1859.

Howay, F. W., ed. *The Dixon-Meares Controversy.* . . . Toronto: Ryerson [1929].

———. *The Early History of the Fraser River Mines.* Archives of British Columbia Memoir no. 6. Victoria: C. F. Banfield, 1926.

———. *The Journal of Captain James Colnett Aboard the "Argonaut" from April 26, 1789 to November 3, 1791.* Toronto: Champlain Society, 1940.

———. *Voyages of the "Columbia" to the Northwest Coast 1787–1790 and 1790–1793.* Boston: Massachusetts Historical Society, 1941.

———. "William Sturgis: The Northwest Fur Trade." *British Columbia Historical Quarterly* 8 (1944): 11–25.

———. *Zimmermann's Captain Cook, an Account of the "Third Voyage of Captain Cook Around the World, 1776–1780," by Henry Zimmermann.* . . . Toronto: Ryerson, 1930.

The Hudson's Bay Question [from the "Colonial Intelligencer"]. London: W. Tweedie, 1857.

Jane, Cecil, trans. *A Spanish Voyage to Vancouver and the North-West Coast of America being the Narrative of the Voyage made in the Year 1792 by the Schooners "Sutil" and "Mexicana" to Explore the Strait of Fuca.* London: The Argonaut Press, 1930.

Jessett, Thomas E., ed. *Reports and Letters of Herbert Beaver 1836–1838, Chaplain to the Hudson's Bay Company and Missionary to the Indians at Fort Vancouver.* Portland, Ore.: Champoeg Press, 1959.

Jewitt, John R. *A Journal Kept at Nootka Sound.* . . . Boston: J. Jewitt, 1807.

————. *A Narrative of the Adventures and Sufferings of John R. Jewitt*.... Middletown: Loomis & Richards, 1815.

Johnson, Ebenezer. *A Short Account of a Northwest Voyage, Performed in the Years 1796, 1797, and 1798*. Massachusetts: Ebenezer Johnson, 1798.

Johnson, R. Byron. *Very Far West Indeed: A Few Rough Experiences on the North-West Pacific Coast*. London: S. Low, Marston, Low and Searle, 1872.

Kane, Paul. "Incidents of Travel on the North-West Coast, Vancouver's Island, Oregon, etc., etc." *Canadian Journal* 3 (1855): 273–79.

Kaplanoff, Mark D., ed. *Joseph Ingraham's Journal of the Brigantine "Hope" on a Voyage to the Northwest Coast of North America 1790–1792*.... Barre, Mass.: Imprint Society, 1971.

Knaplund, Paul, ed. "Letters from James Fitzgerald to W. E. Gladstone Concerning Vancouver Island and the Hudson's Bay Company, 1848–1850." *British Columbia Historical Quarterly* 13 (1949): 1–21.

Lamb, W. Kaye, ed. "Five Letters of Charles Ross, 1842–1844." *British Columbia Historical Quarterly* 7 (1943): 103–18.

————. "Four Letters Relating to the Cruise of the 'Thetis,' 1852–1853." *British Columbia Historical Quarterly* 6 (1942): 189–206.

————. *Journal of a Voyage to the Northwest Coast of North America During the Years 1811, 1812, 1813 and 1814, by Gabriel Franchère*. Toronto: Champlain Society, 1969.

————. *The Journals and Letters of Sir Alexander Mackenzie*. Cambridge: Hakluyt Society, 1970.

————. *The Letters and Journals of Simon Fraser, 1806–1808*. Toronto: Macmillan of Canada, 1960.

————. *Sixteen Years in Indian Country: The Journal of Daniel Williams Harmon, 1800–1816*. Toronto: Macmillan, 1957.

Langsdorff, G. H. Von. *Voyages and Travels in Various Parts of the World, during the Years 1803, 1804, 1805, 1806, and 1807*. Carlisle: George Philips, 1817.

Ledyard, John. *A Journal of Captain Cook's Last Voyage to the Pacific Ocean, and in Quest of a North-West Passage, between Asia and America; Performed in the Years 1776, 1777, 1778, and 1779*. Chicago: Quadrangle Books, 1963.

Lewis, William S., and Phillips, Paul C. *The Journal of John Work*;.... Cleveland: Arthur H. Clark Company, 1923.

Lord, John Keast. *The Naturalist in Vancouver Island and British Columbia*. 2 vols. London: R. Bentley, 1866.

MacDonald, George Duncan Forbes. *British Columbia and Vancouver's Island*.... London: Longman, Green, Longman, Roberts and Green, 1862.

Macfie, Matthew. *Vancouver Island and British Columbia: Their History Resources and Prospects*. London: Longman, Green, Longman, Roberts and Green, 1865.

McLean, John. *Notes of a Twenty-Five Years' Service in the Hudson's Bay Territory*. 2 vols. London: R. Bentley, 1849.

McLeod, Malcolm, ed. *Peace River. A Canoe Voyage from Hudson's Bay to the Pacific by the Late Sir George Simpson; (Governor Hon. Hudson's Bay Company) in 1828. Journal of the Late Chief Factor Archibald McDonald, (Hon. Hudson's Bay Company), who Accompanied Him*. Ottawa: J. Durie and Son, 1872.

MacLeod, Margaret Arnett, ed. *The Letters of Letitia Hargrave*. Toronto: Champlain Society, 1947.

Martin, R. M. *The Hudson's Bay Territories and Vancouver's Island, with an Exposition of the Chartered Rights, Conduct and Policy of the Honble. Hudson's Bay Corporation*. London: T. and W. Boone, 1849.

Mayne, R. C. *Four Years in British Columbia and Vancouver Island*.... London: J. Murray, 1862.

————. "Report on a Journey in British Columbia in the Districts Bordering on the Thompson, Fraser and Harrison Rivers." *Journal of the Royal Geographical Society* 31 (1861): 213–23.

Meany, Edmond S., ed. *A New Vancouver Journal on the Discovery of Puget Sound by a Member of the "Chatham's" Crew.* Seattle: University of Washington Press, 1915.

Meares, John. *Voyages Made in the Years 1788 and 1789, from China to the North West Coast of America....* London: Logographic Press, 1790.

Melrose, Robert. "The Diary of Robert Melrose." *British Columbia Historical Quarterly* 7 (1943): 119–34, 199–218, 283–95.

Merivale, Herman. *Lectures on Colonization and Colonies Delivered before the University of Oxford in 1839, 1840 & 1841.* London: Longman, Green, Longman, and Roberts, 1861.

Merk, Frederick. *Fur Trade and Empire, George Simpson's Journal, Remarks Connected with the Fur Trade in the Course of a Voyage from York Factory to Fort George and back to York 1824–1825;....* Cambridge, Mass.: Harvard University Press, 1931.

Milton, Henry, ed. *Speeches and Addresses of the Right Honourable Frederick Temple Hamilton Earl of Dufferin.* London: John Murray, 1882.

Milton, Viscount, and Cheadle, W. B. *The North-West Passage by Land. Being the Narrative of an Expedition from the Atlantic to the Pacific....* London: Cassell, Petter, and Galpin [1865].

Missions de la Congrégation des Missionaires Oblats de Marie Immaculée. Paris: A. Hennuyer, 1862–70.

Moberly, Walter. *The Rocks and Rivers of British Columbia.* London: H. Blacklock and Company, 1885.

Moresby, Admiral John. *Two Admirals: Sir Fairfax Moresby John Moresby a Record of a Hundred Years.* London: Methuen, 1913.

Morris, Alexander. *The Treaties of Canada with the Indians of Manitoba and the North-West Territories Including the Negotiations on which they were Based, and other Information Relating Thereto.* Toronto: Belfords, Clark & Co., 1880.

Mourelle, Don Francisco Antonio. *Voyage of the "Sonora" in the Second Bucareli Expedition ... the Journal Kept in 1775 on the "Sonora" by Don Francisco Antonio Mourelle.* Translated by Daines Barrington. San Francisco: T. C. Russell, 1920.

Moziño, Jose Mariño. *Noticias de Nutka: An Account of Nootka Sound in 1792.* Toronto and Montreal: McClelland and Stewart, 1970.

Nesbitt, James K., ed. "The Diary of Martha Cheney Ella, 1853–1856." *British Columbia Historical Quarterly* 13 (1949): 91–112, 257–70.

Newcombe, C. F., ed. *Menzies' Journal of Vancouver's Voyage, April to October 1792.* Archives of British Columbia Memoir no. 5. Victoria: W. H. Cullin, 1923.

[Nicol, John]. *The Life and Adventures of John Nicol Mariner.* Edinburgh and London: W. Blackwood, 1822.

Notices and Voyages of the Famed Quebec Mission to the Pacific Northwest.... Portland: Oregon Historical Society, 1956.

Nunis, Doyce B., Jr., ed. *The Golden Frontier: The Recollections of Herman Francis Reinhart 1851–1869.* Austin: University of Texas Press, 1962.

[Ogden, Peter Skene?]. *Traits of American-Indian Life and Character, by a Fur Trader.* London: Smith, Elder, 1853.

"Old Letters from Hudson's Bay Company Officials and Employees from 1829–1840." *Washington Historical Quarterly* 1 (1907): 256–66, 2 (1907–1908): 40–43, 161–68, 254–64.

Palmer, H. Spencer. *British Columbia. Williams Lake and Cariboo....* New Westminster: Royal Engineer Press, 1863.

————. "Remarks on the Geography and Natural Capabilities of British Columbia, and the Condition of its Principal Gold Fields." *Journal of the Royal Geographical Society* 34 (1864): 171–95.

————. *Report of a Journey from Victoria to Fort Alexandria via Bentinck Arm.* New Westminster: Royal Engineer Press, 1863.

Patterson, Samuel. *Narrative of the Adventures and Sufferings of Samuel Patterson....* Fairfield: Ye Galleon Press, 1967.

Pemberton, J. Despard. *Facts and Figures Relating to Vancouver Island and British Columbia....* London: Longman, Green, Longman, and Roberts, 1860.

Poole, Francis. *Queen Charlotte Islands: A Narrative of Discovery and Adventure in the North Pacific.* London: Hurst and Blackett, 1872.

Portlock, Nathaniel. *A Voyage Round the World; but more Particularly to the North-West Coast of America: Performed in 1785, 1786, 1787,* and *1788....* London: J. Stockdale, 1789.

Rattray, Alexander. *Vancouver Island and British Columbia....* London: Smith, Elder, 1862.

Reynolds, Stephen. *The Voyage of the "New Hazard" to the North-West Coast, Hawaii, and China, 1810–1813....* Edited by F. W. Howay. Salem, Mass.: Peabody Museum, 1938.

Rich, E. E., ed. *Journal of a Voyage from Rocky Mountain Portage in Peace River to the Sources of Finlay's Branch and North West Ward in Summer 1824* [*by Samuel Black*]. London: Hudson's Bay Record Society, 1955.

————. *Journal of Occurrences in the Athapaska Department by George Simpson, 1820 and 1821, and Report.* London: Hudson's Bay Record Society, 1938.

————. *The Letters of John McLoughlin from Fort Vancouver to the Governor and Committee, First Series, 1825–1838.* London: Hudson's Bay Record Society, 1941.

————. *The Letters of John McLoughlin from Fort Vancouver to the Governor and Committee, Second Series, 1839–1844.* London: Hudson's Bay Record Society, 1943.

————. *The Letters of John McLoughlin from Fort Vancouver to the Governor and Committee, Third Series, 1844–1846.* London: Hudson's Bay Record Society, 1944.

————. *London Correspondence Inward from Eden Colvile, 1849–1852.* London: Hudson's Bay Record Society, 1956.

————. *Part of a Despatch from George Simpson Esqr. Governor of Ruperts Land to the Governor & Committee of the Hudson's Bay Company London March 1, 1829. Continued and Completed March 24 and June 5, 1829.* London: Hudson's Bay Record Society, 1947.

————. *Peter Skene Ogden's Snake Country Journals 1824–25 and 1825–26.* London: Hudson's Bay Record Society, 1950.

[Rickman, John]. *Journal of Captain Cook's Last Voyage to the Pacific Ocean on Discovery Performed in the Years 1776, 1777, 1778, 1779....* London: E. Newbery, 1781.

Roe, Michael, ed. *The Journal and Letters of Captain Charles Bishop on the North-West Coast of America, in the Pacific and in New South Wales 1794–1799.* Cambridge: Hakluyt Society, 1967.

Rohner, Ronald P., ed. *The Ethnography of Franz Boas: Letters and Diaries of Franz Boas Written on the Northwest Coast from 1886 to 1931.* Chicago and London: University of Chicago Press, 1969.

Roquefeuil, M. Camille de. *A Voyage Round the World, between the Years 1816–1819.* London: Sir R. Phillips and Co., 1823.

Ross, Alexander. *Adventures of the First Settlers on the Oregon or Columbia River....* London: Smith, Elder, 1849.

Scouler, Dr. John. "Dr. John Scouler's Journal of a Voyage to N.W. America."

Quarterly of the Oregon Historical Society 6 (1905): 54–76, 159–205, 276–89.
———. "Observations of the Indigenous Tribes of the N.W. Coast of America." *Journal of the Royal Geographical Society of London* 11 (1841): 215–50.
———. "On the Indian Tribes Inhabiting the North-West Coast of America." *Journal of the Ethnological Society of London* 1 (1848): 228–52.
Seemann, Berthold. *Narrative of the Voyage of H.M.S. "Herald" during the Years 1845–1851 under the Command of Captain Henry Kellett. . . .* Vol. 1. London: Reeve and Co., 1853.
[Sheridan, P. H.]. *Personal Memoirs of P. H. Sheridan, General United States Army.* Vol. 1. New York: C. L. Webster and Company, 1888.
Simpson, Sir George. *Narrative of a Journey Around the World during the Years 1841 and 1842.* 2 vols. London: H. Colburn, 1847.
Smith, Dorothy Blakey, ed. "The Journal of Arthur Thomas Bushby, 1858–1859." *British Columbia Historical Quarterly* 21 (1957–1958): 83–198.
———. *The Reminiscences of Doctor John Sebastian Helmcken.* Vancouver: University of British Columbia Press, 1975.
Snow, Capt. Elliot, ed. *The Sea, the Ship, and the Sailor: Tales of Adventure from Log Books and Original Narratives.* Salem, Mass.: Marine Research Society, 1925.
[Society for the Propagation of the Gospel]. *Report of the Incorporated Society for the Propagation of the Gospel in Foreign Parts, 1860–1875.* London: The Society for the Propagation of the Gospel, 1860–1876.
[Sproat, Gilbert Malcolm]. *British Columbia. Information for Emigrants.* London: W. Clowes, 1873.
———. *Memorandum on Indian Reserves in the District of Yale.* Victoria: Colonist Steam Press, 1878.
———. "On the Probability of a Bone Age." *Transactions of the Ethnological Society of London,* n.s. 6 (1868): 253–59.
———. *Scenes and Studies of Savage Life.* London: Smith, Elder, 1868.
———. "The West Coast Indians in Vancouver Island." *Transactions of the Ethnological Society of London,* n.s. 5 (1867): 243–54.
Stanley, George F. G., ed. *Mapping the Frontier: Charles Wilson's Diary of the Survey of the 49th Parallel, 1858–1862, while Secretary of the British Boundary Commission.* Toronto: Macmillan, 1970.
Steele, Colonel S. B. *Forty Years in Canada: Reminiscences of the Great North-West. . . .* Toronto: McClelland, Goodchild, Stewart, 1918.
[Stock, Eugene]. *Metlakahtla and the North Pacific Mission of the Church Missionary Society.* London: Church Missionary House, 1881.
Strange, James. *James Strange's Journal and Narrative of the Commercial Expedition from Bombay to the North-West Coast of America. . . .* Madras: Government Press, 1929.
Swan, James G. *Almost out of the World: Scenes from Washington Territory the Strait of Juan de Fuca 1859–1861.* Edited by William A. Katz. Tacoma: Washington State Historical Society, 1971.
———. *The Northwest Coast, or Three Year's Residence in Washington Territory.* Seattle and London: University of Washington Press, 1972.
Teichmann, Oskar, ed. *A Journey to Alaska in the Year 1868: Being a Diary of the Late Emil Teichmann.* New York: Argosy-Antiquarian, 1963.
Tolmie, W. F. *The Journals of William Fraser Tolmie: Physician and Fur Trader.* Vancouver: Mitchell Press, 1963.
Vancouver, George. *A Voyage of Discovery to the North Pacific Ocean, and Round the World; . . . Performed in the Years 1790, 1791, 1792, 1793, 1794, and 1795, in the "Discovery" Sloop of War, and Armed Tender "Chatham," under the Command of Captain George Vancouver.* 3 vols. London: G. G. and J. Robinson, 1798.

Vancouver Island. *A Collection of the Public General Statutes of the Colony of Vancouver Island Passed in the Years 1859, 1860, 1861, 1862, and 1863.* Victoria: Evening Press, 1864.

————. *House of Assembly Correspondence Book. August 12, 1856 to July 6, 1859.* Archives of British Columbia Memoir no. 4. Victoria: W. H. Cullin, 1918.

————. *Minutes of the Council of Vancouver Island Commencing August 30, 1851, and Terminating with the Prorogation of the House of Assembly, February 6, 1861.* Archives of British Columbia Memoir no. 2. Victoria: W. H. Cullin, 1918.

Venn, Henry. *Retrospect and Prospect of the Operations of the Church Missionary Society.* London: Seeley, Jackson and Halliday, 1865.

Waddington, Alfred. *The Fraser Mines Vindicated, or the History of Four Months.* Victoria: De Garro, 1858.

[————]. *Judicial Murder* [Victoria, 1860].

Wagner, Henry R., ed. *Journal of Tomás de Suría of his Voyage with Malaspina to the Northwest Coast of America in 1791.* Glendale, Calif.: A. H. Clark Co., 1936.

Whymper, Frederick. *Travel and Adventure in the Territory of Alaska,...and in Various Other Parts of the North Pacific.* London: J. Murray, 1868.

Wilkes, Charles. *Narrative of the United States Exploring Expedition, During the Years 1838, 1839, 1840, 1841, 1842.* Vols. 4 and 6. London: Whittaker, 1845.

Williams, Glyndwr, ed. *Peter Skene Ogden's Snake Country Journals 1827–28 and 1828–29.* London: Hudson's Bay Record Society, 1971.

3. Newspapers and Periodicals

The Atlantic Monthly. March 1878.

The British Colonist (also *The Daily British Colonist*). 1858–1890.

The British Columbian (also *Daily British Columbian*). 1863–1890.

The Cariboo Sentinel. 1865–1875.

The Church Missionary Intelligencer. 1856–1885.

The Church Missionary Record. 1859–1874.

The Christian Guardian. 1859–1863.

Daily Victoria Gazette (also *The Victoria Gazette*). 1858–1860.

Evening Express (also *Daily Evening Express*). 1863–1865.

The Government Gazette. 1863–1870.

The Inland Sentinel. 1880–1890.

Mainland Guardian. 1870–1888.

The Press (also *Daily Press*). 1861–1862.

Proceedings of the Royal Geographical Society of London. April and May 1857.

Puget Sound Gazette (various titles). 1863–1867.

The Times. 1858–1862.

The Victoria Daily Standard. 1870–1890.

The Victoria Daily Times. 1884–1890.

Weekly Manitoban. 1870–1874.

B. Secondary

1. *Published*

Ajayi, J. F. Ade. *Christian Missions in Nigeria 1841–1891. The Making of a New Elite*. Evanston, Ill.: Northwestern University Press, 1965.

Allport, Gordon W. *The Nature of Prejudice*. New York: Doubleday, 1958.

Archer, Criston I. "The Transient Presence: A Re-Appraisal of Spanish Attitudes toward the Northwest Coast in the Eighteenth Century." *BC Studies* 18 (1973): 3–32.

Arctander, J. W. *The Apostle of Alaska: The Story of William Duncan of Metlakahtla*. New York: Flemming H. Reveli, 1909.

Bancroft, Hubert Howe. *History of British Columbia*. San Francisco: History Company, 1890.

———. *History of the Northwest Coast*. 2 vols. San Francisco: A. L. Bancroft & Co., 1884, 1886.

Barbeau, Marius. *The Downfall of Temlaham*. Toronto: Macmillan, 1928.

———. "How Totem Poles Originated." *Queen's Quarterly* 46 (1939): 304–11.

———. "Old Port Simpson." *The Beaver*, outfit 271 (1940): 20–23.

———. "Totem Poles: A By Product of the Fur Trade." *Scientific Monthly*, December 1942, pp. 507–14.

———. *Totem Poles of the Gitksan, Upper Skeena River, British Columbia*. National Museum of Canada Bulletin no. 61. Ottawa: F. A. Acland, 1929.

Barnett, H. G. "Applied Anthropology in 1860." *Applied Anthropology* 1 (1942): 19–32.

———. *The Coast Salish of British Columbia*. Eugene: University of Oregon Press, 1955.

———. "The Coast Salish of Canada." *American Anthropologist*, n.s. 40 (1938): 118–41.

———. *Innovation: The Basis of Cultural Change*. New York: McGraw-Hill, 1953.

———. "The Nature of the Potlatch." *American Anthropologist*, n.s. 40 (1938): 349–58.

———. "Social Forces, Personal Conflicts, and Cultural Change." *Social Forces* 20 (1941): 160–71.

Begg, Alexander. *History of British Columbia from its Earliest Discovery to the Present Time*. Toronto: W. Briggs, 1894.

———. *A Sketch of the Successful Missionary Work of William Duncan amongst the Indian Tribes of Northern British Columbia from 1858 to 1901*. Victoria, 1901.

Benedict, Ruth. *Patterns of Culture*. Boston: Houghton Mifflin [1959].

Berkhofer, Robert F., Jr. "Protestants, Pagans, and Sequence among the North American Indians, 1760–1860." *Ethnohistory* 10 (1963): 201–32.

———. *Salvation and the Savage: An Analysis of Protestant Missions and American Indian Response, 1787–1862*. Lexington: University of Kentucky Press, 1965.

Bescoby, Isabel. "A Colonial Administration an Analysis of Administration in British Columbia, 1869–1871." *Canadian Public Administration* 10 (1967): 49–104.

———. "Society in Cariboo during the Gold Rush." *Washington Historical Quarterly* 24 (1933): 195–207.

Beynon, William. "The Tsimshian of Metlakatla, Alaska." *American Anthropologist*, n.s. 43 (1941): 83–88.

Binney, Judith. *The Legacy of Guilt: A Life of Thomas Kendall*. Auckland: Auckland-Oxford University Press, 1968.

Binns, Archie. *Peter Skene Ogden: Fur Trader*. Portland, Ore. Binfords and Mort, 1967.

Boas, Franz. "Census and Reservations of the Kwakiutl Nation." *Bulletin of the American Geographical Society* 19 (1887): 225–32.

———. "The Indians of British Columbia." *Bulletin of the American Geographical Society* 28 (1896): 229–43.

———. "The Indians of British Columbia." *Transactions of the Royal Society of Canada* 4, section 2 (1888): 47–57.

———. *Kwakiutl Ethnography*. Edited by Helen Codere. Chicago and London: University of Chicago Press, 1966.

———. "The Methods of Ethnology." *American Anthropologist*, n.s. 22 (1920): 311–21.

Bolt, Christine. *Victorian Attitudes Towards Race*. London and Toronto: Routledge and Kegan Paul, 1971.

Bolton, Herbert Eugene. *Fray Juan Crespi Missionary Explorer on the Pacific Coast 1769–1774*. Berkeley: University of California Press, 1927.

Brathwaite, Jean, and Folan, W. J. "The Taking of the Ship 'Boston': An Ethnohistoric Study of Nootkan-European Conflict." *Syesis* 5 (1972): 259–66.

Broom, Leonard, et al. "Acculturation: an Exploratory Formulation, . . ." *American Anthropologist*, n.s. 56 (1954): 973–1002.

Brown, G. Gordon. "Missions and Social Diffusion." *American Journal of Sociology* 50 (1944): 214–19.

Brown, George D., Jr., and Lamb, W. Kaye. "Captain St. Paul of Kamloops." *British Columbia Historical Quarterly* 3 (1939): 115–27.

Buell, Robert Kingery, and Skadal, Charlotte Northcote. *Sea Otters and the China Trade* [New York]: D. McKay Co., 1968.

Burns, Robert Ignatius. *The Jesuits and the Indian Wars of the Northwest*. New Haven and London: Yale University Press, 1966.

Cail, Robert E. *Land, Man, and the Law: The Disposal of Crown Lands in British Columbia, 1871–1913*. Vancouver: University of British Columbia Press, 1974.

Cairns, H. Alan C. *Prelude to Imperialism: British Reactions to Central African Society 1840–1890*. London: Routledge and Kegan Paul, 1965.

Cell, John W. *British Colonial Administration in the Mid-Nineteenth Century: The Policy Making Process*. New Haven and London: Yale University Press, 1970.

Coan, C. F. "The Adoption of the Reserve Policy in Pacific Northwest, 1853–1855." *Quarterly of the Oregon Historical Society* 23 (1922): 1–38.

———. "The First Stage of Federal Indian Policy in the Pacific Northwest, 1849–1852." *Quarterly of the Oregon Historical Society* 22 (1921): 46–86.

Coats, Robert Hamilton, and Gosnell, R. E. *Sir James Douglas: The Makers of Canada*. Toronto: Morang, 1909.

Codere, Helen. *Fighting with Property: A Study of Kwakiutl Potlatching and Warfare 1792–1930*. Monographs of the American Ethnological Society no. 18. Seattle and London: University of Washington Press, 1966.

Collins, June McCormick. "Growth of Class Distinctions and Political Authority among the Skagit Indians during the Contact Period." *American Anthropologist* 52 (1950): 331–42.

Cook, Warren L. *Flood Tide of Empire: Spain and the Pacific Northwest, 1543–1819*. New Haven and London: Yale University Press, 1973.

Cowan, Ian McTaggart. "The Fur Trade and the Fur Cycle: 1825–1857." *British Columbia Historical Quarterly* 2 (1938): 19–30.

Creighton, Donald. *The Empire of the St. Lawrence*. Toronto: Macmillan, 1970.

Cronin, Kay. *Cross in the Wilderness*. Vancouver: Mitchell, 1960.

Cumming, Peter A., and Mickenberg, Neil H., eds. *Native Rights in Canada*. Toronto: Indian-Eskimo Association of Canada, 1972.

Curtin, Phillip D. *The Image of Africa: British Ideas and Action, 1780–1850*. Madison: University of Wisconsin Press, 1964.

Dalzell, Kathleen. *The Queen Charlotte Islands 1774–1966*. Terrace, B.C.: C. M. Adam, 1968.

Davidson, Donald C. "Relations of the Hudson's Bay Company with the Russian American Company on the Northwest Coast." *British Columbia Historical Quarterly* 5 (1941): 33–51.

Davis, George. *Metlakahtla: A True Narrative of the Red Man*. Chicago: Ram's Horn Company, 1904.

Dawson, George M. "Notes and Observations on the Kwakiool People of the Northern Part of Vancouver Island and Adjacent Coasts, made during the Summer of 1885; . . . ." *Transactions of the Royal Society of Canada* 5, section 2 (1887): 63–98.

Dee, Henry Drummond. "An Irishman in the Fur Trade: The Life and Journals of John Work." *British Columbia Historical Quarterly* 7 (1943): 229–70.

Dictionary of Canadian Biography. Edited by Marc La Terreur. Vol. 10. Toronto: University of Toronto Press, 1972.

Dixon, C. W. *Smallpox*. London: Churchill, 1962.

Down, Sister Mary Margaret. *A Century of Service 1858–1958: A History of the Sisters of Saint Ann. . . .* Victoria: Sisters of Saint Ann, 1966.

Dozier, Edward P. "Differing Reactions to Religious Contacts among North American Indian Societies." *International Congress of Americanists* 34 (1960): 161–71.

————. "Forced and Permissive Acculturation." *American Indian* 7 (1955): 38–44.

Drucker, Phillip. "The Antiquity of the Northwest Coast Totem Pole." *Journal of the Washington Academy of Sciences* 38 (1948): 389–97.

————. *Cultures of the North Pacific Coast*. San Francisco: Chandler Publishing, 1965.

————, and Heizer, Robert F. *To Make my Name Good; A Re-examination of the Southern Kwakiutl Potlatch*. Berkeley and Los Angeles: University of California Press, 1967.

————. *The Northern and Central Nootkan Tribes*, Smithsonian Institution Bureau of American Ethnology Bulletin 144. Washington, D.C.: U.S. Government Printing Office, 1951.

————. "Rank, Wealth, and Kinship in Northwest Coast Society." *American Anthropologist*, n.s. 41 (1939): 55–65.

Duff, Wilson, and Kew, Michael. *Anthony Island, a Home of the Haidas*. Report of the Provincial Museum of Natural History and Anthropology. Victoria: Provincial Museum, 1957.

Duff, Wilson. "Contributions of Marius Barbeau to West Coast Ethnography." *Anthropologica* 6 (1964): 63–96.

————. "The Fort Victoria Treaties." *BC Studies* 3 (1969): 3–57.

————, ed. *Histories, Territories, and Laws of the Kitwancool*. Anthropology in British Columbia Memoir no. 4. Victoria: Provincial Museum, 1959.

————. *The Indian History of British Columbia: Vol. 1. The Impact of the White Man*. Anthropology in British Columbia Memoir no. 5. Victoria: Provincial Museum, 1964.

————. *The Upper Stalo Indians of the Fraser Valley, British Columbia*. Anthropology in British Columbia Memoir no. 1. Victoria: Provincial Museum, 1952.

Fisher, Robin. "Arms and Men on the Northwest Coast, 1774–1825." *BC Studies* 29 (1976): 3–18.

————. "An Exercise in Futility: The Joint Commission on Indian Land in British

Columbia, 1875–1880." Canadian Historical Association, *Historical Papers* (1975): 79–94.

———. "Joseph Trutch and Indian Land Policy." *BC Studies* 12 (1971–72): 3–33.

Foster, W. Garland. "British Columbia Indian Lands." *Pacific Northwest Quarterly* 28 (1937): 151–62.

Galbraith, John S. "The Early History of the Puget's Sound Agricultural Company 1838–1843." *Oregon Historical Quarterly* 55 (1954): 234–59.

———. *The Hudson's Bay Company as an Imperial Factor 1821–1869*. Berkeley and Los Angeles: University of California Press, 1957.

———. "James Edward Fitzgerald Versus the Hudson's Bay Company: The Founding of Vancouver Island." *British Columbia Historical Quarterly* 16 (1952): 191–207.

Garfield, Viola E. *Tsimshian Clan and Society*. Seattle: University of Washington Press, 1939.

———, and Wingert, P. S. *The Tsimshian Indians and their Arts*. Seattle and London: University of Washington Press, n.d.

Gladstone, Percy. "Native Indians and the Fishing Industry of British Columbia." *Canadian Journal of Economics and Political Science* 19 (1953): 20–34.

Gossett, Thomas F. *Race: The History of an Idea in America*. New York: Shocken Books, 1965.

Gough, Barry M. *The Royal Navy and the Northwest Coast of America, 1810–1914: A Study of British Maritime Ascendancy*. Vancouver: University of British Columbia Press, 1971.

———. " 'Turbulent Frontiers' and British Expansion: Governor Douglas, the Royal Navy, and the British Columbia Gold Rushes." *Pacific Historical Review* 41 (1972): 15–32.

Graham, Hugh Davis, and Gurr, Ted Robert, eds. *Violence in America: Historical and Comparative Perspectives*. New York: Bantam Books, 1969.

Gunther, Erna. *Indian Life on the Northwest Coast of North America as Seen by the Early Explorers and Fur Traders during the Last Decades of the Eighteenth Century*. Chicago and London: University of Chicago Press, 1972.

Hawthorn, H. B.; Belshaw, C. S.; and Jamieson, S. M. *The Indians of British Columbia; A Study of Contemporary Social Adjustment*. Toronto: University of Toronto Press, 1958.

Herskovits, Melville J. *Acculturation, the Study of Culture Contact*. New York: J. J. Augustin, 1938.

———. *Franz Boas. The Science of Man in the Making*. New York and London: Scribner, 1953.

Hewlett, Edward Sleigh. "The Chilcotin Uprising of 1864." *BC Studies* 19 (1973): 50–72.

Hill, J. M. "The Most Reverend Modeste Demers, D. D. First Bishop of Vancouver Island." *Canadian Catholic Church Historical Association Report* (1953): 29–35.

Howard, Joseph Kinsey. *Strange Empire*. Toronto: Swan, 1965.

Howay, F. W. "Authorship of Traits of Indian Life," *Oregon Historical Quarterly* 35 (1934): 42–49.

———. "The Ballad of the Bold Northwestman: An Incident in the Life of Captain John Kendrick." *Washington Historical Quarterly* 20 (1929): 114–23.

———; Sage, W. N.; and Angus, H. F. *British Columbia and the United States: The North Pacific Slope from Fur Trade to Aviation*. Toronto: Ryerson, 1942.

———. "Early Days of the Maritime Fur Trade on the Northwest Coast." *Canadian Historical Review* 4 (1923): 26–44.

———. "Early Followers of Captain Grey." *Washington Historical Quarterly* 18 (1927): 11–20.

————. "An Early Account of the Loss of the *Boston* in 1803." *Washington Historical Quarterly* 17 (1926): 280–88.

————. "Indian Attacks upon Maritime Fur Traders of the North-West Coast, 1785–1805." *Canadian Historical Review* 6 (1925): 287–309.

————. "International Aspects of the Maritime Fur Trade." *Transactions of the Royal Society of Canada*, 3d ser. 36, section 2 (1942): 59–78.

————. "The Introduction of Intoxicating Liquors amongst the Indians of the Northwest Coast." *British Columbia Historical Quarterly* 6 (1942): 157–69.

————. "A List of Trading Vessels in the Maritime Fur Trade, 1785–1794." *Transactions of the Royal Society of Canada*, 3d ser. 24, section 2 (1930): 111–34.

————. "A List of Trading Vessels in the Maritime Fur Trade, 1795–1804." *Transactions of the Royal Society of Canada*, 3d ser. 25, section 2 (1931): 117–49.

————. "A List of Trading Vessels in the Maritime Fur Trade, 1805–1814." *Transactions of the Royal Society of Canada*, 3d ser. 26, section 2 (1932): 43–86.

————. "A List of Trading Vessels in the Maritime Fur Trade, 1815–1819." *Transactions of the Royal Society of Canada*, 3d ser. 27, section 2 (1933): 119–47.

————. "A List of Trading Vessels in the Maritime Fur Trade, 1820–1825." *Transactions of the Royal Society of Canada*, 3d ser. 28, section 2 (1934): 11–49.

————. "The Loss of the *Tonquin*." *Washington Historical Quarterly* 13 (1922): 83–92.

————. "An Outline Sketch of the Maritime Fur Trade." Canadian Historical Association, *Report* (1932): 5–14.

————. "Potatoes: Records of Some Early Transactions at Fort Simpson, B.C." *The Beaver*, outfit 259 (1929): 155–56.

————. "The Raison d'Etre of Forts Yale and Hope." *Transactions of the Royal Society of Canada*, 3d ser. 16, section 2 (1922): 49–64.

————. "The Spanish Settlement at Nootka." *Washington Historical Quarterly* 8 (1917): 163–71.

————. "The Trading Voyages of the *Atahualpa*." *Washington Historical Quarterly* 19 (1928): 3–12.

————. "The Voyage of the *Hope*: 1790–1792." *Washington Historical Quarterly* 11 (1920): 3–28.

————. "Voyages of Kendrick and Gray in 1787–90." *Oregon Historical Quarterly* 30 (1929): 89–94.

————. "A Yankee Trader on the Northwest Coast, 1791–1795." *Washington Historical Quarterly* 21 (1930): 83–94.

Hussey, John A. *The History of Fort Vancouver and its Physical Structure*. Tacoma: Washington State Historical Society, 1957.

Innis, Harold A. *The Fur Trade in Canada: An Introduction to Canadian Economic History*. Toronto: University of Toronto Press, 1956.

Ireland, Willard E. "The Appointment of Governor Blanshard." *British Columbia Historical Quarterly* 8 (1944): 213–26.

————. "Captain Walter Colquhoun Grant: Vancouver Island's First Independent Settler." *British Columbia Historical Quarterly* 17 (1953): 87–121.

————. "The Evolution of the Boundaries of British Columbia." *British Columbia Historical Quarterly* 3 (1939): 263–82.

Jacobs, Wilbur R. *Dispossessing the American Indian: Indians and Whites on the Colonial Frontier*. New York: Scribners, 1972.

————. "The Fatal Confrontation: Early Native-White Relations on the Frontiers of Australia, New Guinea, and America—a Comparative Study." *Pacific Historical Review* 40 (1971): 283–309.

————. "Frontiersmen, Fur Traders, and other Varmints, an Ecological Appraisal of the Frontier in American History." *American Historical Association Newsletter* (November 1970): 5–11.

Jenness, Diamond. *The Carrier Indians of the Bulkley River: Their Social and Religious Life*, Smithsonian Institution Bureau of American Ethnology Anthropological Paper, no. 25. Washington, 1943.

———. *The Indian Background of Canadian History*. Canada, Department of Mines and Resources Bulletin no. 86. Ottawa: J. O. Patenaude, 1937.

———. *The Indians of Canada*, National Museum of Canada Bulletin no. 65. Ottawa: Queen's Printer, 1960.

———. *The Sekani Indians of British Columbia*. Canada, Department of Mines and Resources Bulletin no. 84. Ottawa: J. O. Patenaude, 1937.

Johansen, Dorothy O. "McLoughlin and the Indians." *The Beaver*, outfit 277 (1946): 18–21.

Johnson, Edward Philip. "The Early Years of Ashcroft Manor." *BC Studies* 5 (1970): 3–23.

Johnson, Patricia M. "Fort Rupert." *The Beaver*, outfit 302 (1972): 4–15.

Josephy, Alvin M., Jr. *The Nez Percé Indians and the Opening of the Northwest*. New Haven and London: Yale University Press, 1965.

Knaplund, Paul. "James Stephen on Granting Vancouver Island to the Hudson's Bay Company." *British Columbia Historical Quarterly* 9 (1945): 259–71.

Krause, Aurel. *The Tlingit Indians: Results of a Trip to the Northwest Coast of America and Bering Straits*. Translated by Erna Gunther. Seattle and London: University of Washington Press, 1970.

Laing, Lionel H. "The Family-Company-Compact." *Washington Historical Quarterly* 22 (1931): 117–28.

Lamb, W. Kaye. "The Founding of Fort Victoria." *British Columbia Historical Quarterly* 7 (1943): 71–92.

———. "The Governorship of Richard Blanshard." *British Columbia Historical Quarterly* 14 (1950): 1-40.

———. "The Mystery of Mrs Barkley's Diary. Notes on the Voyage of the 'Imperial Eagle' 1786–1787." *British Columbia Historical Quarterly* 6 (1942): 31–59.

LaViolette, Forrest. "Missionaries and the Potlatch." *Queen's Quarterly* 58 (1951): 237–51.

———. *The Struggle for Survival: Indian Cultures and the Protestant Ethic in British Columbia*. Toronto: University of Toronto Press, 1961.

Leacock, Eleanor. *The Montagnais "Hunting Territory" and the Fur Trade*. American Anthropological Memoir no. 78. Menasha, Wis.: American Anthropological Association, 1954.

Lemert, Edwin M. *Alcohol and the Northwest Coast Indians*. University of California Publications in Culture and Society. Berkeley and Los Angeles: University of California Press, 1954.

———. "The Life and Death of an Indian State." *Human Organization* 13 (1954): 23–27.

Lewis, Oscar. *The Effects of White Contact upon Blackfoot Culture with Special Reference to the Fur Trade*. Monographs of the American Ethnological Society. Seattle and London: University of Washington Press, 1966.

Linton, Ralph, ed. *Acculturation in Seven American Indian Tribes*. Gloucester, Mass.: Peter Smith, 1963.

———. "Nativistic Movements." *American Anthropologist*, n.s. 45 (1943): 230–40.

Lotz, Pat, and Lotz, Jim, eds. *Pilot not Commander: Essays in Memory of Diamond Jenness (Anthropologica, n.s. 13, 1971)*. Ottawa, 1971.

Lugrin, N. de Bertrand. *The Pioneer Women of Vancouver Island 1843–1866*. Victoria: Women's Canadian Club, 1928.

Lynch, H. R. "Sir Joseph William Trutch, a British American on the Pacific Coast." *Pacific Historical Review* 30 (1961): 243–55.

Lyons, Cicely. *Salmon Our Heritage*: *The Story of a Province and an Industry.* Vancouver: British Columbia Packers, 1969.

McArthur, Norma. *Island Populations of the Pacific.* Canberra: Australian National University Press, 1967.

McKechnie, Robert E. *Strong Medicine*: *History of Healing on the Northwest Coast.* Vancouver: J. J. Douglas, 1972.

McKelvie, B. A. "Lieutenant-Colonel Israel Wood Powell, M.D., C.M." *British Columbia Historical Quarterly* 11 (1947): 33–54.

——. *Maquinna the Magnificent.* Vancouver: Vancouver Daily Province, 1946.

——, and Ireland, Willard. "The Victorian Voltigeurs." *British Columbia Historical Quarterly* 20 (1956): 221–39.

MacLeod, William Cristie. *The American Indian Frontier.* London: Dawson of Pall Mall, 1928.

Manning, William Ray. *The Nootka Sound Controversy.* Annual Report of the American Historical Association for the Year 1904. Washington, 1905.

Mannoni, O. *Prospero and Caliban*: *The Psychology of Colonization.* Translated by P. Powesland. New York: Praeger, 1964.

Mason, Philip. *Patterns of Dominance.* London: Oxford University Press, 1970.

Moorehead, Alan. *The Fatal Impact*: *An Account of the Invasion of the South Pacific 1767–1840.* New York: Harper and Row, 1966.

Morice, A. G. *History of the Catholic Church in Western Canada, from Lake Superior to the Pacific, 1659–1895.* 2 vols. Toronto: Musson, 1910.

——. *The History of the Northern Interior of British Columbia Formerly New Caledonia [1660–1880].* Toronto: William Briggs, 1904.

Morison, Samuel Eliot. *The Maritime History of Massachusetts, 1783–1860.* Boston and New York: Houghton Mifflin, 1921.

Morrell, W. P. *British Colonial Policy in the Age of Peel and Russell.* London: Clarendon Press, 1930.

——. *British Colonial Policy in the Mid-Victorian Age.* London: Clarendon Press, 1969.

——. *The Gold Rushes.* London: A. and C. Black, 1940.

Morton, Arthur S. *A History of the Canadian West to 1870–71.* . . . Edited by Lewis G. Thomas. Toronto: University of Toronto Press, 1973.

——. "The Northwest Company's Columbia Enterprise and David Thompson." *Canadian Historical Review* 17 (1936): 266–88.

Morton, W. L., ed. *The Shield of Achilles*: *Aspects of Canada in the Victorian Age.* Toronto and Montreal: McClelland and Stewart, 1968.

Murdock, George Peter. "Kinship and Social Behaviour Among the Haida." *American Anthropologist,* n.s. 36 (1934): 355–85.

——. *Rank and Potlatch among the Haida.* Yale University Publications in Anthropology no. 13. New Haven: Yale University Press, 1936.

Murphy, Robert F., and Steward, Julian H. "Tappers and Trappers: Parallel Process in Acculturation." *Economic Development and Cultural Change* 4 (1956): 335–55.

Nash, Gary B., and Weiss, Richard, eds. *The Great Fear*: *Race in the Mind of America.* New York: Holt, Rinehart, and Winston, 1970.

Nash, Gary B. "The Image of the Indian in the Southern Colonial Mind." *William and Mary Quarterly,* 3d ser. 29 (1972): 197–230.

Niblack, A. P. *The Coast Indians of Southern Alaska and Northern British Columbia.* N.p. [1890].

Norris, John. *Strangers Entertained*: *A History of Ethnic Groups of British Columbia.* Vancouver: Evergreen Press, 1971.

O'Callaghan, J. A. "Extinguishing Indian Titles on the Oregon Coast." *Oregon Historical Quarterly* 52 (1951): 139–44.

Ogden, Adele. *The California Sea Otter Trade, 1784–1848.* University of California Publications in History, vol. 26. Berkeley and Los Angeles: University of California Press, 1941.

Oliver, Douglas L. *The Pacific Islands.* Cambridge, Mass.: Harvard University Press, 1961.

O'Meara, Walter. *Daughters of the Country: The Women of Fur Traders and Mountain Men.* New York: Harcourt, Brace, and World, 1968.

O'Neil, Marion. "The Maritime Activities of the North West Company, 1813 to 1821." *Washington Historical Quarterly* 21 (1930): 343–67.

Ormsby, Margaret A. *British Columbia: a History.* Toronto: Macmillan, 1971.

————. "Some Irish Figures in Colonial Days." *British Columbia Historical Quarterly* 14 (1950): 61–82.

Patterson, E. Palmer, II. *The Canadian Indian: A History Since 1500.* Don Mills, Ont.: Collier-Macmillan Canada, 1972.

Peake, Frank A. *The Anglican Church in British Columbia.* Vancouver: Mitchell, 1959.

Pearce, Roy Harvey. *The Savages of America: A Study of the Indian and the Idea of Civilization.* Baltimore: Johns Hopkins Press, 1965.

Peckham, Howard, and Gibson, Charles, eds. *Attitudes of Colonial Powers Toward the American Indian.* Salt Lake City: University of Utah Press, 1969.

Pethick, Derek. *James Douglas: Servant of Two Empires.* Vancouver: Mitchell, 1969.

Phillips, Paul Chrisler. *The Fur Trade.* Vol. 2. Norman: University of Oklahoma Press, 1961.

Pitt-Rivers, George Henry Lane-Fox. *The Clash of Cultures and the Contact of Races. . . .* London: George Routledge and Sons, 1927.

Prosch, Thomas W. "The Indian War in Washington Territory." *Quarterly of the Oregon Historical Society* 16 (1915): 1–23.

Quimby, George I. "Culture Contact on the Northwest Coast, 1785–1795." *American Anthropologist,* n.s. 50 (1948): 147–55.

Ranger, T. O. *Revolt in Southern Rhodesia 1896–1897: A Study in African Resistance.* Evanston, Ill.: Northwestern University Press, 1967.

Ray, Verne F. *Cultural Relations in the Plateau of Northwestern America.* Publications of the Frederick Webb Hodge Anniversary Publication Fund. Vol. 3. Los Angeles; Southwest Museum, 1939.

Reid, Robie. "Early Days at Old Fort Langley." *British Columbia Historical Quarterly* 1 (1937): 71–85.

Rich, E. E. *The History of the Hudson's Bay Company 1670–1870. Vol. 2: 1763–1870.* London: Hudson's Bay Record Society, 1959.

————. "Trade Habits and Economic Motivations among the Indians of North America." *Canadian Journal of Economics and Political Science* 26 (1960): 35–53.

Rickard, T. A. "Gilbert Malcolm Sproat." *British Columbia Historical Quarterly* 1 (1937): 21–32.

————. "Indian Participation in the Gold Discoveries." *British Columbia Historical Quarterly* 2 (1938): 3–18.

————. "The Sea-Otter in History." *British Columbia Historical Quarterly* 11 (1947): 15–31.

————. "The Use of Iron and Copper by the Indians of British Columbia." *British Columbia Historical Quarterly* 3 (1939): 25–50.

Robin, Martin. *The Rush for Spoils: The Company Province 1871–1933.* Toronto: McClelland and Stewart, 1972.

Ross, Frank E. "The Retreat of the Hudson's Bay Company in the Pacific North-West." *Canadian Historical Review* 18 (1937): 262–80.

Ryerson, Stanley B. *The Founding of Canada: Beginnings to 1815.* Toronto: Progress Books, 1960.

Sage, Walter N. "The North-West Mounted Police and British Columbia." *Pacific Historical Review* 18 (1949): 345–61.

———. *Sir James Douglas and British Columbia.* Toronto: University of Toronto Press, 1930.

———. "Sir James Douglas: Fur Trader and Governor." *Canadian Historical Association, Annual Report* (1925): 49–55.

———. "James Douglas on the Columbia, 1830–1849." *Oregon Historical Quarterly* 27 (1926): 365–80.

Saum, Lewis O. *The Fur Trader and the Indian.* Seattle and London: University of Washington Press, 1965.

Saywell, John Tupper. "Sir Joseph Trutch: British Columbia's First Lieutenant-Governor." *British Columbia Historical Quarterly* 19 (1955): 71–92.

Scholefield, E. O. S., and Howay, F. W. *British Columbia from the Earliest Times to the Present.* 4 vols. Vancouver: S. J. Clarke, 1914.

Scott, Leslie M. "Indian Diseases as Aids to Pacific Northwest Settlement." *Oregon Historical Quarterly* 29 (1928): 144–61.

Sharp, Paul. "Three Frontiers: Some Comparative Studies of Canadian, American, and Australian Settlement." *Pacific Historical Review* 24 (1955): 369–77.

Sheehan, Bernard W. "Indian-White Relations in Early America: A Review Essay." *William and Mary Quarterly* 26 (1969): 267–86.

Shelton, George W., ed. *British Columbia and Confederation.* Victoria: University of Victoria, 1967.

Shineberg, Dorothy. *They Came for Sandalwood: A Study of the Sandalwood Trade in the South-West Pacific.* Melbourne: Melbourne University Press, 1967.

Shortt, Adam, and Doughty, Arthur G., eds. *Canada and Its Provinces. . . .* Vols. 5 and 7. Toronto: Glasgow, Brook and Company, 1913.

Slater, G. Hollis. "New Light on Herbert Beaver." *British Columbia Historical Quarterly* 6 (1942): 13–29.

———. "Rev. Robert John Staines, Priest, Pedagogue, and Political Agitator." *British Columbia Historical Quarterly* 14 (1950): 187–240.

Smith, James Morton, ed. *Seventeenth-Century America: Essays in Colonial History.* Chapel Hill: University of North Carolina Press, 1959.

Sorrenson, M. P. K. "Land Purchase Methods and their Effect on Maori Population, 1865–1901." *Journal of the Polynesian Society* 65 (1956): 183–99.

Spicer, Edward H. *Cycles of Conquest, the Impact of Spain, Mexico, and the United States on the Indians of the Southwest, 1533–1960.* Tucson: University of Arizona Press, 1962.

———, ed. *Perspectives in American Indian Culture Change.* Chicago and London: University of Chicago Press, 1961.

Stanley, George F. G. "The Indian Background of Canadian History." *Canadian Historical Association, Report* (1952): 14–21.

———. "Western Canada and the Frontier Thesis." *Canadian Historical Association, Report* (1940): 105–14.

Stanton, William. *The Leopard's Spots: Scientific Attitudes Towards Race in America 1815–1859.* Chicago: University of Chicago Press, 1960.

Stearn, E. Wagner, and Stearn, Allan E. *The Effect of Smallpox on the Destiny of the Amerindian.* Boston: Humphries, 1945.

Stephens, H. Morse, and Bolton, Herbert E. *The Pacific Ocean in History: Papers and Addresses Presented at the Panama-Pacific Historical Congress Held at San Francisco, Berkeley, and Palo Alto, California July 19–23, 1915.* New York: Macmillan, 1917.

Stock, Eugene. *The History of the Church Missionary Society, its Environment, its Men and its Work.* Vols. 2 and 3. London: Church Missionary Society, 1899.

Suttles, Wayne. "Affinal Ties, Subsistence, and Prestige among the Coast Salish." *American Anthropologist*, n.s. 62 (1960): 296–305.

———. "The Early Diffusion of the Potato among the Coast Salish." *Southwestern Journal of Anthropology* 7 (1951): 272–88.

———. "The Persistence of Intervillage Ties among the Coast Salish." *Ethnology* 2 (1963): 512–25.

———. "The Plateau Prophet Dance among the Coast Salish." *Southwestern Journal of Anthropology* 13 (1957): 352–96.

———. "Post-Contact Culture Change among the Lummi Indians." *British Columbia Historical Quarterly* 18 (1954): 29–102.

Swanton, John R. *Contributions to the Ethnology of the Haida.* Memoir of the American Museum of Natural History. New York: G. E. Stechert, 1905.

Taylor, Herbert C., Jr., and Duff, Wilson. "A Post-Contact Southward Movement of the Kwakiutl." *Research Studies of the State College of Washington* 24 (1956): 56–66.

Teit, James. *The Lillooet Indians.* Memoir of the American Museum of Natural History. Edited by Franz Boas. New York: G. E. Stechert, 1906.

———. *The Salishan Tribes of the Western Plateaus.* Extract from Forty-Fifth Annual Report of the Bureau of American Ethnology. Edited by Franz Boas. Washington, 1930.

———. *The Shuswap.* Memoir of the American Museum of Natural History. Edited by Franz Boas. New York: G. E. Stechert, 1909.

———. *The Thompson Indians of British Columbia.* Memoir of the American Museum of Natural History. Edited by Franz Boas. N.p., 1900.

Temperly, Howard. *British Antislavery, 1833–1870.* London: Longmans, 1972.

Thompson, Rev. H. P. *Into All Lands: The History of the Society for the Propagation of the Gospel in Foreign Parts 1701–1950.* London: Society for the Propagation of Christian Knowledge, 1951.

Trimble, W. J. "American and British Treatment of the Indians of the Pacific Northwest." *Washington Historical Quarterly* 5 (1914): 32–54.

———. "The Indian Policy of the Colony of British Columbia in Comparison with that of Adjacent American Territories." *Proceedings of the Mississippi Valley Historical Association for the Year 1912–1913* 6: 276–86.

———. *The Mining Advance into the Inland Empire.* . . . Bulletin of the University of Wisconsin no. 638. Madison: University of Wisconsin, 1914.

Turner, Frederick Jackson. *The Frontier in American History.* New York: Holt, Rinehart and Winston, 1962.

Turney-High, Harry Holbert. *Ethnography of the Kutenai.* Memoirs of the American Anthropological Association no. 56. Menasha, Wis., 1941.

Usher, Jean. "Apostles and Aborigines: The Social Theory of the Church Missionary Society." *Social History* 7 (1971): 28–52.

———. *William Duncan of Metlakatla: A Victorian Missionary in British Columbia.* National Museum of Man Publications in History, no. 5. Ottawa: National Museums of Canada, 1974.

Wagner, Henry R. *The Cartography of the Northwest Coast of America to the Year 1800.* Vol. 1. Berkeley: University of California Press, 1937.

Walbran, John T. *British Columbia Coast Names 1592–1906.* . . . Ottawa: Government Printing Bureau, 1909.

Walkem, Wymond W. *Stories of Early British Columbia.* Vancouver, B.C.: News-Advertiser, 1914.

Walker, James St. G. "The Indian in Canadian Historical Writing." Canadian Historical Association, *Historical Papers* (1971): 21–51.

Washburn, Wilcomb. "The Writing of American Indian History: A Status Report." *Pacific Historical Review* 40 (1971): 261–81.

Wellcome, H. S. *The Story of Metlakahtla.* London: Saxon, 1887.

White, Hester E. "John Carmichael Haynes." *British Columbia Historical Quarterly* 4 (1940): 183–201.
Wike, Joyce. "More Puzzles on the Northwest Coast." *American Anthropologist*, n.s. 59 (1957): 301–17.
———. "Problems in Fur Trade Analysis: The Northwest Coast." *American Anthropologist*, n.s. 60 (1958): 1086–1101.
———. "Social Stratification among the Nootka." *Ethnohistory* 5 (1958): 219–41.
Wild, Ronald. *Amor De Cosmos*. Toronto: Ryerson, 1958.
Winks, Robin W. *The Blacks in Canada: A History*. Montreal: Yale University Press, 1971.
Yarmie, Andrew H. "Smallpox and the British Columbia Indians, Epidemic of 1862." *British Columbia Library Association Quarterly* 31 (1968): 13–21.
Zaslow, Morris. "The Missionary as Social Reformer: The Case of William Duncan." *Journal of the Canadian Church Historical Society* 8 (1966): 52–69.
———. *The Opening of the Canadian North 1870–1914*. The Canadian Centenary Series. Toronto and Montreal: McClelland and Stewart, 1971.

2. *Unpublished*

Annakin, Virgil Dewey. "The Missionary, an Agent of Cultural Diffusion." Ph.D. dissertation, Ohio State University, 1940.
Baker, Mildred M. "The Relations of the Early Fur Companies with the Indians of the Pacific Northwest." Honors thesis, University of Oregon, 1929.
Barbeau, Marius. "The Potlatch among the B.C. Indians and Section 149 of the Indian Act." TS prepared for the superintendent of Indian affairs, 1934.
———, and Beynon, William. "Unpublished field notes, (selections from the 'Tsimshian file')." TS in the possession of the Department of Anthropology, University of British Columbia.
Darling, J. D. "The Effects of Culture Contact on the Tsimshian System of Land Tenure during the Nineteenth Century." M.A. thesis, University of British Columbia, 1955.
Frawley, Carol Mavis. "Continuity and Change: The Role of the Hudson's Bay Company in Oregon and Vancouver Island, 1824–1859." M.A. thesis, University of Victoria, 1971.
Gilliland, Henry Cecil. "The Early Life and Early Governorships of Sir Arthur Edward Kennedy." M.A. thesis, University of British Columbia, 1951.
Gormly, Mary. "Early Culture Contact on the Northwest Coast, 1774–1795. Analysis of Spanish Material." Master of Librarianship thesis, University of Washington, 1959.
Gough, Barry M. "The Power to Compel: White-Indian Conflict in British Columbia during the Colonial Period, 1849–1871." Paper given at the Canadian Historical Association Annual Meeting, June 1972.
Gunson, W. N. "Evangelical Missionaries in the South Seas, 1797–1860." Ph.D. dissertation, Australian National University, 1959.
Hanley, Phillip. "The Catholic Ladder and Missionary Activity in the Pacific Northwest." M.A. thesis, University of Ottawa, 1965.
Hatch, Frederick John. "The British Columbia Police, 1858–1871." M.A. thesis, University of British Columbia, 1955.

Hewlett, Edward Sleigh. "The Chilcotin Uprising: A Study of Indian-European Relations in Nineteenth Century British Columbia." M.A. thesis, University of British Columbia, 1972.

Johnson, Margaret Olive. "Spanish Exploration of the Pacific Coast by Juan Perez in 1774." Master of Letters thesis, University of California, Berkeley, 1911.

Kennedy, Jacqueline Judith. "Roman Catholic Missionary Effort and Indian Acculturation in the Fraser Valley 1860–1900." B.A. essay, University of British Columbia, 1969.

Kopas, Leslie Clifford. "Political Action of the Indians of British Columbia." M.A. thesis, University of British Columbia, 1972.

Laing, F. W. "Colonial Farm Settlers on the Mainland of British Columbia" (TS, UBCL). Victoria, 1939.

Lane, Robert Brockstedt. "Cultural Relations of the Chilcotin Indians of West Central British Columbia." Ph.D. dissertation, University of Washington, 1953.

Little, Margaret. "Early Days of the Maritime Fur Trade, 1785–1794." M.A. thesis, University of British Columbia, 1934.

Lorimer, Douglas Alexander. "British Attitudes to the Negro, 1850–1870." Ph.D. dissertation, University of British Columbia, 1972.

Lynch, Hollis. "A Biography of Sir Joseph Trutch." B.A. essay, University of British Columbia, 1960.

McInnis, T. R. E. "Report on the Indian Title in Canada with Special Reference to British Columbia, House of Commons Sessional Paper no. 47, 1914 (unpublished)." TS, Department of Indian Affairs, Ottawa.

Mathes, Valarie L. "Wikaninish; A Vancouver Island Chieftain, his Life as Told by Foreign Visitors." M.A. thesis, University of New Mexico, 1965.

Matheson, G. M. "Resumé of British Columbia Land Question (Blue Book)" [1921]. TS, Department of Indian Affairs, Ottawa.

Mercer, N. J. "Dr. Israel Wood Powell." B.A. essay, University of British Columbia, 1959.

Mikkelsen, Phyllis. "Land Settlement Policy on the Mainland of British Columbia, 1858–1874." M.A. thesis, University of British Columbia, 1950.

Mills, John Edwin. "The Ethnohistory of Nootka Sound, Vancouver Island." Ph.D. dissertation, University of Washington, 1955.

Mitchell, Bruce. "Exploration and Settlement in Southwestern British Columbia before 1900" (TS, UBCL). Vancouver, 1966.

Oberg, Kalervo. "The Social Economy of the Tlingit Indians." Ph.D. dissertation, University of Chicago, 1937.

Ormsby, M.A. "The Relations between British Columbia and the Dominion of Canada, 1871–1885." Ph.D. dissertation, Bryn Mawr College [1937].

Pine, Francis. "The Power and Authority of Haida Women." B.A. essay, University of British Columbia, 1973.

Rumley, Hilary Eileen. "Reactions to Contact and Colonization: An Interpretation of Religious and Social Change among the Indians of British Columbia." M.A. thesis, University of British Columbia, 1973.

Shankel, G. E. "The Development of Indian Policy in British Columbia." Ph.D. dissertation, University of Washington, 1945.

Suttles, W. P. "Economic Life of the Coast Salish of Haro and Rosario Straits." Ph.D. dissertation, University of Washington, 1951.

Tanner, Adrian. "The Structure of Fur Trade Relations." M.A. thesis, University of British Columbia, 1965.

Trennert, Robert Anthony. "The Far Western Indian Frontier and the Beginnings of the Reservation System, 1846–1851." Ph.D. dissertation, University of California, Santa Barbara, 1969.

Verma, Behari L. "The Squamish: A Study of Changing Political Organization." M.A. thesis, University of British Columbia, 1954.

Wike, J. A. "The Effect of the Maritime Fur Trade on Northwest Coast Indian Society." Ph.D. dissertation, Columbia University [1951].

Wrinch, Leonard A. "Land Policy of the Colony of Vancouver Island, 1849–1866." M.A. thesis, University of British Columbia, 1932.

Young, Walter Douglas. "Pioneer Methodist Missionaries in British Columbia, 1859–1871." B.A. essay, University of British Columbia [1955].

Index